T0288692

How to Pay for Your Degree in Business & Related Fields 2004-2006

Second Edition

Gail Ann Schlachter
R. David Weber

A List of: Scholarships, Fellowships, Grants, Awards, and
Other Funding Programs Set Aside to Support Study,
Training, Research, and Creative Activities for Students
Working on a Degree in Business or a Related Field. Plus
a Set of Five Indexes: Sponsor, Residency, Tenability,
Specialty, and Deadline.

Reference Service Press
2004

©2004 Gail Ann Schlachter

All rights reserved. No part of this publication may be reproduced, stored in a retrieval system, or transmitted, in any form or by any means, electronic, mechanical, photocopying, recording, or otherwise, except for the inclusion of brief quotations in a review, without the prior permission in writing from the publisher. Reference Service Press vigorously defends its copyright.

ISBN 1-58841-103-6

10 9 8 7 6 5 4 3 2 1

Reference Service Press (RSP) began in 1977 with a single financial aid publication *(Directory of Financial Aids for Women)* and now specializes in the development of financial aid resources in multiple formats, including books, large print books, disks, CD-ROMs, print-on-demand reports, eBooks, and online sources. Long recognized as a leader in the field, RSP has been called, by the *Simba Report on Directory Publishing,* "a true success in the world of independent directory publishers." Both Kaplan Educational Centers and Military.com have hailed RSP as "the leading authority on scholarships."

Reference Service Press
El Dorado Hills Business Park
5000 Windplay Drive, Suite 4
El Dorado Hills, CA 95762-9600
    (916) 939-9620
    Fax: (916) 939-9626
    E-mail: findaid@aol.com
Visit our web site: www.rspfunding.com

Manufactured in the United States of America

Price: $30.00, plus $5 shipping

SCHOOLS OF BUSINESS, ORGANIZATIONS, AND OTHER QUANTITY BUYERS:
discounts on this book are available for bulk purchases. Write or call for information on our discount program.

Contents

Introduction

WHY THIS DIRECTORY IS NEEDED

Are you planning to get an undergraduate or graduate degree in business, economics, finance, or a related field? Congratulations. You have made a wise decision. Not only will you find these careers personally and intellectually challenging, you will also find them financially rewarding. In the National Association of Colleges and Employers' latest annual survey, the average beginning salary for business school graduates was well over $50,000. And, according to the Barron's *Guide to Graduate Business Schools,* it is "not unusual" for business school graduates "to receive salaries over $100,000 a year, plus signing-on bonuses that could be in the $10,000 to $25,000 range."

Getting your degree in business or related fields, however, is expensive. It can cost $100,000 or more just to complete a bachelor's degree, and that amount or more for a master's and doctoral degree. That's more than most students can afford to pay on their own.

Fortunately, hundreds of financial aid programs, representing billions of dollars, are available to help undergraduate and graduate students prepare for a career in business or a related field. How can students find out about this funding? In the past, general financial aid directories haven't offered much assistance. *Scholarships, Fellowships, and Loans* (published by Gale Group) and *Chronicle Financial Aid Guide* (published by Chronicle Guidance) are representative; each just scratches the surface, identifying only a few dozen of the hundreds of available funding opportunities. Similarly, the handful of publications that have focused specifically on financial aid for students in business-related fields tend to be either out of date or limited in scope; for example, neither *Dollars for College: The Quick Guide to Financial Aid for Business and Related Fields* nor *Financial Aid for Minorities in Business and Law* (both published by Ferguson) have been updated in the past seven years. As a result, many students working on an undergraduate or graduate degree in a business-related field (along with the counselors and librarians trying to serve them) have been unaware of the hundreds of scholarships, fellowships, loans, forgivable loans, grants, and awards available specifically to them.

That's why this updated edition of *How to Pay for Your Degree in Business & Related Fields* is so important. Here, in just one place, you'll be able to find detailed information on 675 scholarships, fellowships, grants, awards, and other funding opportunities available to support undergraduate and graduate study and research in any business-related field. All appropriate areas are covered, including accounting, actuarial science, agricultural economics, banking, business administration, economics, finance, management, marketing and sales, personnel administration, and real estate.

WHAT'S INCLUDED?

How to Pay for Your Degree in Business & Related Fields is unlike any other financial aid listing. Not only does it provide the most comprehensive coverage of business-related funding opportunities (675 entries), but it also offers the most informative program descriptions (on the average, twice the detail found in any other source).

In addition, only funding set aside for high school seniors, high school graduates, current college students, returning college students, and graduate students working on a degree in a business-related field is included. If a program doesn't support study, training, research, or creative activities for these students, it is not covered here.

Third, only the biggest and best funding programs are described in this book. To be listed here, a program has to offer students in business or related fields at least $500 per year. More than 90 percent go way beyond that, paying up to $20,000 or more annually, or covering the full cost of college attendance. And, all of this is "free" money; not one of these programs requires you to pay back any funds (provided, of course, that you meet the program requirements).

Fourth, you can take the money awarded by these funding programs to any number of locations. Unlike other financial aid directories, which often list large numbers of scholarships available only to students enrolled at one specific school, all of the entries in this book are "portable" (although some portability may be restricted by other program parameters). Another plus: many of the programs listed here have never been covered in other financial aid directories. So, even if you have checked elsewhere, you will want to look at *How to Pay for Your Degree in Business & Related Fields* for additional leads.

Fifth, unlike other funding directories, which tend to follow a straight alphabetical arrangement, this one groups entries by the various types of financial aid available to help you pay for your degree in a business-related field:

- *Scholarships.* Programs that support study and training at the undergraduate level in the United States. Usually no return of service or repayment is required. For information on funding for business-related research on the undergraduate level, see the Grants category below.

- *Fellowships.* Programs that support study and training at the graduate level in the United States. Usually no return of service or repayment is required. For information on funding for business-related research on the graduate level, see the Grants category below.

- *Grants.* Programs that provide funding to support innovative efforts, projects, creative activities, or research at the undergraduate or graduate school level in the United States. Usually no return of service or repayment is required.

- *Awards.* Competitions, prizes, and honoraria granted in recognition of personal accomplishments, research results, creative writing, or other achievements. Prizes received solely as the result of entering contests are excluded.

This arrangement, by type of funding, is designed to facilitate your search for appropriate programs. The same convenience is available in the indexes, where sponsoring organization, residency, tenability, specialty, and deadline date entries are each subdivided by type of funding offered.

Finally, we have tried to anticipate all the ways you might wish to search for funding; we organized the volume so you can identify programs not only by funding type, but by program title, sponsor, business specialty, where you live, where you want to go to school or conduct research, and when you plan to apply for funding. Plus, we've included all the information you will need to decide if a program is right for you: purpose, eligibility requirements, financial data, duration, special features, limitations, number awarded, and application date. You even get fax numbers, toll-free numbers, e-mail addresses, and web sites (when available), along with complete contact information.

WHAT'S EXCLUDED?

The focus of *How to Pay for Your Degree in Business & Related Fields* is on portable programs aimed specifically at high school seniors, high school graduates, current college students, returning college students, and graduate students interested in working on a degree in business-related fields at any school in the United States. While the directory is intended to be the most current and comprehensive source of information on available funding, there are some programs we've specifically excluded from the listing:

SAMPLE ENTRY

(1) **[5]**

(2) **ACCOUNTEMPS/AICPA STUDENT SCHOLARSHIP**

(3) American Institute of Certified Public Accountants
Attn: Academic and Career Development Division
1211 Avenue of the Americas
New York, NY 10036-8775
(212) 596-6223   Fax: (212) 596-6292
E-mail: educat@aicpa.org
Web site: www.aicpa.org

(4) **Purpose** To provide financial assistance to student affiliate members of the American Institute of Certified Public Accountants (AICPA) who are majoring in accounting, finance, or information systems.

(5) **Eligibility** Applicants must meet all of the following criteria: be AICPA student affiliate members; have a declared major in accounting, finance, or information systems; have a grade point average of 3.0 or higher; have completed at least 30 semester hours, including at least 6 semesters in accounting; be enrolled full time as an undergraduate student at a 4-year college or university; and be a U.S. citizen. Students who will be transferring to a 4-year school must include an acceptance letter from that school. Selection is based on outstanding academic achievement, leadership, and future career interests.

(6) **Financial data** The stipend is $2,500.

(7) **Duration** 1 year.

(8) **Additional information** No application materials should be sent to Accountemps.

(9) **Number awarded** 2 each year.

(10) **Deadline** March of each year.

DEFINITION

(1) **Entry number:** Consecutive number assigned to the references and used to index the entry.

(2) **Program title:** Title of scholarship, fellowship, grant, or award.

(3) **Sponsoring organization:** Name, address, and telephone number, toll-free number, fax number, e-mail address, and/or web site (when information was supplied) for organization sponsoring the program.

(4) **Purpose:** Basic program requirements; read the rest of the entry for additional detail

(5) **Eligibility:** Qualifications required of applicants and factors considered in the selection process.

(6) **Financial data:** Financial details of the program, including fixed sum, average amount, or range of funds offered, expenses for which funds may and may not be applied, and cash-related benefits supplied (e.g., room and board).

(7) **Duration:** Period for which support is provided; renewal prospects.

(8) **Additional information:** Any benefits, features, restrictions, or limitations (generally nonmonetary) associated with the program.

(9) **Number of awards:** Total number of recipients each year or other specified period.

(10) **Deadline:** The month by which applications must be submitted.

- *Programs not focused on business or related fields:*   Only funding opportunities set aside specifically for business-related fields are described here. If you are looking for money to support study, training, research, or creative activities in other, or broader, subject areas, check out the list of Reference Service Press's award-winning directories on the inside of the front cover. You can also look for general or other financial aid directories at your library or bookstore.

- *Programs that do not accept applications from U.S. citizens or residents:*   If a program is open only to foreign nationals or excludes Americans from applying, it is not covered.

- *Programs that do not award funds specifically to help students pay for their degree:*   While financial aid programs available to students working on a degree related to business are covered comprehensively in this directory, work-related opportunities (e.g., cooperative education, internships) are excluded—unless as part of their compensation students receive scholarships or other college funding. To find out about paid and unpaid work experience programs, use a source like Peterson's *Internships* directory.

- *School-based programs:* The directory identifies portable programs—ones that can be used at any number of schools. Financial aid administered by individual schools solely for the benefit of their incoming or continuing students is not covered. Write directly to the schools you are considering to get information on their offerings.

- *Money for study outside the United States:* Since there are comprehensive and up-to-date directories that describe all available funding for study and research abroad (see *Financial Aid for Research and Creative Activities Abroad* and *Financial Aid for Study and Training Abroad,* both published by Reference Service Press), only programs that support study or research in the United States are covered here.

- *Very restrictive programs:* In general, programs are excluded if they are open only to a limited geographic area (less than a state), are available to a very limited membership group (e.g., a local union or a tightly targeted organization), or offer very limited financial support (under $500).

- *Programs that did not respond to our research inquiries:* Program are included in *How to Pay for Your Degree in Business & Related Fields* only if the sponsors responded to our research requests for up-to-date information (see below for details).

WHAT'S UPDATED?

The preparation of each new edition of *How to Pay for Your Degree in Business & Related Fields* involves extensive updating and revision. To make sure that the information included here is both reliable and current, the editors at Reference Service Press 1) reviewed and updated all relevant programs currently in our funding database and 2) searched exhaustively for new program leads in a variety of sources, including directories, news reports, newsletters, annual reports, and sites on the Internet. Since we only include program descriptions that are written directly from information supplied by the sponsoring organization (no information is ever taken from secondary sources), we sent up to four collection letters (followed by up to three telephone inquiries, if necessary) to each sponsor identified in the process. Despite our best efforts, however, some sponsoring organizations still failed to respond and, as a result, their programs are not included in this edition of the directory.

The 2004-2006 edition of *How to Pay for Your Degree in Business & Related Fields* completely revises and updates the previous (first) edition. Programs that have ceased operation have been dropped. Similarly, programs that have broadened their scope and no longer focus on business-related fields have also been removed from the listing. Profiles of continuing programs have been rewritten to reflect current requirements; nearly 85 percent of the continuing programs reported subsequent changes in their locations, deadlines, or benefits since 2002. In addition, more than 360 new entries have been added. The result is a listing of 675 scholarships, fellowships, grants, awards, and other funding opportunities available to students working on a degree in business or related fields.

HOW THE DIRECTORY IS ORGANIZED

How to Pay for Your Degree in Business & Related Fields is divided into two sections: 1) a detailed list of funding opportunities open to students working on an undergraduate or graduate degree in such fields as accounting, actuarial science, agricultural economics, banking, business administration, economics, finance, management, marketing and sales, personnel administration, and real estate; and 2) a set of indexes to help you pinpoint available funding programs.

Funding for Students Working on a Degree in Business and Related Fields. The first section of the directory describes 675 scholarships, fellowships, grants, and awards for students working on an undergraduate or graduate degree in business-related fields. The programs listed are sponsored by 500 different federal and state government agencies, professional organizations, foundations, educational associations, and military/veterans organizations. All business-related fields are covered, including accounting, actuarial science, agricultural economics, banking, business administration, economics, finance, management, marketing and sales, personnel administration, and real estate. The focus is on programs tenable in the United States that are open to students who are U.S. citizens or permanent residents.

To help you tailor your search, the entries in this section are grouped into four main categories: scholarships, fellowships, grants, and awards. Programs that supply more than one type of assistance are listed in all relevant categories. For example, both undergraduate and graduate students may apply for the Ralph and Valerie Thomas Scholarship, so the program is described in the Scholarships and the Fellowships subsections.

Entries in each of the subsections appear alphabetically by program title. Each program entry has been designed to provide a concise profile that, as the sample on page 7 illustrates, includes information (when available) on organization address and telephone numbers (including fax and toll-free numbers), e-mail address and web site, purpose, eligibility, money awarded, duration, special features, limitations, number of awards, and application deadline.

The information provided for each of the programs covered in this section was supplied by sponsoring organizations in response to questionnaires we sent through mid-2004. While *How to Pay for Your Degree in Business & Related Fields* is intended to cover available funding as comprehensively as possible, some sponsoring organizations did not respond to our research inquiries and, consequently, are not included in the first edition of the directory.

Indexes. To help you find the aid you need, we have constructed five indexes; these will let you access the listings by sponsoring organization, residency, tenability, specialty, and deadline date. These indexes use a word-by-word alphabetical arrangement. Note: numbers in the index refer to entry numbers, not to page numbers in the book.

Sponsoring Organization Index. This index makes it easy to identify agencies that offer funding to students working on an undergraduate or graduate degree in a business related field. More than 500 sponsoring organizations are listed alphabetically, word by word. In addition, we've used a code to help you identify the type of funding offered by these organizations (e.g., "F" = Fellowships; "A" = Awards).

Residency Index. Some programs listed in this book are restricted to residents of a particular state or region. Others are open to students wherever they live. This index helps you identify programs available only to residents in your area as well as programs that have no residency restrictions.

Tenability Index. Some programs in this book can be used only in specific cities, counties, states, or regions. Others may be used anywhere in the United States (or even abroad). Use this index to find out what programs are available to support your studies in a particular geographic area.

Specialty Index. Refer to this index when you want to identify funding opportunities for undergraduate or graduate students working on a degree in a specific business-related field, including accounting, actuarial science, agricultural economics, banking, business administration, economics, finance, management, marketing and sales, personnel administration, and real estate.

Calendar Index. Since most financial aid programs have specific deadline dates, some may have closed by the time you begin to look for funding. You can use the Calendar Index to identify which programs are still open. This index is arranged by type of funding offered (e.g., scholarship, grant) and divided by month during which the deadline falls. Filing dates can and quite often do vary from year to year; consequently, the dates in this index should be viewed as only approximations after mid-2006. It is important to note that not all sponsoring organizations supplied information on application deadline, so some of the programs described in the directory are not listed here.

HOW TO USE THE DIRECTORY

Here are some tips to help you get the most out of the financial aid listings in *How to Pay for Your Degree in Business & Related Fields:*

To Locate Programs Offering a Particular Type of Financial Assistance. If you are looking for programs offering a particular type of financial aid (e.g., a scholarship for undergraduate study, a grant for independent research), turn first to the definitions of these program types on page 6 and then browse through the entries in each of the appropriate categories in the first section of the directory. Keep in mind that more than one of these subsections may contain funding leads for you. For example, if you are a graduate student looking for money to help you pay for the educational and research costs associated with your master's degree, you will not want to overlook the opportunities described in the Fellowships, Grants, and even Awards subsections. Since programs with multiple purposes are listed in every appropriate category, each subsection functions as a self-contained entity. In fact, you can browse through any of the subsections in the directory without first consulting an index.

To Find Information on a Particular Financial Aid Program. If you know both the name of a particular financial aid program and the type of assistance offered by the program (scholarship, fellowship, etc.), then go directly to the appropriate category in the first section of the directory, where you'll find program profiles arranged alphabetically by title.

To Browse Quickly Through the Listings. Turn to the type of funding category that interests you (scholarships, fellowships, etc.) and read the "Purpose" field in each entry. In seconds, you'll know if this is an opportunity that might apply to you. If it is, read the rest of the information in the entry to make sure you meet all of the program requirements before writing for an application form. Remember: don't apply if you don't qualify!

To Locate Financial Aid Programs Sponsored by a Particular Organization. The Sponsoring Organization Index makes it easy to determine which groups are providing funding to undergraduate and graduate students working on a degree in a business-related fields (more than 500 are listed here) and to identify specific financial aid programs offered by a particular sponsor. Each entry number in the index is coded to indicate funding type, to help you target appropriate entries.

To Locate Financial Aid Based on Residency or Where You Want to Study. Use the Residency Index to identify funding that has been set aside to support applicants from your area. If you are looking for funding to support studies in a particular city, county, state, or region, turn to the Tenability Index. Both of these indexes are subdivided by type of funding (scholarships, fellowships, etc.), to help you identify various ways to pay for your degree in business or related fields. When using these indexes, always check the listings under the term "United States," since the programs indexed there have no geographic restrictions and can be used in any area.

To Locate Financial Aid for Study or Research in a Specific Business-Related Field. Turn to the Specialty Index first if you are interested in identifying available funding in a specific business-related field, including accounting, actuarial science, agricultural economics, banking, business administration, economics, finance, management, marketing and sales, personnel administration, and real estate. Each index entry indicates the type of funding available: scholarships, fellowships, grants, or awards.

To Locate Financial Aid by Deadline Date. If you are working with specific time constraints and want to weed out financial aid programs whose filing dates you won't be able to meet, turn first to the Calendar Index and check the program references listed under the appropriate program type and month. Note: not all sponsoring organizations supplied deadline information, so not all programs are covered in this index. To identify every relevant financial aid program, regardless of filing dates, read through all the entries in each of the program subsections (Scholarships, Fellowships, etc.) that apply.

PLANS TO UPDATE THE DIRECTORY

This is the second biennial edition of *How to Pay for Your Degree in Business & Related Fields.* The next edition will cover the years 2006-2008 and will be released in mid-2006.

OTHER RELATED PUBLICATIONS

How to Pay for Your Degree in Business & Related Fields is one of a dozen financial aid titles published by Reference Service Press that deal with specific subject areas, including *How to Pay for Your Degree in Education & Related Fields* and *Money for Graduate Students in the Social & Behavioral Sciences.* For more information on these and other award-winning financial aid directories, you can 1) write to Reference Service Press's marketing department at 5000 Windplay Drive, Suite 4, El Dorado Hills, CA 95762; 2) call us at (916) 939-9620; 3) fax us at (916) 939-9626; 4) send us an e-mail at findaid@aol.com; or 5) visit our web site: http://www.rspfunding.com.

ACKNOWLEDGEMENTS

A debt of gratitude is owed all the organizations that contributed information to this edition of *How to Pay for Your Degree in Business & Related Fields.* Their generous cooperation has helped to make the second edition of this publication a current and comprehensive survey of available funding.

ABOUT THE AUTHOR

Dr. Gail Ann Schlachter has worked for more than three decades as a library administrator, a library educator, and an administrator of library-related publishing companies. Among the reference books to her credit are the biennially-issued *College Student's Guide to Merit and Other No-Need Funding* (named by *Choice* as one of the outstanding reference titles of the year) and two award-winning bibliographic guides: *Minorities and Women: A Guide to Reference Literature in the Social Sciences* (which also was chosen as an "Outstanding Reference Book of the Year" by *Choice)* and *Reference Sources in Library and Information Services* (which won the first Knowledge Industry Publications "Award for Library Literature"). She was the reference book review editor for *RQ* (now *Reference and User Services Quarterly)* for 10 years, is a past president of the American Library Association's Reference and User Services Association, is the former editor of the *Reference and User Services Association Quarterly,* and recently was elected to her third term on the American Library Association's governing council. In recognition of her outstanding contributions to reference service, Dr. Schlachter has been awarded both the Isadore Gilbert Mudge Citation and the Louis Shores/Oryx Press Award.

Dr. R. David Weber has been teaching economics and history at Los Angeles Harbor College (Wilmington, California) since 1975. He is the author of a number of critically-acclaimed reference works, including *Dissertations in Urban History* and the three-volume *Energy Information Guide.* With Gail Schlachter, he is the author of Reference Service Press's award-winning *High School Senior's Guide to Merit and Other No-Need Funding* and a number of other financial aid titles, including *Financial Aid for Veterans, Military Personnel, and Their Dependents* and *Financial Aid for the Disabled and Their Families,* which was selected as one of the "Best Reference Books of the Year" by *Library Journal.*

How to Pay for Your Degree in Business & Related Fields

Scholarships •
Fellowships •
Grants •
Awards •

Scholarships

Described here are 416 funding opportunities designed to support undergraduates majoring in a business-related field, including accounting, actuarial science, agricultural economics, banking, business administration, economics, finance, management, marketing and sales, personnel administration, and real estate. Usually no return of service or repayment is required. Note: other funding opportunities for undergraduate students working on a degree in business or a related field are also described in the Grants and Awards subsections.

[1]
AARP FOUNDATION FOUNDER'S SCHOLARS AWARD

Association for Gerontology in Higher Education
1030 15th Street, N.W., Suite 240
Washington, DC 20005-1503
(202) 289-9806   Fax: (202) 289-9824
E-mail: info@aghe.org
Web: www.aghe.org

Purpose To provide financial assistance to undergraduate students who are interested in preparing for a career related to the financial aspects of the process of aging.

Eligibility Only nominations from faculty at academic institutions are accepted; the institution must be accredited, be located in the United States, and offer a program in gerontology and finance (including economics and business). Nominees must 1) have a GPA of 3.0 or higher; 2) be planning to work in the field of aging; and 3) exhibit interest in financial issues that affect work and retirement throughout the life process and concerns of older consumers (this interest can be demonstrated by course work, independent study, volunteer activities, internships, research publications, prior or current work experience, and/or career plans). Selection is based on academic record, academic honors received, membership in honorary societies, faculty recommendations, and career commitment (as evidenced by course work, independent study, volunteer activities, internships, research, publications, and work experience). Preference is given to students attending institutions belonging to the Association for Gerontology in Higher Education.

Financial data The stipend is $4,000. Funds are to be used for tuition, fees, and books. If tuition and fees at the recipient's institution are less than $5,000 per year, a stipend to cover living expenses may be included in the award. Recipients also receive a $1,000 award to travel to the annual professional meeting of the Gerontological Society of America (GSA).

Duration 1 year; nonrenewable.

Additional information Funding for this program is provided by the AARP Foundation. Although students may be enrolled part time at the time of application, they will be expected to enroll on a full-time basis if they are awarded the scholarship. Recipients are required to write a research paper on some aspects of aging and finance in conjunction with a faculty mentor and report on the progress of the paper at the GSA meeting.

Number awarded 1 each year.

Deadline June of each year.

[2]
ACCOUNTANCY BOARD OF OHIO EDUCATION ASSISTANCE PROGRAM

Accountancy Board of Ohio
77 South High Street, 18th Floor
Columbus, OH 43215-6128
(614) 466-4135   Fax: (614) 466-2628
Web: acc.ohio.gov/edrule.html

Purpose To provide financial assistance to minority and financially disadvantaged students enrolled in an accounting education program at Ohio academic institutions approved by the Accountancy Board of Ohio.

Eligibility This program is open to minority and financially disadvantaged Ohio residents enrolled full time as sophomores, juniors, or seniors in an accounting program at an accredited college or university in the state. Students who remain in good standing at their institutions and who enter a qualified fifth-year program are also eligible if funds are available. Minority is defined as people with significant ancestry from Africa (excluding the Middle East), Asia (excluding the Middle East), Central America and the Caribbean islands, South America, and the islands of the Pacific Ocean. Financial disadvantage is defined according to information provided on the Free Application for Federal Student Aid (FAFSA). U.S. citizenship or permanent resident status is required.

Financial data The amount of the stipend is determined annually but does not exceed the in-state tuition at Ohio public universities.

Duration 1 year; nonrenewable.

Number awarded Several each year.

Deadline May or November of each year.

[3]
ACCOUNTEMPS/AICPA STUDENT SCHOLARSHIP

American Institute of Certified Public Accountants
Attn: Academic and Career Development Division
1211 Avenue of the Americas
New York, NY 10036-8775
(212) 596-6223   Fax: (212) 596-6292
E-mail: educat@aicpa.org
Web: www.aicpa.org

Purpose To provide financial assistance to student affiliate members of the American Institute of Certified Public Accountants (AICPA) who are working on an undergraduate or graduate degree in accounting, finance, or information systems.

Eligibility This program is open to full-time undergraduate and graduate students who are AICPA student affiliate members with a declared major in accounting, finance, or information systems. Applicants must have completed at least 30 semester hours, including at least 6 semesters in accounting, with a GPA of 3.0 or higher and be a U.S. citizen. Students who will be transferring to a 4-year school must include an acceptance letter from that school. Selection is based on outstanding academic achievement, leadership, and future career interests.

Financial data The stipend is $2,500.

Duration 1 year.

Number awarded 2 each year.

Deadline March of each year.

[4]
ACCOUNTING CAREERS UIL SCHOLARSHIPS

Texas Society of Certified Public Accountants
Attn: Accounting Education Foundation
14860 Montfort Drive, Suite 150
Dallas, TX 75240-6705
(972) 687-8500   Toll-free: (800) 428-0272, ext. 233
Fax: (972) 687-8646   E-mail: Sking@tscpa.net
Web: www.tscpa.org

Purpose To provide financial assistance to high school students in Texas who plan to attend a university in the state and major in accounting.

Eligibility This program is open to high school seniors in Texas who participate in the state University Interscholastic League (UIL) competition. Applicants must plan to major in accounting at 1 of 52 Texas colleges and universities and rank in the top 10% of their high school graduating class.

Financial data The stipend is $1,000 per year.

Duration Up to 5 years.

Number awarded 5 each year: 1 in each of the 5 UIL competition divisions in the state.

[5]
ADELA R. SCHARR MEMORIAL SCHOLARSHIP

Adela R. Scharr Memorial Scholarship Fund
c/o Jan Pocock
224 New Ballwin Road
Ballwin, MO 63021

Purpose To provide financial assistance to women currently enrolled in a mid-central U.S. college or university and planning to prepare for a career in aviation.

Eligibility This program is open to women majoring in engineering, science, liberal arts, business, or flight/maintenance training. Applicants must have completed at least 1 year of college at a mid-central U.S. school with a GPA of 2.0 or higher. They must be interested in preparing for a career in aviation.

Financial data The stipend is $500.

Duration 1 year.

Number awarded 1 each year.

[6]
ADVANTAGE PAYROLL SCHOLARSHIP

Maine Society of CPAs
Attn: Executive Director
153 U.S. Route 1, Suite 8
Scarborough, ME 04074-9053
(207) 883-6090   Toll-free: (800) 660-2721 (within ME)
Fax: (207) 883-6211   E-mail: wwhiting@mecpa.org
Web: www.mecpa.org

Purpose To provide financial assistance to students in Maine majoring in accounting.

Eligibility This program is open to college students majoring in accounting in Maine. Applicants must have a GPA of 3.0 or higher, be able to demonstrate writing skills, and have participated in community activities. Selection is based on academic achievement, writing skills, extracurricular activities, work experience, career goals, and financial need.

Financial data The stipend is $1,000.

Duration 1 year.

Number awarded 1 each year.

[7]
A&E INCORPORATED COLLEGE-TO-WORK SCHOLARSHIP

Wisconsin Foundation for Independent Colleges, Inc.
735 North Water Street, Suite 800
Milwaukee, WI 53202-4100
(414) 273-5980   Fax: (414) 273-5995
E-mail: info@wficweb.org
Web: www.wficweb.org/documents/coll_work.htm

Purpose To provide financial assistance and work experience to students at designated private colleges in Wisconsin who are interested in preparing for a career in a field related to business or engineering.

Eligibility This program is open to full-time sophomores, juniors, and seniors at the following independent colleges in Wisconsin: Alverno College, Cardinal Stritch University, Carthage College, Marquette University, Milwaukee School of Engineering, Mount Mary College, and Wisconsin Lutheran College. Applicants must be preparing for a career in accounting, human resources, sales, production control, quality control, computer science, communications, marketing, or engineering. They must have a GPA of 3.0 or higher and be interested in an internship with A&E Incorporated. Along with their application, they must submit a 1-page autobiography, transcripts, a list of campus involvement and academic honors, a resume including 3 references, and 2 letters of recommendation.

Financial data The scholarship stipend is $1,500. The internship is paid hourly.

Duration 1 year for the scholarship; 10 weeks during the summer for the internship.

Additional information This program is sponsored by A&E Incorporated in association with the Lang Family Foundation.

Number awarded 1 each year.

Deadline January of each year.

[8]
AFSCME/UNCF UNION SCHOLARS PROGRAM

United Negro College Fund
Attn: Corporate Scholars Program
P.O. Box 1435
Alexandria, VA 22313-9998
Toll-free: (866) 671-7237   E-mail: internship@uncf.org
Web: www.uncf.org/Scholarship/CorporateScholars.asp

Purpose To provide financial assistance and work experience to students of color who are interested in working during the summer on an organizing campaign for the American Federation of State, County and Municipal Employees (AFSCME).

Eligibility This program is open to students of color, including African Americans, Hispanic Americans, Asian/Pacific Islander Americans, and American Indians/Alaskan Natives. Applicants must be second semester sophomores or juniors and majoring in ethnic studies, women's studies, labor studies, American studies, sociology, anthropology, history, political science, psychology, social work, or economics. They must have a GPA of 2.5 or higher and be interested in working on a union organizing campaign at 1 of several locations in the United States.

Financial data The program provides a stipend of $4,000, on-site housing at their location, a week-long orientation and training, and (based on successful performance during the organizing campaign) a $5,000 scholarship.

Duration 10 weeks for the organizing assignment; 1 year for the scholarship.

Number awarded Varies each year.

Deadline February of each year.

[9]
AG SERVICES OF AMERICA SCHOLARSHIPS

National FFA Organization
Attn: Scholarship Office
6060 FFA Drive
P.O. Box 68960
Indianapolis, IN 46268-0960
(317) 802-4321   Fax: (317) 802-5321
E-mail: scholarships@ffa.org
Web: www.ffa.org

Purpose To provide financial assistance to FFA members who are interested in studying agriculture or related fields (including agricultural economics) in college.

Eligibility This program is open to members who are graduating high school seniors planning to enroll full time in college. Applicants must be interested in working on a 2- or 4-year degree in agricultural production, agricultural systems management, agricultural economics, or a related discipline. Preference is given to those who receive 50% of their family income from production agriculture and those whose chapters participate in the data center on www.powerfarm.com. Selection is based on academic achievement (10 points for GPA, 10 points for SAT or ACT score, 10 points for class rank), leadership in FFA activities (30 points), leadership in community activities (10 points), and participation in the Supervised Agricultural Experience (SAE) program (30 points). U.S. citizenship is required.

Financial data The stipend is $1,000. Funds are paid directly to the recipient.

Duration 1 year; nonrenewable.

Additional information Funding for this program is provided by Ag Services of America, Inc. of Cedar Falls, Iowa.

Number awarded 3 each year.

Deadline February of each year.

[10]
AGCO CORPORATION SCHOLARSHIPS

National FFA Organization
Attn: Scholarship Office
6060 FFA Drive
P.O. Box 68960
Indianapolis, IN 46268-0960
(317) 802-4321   Fax: (317) 802-5321
E-mail: scholarships@ffa.org
Web: www.ffa.org

Purpose To provide financial assistance to FFA members interested in studying an agricultural field (including agribusiness) in college.

Eligibility This program is open to members who are graduating high school seniors planning to enroll full time in college. Applicants must be planning to work on a 4-year college degree in agricultural engineering, agricultural mechanization, agricultural economics, agricultural communications, or agri-

business. Selection is based on academic achievement (10 points for GPA, 10 points for SAT or ACT score, 10 points for class rank), leadership in FFA activities (30 points), leadership in community activities (10 points), and participation in the Supervised Agricultural Experience (SAE) program (30 points). U.S. citizenship is required.

Financial data The stipend is $2,000. Funds are paid directly to the recipient.

Duration 1 year; nonrenewable.

Additional information Funding for these scholarships is provided by AGCO Corporation.

Number awarded 4 each year.

Deadline February of each year.

[11]
AIMR 11 SEPTEMBER MEMORIAL
SCHOLARSHIP FUND

Association for Investment Management and Research
Attn: Research Foundation of AIMR
560 Ray C. Hunt Drive
P.O. Box 3668
Charlottesville, VA 22903-0668
(434) 951-5391   Toll-free: (800) 247-8132
Fax: (434) 951-5370
E-mail: 11septemberfund@aimr.org
Web: www.aimr.org

Purpose To provide financial assistance to disabled victims of the September 11, 2001 terrorist attack and the family members of victims who are interested in majoring in a business-related field.

Eligibility This program is open to 1) victims of the September 11, 2001 terrorist attacks who are permanently disabled, and 2) children, spouses, and domestic partners of persons who died or were permanently disabled as a direct result of the attacks. Applicants must be planning to study finance, economics, accounting, or business ethics at an accredited undergraduate or graduate institution. They may come from any country and may study at any qualifying college or university in the world. Selection is based on financial need, academic record, and demonstrated commitment to high levels of professional ethics.

Financial data The stipend is $5,000 per year.

Duration 1 year; may be renewed up to 4 additional years.

Additional information This program is administered by Scholarship Management Services of Scholarship America, One Scholarship Way, P.O. Box 297, St. Peter, MN 56082, (507) 931-1682, (800) 537-4180, Fax: (507) 931-9168, E-mail: smsinfo@csfa.org.

Number awarded Varies each year.

Deadline May of each year.

[12]
ALBUQUERQUE CPA CHAPTER SCHOLARSHIPS

New Mexico Society of Certified Public Accountants
Attn: Scholarships in Accounting
1650 University N.E., Suite 450
Albuquerque, NM 87102-1733
(505) 246-1699   Toll-free: (800) 926-2522
Fax: (505) 246-1686   E-mail: nmcpa@nmcpa.org
Web: www.nmcpa.org

Purpose To provide financial assistance to accounting students at New Mexico universities and colleges.

Eligibility This program is open to full-time students at New Mexico colleges and universities who have completed 12 semester hours in accounting, are currently enrolled in 6 or more accounting hours, have completed 75 hours overall, and have a cumulative GPA of 3.0 or higher. Applicants must have a permanent home address in the Albuquerque metropolitan area. Selection is based on academic achievement, extracurricular activities, career objectives and goals in accounting, and financial need.

Financial data The stipend is $750.

Duration 1 year; may be renewed 1 additional year.

Number awarded Varies each year.

Deadline September of each year.

[13]
ALEX POSTLETHWAITE SCHOLARSHIP

Society of Louisiana Certified Public Accountants
Attn: LCPA Education Foundation
2400 Veterans Boulevard, Suite 500
Kenner, LA 70062-4739
(504) 464-1040   Toll-free: (800) 288-5272
Fax: (504) 469-7930
Web: www.lcpa.org/LCPAScholarships.html

Purpose To provide financial assistance to currently-enrolled college students in Louisiana who are interested in becoming certified public accountants.

Eligibility This program is open to Louisiana residents who are currently enrolled full time in an accounting program at a 4-year college or university in Louisiana. Applicants must have completed at least 4 semesters by the fall of the academic year in which the application is filed and have a GPA of 2.5 or higher. Along with their application, they must submit a 2-page essay on their perception of the CPA's role on the job and in the community, including how they plan to contribute to the profession and to the community.

Financial data The stipend is $1,000.

Duration 1 year.

Number awarded 1 each year.

[14]
ALL STUDENT LOAN GROUP COLLEGE SCHOLARSHIP PROGRAM FOR BUSINESS STUDENTS

All Student Loan Group
12100 Wilshire Boulevard, Suite 1200
Los Angeles, CA 90025-7122
Toll-free: (888) 271-9721   E-mail: info@allslg.org
Web: www.allstudentloan.org

Purpose To provide financial assistance to business students who are members of designated organizations.

Eligibility This program is open to high school seniors and college business students who are members of Future Business Leaders of America-Phi Beta Lambda, Business Professionals of America, or DECA. Applicants must be enrolled or planning to enroll in an institution that participates in the Federal Family Education Loan Program. They must submit a 500-word essay on "How Will You Manage Your Collegiate Financial Responsibilities?" Selection is based primarily on participation in the qualifying student organization.

Financial data The stipend is $500.

Duration 1 year.

Number awarded 2 each year.

Deadline May of each year.

[15]
ALLISON TRANSMISSION AND INDIANAPOLIS METAL CENTER SCHOLARSHIPS

National FFA Organization
Attn: Scholarship Office
6060 FFA Drive
P.O. Box 68960
Indianapolis, IN 46268-0960
(317) 802-4321   Fax: (317) 802-5321
E-mail: scholarships@ffa.org
Web: www.ffa.org

Purpose To provide financial assistance to FFA members who are from an ethnic minority group interested in majoring in selected fields.

Eligibility This program is open to members who are graduating high school seniors planning to enroll full time in college. Applicants must be members of ethnic minority groups interested in working on a 4-year degree in the following areas of agriculture: management, finance, science, engineering, and related specialties, although non-agricultural majors are also eligible. They must have a GPA of 3.0 or higher and be able to demonstrate financial need. Selection is based on academic achievement (10 points for GPA, 10 points for SAT or ACT score, 10 points for class rank), leadership in FFA activities (30 points), leadership in community activities (10 points), and participation in the Supervised Agricultural Experience (SAE) program (30 points). U.S. citizenship is required.

Financial data The stipend is $5,000 per year. Funds are paid directly to the recipient.

Duration 1 year; nonrenewable.

Additional information Funding for these scholarships is provided by the Allison Transmission and Indianapolis Metal Center of General Motors Corporation.

Number awarded 2 each year.

Deadline February of each year.

[16]
AMERICAN COUNCIL OF THE BLIND OF TEXAS SCHOLARSHIPS

American Council of the Blind of Texas
c/o Chris Prentice, President
109 East Sixth Street
Plainview, TX 79072
(806) 839-2901   E-mail: chris@attorney-prentice.com
Web: www.acbtexas.org/scholarshipinfo.html

Purpose To provide financial assistance for college to blind and visually impaired residents of Texas.

Eligibility This program is restricted to legally or totally blind Texas residents (documentation requested). Applicants may be high school seniors, high school graduates, or currently-enrolled college students (including students at technical and vocational institutions of higher learning). All applicants (high school or college) must have a GPA of 3.0 or higher. Required as part of the application process are: a transcript, a copy of the acceptance letter (if not yet attending college), 2 to 3 letters of recommendation not more than 12 months old, and a completed application form signed by a member of the Texas council. Selection is based on academic achievement, community service, and financial need.

Financial data Stipends range from $250 to $1,000 per year. Funds may be used for any educational purpose, including tuition, books, housing, and transportation.

Duration 1 year; recipients may reapply.

Additional information Recipients do not need to study in a field related to blindness; in general, they may major in any field (although 1 of the scholarships is specifically for a student interested in majoring in food service and another is specifically for a student majoring in business administration). Information is also available from Nolan Dyer, Roy Road, Texarkana, TX 75501, (903) 832-5038.

Number awarded 8 each year: 1 at $1,000; 3 at $500; and 4 at $250.

Deadline April of each year.

[17]
AMERICAN SOCIETY OF MILITARY COMPTROLLERS NATIONAL SCHOLARSHIP PROGRAM

American Society of Military Comptrollers
Attn: National Awards Committee
2034 Eisenhower Avenue, Suite 145
Alexandria, VA 22314-4650
(703) 549-0360   Toll-free: (800) 462-5637
E-mail: asmchq@aol.com
Web: www.asmconline.org

Purpose To provide financial assistance to high school seniors and recent graduates interested in preparing for a career in financial management.

Eligibility This program is open to high school seniors and to people who graduated from high school during the preceding 6 months. Applicants must be planning to enter college in a field of study directly related to financial resource management, including business administration, economics, public administration, computer science, or operations research related to financial management, accounting, and finance. They must be endorsed by a chapter of the American Society of Military Comptrollers (ASMC). Selection is based on scholastic achievement, leadership ability, extracurricular activities, career and academic goals, and financial need.

Financial data Stipends are $2,000 or $1,000 per year.

Duration 1 year.

Additional information The ASMC is open to all financial management professionals employed by the U.S. Department of Defense and Coast Guard, both civilian and military.

Number awarded 10 each year: 5 at $2,000 and 5 at $1,000.

Deadline March of each year.

[18]
AMERICAN SOCIETY OF WOMEN ACCOUNTANTS SCHOLARSHIPS

American Society of Women Accountants
Attn: Administrative Director
8405 Greensboro Drive, Suite 800
McLean, VA 22102
(703) 506-3265   Toll-free: (800) 326-2163
Fax: (703) 506-3266   E-mail: aswa@aswa.org
Web: www.aswa.org/scholarship.html

Purpose To provide financial assistance to undergraduate and graduate women interested in preparing for a career in accounting.

Eligibility This program is open to women who are enrolled in a college, university, or professional school as either part-time or full-time students working on a bachelor's or master's degree in accounting. Applicants must have completed at least 60 semester hours with a declared accounting major. Selection is based on career goals, communication skills, GPA, personal circumstances, and financial need. Membership in the American Society of Women Accountants (ASWA) is not required. Applications must be submitted to a local ASWA chapter.

Financial data The stipends range from $1,500 to $4,500 each.

Duration 1 year; recipients may reapply.

Additional information Founded in 1938 to assist women C.P.A.s, the organization has nearly 5,000 members in 30 chapters. Some chapters offer scholarships on the local/regional level. Funding for this program is provided by the Educational Foundation for Women in Accounting.

Number awarded Varies each year: recently, 8 of these scholarships were available, with a total value of $14,000.

Deadline Local chapters must submit their candidates to the national office by February of each year.

[19]
ANNA M. WINSTON FOUNDERS' SCHOLARSHIPS

National Association of Black Accountants
Attn: Director, Center for Advancement of Minority
    Accountants
7249-A Hanover Parkway
Greenbelt, MD 20770
(301) 474-NABA, ext. 114   Fax: (301) 474-3114
E-mail: cquinn@nabainc.org
Web: www.nabainc.org

Purpose To provide financial assistance to student members of the National Association of Black Accountants (NABA) who are working on an undergraduate or graduate degree in a field related to accounting.

Eligibility This program is open to NABA members who are members of ethnic minority groups enrolled full time as 1) an undergraduate freshman, sophomore, junior, or first-semester senior majoring in accounting, business, or finance; or 2) a graduate student working on a master's degree in accounting. Applicants must have a GPA of 3.5 or higher in their major and 3.3 or higher overall. Selection is based on grades, financial need, and a 500-word autobiography that discusses career objectives, leadership abilities, community activities, and involvement in NABA.

Financial data The stipend is $500 per year.

Duration 1 year.

Number awarded Varies each year.

Deadline December of each year.

[20]
APPRAISAL INSTITUTE EDUCATION TRUST SCHOLARSHIP

Appraisal Institute
Attn: Appraisal Institute Education Trust
550 West Van Buren Street, Suite 1000
Chicago, IL 60607
(312) 335-4100   Fax: (312) 335-4400
E-mail: ocarreon@appraisalinstitute.org
Web: www.appraisalinstitute.org

Purpose To provide financial assistance to graduate and undergraduate students majoring in real estate or allied fields.

Eligibility This program is open to U.S. citizens who are graduate or undergraduate students majoring in real estate appraisal, land economics, real estate, or related fields. Applicants must submit a statement regarding their general activities and intellectual interests in college; college training; activities and employment outside of college; contemplated line of study for a degree; and career they expect to follow after graduation. Selection is based on academic excellence.

Financial data The stipend is $3,000 for graduate students or $2,000 for undergraduate students.

Duration 1 year.

Number awarded At least 1 each year.

Deadline March of each year.

[21]
APPRAISAL INSTITUTE MINORITIES AND WOMEN EDUCATIONAL SCHOLARSHIP PROGRAM

Appraisal Institute
Attn: Minorities and Women Scholarship Fund
550 West Van Buren Street, Suite 1000
Chicago, IL 60607
(312) 335-4121   Fax: (312) 335-4118
E-mail: sbarnes@appraisalinstitute.org
Web: www.appraisalinstitute.org

Purpose To provide financial assistance to women and minority undergraduate students majoring in real estate or allied fields.

Eligibility This program is open to members of groups underrepresented in the real estate appraisal profession.

Those groups include women, American Indians, Alaska Natives, Asians, Black or African Americans, Hispanics or Latinos, and Native Hawaiians or other Pacific Islanders. Applicants must be full- or part-time students enrolled in real estate courses within a degree-granting college, university, or junior college. They must submit evidence of demonstrated financial need and a GPA of 2.5 or higher. U.S. citizenship is required.

Financial data The stipend is $1,000 per year. Funds are paid directly to the recipient's institution to be used for tuition and fees.

Duration 1 year.

Number awarded At least 1 each year.

Deadline April of each year.

[22]
APWA HORIZONS FRONT RANGE SCHOLARSHIP

American Public Works Association-Colorado Chapter
c/o Paul A. Hindman
Urban Drainage and Flood Control District
2480 West 26th Avenue, Suite 156-B
Denver, CO 80211
(303) 455-6277   Fax: (303) 455-7880
E-mail: coloapwa@eazy.net
Web: www.coloapwa.org/scholarships/scholar.html

Purpose To provide financial assistance to high school seniors in Colorado who plan to attend a college or university in the state to prepare for a career in public works.

Eligibility This program is open to seniors graduating from high schools in Colorado who plan to attend a college, university, or junior college in the state. Applicants must be planning to major in accounting, architecture, biology, business, chemistry, construction management, engineering, finance, management, or other field associated with public works. They must have completed a course in trigonometry and have a GPA of 3.0 or higher. Preference is given to applicants preparing for a career that promotes the public sector. Financial need is not considered in the selection process.

Financial data The stipend is $1,500.

Duration 1 year.

Additional information Recipients are given the name of a public works professional who works near their home and works in the area of local government, private consulting, or construction. Students must contact that professional and arrange to "shadow" them for half a day. Following completion of that assignment, they receive the scholarship funds, made payable to the college or university.

Number awarded 1 or more each year.

Deadline March of each year.

[23]
ARIZONA PRIVATE SCHOOL ASSOCIATION SCHOLARSHIP

Arizona Private School Association
202 East McDowell Road, Suite 273
Phoenix, AZ 85004-4536
(602) 254-5199   Fax: (602) 254-5073
E-mail: apsa@eschelon.com
Web: www.arizonapsa.org/scholarships.html

Purpose To provide financial assistance to high school seniors in Arizona who are interested in attending a career college to prepare for jobs in selected fields.

Eligibility Open to high school seniors in Arizona who are interested in attending a career college in the state, to prepare for a career in such fields as computer or information technology, health care, cosmetology, massage, business, criminal justice, or health occupations. The sponsor provides 2 scholarships to each high school in the state. Recipients are then selected by the scholarship directors or counselors at their high school.

Financial data The stipend is a $1,000 award certificate to be used to pay for tuition at a career college in Arizona.

Duration 1 year.

Number awarded 2 each year at each high school in Arizona.

[24]
ASMC MEMBERS' CONTINUING EDUCATION PROGRAM AWARD

American Society of Military Comptrollers
Attn: National Awards Committee
2034 Eisenhower Avenue, Suite 145
Alexandria, VA 22314-4650
(703) 549-0360   Toll-free: (800) 462-5637
E-mail: asmchq@aol.com
Web: www.asmconline.org

Purpose To provide financial assistance for continuing education to members of the American Society of Military Comptrollers (ASMC).

Eligibility Applicants for this assistance must have been members of the society for at least 2 full years and must have been active in the local chapter at some level (board member, committee chair or member, volunteer for chapter events, etc.). They must be enrolled in or planning to enroll in an academic institution in a field of study directly related to financial resource management, including business administration, economics, public administration, computer science, or operations research related to financial management, accounting, and finance. As part of the selection process, they must submit an essay of up to 500 words on their academic and career goals and financial need.

Financial data Stipends are $1,000 per year.

Duration 1 year.

Additional information The ASMC is open to all financial management professionals employed by the U.S. Department of Defense and Coast Guard, both civilian and military. The applicant whose service to the society is judged the most exceptional is designated the Dick Vincent Scholarship Winner.

Number awarded Up to 15 each year.

Deadline February of each year.

[25]
ASPARAGUS CLUB SCHOLARSHIPS

Baton Rouge Area Foundation
Attn: Scholarship Programs
402 North Fourth Street
Baton Rouge, LA 70802
(225) 387-6126   Toll-free: (877) 387-6126
Fax: (225) 387-6153   E-mail: rsayes@braf.org
Web: www.braf.org

Purpose To provide financial assistance to college students interested in preparing for a career in the grocery industry.

Eligibility This program is open to college sophomores and juniors who are working on a degree in an academic discipline relevant to the grocery industry. Their field of study may relate to retailing (including supermarket management, convenience store management, produce management, advertising, accounts management, marketing, public relations), processing and manufacturing (including food plant management, personnel management, purchasing management, sales management, packaging, new product development), or wholesaling (including merchandising, marketing, accounting, store construction and remodeling, computer applications). Applicants must submit a letter of recommendation from a professor in the food management and/or business school, transcripts, ACT and/or SAT scores, and documentation of financial need.

Financial data Stipends range up to $1,500 per year. Funds are sent directly to the student with a check payable to him or her and the university to be used for tuition and fees.

Duration 1 year; may be renewed if the recipient maintains a GPA of 2.5 or higher.

Additional information The Asparagus Club was founded in 1909 to generate a spirit of cooperation and unity among all segments of the grocery industry. Its scholarship fund has been administered by the Baton Rouge Area Foundation since 2002.

Number awarded Varies each year

Deadline May of each year.

[26]
ASSOCIATION FOR THE ADVANCEMENT OF COST ENGINEERING INTERNATIONAL COMPETITIVE SCHOLARSHIPS

Association for the Advancement of Cost Engineering
209 Prairie Avenue, Suite 100
Morgantown, WV 26505
(304) 296-8444   Toll-free: (800) 858-COST
Fax: (304) 291-5728   E-mail: info@aacei.org
Web: www.aacei.org/education/scholarship.shtml

Purpose To provide financial assistance to undergraduate and graduate students in the United States or Canada working on a degree related to total cost management (the effective application of professional and technical expertise to plan and control resources, costs, profitability, and risk).

Eligibility Applicants may be undergraduate students (second year standing or higher) or graduate students. They must be enrolled full time in a degree program in the United States or Canada that is related to the field of cost management/cost engineering, including engineering, construction, manufacturing, technology, business, and computer science. Selection is based on academic record (35%), extracurricular activities

(35%), and an essay (30%) on why the study of cost engineering or total cost management is important to their academic objectives and career goals.

Financial data Stipends range from $750 to $3,000 per year.

Duration 1 year.

Number awarded Varies each year; recently, 28 of these scholarships were awarded.

Deadline October of each year.

[27]
ASSOCIATION OF GOLF MERCHANDISERS SCHOLARSHIPS

Association of Golf Merchandisers
P.O. Box 7247
Phoenix, AZ 85011-7247
(602) 604-8250   Fax: (602) 604-8251
E-mail: info@agmgolf
Web: www.agmgolf.org

Purpose To provide financial assistance to college students interested in a career in golf merchandising.

Eligibility This program is open to students who are currently enrolled at a college, university, or technical institute and are actively preparing for a golf merchandising career. Applicants must have completed at least their sophomore year with a GPA of 2.5 or higher.

Financial data The stipend is $1,000.

Duration 1 year.

Number awarded Several each year.

[28]
ASSOCIATION OF GOVERNMENT ACCOUNTANTS ACADEMIC MERIT SCHOLARSHIPS

Association of Government Accountants
Attn: National Awards Committee
2208 Mount Vernon Avenue
Alexandria, VA 22301-1314
(703) 684-6931   Toll-free: (800) AGA-7211, ext. 131
Fax: (703) 548-9367   E-mail: rortiz@agacgfm.org
Web: www.agacgfm.org/membership/awards

Purpose To provide financial assistance to members of the Association of Government Accountants (AGA) and their families who wish to work on a degree in financial management.

Eligibility This program is open to members of the association and their spouses, children, and grandchildren. Applicants may be pursuing or intending to pursue an undergraduate or graduate degree in a financial management discipline, including accounting, auditing, budgeting, economics, finance, information technology, or public administration. As part of the selection process, they must submit a 2-page essay on "Why I want a career in public financial management," high school or college transcripts, and a letter of recommendation from an AGA member. Financial need is not considered.

Financial data The annual stipends are $1,000 for full-time study or $500 for part-time study.

Duration 1 year; renewable.

Number awarded 16 each year: 8 to high school seniors and graduates (6 for full-time study and 2 for part-time study) and 8 to undergraduate and graduate students (6 for full-time study and 2 for part-time study).

Deadline March of each year.

[29]
ASSOCIATION OF LATINO PROFESSIONALS IN FINANCE AND ACCOUNTING SCHOLARSHIPS

Association of Latino Professionals in Finance and
   Accounting
Attn: Scholarships
510 West Sixth Street, Suite 400
Los Angeles, CA 90017
(213) 243-0004   Fax: (213) 243-0006
E-mail: scholarships@national.alpfa.org
Web: www.alpfa.org

Purpose To provide financial assistance to undergraduate and graduate students of Hispanic descent who are preparing for a career in a field related to finance or accounting.

Eligibility This program is open to full-time undergraduate and graduate students who have completed at least 15 undergraduate units at a college or university in the United States or Puerto Rico with a GPA of 3.0 or higher. Applicants must be of Hispanic heritage, defined as having 1 parent fully Hispanic or both parents half Hispanic. They must be working on a degree in accounting, finance, information technology, or a related field. Along with their application, they must submit a 2-page personal statement that addresses their Hispanic heritage and family background, personal and academic achievements, academic plans and career goals, efforts and plans for making a difference in their community, and financial need. U.S. citizenship or permanent resident status is required.

Financial data Stipends range from $1,000 to $5,000.

Duration 1 year.

Additional information The sponsoring organization was formerly named the American Association of Hispanic Certified Public Accountants. This program is administered by the Hispanic College Fund, 1717 Pennsylvania Avenue, Suite 460, Washington, DC 20006, (202) 296-5400, (800) 644-4223, Fax: (202) 296-3774, E-mail: hcf-info@hispanicfund.org.

Number awarded Varies each year; recently, 78 of these scholarships, worth $195,000, were awarded.

Deadline April of each year.

[30]
AVIATION COUNCIL OF PENNSYLVANIA SCHOLARSHIP

Aviation Council of Pennsylvania
Attn: Scholarship Program
3111 Arcadia Avenue
Allentown, PA 18103-6903
(610) 797-6911   Fax: (610) 797-8238
Web: www.acpfly.com

Purpose To provide financial assistance for college to students from Pennsylvania preparing for a career in aviation or aviation management.

Eligibility This program is open to students who are interested in preparing for a career in aviation technology, aviation management, or the professional pilot field. Applicants must be residents of Pennsylvania. If they are applying for the aviation management scholarship, they may attend college in any state. Applicants for the aviation technology and professional pilot scholarships must attend school in Pennsylvania. Financial need is considered in the selection process.

Financial data Typically, the stipend is $1,000 (although the amount may vary).

Duration 1 year.

Additional information The scholarship in aviation management is named the Wilfred M. "Wiley" Post Scholarship; the scholarships for professional pilots are named the John W. "Reds" Macfarlane Scholarship and the Arnold Palmer Scholarship.

Number awarded 4 each year: 1 for aviation technology, 1 for aviation management, and 2 for professional pilots.

Deadline July of each year.

[31]
A.W. PERIGARD FUND SCHOLARSHIP

Society of Satellite Professionals International
Attn: Scholarship Program
New York Information Technology Center
55 Broad Street, 14th Floor
New York, NY 10004
(212) 809-5199   Fax: (212) 825-0075
E-mail: sspi@sspi.org
Web: www.sspi.org/html/scholarship.html

Purpose To provide financial assistance to students interested in majoring in satellite-related disciplines (including business) in college or graduate school.

Eligibility This program is open to high school seniors, undergraduates, and graduate students majoring or planning to major in fields related to satellite technologies, policies, or applications. Fields of study in the past have included broadcasting, business, distance learning, energy, government, imaging, meteorology, navigation, remote sensing, space law, and telecommunications. Applicants may be from any country. Selection is based on academic and leadership achievement, commitment to pursue educational and career opportunities in the satellite communications industry, potential for significant contribution to that industry, a personal statement of 500 to 750 words on interest in satellite communications and why they deserve the award, and a creative work (such as a research report, essay, article, videotape, artwork, computer program, or scale model of an antenna or spacecraft design) that reflects the applicant's interests and talents. Financial need is also considered.

Financial data The stipend is $2,000.

Duration 1 year.

Number awarded 1 each year.

Deadline May of each year.

[32]
AWIC-DC SCHOLARSHIP

Association for Women in Communications-Washington DC Area Chapter
Attn: Frappa Stout, Vice President of Student Affairs
USA Weekend
7950 Jones Branch Drive
McLean, VA 22108-0001
Toll-free: (800) 487-2956   Fax: (703) 854-2122
E-mail: fstout@usaweekend.com
Web: www.awic-dc.org/student_affairs.shtml

Purpose To provide financial assistance to women who are working on undergraduate degrees in a communications-related field at universities in the Washington, D.C. area.

Eligibility This program is open to female sophomores and juniors attending a Washington, D.C. area university or college studying advertising, communications, graphic arts, journalism, marketing, public relations, or a related field. Applicants must have an overall GPA of 3.0 or higher and work experience in communications or a related field. They must be active in extracurricular activities, including family obligations, volunteer work, clubs, and organizations, and their involvement must show versatility and commitment. Selection is based on a 500-word essay on their career plans and goals in communications, at least 2 letters of recommendation, and official transcripts; financial need is not considered.

Financial data The stipend is $1,000.

Duration 1 year.

Number awarded 1 each year.

Deadline March of each year.

[33]
AYLESWORTH FOUNDATION FOR THE ADVANCEMENT OF MARINE SCIENCE SCHOLARSHIPS

Florida Sea Grant College Program
Attn: Director
University of Florida
P.O. Box 110400
Gainesville, FL 32611-0400
(352) 392-5870   Fax: (352) 392-5113
Web: www.flseagrant.org

Purpose To provide financial assistance to undergraduate or graduate students working on a degree in a marine science-related field at any Florida university that participates in the Florida Sea Grant College Program.

Eligibility Eligible to be nominated by their department chair are undergraduate or graduate students who are working on a degree in an academic discipline that has direct application in marine science (ranging from biology and engineering to economics and food science) at a university or college in Florida that participates in the Florida Sea Grant College Program. These include: Florida A&M University, Florida Gulf Coast University, Florida Atlantic University, Florida Institute of Technology, Florida International University, Florida State University, Harbor Branch Oceanographic Institution, University of Miami, University of North Florida, University of South Florida, University of West Florida, Nova Southeastern University, University of Central Florida, and University of Florida. Financial need is the principal factor used in the selection process, although academic record, leadership, and personal character are also considered. Florida residents are given preference.

Financial data The maximum stipend awarded is 65% of the annual official university or college cost of attendance or $4,500, whichever is less.

Duration 1 year; renewable until the recipient completes the degree.

Additional information Since 1986, when the program was established, more than 60 students in 9 Florida universities have received funding.

Number awarded Generally, 4 or more each year.

Deadline November of each year.

[34]
BANK OF AMERICA ADA ABILITIES SCHOLARSHIP PROGRAM

The Center for Scholarship Administration, Inc.
Attn: Bank of America ADA Abilities Scholarship Program
P.O. Box 1465
Taylors, SC 29687-1465
(864) 268-3363   Fax: (864) 268-7160
E-mail: cfsainc@bellsouth.net
Web: www.scholarshipprograms.org

Purpose To provide financial assistance to disabled high school seniors or college students from selected states who are interested in preparing for a career with a banking institution.

Eligibility This program is open to high school seniors, high school graduates, and currently-enrolled college students who have a disability (must have written documentation from an appropriate provider that the candidate meets the definition of disabled in the Americans with Disabilities Act). Applicants must be U.S. citizens and permanent residents of 1 of the following states: Arizona, Arkansas, California, Florida, Georgia, Idaho, Illinois, Iowa, Kansas, Maryland, Missouri, Nevada, New Mexico, North Carolina, Oklahoma, Oregon, South Carolina, Tennessee, Texas, Virginia, Washington, or the District of the Columbia. They must 1) have a cumulative GPA of 3.0 or higher; 2) be majoring in finance, business, or computer systems; 3) be younger than 40 years of age; and 4) be planning a career with a banking institution.

Financial data The maximum stipend is $5,000, depending on financial need, the annual cost of the recipient's institution, and any other financial aid (excluding loans) received by the student.

Duration 1 year.

Additional information This program is administered by The Center for Scholarship Administration on behalf of the Bank of America Foundation.

Number awarded Varies each year.

Deadline February of each year.

[35]
BANK ONE/UNCF CORPORATE SCHOLARS PROGRAM

United Negro College Fund
Attn: Corporate Scholars Program
P.O. Box 1435
Alexandria, VA 22313-9998
Toll-free: (866) 671-7237   E-mail: internship@uncf.org
Web: www.uncf.org/internships/index.asp

Purpose To provide financial assistance and work experience in banking to undergraduates at colleges and universities that are members of the United Negro College Fund (UNCF).

Eligibility This program is open to sophomores and juniors at UNCF-member colleges and universities. All majors are welcome, but preference is given to applicants studying accounting, business, finance, or retailing. They must have a GPA of 3.0 or higher and be able to demonstrate financial need. Along with their application, they must submit an official school transcript, a letter of recommendation from a faculty member, a resume, a personal statement of career interest, and a financial need statement. Finalists are interviewed by representatives of Bank One, the program's sponsor.

Financial data Recipients are assigned paid internships at a Bank One location in Arizona, Delaware, Illinois, Indiana, Louisiana, Michigan, Ohio, or Texas. Following successful completion of the internship, they receive a scholarship up to $10,000 to cover school expenses.

Duration 8 to 10 weeks for the internship; 1 academic year for the scholarship.

Number awarded Approximately 12 each year.

Deadline January of each year.

[36]
BANTA COLLEGE-TO-WORK SCHOLARSHIP

Wisconsin Foundation for Independent Colleges, Inc.
735 North Water Street, Suite 800
Milwaukee, WI 53202-4100
(414) 273-5980   Fax: (414) 273-5995
E-mail: info@wficweb.org
Web: www.wficweb.org/documents/coll_work.htm

Purpose To provide financial assistance and work experience to students (especially those with learning disabilities) majoring in fields related to business and engineering at private colleges in Wisconsin.

Eligibility This program is open to full-time juniors and seniors at the 20 independent colleges or universities in Wisconsin. Students with learning disabilities are encouraged to apply. Applicants may be majoring in any liberal arts field, but they must be preparing for a career in accounting, production management, marketing, human resources, information technology, computer sciences, graphic design, or mechanical, electrical or industrial engineering. They must have a GPA of 3.0 or higher (waived for students with learning disabilities) and be interested in an internship at a Banta Corporation location, including Chicago and Menasha, Wisconsin. Along with their application, they must submit a 1-page autobiography, transcripts, a list of campus involvement and academic honors, a resume including 3 references, and 2 letters of recommendation.

Financial data The stipends are $3,500 for the scholarship and $1,500 for the internship.

Duration 1 year for the scholarship; 10 weeks during the summer for the internship.

Additional information The participating schools are Alverno College, Beloit College, Cardinal Stritch University, Carroll College, Carthage College, Concordia University of Wisconsin, Edgewood College, Lakeland College, Lawrence University, Marian College, Marquette University, Milwaukee Institute of Art & Design, Milwaukee School of Engineering, Mount Mary College, Northland College, Ripon College, St. Norbert College, Silver Lake College, Viterbo University, and Wisconsin Lutheran College. This program is sponsored by Banta Corporation.

Number awarded 2 each year.

Deadline January of each year.

[37]
BETTY RENDEL SCHOLARSHIPS

National Federation of Republican Women
Attn: Scholarship Coordinator
124 North Alfred Street
Alexandria, VA 22314-3011
(703) 548-9688   Fax: (703) 548-9836
E-mail: mail@nfrw.org
Web: www.nfrw.org/programs/scholarships.htm

Purpose To provide financial assistance to undergraduate Republican women who are majoring in political science, government, or economics.

Eligibility This program is open to Republican women who have completed at least 2 years of college. Applicants must be majoring in political science, government, or economics. A complete application must include the following: the application form, 3 letters of recommendation, an official transcript, a 1-page essay on why the applicant should be considered for the scholarship, and a 1-page essay on career goals. Optionally, a photograph may be supplied. Applications must be submitted to the federation president in the applicant's state. Each president chooses 1 application from her state to submit for scholarship consideration. Financial need is not a factor in the selection process.

Financial data The stipend is $1,000.

Duration 1 year; nonrenewable.

Additional information This program was established in 1985.

Number awarded 3 each year.

Deadline July of each year.

[38]
BI-LO MINORITY SCHOLARSHIP PROGRAM

The Center for Scholarship Administration, Inc.
Attn: BI-LO Minority Scholarship Program
P.O. Box 1465
Taylors, SC 29687-1465
(864) 268-3363   Fax: (864) 268-7160
E-mail: cfsainc@bellsouth.net
Web: www.scholarshipprograms.org

Purpose To provide financial assistance to high school seniors who are interested in attending a designated Histori-

cally Black College and University (HBCU) to prepare for a career in the food retail industry.

Eligibility This program is open to high school seniors of color who have applied for full-time enrollment in at least 1 of the following institutions: Benedict College (Columbia, South Carolina), Claflin University (Orangeburg, South Carolina), Morris College (Sumter, South Carolina), North Carolina A&T State University (Greensboro, North Carolina), or South Carolina State University (Orangeburg, South Carolina). Applicants must have a cumulative GPA of 3.0 or higher and an SAT score of 900 or higher. They must be interested in pursuing a course of study and career in the food retail industry (e.g., accounting, business management, marketing, distribution management, communications, pharmacy, human resources, information systems, advertising, finance). Along with their application, they must submit an essay in which they describe themselves, including the kind of person they are, their strengths, and their most important achievements in school and in their community; they may also include their hobbies, interests, sports, volunteer work, employment, future plans, or career goals. In addition to the essay, academic honors, leadership activities, extracurricular activities, and financial need are considered in the selection process.

Financial data The stipend is $1,250 per year. Funds are sent directly to the recipient's college or university.

Duration 2 years (the freshman and sophomore year of college), provided the recipient maintains full-time enrollment at 1 of the designated institutions and a GPA of 3.0 or higher.

Additional information This program is administered by The Center for Scholarship Administration on behalf of BI-LO Incorporated. Recipients must be willing to commit to 1 semester of participation in BI-LO's cooperative education program.

Number awarded 5 each year.

Deadline February of each year.

[39]
BICK BICKSON SCHOLARSHIP FUND

Hawai'i Community Foundation
Attn: Scholarship Department
1164 Bishop Street, Suite 800
Honolulu, HI 96813
(808) 537-6333   Toll-free: (888) 731-3863
Fax: (808) 521-6286
E-mail: scholarships@hcf-hawaii.org
Web: www.hawaiicommunityfoundation.org

Purpose To provide financial assistance to Hawaii residents who are interested in studying marketing, law, or travel industry management in college or graduate school.

Eligibility This program is open to Hawaii residents who are interested in majoring in marketing, law, or travel industry management on the undergraduate or graduate school level. They must be able to demonstrate academic achievement (GPA of 2.7 or higher), good moral character, and financial need. In addition to filling out the standard application form, applicants must write a short statement indicating their reasons for attending college, their planned course of study, and their career goals.

Financial data The amounts of the awards depend on the availability of funds and the need of the recipient; recently, stipends averaged $1,250.

Duration 1 year.

Additional information Recipients may attend college in Hawaii or on the mainland. Recipients must be full-time students.

Number awarded Varies each year; recently, 2 of these scholarships were awarded.

Deadline February of each year.

[40]
BLUE CROSS AND BLUE SHIELD UNITED OF WISCONSIN COLLEGE-TO-WORK SCHOLARSHIP

Wisconsin Foundation for Independent Colleges, Inc.
735 North Water Street, Suite 800
Milwaukee, WI 53202-4100
(414) 273-5980   Fax: (414) 273-5995
E-mail: info@wficweb.org
Web: www.wficweb.org/documents/coll_work.htm

Purpose To provide financial assistance and work experience to students majoring in fields related to business at private colleges in Wisconsin.

Eligibility This program is open to full-time juniors and seniors at the 20 independent colleges or universities in Wisconsin. Applicants must be preparing for a career in accounting, sales, marketing, or computer sciences and have a GPA of 3.2 or higher. They must also be interested in an internship at Blue Cross and Blue Shield (BC&BS) United of Wisconsin some time during the year. Along with their application, they must submit a 1-page autobiography, transcripts, a list of campus involvement and academic honors, a resume including 3 references, and 2 letters of recommendation.

Financial data The stipends are $3,500 for the scholarship and $1,500 for the internship.

Duration 1 year for the scholarship; 10 weeks for the internship.

Additional information The participating schools are Alverno College, Beloit College, Cardinal Stritch University, Carroll College, Carthage College, Concordia University of Wisconsin, Edgewood College, Lakeland College, Lawrence University, Marian College, Marquette University, Milwaukee Institute of Art & Design, Milwaukee School of Engineering, Mount Mary College, Northland College, Ripon College, St. Norbert College, Silver Lake College, Viterbo University, and Wisconsin Lutheran College. This program is sponsored by Blue Cross & Blue Shield United of Wisconsin.

Number awarded 9 each year: 3 to students majoring in accounting and 2 each to students majoring in sales, marketing, and computer science.

Deadline January of each year.

[41]
BNSF SCHOLARSHIP PROGRAM

Hispanic College Fund
Attn: National Director
1717 Pennsylvania Avenue, N.W., Suite 460
Washington, D.C. 20006
(202) 296-5400   Toll-free: (800) 644-4223
Fax: (202) 296-3774 E-mail: hcf-info@hispanicfund.org
Web: www.hispanicfund.org

Purpose To provide financial assistance to Hispanic American undergraduate students from designated states who are interested in preparing for a career in a business-related field.

Eligibility This program is open to U.S. citizens of Hispanic background (at least 1 grandparent must be 100% Hispanic) who are entering their freshman, sophomore, junior, or senior year of college. Applicants must be residents of Arizona, California, Colorado, Illinois, Kansas, Missouri, New Mexico, or Texas. They must be working on a bachelor's degree in accounting, economics, engineering, finance, information systems, marketing, or a related major and have a cumulative GPA of 3.0 or higher. They must be applying to or enrolled in a college or university in the 50 states or Puerto Rico as a full-time student. Financial need is considered in the selection process.

Financial data Stipends range from $500 to $5,000, depending on the need of the recipient, and average approximately $3,000. Funds are paid directly to the recipient's college or university to help cover tuition and fees.

Duration 1 year; recipients may reapply.

Additional information This program is sponsored by the Burlington Northern Santa Fe (BNSF) Foundation and administered by the Hispanic College Fund (HCF). All applications must be submitted online; no paper applications are available.

Number awarded Varies each year.

Deadline April of each year.

[42]
BOOZ ALLEN HAMILTON/WILLIAM F. STASIOR SCHOLARSHIP PROGRAM

United Negro College Fund
Attn: Corporate Scholars Program
P.O. Box 1435
Alexandria, VA 22313-9998
Toll-free: (866) 671-7237   E-mail: internship@uncf.org
Web: www.uncf.org/internships/index.asp

Purpose To provide financial assistance and work experience in consulting to students at colleges and universities that are members of the United Negro College Fund (UNCF).

Eligibility This program is open to rising juniors and seniors at UNCF-member colleges and universities who are majoring in business management, computer science, economics, engineering, information systems technology, or mathematics. Applicants must have a GPA of 3.3 or higher and be interested in a summer internship with Booz Allen Hamilton. They must be able to demonstrate leadership experience in collegiate and non-collegiate activities, honors and awards, community service, and interests outside their major.

Financial data Recipients are assigned paid internships at a Booz Allen Hamilton location. Following successful completion of the internship, they receive a need-based scholarship up to $10,000 to cover school expenses.

Duration 8 weeks for the internship; 1 academic year for the scholarship.

Number awarded Varies each year.

Deadline February of each year.

[43]
BOSTON AFFILIATE SCHOLARSHIP

American Woman's Society of Certified Public
  Accountants-Boston Affiliate
c/o Julie Mead
Ziner, Kennedy & Lehan
2300 Crown Colony Drive
Quincy, MA 02169
E-mail: julie.m.mead@aexp.com
Web: www.awscpa.org

Purpose To provide financial assistance to women who are working on an undergraduate or graduate degree in accounting at a college or university in New England.

Eligibility This program is open to women who are attending a college in New England and majoring in accounting. Applicants must have completed at least 12 semester hours of accounting or tax courses and have a cumulative GPA of 3.0 or higher. They must be planning to graduate between May of next year and May of the following year or, for the 15-month graduate program, before September of the current year.

Financial data A stipend is awarded (amount not specified).

Duration 1 year.

Number awarded 1 or more each year.

Deadline April of each year.

[44]
BROADCAST CABLE FINANCIAL MANAGEMENT ASSOCIATION SCHOLARSHIP

Broadcast Cable Financial Management Association
932 Lee Street, Suite 204
Des Plaines, Il 60016
(847) 296-0200   Fax: (847) 296-7510
Web: www.bcfm.com

Purpose To provide financial assistance to members of the Broadcast Cable Financial Management Association who are interested in working on an undergraduate or graduate degree.

Eligibility All fully-paid members in good standing are eligible to apply for the scholarship. They must be interested in working on an undergraduate or graduate degree at an accredited college or university that has some relevance to their current job and/or to the broadcast or cable industries. To apply, individuals must submit an application, attach a current resume, include 2 letters of reference, and submit a 1-page essay that addresses the following: their current job responsibilities, the courses they intend to take, and a description of their career goals.

Financial data The stipend is generally $1,000.

Duration 1 year; recipients may reapply.

Number awarded Varies each year; a total of $5,000 is distributed annually.

Deadline March of each year.

[45]
BURLINGTON NORTHERN SANTA FE FOUNDATION SCHOLARSHIP

American Indian Science and Engineering Society
Attn: Higher Education Program Manager
2305 Renard, S.E., Suite 200
P.O. Box 9828
Albuquerque, NM 87119-9828
(505) 765-1052, ext. 106   Fax: (505) 765-5608
E-mail: shirley@aises.org
Web: www.aises.org/scholarships

Purpose To provide financial assistance for college to outstanding American Indian high school seniors from designated states who are members of American Indian Science and Engineering Society (AISES).

Eligibility This program is open to AISES members who are high school seniors planning to attend an accredited 4-year college or university and major in business, engineering, mathematics, medicine, natural resources, physical science, science, or technology. Applicants must submit 1) proof of tribal enrollment or a Certificate of Degree of Indian Blood; 2) evidence of residence in the service area of the Burlington Northern and Santa Fe Corporation (Arizona, California, Colorado, Kansas, Minnesota, Montana, New Mexico, North Dakota, Oklahoma, Oregon, South Dakota, and Washington); 3) a statement of financial need; 4) a 500-word essay on why they chose their particular field of study, their career aspirations, an evaluation of past scholastic performance, obstacles faced as a student, and involvementin and commitment to tribal community life; and 5) high school transcripts showing a GPA of 2.0 or higher.

Financial data Stipends range from $1,000 to $2,500 per year.

Duration 4 years or until completion of a baccalaureate degree, whichever occurs first.

Additional information This program is funded by the Burlington Northern Santa Fe Foundation and administered by AISES.

Number awarded 5 new awards are made each year.

Deadline April of each year.

[46]
CAEOP HIGH SCHOOL SENIOR SCHOLARSHIPS

California Association of Educational Office Professionals
Attn: Scholarship/Awards Chair
P.O. Box 1007
El Cajon, CA 92022
(619) 588-3111   E-mail: hensle@gwise.cajon.k12.ca.us

Purpose To provide financial assistance to high school seniors in the state of California or Clark County, Nevada who are interested in preparing for a career in business, preferably in the field of education.

Eligibility This program is open to seniors graduating from high schools in California or Clark County, Nevada who are interested in preparing for a career in business, preferably in the field of business education. They must be U.S. citizens who have an overall GPA of 2.0 or higher in high school and 3.0 or higher in high school business courses. They must complete an application form, attach a 1-page biographical sketch on "Why I am Choosing a Career in Business," include an official transcript (which must indicate class rank), and sub mit 3 letters of recommendation. Selection is based on need for assistance, scholastic achievement, initiative, extracurricular activities, and quality and completeness of the application materials.

Financial data The stipend is $1,000.

Duration 1 year.

Additional information This program was established in 1967.

Number awarded 3 each year.

Deadline January of each year.

[47]
CAEOP MEMBER RE-ENTRY SCHOLARSHIP

California Association of Educational Office Professionals
Attn: Scholarship/Awards Chair
P.O. Box 1007
El Cajon, CA 92022
(619) 588-3111   E-mail: hensle@gwise.cajon.k12.ca.us

Purpose To provide financial assistance to members of the California Association of Educational Office Professionals (CAEOP) who want to continue their education in the field of education or business.

Eligibility Applicants must have been CAEOP members for at least 2 years. They must be interested in advancing their career in the field of education or business and plan to take at least 3 semester college units if they receive the scholarship. All applicants must be U.S. citizens, currently employed in an educational office, and able to show financial need.

Financial data The stipend is $500.

Duration 1 year; nonrenewable.

Number awarded 2 each year.

Deadline January of each year.

[48]
CALCPA STATE ACCOUNTING EDUCATION SCHOLARSHIP PROGRAM

California Society of Certified Public Accountants
Attn: Member Relations Division
1235 Radio Road
Redwood City, CA 94065-1217
(650) 802-2600   Toll-free: (800) 9-CALCPA
Fax: (650) 802-2200
Web: www.calcpa.org

Purpose To provide financial assistance to students in California who are preparing for a career as a certified public accountant.

Eligibility This program is open to accounting students in California who have already received a scholarship offered by a chapter of the California Society of Certified Public Accountants (CalCPA). Applicants must be committed to a plan to achieve the 150 semester hours of education required by Pathway 2 for certification as a C.P.A. in California. Along with their application, they must submit a list of all colleges and universities they have attended; transcripts for each of those educational institutions; a description of their accounting interests, including their plan to pursue Pathway 2, in relation to their career goals; and a summary of their work experiences, community service, and extracurricular college activities.

Financial data A stipend is awarded (amount not specified).

Duration 1 year.

Additional information Information is also available from Patti Sustin, 330 North Brand Boulevard, Suite 710, Glendale, CA 91203.

Number awarded Varies each year.

Deadline April of each year.

[49]
CALIFORNIA ASSOCIATION OF REALTORS SCHOLARSHIPS

California Association of Realtors
Attn: Scholarship Foundation
525 South Virgil Avenue
Los Angeles, CA 90020
(213) 739-8200   Fax: (213) 739-7202
E-mail: scholarship@car.org
Web: www.car.org

Purpose To provide financial assistance to students in California who are interested in a career in real estate.

Eligibility This program is open to undergraduate and graduate students enrolled at California colleges and universities who are interested in studying real estate brokerage, real estate finance, real estate management, real estate development, real estate appraisal, real estate planning, real estate law, or other related areas of study. Applicants must have completed at least 12 units prior to applying, be currently enrolled for at least 6 units per semester or term, have a cumulative GPA of 2.6 or higher, and have been legal residents of California for at least 1 year. Real estate licensees who wish to pursue advanced real estate designations, degrees, or credentials are also eligible.

Financial data The stipend is $2,000 for students at 4-year colleges or universities or $1,000 for students at 2-year colleges.

Duration 1 year; may be renewed 1 additional year.

Number awarded Varies each year.

Deadline May of each year.

[50]
CALIFORNIA CATTLEMEN'S ASSOCIATION SCHOLARSHIPS

California Cattlemen's Association
Attn: Director of Member and Office Services
1221 H Street
Sacramento, CA 95814
(916) 444-0845   Fax: (916) 444-2194
E-mail: staff@calcattlemen.org
Web: www.calcattlemen.org/ycc.htm

Purpose To provide financial assistance to members of the California Cattlemen's Association (CCA) and their families who are attending college to prepare for a career in the beef industry.

Eligibility This program is open to students currently attending a junior college, 4-year college, or university in California who are CCA Young Cattlemen members or whose parents are current CCA members. Applicants must be preparing for a career associated with the beef cattle industry, including production, nutrition, trade, agricultural communications, agricultural education and professional services, marketing, and lending. Selection is based on future plans in the beef industry, academic achievement (GPA of 2.5 or higher), community involvement, and knowledge of the beef industry. An interview may be required.

Financial data The stipend is at least $1,000.

Duration 1 year; recipients may reapply.

Additional information Supporters of this program include the CCA Allied Industries Council, the CCA Feeder Council, and Allflex USA.

Number awarded Varies each year; recently, 10 of these scholarships were awarded.

Deadline July of each year.

[51]
CALIFORNIA REAL ESTATE ENDOWMENT FUND SCHOLARSHIP PROGRAM

California Community Colleges
Attn: Student Financial Assistance Programs
1102 Q Street
Sacramento, CA 95814-6511
(916) 324-0925   E-mail: rquintan@cccco.edu
Web: www.cccco.edu

Purpose To provide financial assistance to disadvantaged California community college students who are studying real estate.

Eligibility This program is open to students at community colleges in California who are majoring in real estate or (if their college does not offer a real estate major) business administration with a concentration in real estate. Applicants must have completed at least a 3-unit college course in real estate with a grade of "C" or better and must be enrolled in at least 6 semester units of real estate for the semester of the scholarship. Students must meet 1 of the following financial need criteria: 1) have completed the Free Application for Federal Student Aid (FAFSA) and been determined by their college to have financial need; 2) come from a family with an income less than $12,885 for 1 person, $17,415 for 2 persons, $21,945 for 3 persons, $26,475 for 4 persons, or an additional $4,530 for each additional family member; or 3) come from a family with an income less than $50,000 and be from a disadvantaged group (have low economic status and/or have been denied opportunities in society for reasons of gender, race, ethnicity, economics, language, education, physical disabilities, or other mitigating factors). Scholarships are awarded on a first-come, first-served basis.

Financial data Awards up to $400 per semester are available.

Duration 1 semester; may be renewed if the student remains enrolled in at least 6 units of real estate with a GPA of 2.0 or higher.

Additional information Students apply to their community college, not to the sponsoring organization.

Number awarded From 75 to 90 each year; approximately $60,000 per year is available for this program.

Deadline April of each year.

[52]
CALVIN E. MOORE MEMORIAL SCHOLARSHIP

South Florida Manufacturers Association
1000 West McNab Road, Suite 111
Pompano Beach, FL 33069
(954) 941-3558   Fax: (954) 941-3559
Web: www.sfma.org

Purpose To provide financial assistance for college to high school seniors in Florida whose parents work for a company that belongs to the South Florida Manufacturers Association (SFMA).

Eligibility This program is open to high school seniors in Florida whose parents work at an SFMA-member company and have earned a GPA of 3.0 or higher. Applicants must indicate why they have chosen an engineering, computer science, technical, or business career.

Financial data A stipend is awarded (amount not specified).

Duration 1 year.

Number awarded 1 or more each year.

Deadline April of each year.

[53]
CAREER ADVANCEMENT SCHOLARSHIPS

Business and Professional Women's Foundation
Attn: Scholarships
1900 M Street, N.W., Suite 310
Washington, DC 20036
(202) 293-1100, ext. 173   Fax: (202) 861-0298
E-mail: dfrye@bpwusa.org
Web: www.bpwusa.org

Purpose To provide financial assistance for college or graduate school to mature women who are employed or seeking employment in selected fields.

Eligibility Applicants must be women who are at least 25 years of age, citizens of the United States, within 2 years of completing their course of study, officially accepted into an accredited program or course of study at an American institution (including those in Puerto Rico and the Virgin Islands), in financial need, and planning to use the desired training to improve their chances for advancement, train for a new career field, or enter/reenter the job market. They must be in a transitional period in their lives and be interested in studying 1 of the following fields: biological sciences, business studies, computer science, engineering, humanities, mathematics, paralegal studies, physical sciences, social science, teacher education certification, or for a professional degree (J.D., D.D.S., M.D.). Study at the Ph.D. level and for non-degree programs is not covered.

Financial data The stipend is $1,000 per year.

Duration 1 year; recipients may reapply.

Additional information The scholarship may be used to support part-time study as well as academic or vocational/paraprofessional/office skills training. The program was established in 1969. Scholarships cannot be used to pay for classes already in progress. The program does not cover study at the doctoral level, correspondence courses, postdoctoral studies, or studies in foreign countries. Training must be completed within 24 months.

Number awarded Varies each year; recently, 120 of these scholarships were awarded.

Deadline April of each year.

[54]
CAREER COLLEGES & SCHOOLS OF TEXAS SCHOLARSHIP

Career Colleges & Schools of Texas
P.O. Box 140647
Austin, TX 78714-0647
(512) 454-8626   Fax: (512) 454-3036
E-mail: ccst@assnmgmt.com
Web: www.colleges-schools.org/scholarships.html

Purpose To provide financial assistance to high school seniors in Texas who are interested in attending a career college and majoring in selected fields.

Eligibility Open to high school seniors in Texas who are interested in attending a career college in the state, to prepare for a career in such fields as computer or information technology, health care, cosmetology, massage, business, criminal justice, welding, or health occupations. The sponsor provides 4 scholarships to each of the 1,500 high schools in the state. Recipients are then selected by the scholarship directors or counselors at their high school. Selection criteria vary by school but usually include academic excellence, financial need, and/or student leadership.

Financial data The stipend is a $1,000 award certificate to be used to pay for tuition at any of the 44 career colleges in Texas.

Duration 1 year.

Number awarded 6,000 each year (4 at each of the 1,500 high schools in the state).

[55]
CAREERS THAT WORK! SCHOLARSHIP

Washington Federation of Private Career Schools &
    Colleges
10426 180th Court N.E.
Redmond, WA 87052
(425) 376-0369   Fax: (425) 881-1580
E-mail: exec@washingtonschools.org
Web: www.washingtonschools.org

Purpose To provide financial assistance to high school seniors in Washington who are interested in attending a career college and majoring in selected fields.

Eligibility Open to high school seniors in Washington who are interested in attending 1 of the 26 career colleges in the state, to prepare for a career in such fields as computer or information technology, health care, cosmetology, massage, business, criminal justice, or health occupations. The sponsor provides 3 scholarships to each high school in Washington. Recipients are then selected by the scholarship directors or counselors at their high school.

Financial data The stipend is a $1,000 award certificate to be used to pay for tuition at a career college in Washington.

Duration 1 year.

Additional information This scholarship was established in 1999.

Number awarded 3 each year at each high school in Washington.

[56]
CARL H. MARRS SCHOLARSHIP FUND

Cook Inlet Region, Inc.
Attn: CIRI Foundation
2600 Cordova Street, Suite 206
Anchorage, AK 99503
(907) 263-5582   Toll-free: (800) 764-3382
Fax: (907) 263-5588   E-mail: tcf@ciri.com
Web: www.ciri.com/tcf/designated.html

Purpose To provide financial assistance for undergraduate or graduate studies in business-related fields to Alaska Natives who are original enrollees to Cook Inlet Region, Inc. (CIRI) and their lineal descendants.

Eligibility This program is open to Alaska Native enrollees under the Alaska Native Claims Settlement Act (ANCSA) of 1971 and their lineal descendants of Cook Inlet Region, Inc. There are no Alaska residency requirements or age limitations. Applicants must be accepted or enrolled full time in a 4-year undergraduate or a graduate degree program in business administration, economics, finance, organizational management, accounting, or a similar field. They must have a GPA of 3.7 or higher. Selection is based on academic achievement, rigor of course work or degree program, quality of a statement of purpose, student financial contribution, financial need, grade level, previous work performance, education and community activities, letters of recommendation, seriousness of purpose, and practicality of educational and professional goals.

Financial data The stipend is $18,000 per year.

Duration 1 year; may be renewed.

Additional information This program was established in 2001. Recipients must enroll in school on a full-time basis.

Number awarded 1 or more each year.

Deadline May of each year.

[57]
CARL W. CHRISTIANSEN SCHOLARSHIPS

Rhode Island Society of Certified Public Accountants
45 Royal Little Drive
Providence, RI 02904
(401) 331-5720   Fax: (401) 454-5780
E-mail: rchurch@riscpa.org
Web: www.riscpa.org/student.php

Purpose To provide financial assistance to undergraduates in Rhode Island who are majoring in accounting.

Eligibility This program is open to residents of Rhode Island who are enrolled in college and have expressed an interest in public accounting during their undergraduate years. Applicants must be U.S. citizens who have a GPA of 3.0 or higher. Selection is based on demonstrated potential to become a valued member of the public accounting profession. Finalists are interviewed.

Financial data Stipends are normally $1,000.

Duration 1 year.

Additional information This program was established in 1974.

Number awarded Varies each year; recently, a total of $9,000 was available for this program.

Deadline April of each year.

[58]
CAROLYN HUEY HARRIS SCHOLARSHIP

Alpha Omicron Pi Foundation
Attn: Scholarship Committee
5390 Virginia Way
P.O. Box 395
Brentwood, TN 37024-0395
(615) 370-0920   Fax: (615) 370-4424
E-mail: foundation@alphaomicronpi.org
Web: www.aoiifoundation.org

Purpose To provide financial assistance for college or graduate school to collegiate and alumnae members of Alpha Omicron Pi, especially those from Georgia majoring in fields related to the communications industry.

Eligibility This program is open to collegiate members of Alpha Omicron Pi who wish to continue their undergraduate education and alumnae members who wish to work on a graduate degree. First preference is given to Lambda Sigma chapter members who are juniors or above and majoring in communications (including journalism, public relations, marketing, speech, and media) with a GPA of 3.0 or higher; second preference is given to members from other Georgia colleges; third preference is given to members from other states. Applicants must submit 50-word essays on the following topics: 1) the circumstances that have created their need for this scholarship, and 2) their immediate and long-term life objectives. Selection is based on academic excellence, dedication to serving the community and Alpha Omicron Pi, and financial need.

Financial data A stipend is awarded (amount not specified).

Duration 1 year.

Additional information Undergraduate recipients must enroll full time, but graduate recipients may enroll part time.

Number awarded 1 each year.

Deadline February of each year.

[59]
CARY C. AND DEBRA Y.C. WU SCHOLARSHIP

US Pan Asian American Chamber of Commerce
Attn: Scholarship Coordinator
1329 18th Street, N.W.
Washington, DC 20036
(202) 296-5221   Fax: (202) 296-5225
E-mail: administrator@uspaacc.com
Web: www.uspaacc.net

Purpose To provide financial assistance for college to Asian American high school seniors who are interested in becoming a business leader.

Eligibility This program is open to high school seniors of Asian heritage who are U.S. citizens or permanent residents. Applicants must be planning to begin full-time study at an accredited postsecondary educational institution in the United States. Along with their application, they must submit a 500-word essay on "My role and contribution as a future Asian American business leader." Selection is based on academic excellence (GPA of 3.5 or higher), leadership in extracurricular activities, community service involvement, and financial need.

Financial data The maximum stipend is $5,000. Funds are paid directly to the recipient's college or university.

Duration 1 year.

Additional information Funding is not provided for correspondence courses, Internet courses, or study in a country other than the United States.

Number awarded 1 each year.

Deadline February of each year.

[60]
CASH SCHOLARSHIPS TO ACCOUNTING COMMUNITY COLLEGE STUDENTS

Connecticut Society of Certified Public Accountants
Attn: Educational Trust Fund
845 Brook Street, Building 2
Rocky Hill, CT 06067-3405
(860) 258-4800   Toll-free: (800) 232-2232 (within CT)
Fax: (860) 258-4859   E-mail: cscpa@cs-cpa.org
Web: www.cs-cpa.org

Purpose To provide financial assistance to college students majoring in accounting at community colleges in Connecticut.

Eligibility This program is open to community college students in Connecticut who are majoring in accounting. Applicants must be committed to majoring in accounting at a 4-year school recognized by the Connecticut State Board of Accountancy.

Financial data Modest stipends are awarded.

Duration 1 year.

Number awarded Up to 5 each year.

[61]
CATHY L. BROCK MEMORIAL SCHOLARSHIP

Institute for Diversity in Health Management
Attn: Education Program Coordinator
One North Franklin Street, 30th Floor
Chicago, IL 60606
Toll-free: (800) 233-0996   Fax: (312) 422-4566
E-mail: clopez@aha.org
Web: www.diversityconnection.com

Purpose To provide financial assistance to minority upper-division and graduate students in health care management or business management.

Eligibility This program is open to members of ethnic minority groups who are college juniors, seniors, or graduate students. Applicants must be accepted or enrolled in an accredited program in health care management or business management and have a GPA of 3.0 or higher. They must demonstrate commitment to a career in health services administration, financial need, solid extracurricular and community service activities, and a strong interest and experience in finance. U.S. citizenship or permanent resident status is required.

Financial data The stipend is $1,000.

Duration 1 year.

Number awarded 1 or more each year, depending on the availability of funds.

Deadline June of each year.

[62]
CEDARCREST FARMS SCHOLARSHIP

American Jersey Cattle Association
Attn: Dr. Cherie L. Bayer
6486 East Main Street
Reynoldsburg, OH 43068-2362
(614) 861-3636   Fax: (614) 861-8040
E-mail: cbayer@usjersey.com
Web: www.usjersey.com

Purpose To provide financial assistance to undergraduate and graduate students working on a degree related to the dairy industry.

Eligibility This program is open to undergraduate and graduate students who are working on a degree in large animal veterinary practice, dairy production, dairy manufacturing, or dairy product marketing. Applicants must have significant and extensive experience in breeding, managing, and showing Jersey cattle. They must demonstrate significant progress toward their intended degree and an intention to prepare for a career in agriculture. A GPA of 2.5 or higher is required. Financial need is not considered in the selection process.

Financial data The stipend is approximately $1,000.

Duration 1 year.

Number awarded 1 each year.

Deadline June of each year.

[63]
CENEX HARVEST STATES FOUNDATION SCHOLARSHIPS FOR COOPERATIVE STUDIES

Cenex Harvest States Foundation
Attn: Scholarship Program
5500 Cenex Drive
Inver Grove Heights, MN 55077
(651) 355-5129   Fax: (651) 355-5073
E-mail: william.nelson@chsinc.com
Web: www.chsfoundation.org

Purpose To provide financial assistance to upper-division students at selected universities who are enrolled in courses on cooperative principles and cooperative business practices.

Eligibility This program is open to students who are attending a participating university. Applicants must be attending the school's agriculture college, enrolled in courses on cooperative principles and cooperative business practices. They must be in their junior or senior year in college. Selection is based on scholastic achievement and class work in cooperative studies.

Financial data $750 is awarded to recipients at each participating university. If the award is made during the junior year, students are eligible for an additional $750 in their senior year. If the award is made during the senior year, it is not retroactive to the junior year. A maximum of $1,500 can be awarded to any 1 student in the cooperative studies program.

Duration 1 year; may be renewed for 1 additional year if the student first receives the award as a junior.

Additional information The participating institutions are Colorado State University, the University of Idaho, Iowa State University, Kansas State University, Southwest Minnesota State University, the University of Minnesota at Crookston, the University of Minnesota-Twin Cities, Montana State University, the University of Nebraska, North Dakota State University, Oregon State University, South Dakota State University, Utah State University, Washington State University, the University of Wisconsin at Platteville, the University of Wisconsin at River Falls, the University of Wisconsin at Madison, and the University of Wyoming.

Number awarded More than 140 each year.

Deadline Individual institutions administer this program; recipients are selected in the spring to receive the award in the fall.

[64]
CENTRAL OHIO INSURANCE EDUCATION DAY SCHOLARSHIPS

Griffith Foundation for Insurance Education
172 East State Street, Suite 305A
Columbus, OH 43215-4321
(614) 341-2392   Fax: (614) 442-0402
E-mail: griffithfoundation@attglobal.net
Web: www.griffithfoundation.org

Purpose To provide financial assistance to undergraduate students from Ohio who are preparing for a career in a field related to insurance.

Eligibility This program in open to U.S. citizens from Ohio who are attending a college or university anywhere in the United States. Applicants for the large scholarships must be studying insurance, risk management, or other insurance-related area and be planning to enter an insurance-related field upon graduation. Applicants for the small scholarships must be majoring in business, have a GPA of 3.5 or higher, and agree to take and complete at least 1 college insurance and risk management course. Selection is based on academic achievement, extracurricular activities and honors, work experience, 3 letters of recommendation, and financial need.

Financial data The stipends are $1,000 for the large scholarships and $500 for the small scholarships.

Duration 1 year.

Additional information This program is sponsored by Insurance Women of Columbus, the Midwest Forum Chapter of the Association of Insurance Compliance Professionals, the Columbus Chapter of the Chartered Property Casualty Underwriters Society, the Columbus Association of Insurance & Financial Advisors, the Ohio Insurance Institute, the Central Ohio Chapter of the Risk & Insurance Management Society, the Columbus Chapter of the Society of Financial Service Professionals, and the Griffith Foundation for Insurance Education.

Number awarded 7 each year: 2 large scholarships at $1,000 and 5 small scholarships at $500.

Deadline March of each year.

[65]
CERT SCHOLARSHIPS

Council of Energy Resource Tribes
Attn: Education Program Director
695 South Colorado Boulevard, Suite 10
Denver, CO 80246-8008
(303) 282-7576   Fax: (303) 282-7584
E-mail: info@CERTRedEarth.com
Web: www.CERTRedEarth.com

Purpose To provide financial assistance to American Indian high school seniors who are interested in studying fields related to mathematics, business, science, engineering, or other technical fields in college.

Eligibility Indian high school seniors who are preparing to enter college may enroll in the Tribal Resource Institute in Business, Engineering, and Science (TRIBES) program, an intensive 7-week summer college-level program. TRIBES graduates are eligible to apply for these scholarships.

Financial data Costs of instruction, activities, and room and board for the summer institute are paid by the TRIBES program. The amount of the college scholarship is $1,000 per year.

Duration 1 year; may be renewed up to 4 additional years.

Additional information The TRIBES program runs for 7 weeks during the summer at the University of New Mexico, Native American Programs, Scholes Hall, Room 226, Albuquerque, NM 87131, (505) 277-5725, Fax: (505) 277-0228.

Deadline Applications for the TRIBES program must be submitted by April of each year.

[66]
CHARLES A. NEWMAN FBLA-PBL SCHOLARSHIP

Future Business Leaders of America-Phi Beta Lambda-
Missouri Chapter
c/o Leslie Kerns, State Advisor
Missouri Department of Elementary and Secondary
Education
Division of Career Education–Business Education
205 Jefferson Street
P.O. Box 480
Jefferson City, MO 65102-0480
(573) 751-3926   Fax: (573) 526-4261
E-mail: Leslie.Kerns@dese.mo.us
Web: dese.mo.gov/divcareered/fbla_scholarships.htm

Purpose To provide financial assistance to members of Future Business Leaders of America (FBLA) or Phi Beta Lambda (PBL) majoring in business at a college or university in Missouri.

Eligibility This program is open to current members of FBLA or PBL attending or planning to attend a Missouri college or university. Applicants must be nominated by an instructor who is a current member of the Missouri Business Education Association, have taken at least 3 business classes, and be enrolled or planning to enroll as a business major. Along with their application, they must submit a letter describing their career goals and background. Selection is based on written communication skills as revealed by the letter (10%), neatness and completeness of the application form (10%), letters of recommendation (10%), FBLA-PBL activities (30%), business-related activities (10%), other leadership activities (15%), and scholastic achievement (15%).

Financial data The stipend is $500 per year.

Duration 1 year.

Number awarded 1 each year.

Deadline January of each year.

[67]
CHARLES B. ATCHISON, JR. ENDOWMENT SCHOLARSHIP

Epsilon Sigma Alpha
Attn: ESA Foundation Assistant Scholarship Director
P.O. Box 270517
Fort Collins, CO 80527
(970) 223-2824   Fax: (970) 223-4456
Web: www.esaintl.com/esaf

Purpose To provide financial assistance for college to students from Illinois studying business or computer programming.

Eligibility This program is open to residents of Illinois who are either 1) graduating high school seniors in the top 25% of their class or with minimum scores of 20 on the ACT or 950 on the SAT, or 2) students already enrolled in college with a GPA of 3.0 or higher. Students enrolled for training in a technical school or returning to school after an absence are also eligible. Applicants must be planning to prepare for a career in business or computer programming. Selection is based on character (10%), leadership (20%), service (10%), financial need (30%), and scholastic ability (30%).

Financial data The stipend is $500.

Duration 1 year; may be renewed.

Additional information Epsilon Sigma Alpha (ESA) is a women's service organization, but scholarships are available to both men and women. Information is also available from Kathy Loyd, Scholarship Director, 1222 N.W. 651, Blairstown, MO 64726, (660) 747-2216, Fax: (660) 747-0807, E-mail: kloyd@iland.net. This scholarship was first awarded in 1990. Completed applications must be submitted to the ESA State Counselor who verifies the information before forwarding them to the scholarship director. A $5 processing fee is required.

Number awarded 1 each year.

Deadline January of each year.

[68]
CHARLES P. LAKE-RAIN FOR RENT SCHOLARSHIP

Rain for Rent
P.O. Box 2248
Bakersfield, CA 93303-2248
(661) 399-9124   Fax: (661) 399-1086
Web: www.rainforrent.com/company/scholarship.htm

Purpose To provide financial assistance for college to residents of Arizona, California, and Idaho who are interested in studying agriculture, business, or engineering.

Eligibility Applicants must have completed their freshman year at an approved university with a major in agriculture, business, or engineering. Preference is given to students specializing in irrigation technology, pumps, and fluid dynamics. Selection is based on academic achievements, extracurricular activities, and (if those are equal) financial need.

Financial data The stipend is $1,000.

Duration 1 year.

Additional information Applications must be submitted through the student's university, farm bureau, or other sponsoring organization. The participating organizations include the Arizona Farm Bureau Federation, the Idaho Future Farmers of America, the Idaho Irrigation Equipment Association, the National FFA Foundation, and the Fresno, Imperial, Kern, Monterey, San Joaquin, San Luis Obispo, Tulare, and Yolo County Farm Bureaus in California. The participating universities are California State University at Bakersfield, California State University at Chico, California State Polytechnical University at Pomona, California Polytechnical State University at San Luis Obispo, Fresno State University, Louisiana State University, Texas A&M University, and the University of California at Davis.

Number awarded 1 or more each year.

Deadline June of each year.

[69]
CHARLES W. AND ANNETTE HILL SCHOLARSHIP FUND

American Legion
Attn: Department of Kansas
1314 S.W. Topeka Boulevard
Topeka, KS 66612-1886
(785) 232-9315   Fax: (785) 232-1399

Purpose To provide financial assistance for college to the children of members of the Kansas American Legion, particularly those interested in majoring in the sciences or business.

Eligibility This program is open to graduating seniors at high schools in Kansas who have a GPA of 3.0 or higher. Applicants must be a descendant of a member of the American Legion. Preference is given to applicants planning to major in science, engineering, or business administration at a Kansas college, university, junior college, or trade school. Selection is based on high school transcripts, 3 letters of recommendation, an essay of 250 to 500 words on "Why I want to go to college," and financial need.

Financial data The stipend is $1,000.

Duration 1 year; may be renewed if the recipient maintains a GPA of 3.0 or higher.

Number awarded 1 each year.

Deadline February of each year.

[70]
CHICAGO MERCANTILE EXCHANGE SCHOLARSHIPS

National FFA Organization
Attn: Scholarship Office
6060 FFA Drive
P.O. Box 68960
Indianapolis, IN 46268-0960
(317) 802-4321   Fax: (317) 802-5321
E-mail: scholarships@ffa.org
Web: www.ffa.org

Purpose To provide financial assistance to FFA members interested in studying business or management in college.

Eligibility This program is open to members who are graduating high school seniors planning to enroll full time in college. Applicants must be interested in working on a degree in agricultural business management, including such majors as agricultural economics or agribusiness. Special consideration is given to students whose family's livelihood is connected to the commodity brokerage business. Selection is based on academic achievement (10 points for GPA, 10 points for SAT or ACT score, 10 points for class rank), leadership in FFA activities (30 points), leadership in community activities (10 points), and participation in the Supervised Agricultural Experience (SAE) program (30 points). U.S. citizenship is required.

Financial data The stipend is $1,000 per year. Funds are paid directly to the recipient.

Duration 1 year; nonrenewable.

Additional information Funding for this scholarship is provided by the Chicago Mercantile Exchange.

Number awarded 1 each year.

Deadline February of each year.

[71]
CHRISTOPHER "KIT" SMITH SCHOLARSHIP

Society of Louisiana Certified Public Accountants
Attn: LCPA Education Foundation
2400 Veterans Boulevard, Suite 500
Kenner, LA 70062-4739
(504) 464-1040   Toll-free: (800) 288-5272
Fax: (504) 469-7930
Web: www.lcpa.org/LCPAScholarships.html

Purpose To provide financial assistance to currently-enrolled college students in Louisiana who are interested in becoming certified public accountants.

Eligibility This program is open to Louisiana residents who are currently enrolled full time in an accounting program at a 4-year college or university in Louisiana. Applicants must have completed at least 4 semesters by the fall of the academic year in which the application is filed and have a GPA of 2.5 or higher. Along with their application, they must submit a 2-page essay on their perception of the CPA's role on the job and in the community, including how they plan to contribute to the profession and to the community.

Financial data The stipend is $2,500.

Duration 1 year.

Additional information This program was established in 1996.

Number awarded 1 each year.

[72]
CHUCK PEACOCK MEMORIAL SCHOLARSHIP

Aircraft Electronics Association
Attn: AEA Educational Foundation
4217 South Hocker Drive
Independence, MO 64055-4723
(816) 373-6565   Fax: (816) 478-3100
E-mail: info@aea.net
Web: www.aea.net

Purpose To provide financial assistance to students preparing for a career in aviation management.

Eligibility This program is open to high school seniors and currently-enrolled college students who are attending (or planning to attend) an accredited postsecondary institution in an aviation management program. Applicants must submit an official transcript (cumulative GPA of 2.5 or higher), a statement about their career plans, a description of their involvement in school and community activities, and a 300-word essay on aircraft electronics. Selection is based on merit.

Financial data The stipend is $1,000.

Duration 1 year.

Number awarded 1 each year.
Deadline January of each year.

[73]
CHURCHARMENIA.COM FINANCE AND BUSINESS SCHOLARSHIP

Charles and Agnes Kazarian Eternal
Foundation/ChurchArmenia.com
Attn: Educational Scholarships
30 Kennedy Plaza, Second Floor
Providence, RI 02903
E-mail: info@churcharmenia.com
Web: www.churcharmenia.com/scholarship1.html

Purpose To provide financial assistance to outstanding undergraduate or graduate students of Armenian descent who are working on a degree in business or finance.
Eligibility Applicants must be of Armenian descent and accepted to or qualified for a highly competitive undergraduate or graduate degree (including M.B.A.) program in economics, finance, or other similar field. They must submit a completed application form, official academic transcripts, 3-page personal statement, and up to 3 letters of recommendation. Applicants should provide examples of commitment to the community in terms of business experience or community service.
Financial data The stipend is $5,000.
Duration 1 year.
Number awarded 1 or more each year.

[74]
CIRI FOUNDATION SPECIAL EXCELLENCE SCHOLARSHIPS

Cook Inlet Region, Inc.
Attn: CIRI Foundation
2600 Cordova Street, Suite 206
Anchorage, AK 99503
(907) 263-5582   Toll-free: (800) 764-3382
Fax: (907) 263-5588   E-mail: tcf@ciri.com
Web: www.ciri.com/tcf/scholarship.html

Purpose To provide financial assistance for undergraduate or graduate studies to Alaska Natives who are original enrollees to Cook Inlet Region, Inc. (CIRI) and their lineal descendants.
Eligibility This program is open to Alaska Native enrollees under the Alaska Native Claims Settlement Act (ANCSA) of 1971 and their lineal descendants of Cook Inlet Region, Inc. There are no Alaska residency requirements or age limitations. Applicants must be accepted or enrolled full time in a 4-year undergraduate or a graduate degree program. They must have a GPA of 3.7 or higher. Preference is given to students working on a degree in business, education, mathematics, sciences, health services, or engineering. Selection is based on academic achievement, rigor of course work or degree program, quality of a statement of purpose, student financial contribution, financial need, grade level, previous work performance, education and community activities, letters of recommendation, seriousness of purpose, and practicality of educational and professional goals.
Financial data The stipend is $18,000 per year.
Duration 1 year; may be renewed.

Additional information This program was established in 1997. Recipients must enroll in school on a full-time basis.
Number awarded 1 or more each year.
Deadline May of each year.

[75]
CITIGROUP FELLOWS PROGRAM

United Negro College Fund
Attn: Scholarships and Grants Department
8260 Willow Oaks Corporate Drive
P.O. Box 10444
Fairfax, VA 22031-8044
(703) 205-3466   Toll-free: (800) 331-2244
Fax: (703) 205-3574
Web: www.uncf.org

Purpose To provide financial assistance to freshmen majoring in fields related to business at colleges and universities that are members of the United Negro College Fund (UNCF).
Eligibility Eligible to apply for these scholarships are second-semester freshmen at UNCF-member institutions. Applicants must be majoring in accounting, business management, economics, finance, or information technology. They must have a GPA of 3.0 or higher for high school and 3.2 or higher for their first semester of college. Along with their application, they must submit a 250-word essay on their career interests in business and where they expect to be in their career in 10 years, a 250-word essay on their professional and academic skills and how they will contribute to a successful career in business, transcripts, a letter of recommendation, and documentation of financial need.
Financial data The stipend is $6,400 per year. Fellows are also eligible to receive Citigroup Academic Excellence Awards, which provide up to $4,500 in additional scholarship support.
Duration 1 year; may be renewed for 2 additional years.
Additional information Recipients are assigned a Citigroup mentor and attend an annual leadership conference for fellows and mentors.
Number awarded 10 each year.
Deadline March of each year.

[76]
C.J. "RED" DAVIDSON MEMORIAL SCHOLARSHIPS

Texas FFA Association
614 East 12th Street
Austin, TX 78701
(512) 480-8045   Fax: (512) 472-0555
E-mail: txffa@texasffa.org
Web: www.texasffa.org/ffa/tfa-scho.html

Purpose To provide financial assistance to high school senior members of FFA in Texas who plan to study a field related to agricultural or life sciences (including agribusiness) at a college or university in the state.
Eligibility This program is open to high school seniors in Texas who are FFA members and have been members at least 2 of the 3 previous years. Applicants must be planning to major in a field related to the agricultural or life sciences at a college or university in Texas. They must have completed at least 3 semesters of instruction in agriculture and/or agribu-

siness during high school and scored at least 950 on the SAT or 20 on the ACT. U.S. citizenship and ranking in the top half of their graduating class are also required. Selection is based on class rank (16 points), SAT or ACT scores (14 points), academic achievement in agricultural science and career related instruction (10 points), FFA achievements (30 points), financial need (10 points), and an interview (25 points).

Financial data The stipend is $5,000.

Duration 1 year.

Additional information The list of approved majors includes plant and soil sciences (agronomy, botany, clothing and textiles, floriculture, horticulture, plant science, soil science); natural and environmental sciences (aquaculture, atmospheric science, bioenvironmental science, entomology, forestry, fisheries, mariculture, marine biology, meteorology, range science, soil and water conservation, and wildlife science); human and animal sciences (animal science, dairy science, food and nutrition, food science, food technology, poultry science, preveterinary medicine, scientific nutrition, and zoology); support curriculums (agricultural development, agricultural business, agricultural economics, agricultural education, agricultural engineering, agricultural journalism, agricultural science, agricultural services, agricultural systems, biomedical engineering, chemical engineering, food engineering, land use and planning, landscape architecture, and recreation and parks); and basic sciences (biochemistry, biology, biomedical science, biotechnology, chemistry, genetics, microbiology, and pharmacology). Students may not apply for both 4-H and FFA scholarships.

Number awarded Varies each year.

[77]
CLAUDE E. POPE SCHOLARSHIP

Mortgage Bankers Association of the Carolinas, Inc.
P.O. Box 11721
Charlotte, NC 28220-1721
(704) 552-2860   Toll-free: (800) 451-4872
Web: www.mbac.org

Purpose To provide financial assistance to upper-division students who are preparing for a career in mortgage banking at colleges and universities in the Carolinas.

Eligibility Eligible to apply are rising juniors in either North Carolina or South Carolina who are working on a degree related to mortgage banking or mortgage financing, including real estate and economics. Applicants must be attending a 4-year accredited college or university and have a GPA of 3.0 or higher. Financial need is not considered in the selection process.

Financial data The stipend is $1,500 per year, paid in 2 equal installments.

Duration 2 years.

Additional information This award was established in 1972.

Number awarded 2 each year.

Deadline March of each year.

[78]
CLEVELAND ADVERTISING ASSOCIATION EDUCATION FOUNDATION SCHOLARSHIPS

Cleveland Advertising Association
Attn: Education Foundation
20325 Center Ridge Road, Suite 670
Cleveland, OH 44116
(440) 673-0020   Fax: (440) 673-0025
E-mail: adassoc@clevead.com
Web: www.clevead.com/education/scholarships.php

Purpose To provide financial assistance to undergraduate students who are residents of Ohio majoring in a field related to advertising at a college or university in the state.

Eligibility This program is open to residents of Ohio who are full-time seniors, juniors, or second-semester sophomores at colleges and universities in the state. Applicants must be majoring in advertising or a related communications/marketing field and have a GPA of 3.0 or higher. They must submit transcripts, 2 letters of recommendation, and an essay describing their career goals. Financial need is not considered in the selection process. Some of the scholarships are set aside for U.S. citizens of African, Asian, Hispanic, Native American, or Pacific Island descent.

Financial data Stipends range from $1,000 to $2,500.

Duration 1 year.

Additional information This program includes the following named scholarships: the Arras Group Minority Scholarship, the Wyse Advertising Scholarship, the Thomas Brennan Memorial Scholarship, the Hitchcock Fleming and Associates Scholarship, the Innis Maggiore Scholarship, the Marcus Thomas Scholarship, the Laurie Mitchell and Company Scholarship, and the Plain Dealer Bob Hagley Scholarship.

Number awarded Varies each year. Recently, this program awarded 11 scholarships: 2 at $2,500, 1 at $2,000, 3 at $1,500, and 5 at $1,000.

Deadline October of each year.

[79]
COCA-COLA DECA SCHOLARSHIPS

DECA
1908 Association Drive
Reston, VA 20191-1594
(703) 860-5000   Fax: (703) 860-4013
E-mail: decainc@aol.com
Web: www.deca.org/scholarships/index.html

Purpose To provide financial assistance to DECA members interested in studying business in college.

Eligibility This program is open to DECA members who are interested in working full time on a 2-year or 4-year degree in marketing, business, or marketing education. Applicants must be able to demonstrate evidence of DECA activities, academic achievement, leadership ability, and community service involvement. Selection is based on merit, not financial need.

Financial data The stipend is $1,000.

Duration 1 year.

Additional information This program, established in 2002, is sponsored by the Coca-Cola Company.

Number awarded Up to 5 each year.

Deadline February of each year.

[80]
COLORADO BROADCASTERS ASSOCIATION CONTINUING EDUCATION SCHOLARSHIPS

Colorado Broadcasters Association
Attn: Education Committee
2042 Boreas Pass Road
P.O. Box 2369
Breckenridge, CO 80424
(970) 547-1388   Fax: (970) 547-1384
E-mail: cobroadcasters@earthlink.net
Web: www.e-cba.org/scholarships.htm

Purpose To provide financial assistance for additional study in related fields to employees of broadcast stations that are members of the Colorado Broadcasters Association (CBA).

Eligibility This program is open to full-time employees who have worked for at least 1 year at a broadcast station that is a member of the CBA. Applicants must be interested in improving their education while continuing to work; examples of acceptable projects include 1) undergraduate and graduate courses in broadcasting, media programs at the college level, or academic work in other related fields, such as business or engineering; and 2) workshops and seminars offered by recognized national trade and professional organizations. Preference is given to projects leading to degrees or certificates. Applicants must submit a resume; a description of the course, workshop, or program for which funding is sought; the cost of the course or program; a statement of their continuing educational and professional goals and their qualifications for the scholarship, a letter of recommendation from a supervisor or senior manager, and an explanation of any other special circumstances that might bear on their application.

Financial data The maximum award is $500.

Duration 1 year.

Number awarded Varies each year; a total of $3,000 is available for this program annually.

Deadline Applications may be submitted at any time and are considered on a first-come, first-served basis throughout the fiscal year (which begins in July).

[81]
COLORADO SOCIETY OF CPAS ETHNIC DIVERSITY SCHOLARSHIPS FOR COLLEGE STUDENTS

Colorado Society of Certified Public Accountants
Attn: CSCPA Educational Foundation
7979 East Tufts Avenue, Suite 500
Denver, CO 80237-2845
(303) 741-8613   Toll-free: (800) 523-9082 (within CO)
Fax: (303) 773-6344   E-mail: gmantz@cocpa.org
Web: www.cocpa.org/student_faculty/scholarships.asp

Purpose To provide financial assistance to minority undergraduate or graduate students in Colorado who are studying accounting.

Eligibility This program is open to African Americans, Hispanics, Asian Americans, Native Americans, and Pacific Islanders studying at a college or university in Colorado at the associate, baccalaureate, or graduate level. Applicants must have completed at least 1 intermediate accounting class, be declared accounting majors, have completed at least 8 semester hours of accounting classes, and have a GPA of at least 3.0. Selection is based first on scholastic achievement and second on financial need.

Financial data The stipend is $1,000. Funds are paid directly to the recipient's school to be used for books, tuition, room, board, fees, and expenses.

Duration 1 year; recipients may reapply.

Number awarded 2 each year.

Deadline June of each year.

[82]
COLORADO SOCIETY OF CPAS ETHNIC DIVERSITY SCHOLARSHIPS FOR HIGH SCHOOL STUDENTS

Colorado Society of Certified Public Accountants
Attn: CSCPA Educational Foundation
7979 East Tufts Avenue, Suite 500
Denver, CO 80237-2845
(303) 741-8613   Toll-free: (800) 523-9082 (within CO)
Fax: (303) 773-6344   E-mail: gmantz@cocpa.org
Web: www.cocpa.org/student_faculty/scholarships.asp

Purpose To provide financial assistance to minority high school seniors in Colorado who plan to study accounting in college.

Eligibility This program is open to African American, Hispanic, Asian American, American Indian, and Pacific Islander high school seniors in Colorado planning to major in accounting at a college or university in the state. Applicants must have a GPA of 3.0 or higher. Selection is based primarily on scholastic achievement.

Financial data The stipend is $1,000.

Duration 1 year; nonrenewable.

Number awarded 3 each year.

Deadline February of each year.

[83]
COLVIN SCHOLARSHIP PROGRAM

Certified Angus Beef LLC
Attn: President
206 Riffel Road
Wooster, OH 44691-8588
(330) 345-2333   Toll-free: (800) 725-2333, ext. 279
Fax: (330) 345-0808
E-mail: bbarner@certifiedangusbeef.com
Web: www.certifiedangusbeef.com

Purpose To provide financial assistance to upper-division students working on a degree related to the beef industry.

Eligibility This program is open to students entering their junior or senior year of college. Applicants must have demonstrated a commitment to the beef industry through work on a degree in meat science, food science, animal science, marketing, business, communications, journalism, or other field related to the industry. Along with their application, they must submit a 1,000-word essay on the challenges facing the beef industry and their solutions. They may also submit a statement of financial need. Selection is based on, in this order of importance, activities and scholastic achievement, communication skills (both essay and verbal), and reference letters.

Financial data The stipend is $2,500.

Duration 1 year.

Additional information This program was established in 1999. The recipient may also be offered a paid summer internship with the sponsor.

Number awarded 1 each year.

Deadline November of each year.

[84]
COMMUNITY SERVICE SCHOLARSHIPS

Association of Government Accountants
Attn: National Awards Committee
2208 Mount Vernon Avenue
Alexandria, VA 22301-1314
(703) 684-6931   Toll-free: (800) AGA-7211, ext. 131
Fax: (703) 548-9367   E-mail: rortiz@agacgfm.org
Web: www.agacgfm.org/membership/awards

Purpose To provide financial assistance to undergraduate and graduate students majoring in financial management who are involved in community service.

Eligibility This program is open to graduating high school seniors, high school graduates, college and university undergraduates, and graduate students. Applicants must be working on or planning to work on a degree in a financial management discipline, including accounting, auditing, budgeting, economics, finance, information technology, or public administration. They must have a GPA of 2.5 or higher and be actively involved in community service projects. As part of the selection process, they must submit a 2-page essay on "My community service accomplishments," high school or college transcripts, and a reference letter from a community service organization. Selection is based on community service involvement and accomplishments; financial need is not considered.

Financial data The annual stipend is $1,000.

Duration 1 year; renewable.

Number awarded 2 each year: 1 to a high school senior or graduate and 1 to an undergraduate or graduate student.

Deadline March of each year.

[85]
CONNECTICUT BROADCASTERS ASSOCIATION SCHOLARSHIPS

Connecticut Broadcasters Association
c/o Paul Taff, President
P.O. Box 678
Glastonbury, CT 06033
(860) 633-5031   (860) 657-2491
E-mail: pkt@ctba.org
Web: www.ctba.org

Purpose To provide financial assistance to Connecticut residents who are studying a field related to broadcasting in college.

Eligibility This program is open to Connecticut residents who are entering their junior or senior year in college. Applicants must be majoring in communications, marketing, or other field related to broadcasting. Selection is based on academic achievement, community service, goals in the chosen field, and financial need.

Financial data A stipend is awarded (amount not specified).

Duration 1 year.

Number awarded 1 or more each year.

[86]
CONNECTICUT BUILDING CONGRESS SCHOLARSHIPS

Connecticut Building Congress
Attn: Scholarship Fund
2600 Dixwell Avenue, Suite 7
Hamden, CT 06514-1800
(203) 281-3183   Fax: (203) 248-8932
E-mail: info@cbc-ct.org
Web: www.cbc-ct.org/scholarship.html

Purpose To provide financial assistance to high school seniors in Connecticut who are interested in studying a field related to the construction industry in college.

Eligibility This program is open to graduating seniors at high schools in Connecticut. Applicants must be interested in attending a 2- or 4-year college or university to major in a field related to construction (e.g., architecture, engineering, construction management, planning, drafting). They must submit an essay (up to 500 words) that explains how their planned studies will relate to a career in the construction industry. Selection is based on academic merit, extracurricular activities, potential, and financial need.

Financial data Stipends range from $500 to $2,000 per year.

Duration Up to 4 years.

Number awarded Varies each year.

Deadline February of each year.

[87]
CREDIT SUISSE FIRST BOSTON SCHOLARSHIP

United Negro College Fund
Attn: Scholarships and Grants Department
8260 Willow Oaks Corporate Drive
P.O. Box 10444
Fairfax, VA 22031-8044
(703) 205-3466   Toll-free: (800) 331-2244
Fax: (703) 205-3574
Web: www.uncf.org/scholarships/index.asp

Purpose To provide financial assistance and work experience to freshmen majoring in business-related fields at colleges and universities that are members of the United Negro College Fund (UNCF).

Eligibility This program is open to second-semester freshmen enrolled full time at UNCF-member institutions with a GPA of 3.4 or higher. Applicants may be majoring in any discipline, but they should have course work related to accounting, business, economics, engineering, finance, or mathematics. Along with their application, they must submit a 400-word essay on a significant experience, achievement, or risk they have taken and how it has impacted them. Financial need is not considered in the selection process. Finalists are interviewed.

Financial data The stipend is $8,000 per year. The program includes paid internships in investment banking and securities at an office of Credit Suisse First Boston (CSFB).

Duration 1 year; may be renewed up to 2 additional years provided the recipient maintains a GPA of 3.4 or higher, full-time enrollment, good student standing at their college or university, and good employee standing with CSFB during the internship programs.

Additional information Funds for this program are provided by CSFB.

Number awarded 1 or more each year.

Deadline March of each year.

[88]
CSCPA CANDIDATE'S AWARD

Connecticut Society of Certified Public Accountants
Attn: Educational Trust Fund
845 Brook Street, Building 2
Rocky Hill, CT 06067-3405
(860) 258-4800   Toll-free: (800) 232-2232 (within CT)
Fax: (860) 258-4859   E-mail: cscpa@cs-cpa.org
Web: www.cs-cpa.org

Purpose To provide financial assistance to college students in Connecticut who are majoring in accounting and going on to a fifth year of school.

Eligibility This program is open to college seniors going on to a fifth year in school in compliance with the 150-hour requirement of the Connecticut State Board of Accountancy to sit for the Uniform Certified Public Accountant Examination. Applicants must hold a baccalaureate degree from an accredited college or university, have earned at least a 3.5 overall GPA, and be enrolled in a formal program at a Connecticut college or university intended to satisfy the 150-hour requirement. Applicants must submit a completed application form and an official copy of their college or university academic transcript.

Financial data The stipend is $2,500.

Duration 1 year.

Number awarded 1 each year.

Deadline August of each year.

[89]
CSCPA CHILDREN'S SCHOLARSHIP PROGRAM

Connecticut Society of Certified Public Accountants
Attn: Educational Trust Fund
845 Brook Street, Building 2
Rocky Hill, CT 06067-3405
(860) 258-4800   Toll-free: (800) 232-2232 (within CT)
Fax: (860) 258-4859   E-mail: cscpa@cs-cpa.org
Web: www.cs-cpa.org

Purpose To provide financial assistance to college students majoring in accounting who are the children of members of the Connecticut Society of Certified Public Accountants.

Eligibility This program is open to rising college seniors (those who have just completed their third year in college) whose parent is a member of the society. Applicants must have an overall GPA of at least 2.5 and at least a 3.0 in accounting through and including their junior year. They must be majoring in accounting at a college or university in Connecticut.

Financial data The stipend is $500.

Duration 1 year (the recipient's senior year in college).

Number awarded Up to 5 each year.

Deadline August of each year.

[90]
D. ANITA SMALL SCIENCE AND BUSINESS SCHOLARSHIP

Maryland Federation of Business and Professional
    Women's Clubs, Inc.
c/o Pat Schroeder, Chair
354 Driftwood Lane
Solomons, MD 20688
(410) 326-0167   Toll-free: (877) INFO-BPW
E-mail: patsc@csmd.edu
Web: www.bpwmaryland.org/HTML/scholarships.html

Purpose To provide financial assistance to women in Maryland who are interested in working on an undergraduate or graduate degree in a science or business-related field.

Eligibility This program is open to women in Maryland who are at least 21 years of age and have been accepted to a bachelor's or advanced degree program at an accredited Maryland academic institution. Applicants must be preparing for a career in 1 of the following or a related field: accounting, aeronautics, business administration, computer sciences, engineering, finance, information technology, mathematics, medical sciences (including nursing, laboratory technology, therapy, etc.), oceanography, or physical sciences. They must have a GPA of 3.0 or higher and be able to demonstrate financial need.

Financial data The stipend is $1,000 per year.

Duration 1 year.

Number awarded 1 or more each year.

Deadline May of each year.

[91]
DALLAS CHAPTER UNDERGRADUATE SCHOLARSHIP

National Black MBA Association-Dallas Chapter
Attn: Student Affairs Committee
P.O. Box 797174
Dallas, TX 75379-7174
(214) 853-4497   E-mail: stud_affairs@dallasmbas.org
Web: www.dallasmbas.org

Purpose To provide financial assistance to African American undergraduate students who are working on a degree in business administration in Texas.

Eligibility This program is open to African American students who are Texas residents and/or enrolled full time in the first, second, or third year of a business program at a college or university in Texas. Applicants must submit an official transcript, 2 letters of recommendation, an e-mail address, a resume of extracurricular/volunteer activities, a statement describing their projected college expense schedule, and a 2-page essay on a topic that changes annually but relates to African Americans in business.

Financial data The stipend is $1,000.

Duration 1 year.

Number awarded Varies each year.

Deadline March of each year.

[92]
DARTHE F. NAY SCHOLARSHIPS

American Society of Women Accountants-St. Louis
   Chapter
c/o Joan Warning
Humes & Barrington, P.C.
333 South Kirkwood Road, Suite 300
St. Louis, MO 63122-6161
(314) 966-6622   Fax: (314) 966-0217
E-mail: jwarning@humbar.com
Web: www.aswastlouis.org/scholarships/geninfo.html

Purpose To provide financial assistance to accounting students at colleges and universities in Missouri and eastern Illinois.

Eligibility This program is open to students majoring in accounting at a college or university in Missouri or eastern Illinois. Applicants must have completed 60 semester hours with at least 12 hours in accounting and a GPA of 3.0 or higher. Financial need and classroom attendance are considered in the selection process.

Financial data Stipends are $1,000 or $500. Funds are paid to the university or college.

Duration 1 year.

Number awarded Varies each year. Recently, 3 of these scholarships were awarded: 1 at $1,000 and 2 at $500.

Deadline February of each year.

[93]
DAVID BRODSKY, RUSSELL SCHOFIELD AND MSI SCHOLARSHIP PROGRAM

American Moving and Storage Association
Attn: Moving and Storage Institute Scholarship Fund
1611 Duke Street
Alexandria, VA 22314
(703) 683-7410   Fax: (703) 683-8208
E-mail: csimpson@moving.org
Web: www.promover.org/scholarships/msi.htm

Purpose To provide financial assistance to employees of van lines and moving and storage companies who are working on a college degree in a field related to the moving and storage industry.

Eligibility This program is open to 1) employees affiliated with a van line or moving and storage company; 2) children, grandchildren, and spouses of such an employee; 3) an independent contractor affiliated with a van line or moving and storage company; and 4) children, grandchildren, and spouses of such independent contractors. Applicants must be working full time on a degree in business administration, accounting, or another field related to the moving and storage industry at an accredited college, university, community college, professional school, or technical school. Along with their application they must submit an essay of 500 to 700 words on the importance and role of the moving and storage industry in today's economy or another topic related to the industry. Selection is based on academic achievement, character, integrity, and financial need.

Financial data Stipends range from $1,000 to $2,000 per year. Funds are sent directly to the recipient's institution to be used for tuition only.

Duration 1 year; may be renewed up to 1 additional year provided the recipient maintains full-time enrollment and good academic standing.

Number awarded 1 or more each year.

Deadline January of each year.

[94]
DAVID TATON SCHOLARSHIP AWARDS

Rhode Island School-to-Career
Attn: Director
1511 Pontiac Avenue
Building 72-3
Cranston, RI 02920
(401) 462-8880   Fax: (401) 462-8865
E-mail: lsoderberg@dlt.state.ri.us
Web: www.ristc.org/taton.html

Purpose To provide financial assistance for additional vocational study to students who have participated in Rhode Island School-to-Career (STC) activities.

Eligibility This program is open to high school seniors in Rhode Island who have shown an interest and a high level of participation in STC initiatives while in high school. Applicants must be planning to continue their STC participation by attending a vocational school or college.

Financial data The stipend is $500.

Duration 1 year.

Additional information The Rhode Island STC program prepares students for careers in such fields as health services, biotechnology, information technology, financial services, manufacturing, hospitality and tourism, construction, and automotive technology. While in high school, STC participants engage in career planning, technical training, and workplace skill development activities through partnerships with representatives from industry.

Number awarded 4 each year.

[95]
DCBMBAA CHAPTER UNDERGRADUATE SCHOLARSHIP PROGRAM

National Black MBA Association-Washington, DC
   Chapter
P.O. Box 14042
Washington, DC 20044
(202) 628-0138   E-mail: info@dcbmbaa.org
Web: www.dcbmbaa.org

Purpose To provide financial assistance to African American and other minority students from the Washington, D.C. area who are working on an undergraduate degree in business or management.

Eligibility This program is open to African American and other minority students who are enrolled in a full-time undergraduate business or management program in the United States, working on a bachelor's degree. Applicants must submit a completed application form, a photograph, a current resume, and an essay (up to 2 pages) on a topic that changes annually but focuses on minorities in business.

Financial data The stipend is $1,000.

Duration 1 year.

Number awarded 1 each year.

Deadline March of each year.

[96]
DELAWARE SHRM SCHOLARSHIPS

Delaware Society for Human Resource Management
c/o Noelle C. Robertson, Student Chapter Liaison
630 Martin Luther King Jr. Boulevard
P.O. Box 231
Wilmington, DE 19899-0231
(302) 429-3486   Fax: (302) 429-3816
E-mail: Noelle.Robertson@Connectiv.com
Web: www.shrmde.org

Purpose To provide financial assistance to students working on a bachelor's or master's degree in human resources at colleges and universities in Delaware.

Eligibility This program is open to 1) undergraduate students enrolled in a human resources program or related programs at a Delaware college, and 2) graduate students currently enrolled in a master's degree program at a Delaware college and clearly pursuing an emphasis area in human resources or related programs. Applicants must have a GPA of 3.0 or higher. Along with their application, they must submit a 2-page essay on their future objectives in the human resources field and why they chose this profession. Selection is based on total achievements and need.

Financial data The stipend is $2,500.

Duration 1 year.

Additional information The sponsor is the Delaware affiliate of the Society for Human Resource Management (SHRM).

Number awarded 4 each year.

Deadline September of each year.

[97]
DELL/UNCF CORPORATE SCHOLARS PROGRAM

United Negro College Fund
Attn: Corporate Scholars Program
P.O. Box 1435
Alexandria, VA 22313-9998
Toll-free: (866) 671-7237   E-mail: internship@uncf.org
Web: www.uncf.org/internships/index.asp

Purpose To provide financial assistance and work experience to undergraduate and graduate students, especially minorities, majoring in designated fields and interested in an internship at Dell Computer Corporation's corporate headquarters near Austin, Texas.

Eligibility This program is open to rising juniors and graduate students who are enrolled full time at institutions that are members of the United Negro College Fund (UNCF) or at any other 4-year college and university. Applicants must be majoring in business administration, computer science, engineering (computer, electrical, or mechanical), finance, human resources, management information systems, marketing, or supply chain management with a GPA of 3.0 or higher. Along with their application, they must submit a 1-page essay about themselves and their career goals, including information about their personal background and any particular challenges they have faced. Finalists are interviewed by a team of representatives from Dell, the program's sponsor.

Financial data The program provides a paid summer internship, housing accommodations in Austin, round-trip transportation to and from Austin, and (based on financial need and successful internship performance) a $10,000 scholarship.

Duration 10 to 12 weeks for the internship; 1 year for the scholarship.

Number awarded Varies each year.

Deadline January of each year.

[98]
DELTA MU DELTA SCHOLARSHIP AWARDS

Delta Mu Delta
Attn: Scholarship Chair
2 Salt Creek Lane LL6
Hinsdale, IL 60521
(630) 321-9522   Fax: (630) 214-6080
E-mail: dmd@dmd-ntl.org
Web: www.deltamudelta.org/scholarships.html

Purpose To provide financial assistance to undergraduate or graduate students majoring in business administration.

Eligibility This program is open to undergraduate and graduate students who are in at least the final term of their sophomore year and working on a degree in business administration. Although membership in Delta Mu Delta (a national honor society in business administration) is not required, applicants must be attending a school with a chapter of the society. Selection is based on scholarship, leadership, character, motivation, potential, and need.

Financial data Stipends are $2,000, $1,500, $1,000, $750, or $500.

Duration 1 year.

Number awarded Varies each year; recently, 39 of these scholarship were awarded: 1 at $2,000 (the Mildred R. Marion Award), 2 at $1,500 (the Albert J. Escher Award and the A.J. Foranoce Award), 4 at $1,000, 11 at $750 (including the Helen D. Snow Award, the Balwant Singh Award, and the Abderrahman Robana Award), and 21 at $500 (including the Eta Chapter Award).

Deadline February of each year.

[99]
DENNY'S SCHOLARSHIP PROGRAM

Hispanic College Fund
Attn: National Director
1717 Pennsylvania Avenue, N.W., Suite 460
Washington, D.C. 20006
Toll-free: (800) 644-4223   Fax: (202) 296-3774
E-mail: hispaniccollegefund@earthlink.net
Web: www.hispanicfund.org

Purpose To provide financial assistance to Hispanic American undergraduate students who are interested in preparing for a career in business, computer science, or engineering.

Eligibility This program is open to U.S. citizens of Hispanic background (at least 1 grandparent must be 100% Hispanic) who are entering their freshman, sophomore, junior, or senior year of college. Applicants must be working on a bachelor's degree in business, computer science, engineering, or a business-related major and have a cumulative GPA of 3.0 or higher. They must be applying to or enrolled in a college or university in the 50 states or Puerto Rico as a full-time student. Financial need is considered in the selection process.

Financial data Stipends range from $500 to $5,000, depending on the need of the recipient. The sponsor's goal is to have the average award be $3,000. Funds are paid directly to the recipient's college or university to help cover tuition and fees.

Duration 1 year; recipients may reapply.

Additional information This program, which began in 1996, is sponsored by Denny's. All applications must be submitted online; no paper applications are available.

Number awarded Varies each year; recently, 44 of these scholarships were awarded.

Deadline April of each year.

[100]
DENVER CHAPTER SCHOLARSHIPS

American Society of Women Accountants-Denver
  Chapter
c/o Nicolette Rounds, Scholarship Trustee
3773 Cherry Creek Drive North, Suite 575
Denver, CO 80209
(303) 377-4282   E-mail: roundscpa@qwest.net
Web: www.aswadenver.org

Purpose To provide financial assistance to women working on a degree in accounting at a college or university in Colorado.

Eligibility This program is open to women who have completed at least 60 semester hours toward a degree in accounting with a GPA of 3.0 or higher. Applicants must be attending a college or university in Colorado. Selection is based on academic achievement, extracurricular activities, honors, a statement of career goals and objectives, 3 letters of recommendation, and financial need.

Financial data A total of $7,000 in scholarships is awarded each year.

Duration 1 year.

Number awarded Several each year.

Deadline June of each year.

[101]
DEREK HUGHES/NAPSLO EDUCATIONAL FOUNDATION INSURANCE SCHOLARSHIP

NAPSLO Educational Foundation
Attn: Insurance Scholarship Committee
6405 North Cosby Avenue, Suite 201
Kansas City, MO 64151
(816) 741-3910   Fax: (816) 741-5409
E-mail: foundation@napslo.org
Web: www.napslo.org

Purpose To provide financial assistance to undergraduate and graduate students working on a adegree in a field of importance to the insurance industry.

Eligibility This program is open to students who are enrolled or accepted for enrollment in an undergraduate or graduate program, working on a degree in actuarial science, business, economics, insurance, finance, management, risk management, statistics, or any field that relates to a career in insurance. They must have a GPA of 3.0 or higher (entering freshmen must also rank in the top 25% of their high school class). Students must submit a completed application, a col-

lege transcript, an essay, and 2 letters of recommendation. Financial need is considered in the selection process.

Financial data The stipend is $2,000.

Duration 1 year; recipients may reapply.

Additional information This program includes several named scholarships: Rolland L. Wiegers, Herbert Kaufman, Kevin A. McLaughlin, and Scott W. Polley Memorial Scholarship (for students majoring in insurance who qualify based on a combination of merit and financial need). Also offered as part of the program is the September 11 Scholarship, for children of insurance professionals killed in the 2001 terrorist attacks. This program is sponsored by the National Association of Professional Surplus Lines Offices (NAPSLO) Educational Foundation.

Number awarded 10 to 12 each year.

Deadline May of each year.

[102]
DIRECT MARKETING SCHOLARSHIP

New England Direct Marketing Association
Attn: NEDMA Foundation
193 Haverhill Street
North Reading, MA 01864
(978) 664-3877   Fax: (978) 664-2835
E-mail: mke@theworld.com
Web: www.nedma.com/foundation.html

Purpose To provide financial assistance and work experience to upper-division students in New England who are preparing for a career in direct marketing.

Eligibility This program is open to students who have completed their sophomore or junior year at a college or university in New England. Applicants must be majoring in marketing, advertising, communications, or other field designed to prepare them for a career in direct marketing. Along with their application, they must submit an essay covering such topics as why they are applying for this scholarship, what courses in their major have interested them the most and why, the extracurricular activities in which they have participated, their employment or internship experiences (especially those related to marketing, advertising, or journalism), their special interest in the field, how they believe this scholarship will affect their short- and long-term goals, and what direct marketing means to them. Financial need is not considered in the selection process.

Financial data The award includes a stipend of $3,000 to be applied to college tuition, attendance at a nationally sponsored seminar on the basics of direct marketing, a paid summer internship at a New England firm that represents a segment of the direct marketing industry, and attendance at the annual conference of the New England Direct Marketing Association (NEDMA).

Duration 1 year.

Number awarded 1 each year.

Deadline February of each year.

[103]
DISTRICT OF COLUMBIA AREA CHAPTER SCHOLARSHIPS

American Society of Women Accountants-District of
Columbia Area Chapter
c/o Marlane Perry, President
6307 Long Meadow Road
McLean, VA 22101
E-mail: mperry@keipearson.com
Web: www.aswa-dc.org

Purpose To provide financial assistance to students majoring in accounting at colleges and universities in the Washington, D.C. area.

Eligibility This program is open to students working on a degree in accounting at a college, university, or professional school of accounting in the Washington area (including suburbs in nearby Maryland and northern Virginia). Applicants must have completed sufficient courses in accounting to demonstrate their aptitude and intention to continue in a career in the field. Selection is based primarily on personal interviews and financial need.

Financial data The stipend is $1,000.

Duration 1 year.

Additional information The highest-ranked applicant receives the Past President's Award and is entered into the national competition for scholarships that range from $1,500 to $4,500. The second-ranked applicant receives the Board of Trustee's Award and the third-ranked applicant (if awarded) receives the June P. Blair Memorial Award.

Number awarded Varies each year; recently, 2 of these scholarships were awarded.

[104]
DONALD R. PLANT MEMORIAL PROFESSIONAL ADVANCEMENT AWARD

Healthcare Financial Management Association-Oklahoma
Chapter
c/o Regan Calhoun
Saint Francis Health Systems
6161 South Yale Avenue
Tulsa, OK 74136
(918) 494-7359   E-mail: rdcalhoun@saintfrancis.com
Web: www.ohfma.org

Purpose To provide financial assistance to students and professionals in Oklahoma who are interested in preparing for a career in health care finance.

Eligibility This program is open to Oklahoma students and professionals who are preparing for a career in health care finance.

Financial data The award includes a $500 stipend, 1-year membership in the Healthcare Financial Management Association (HFMA), and waiver of all Oklahoma HFMA program fees for 1 year.

Duration 1 year.

Number awarded 4 each year.

Deadline March of each year.

[105]
DR. FELIX H. REYLER MEMORIAL SCHOLARSHIP

Dade Community Foundation
Attn: Director of Development and Communications
200 South Biscayne Boulevard, Suite 505
Miami, FL 33131-2343
(305) 371-2711   Fax: (305) 371-5342
E-mail: joe.pena@dadecommunityfoundation.org
Web: www.dadecommunityfoundation.org

Purpose To provide financial assistance to upper-division students who are Florida residents and working on a degree in international business.

Eligibility This program is open to juniors and seniors who are enrolled full time in a 4-year college or university in Florida and have a GPA of 3.0 or higher. Applicants must be Florida residents (this includes individuals who have resided in Florida long enough to be granted resident status in the state university system), be U.S. citizens or permanent residents, and be working on an undergraduate degree in international business or finance. Selection is based on financial need, academic achievement, personal aspirations, career goals and interests in international business and finance, volunteer experience, work experience, and school activities.

Financial data The stipend is $2,500.

Duration 1 year; juniors may reapply.

Additional information This program was established in 1993 by the Florida International Bankers Association.

Number awarded At least 2 each year.

Deadline May of each year.

[106]
DR. LISA BURKE SCHOLARSHIP

Society for Human Resource Management
Attn: Student Program Manager
1800 Duke Street
Alexandria, VA 22314-3499
(703) 535-6084   Toll-free: (800) 283-SHRM
Fax: (703) 739-0399   TDD: (703) 548-6999
E-mail: SHRMStudent@shrm.org
Web: www.shrm.org/students/ags_published

Purpose To provide financial assistance to undergraduate student members of the Society for Human Resource Management (SHRM) who are paying their own way through college.

Eligibility This program is open to undergraduate students who have completed their sophomore year, have maintained a GPA of 2.0 or higher, are majoring in human resources or a related subject, are national student members of the society, and are paying more than 50% of their college expenses. Selection is based on "true passion for the HR profession," scholastic average and standing, campus and charitable activities, leadership positions held, and financial need.

Financial data The winner receives a $1,000 honorarium, a commemorative plaque, and complimentary registration to the society's annual conference and exposition.

Duration 1 year.

Number awarded 1 each year.

Deadline February of each year.

[107]
DR. WILLIAM R. GILES MEMORIAL SCHOLARSHIP

United Negro College Fund
Attn: Scholarships and Grants Department
8260 Willow Oaks Corporate Drive
P.O. Box 10444
Fairfax, VA 22031-8044
(703) 205-3466   Toll-free: (800) 331-2244
Fax: (703) 205-3574
Web: www.uncf.org/scholarships/index.asp

Purpose To provide financial assistance to students from New Jersey who are majoring in business at colleges and universities that are members of the United Negro College Fund (UNCF).

Eligibility This program is open to residents of New Jersey who are majoring in business at UNCF-member institutions. Applicants must have a GPA of 3.0 or higher and be able to demonstrate financial need.

Financial data The amount of the stipend is based on the cost of tuition and room and board at the UNCF-member institution the recipient attends.

Duration 1 year.

Number awarded 1 or more each year.

[108]
D.W. SIMPSON & COMPANY ACTUARIAL SCIENCE SCHOLARSHIP

D.W. Simpson & Company
1800 West Larchmont Avenue
Chicago, IL 60613
(312) 867-2300   Toll-free: (800) 837-8338
Fax: (312) 951-8386
E-mail: actuaries@dwsimpson.com
Web: www.actuaryjobs.com/scholar.html

Purpose To provide financial assistance to college seniors majoring in actuarial science.

Eligibility This program is open to students who are entering their senior year of undergraduate study in actuarial science. Applicants must have a GPA of 3.0 or higher, have passed at least 1 actuarial examination, and be eligible to work in the United States. Financial need is not considered in the selection process.

Financial data The stipend is $1,000 per semester.

Duration 1 semester; nonrenewable.

Number awarded 2 each year (1 per semester).

Deadline April of each year for the fall scholarship; October of each year for the spring scholarship.

[109]
DWIGHT P. JACOBUS SCHOLARSHIPS

Association of School Business Officials of Maryland and the District of Columbia
Attn: Executive Director
P.O. Box 451
Jarrettsville, MD 21084-0451
(410) 591-3886   Fax: (410) 692-6564
E-mail: jcase@erols.com
Web: asbo.net/scholarship.htm

Purpose To provide financial assistance to the residents of Maryland and the District of Columbia who are interested in majoring in business or education at a college or university in the area.

Eligibility This program is open to students who have been residents of Maryland or the District of Columbia for at least 1 year, have been accepted as a full-time student at an accredited institution of higher education within Maryland or the District, are able to demonstrate financial need, and have a GPA of 3.0 or higher. Both high school seniors and currently-enrolled college students may apply. They must be preparing for a career in business or in education. Selection is based on scholastic achievement, financial need, SAT or ACT scores, and quality of extracurricular achievements.

Financial data The stipend is $1,000. Funds are paid directly to the recipient's school.

Duration 1 year; may be renewed up to 3 additional years provided the recipient remains enrolled full time with a GPA of 3.0 or higher.

Number awarded 6 each year; at least 1 of these will go to a student enrolled in an approved program leading to teacher certification.

Deadline March of each year.

[110]
EARL G. GRAVES NAACP SCHOLARSHIP

National Association for the Advancement of Colored People
Attn: Education Department
4805 Mt. Hope Drive
Baltimore, MD 21215-3297
(410) 580-5760   Toll-free: (877) NAACP-98
E-mail: youth@naacpnet.org
Web: www.naacp.org

Purpose To provide financial assistance to upper-division and graduate students majoring in business.

Eligibility This program is open to full-time juniors, seniors, and graduate students majoring in business. Applicants must be currently in good academic standing, making satisfactory progress toward an undergraduate or graduate degree, and in the top 20% of their class. Along with their application, they must submit a 1-page essay on their interest in their major and a career, their life's ambition, what they hope to accomplish in their lifetime, and what they consider their most significant contribution to their community. Financial need is not considered in the selection process.

Financial data The stipend is $5,000 per year.

Duration 1 year.

Additional information Information is also available from the United Negro College Fund, Scholarships and Grants

Administration, 8260 Willow Oaks Corporate Drive, Fairfax, VA 22031, (703) 205-3400.

Number awarded Varies each year; recently, 20 of these scholarships were awarded.

Deadline April of each year.

[111]
EASTERN STATES WOMEN'S TRAFFIC CONFERENCE SCHOLARSHIP

Eastern States Women's Traffic Conference
c/o Susan E. Ringer, Scholarship Committee Chair
Ringer Enterprises, Inc.
2121 Russell Street
Baltimore, MD 21230
(410) 837-0547   Toll-free: (800) 992-0294

Purpose To provide financial assistance to college students in the East who are majoring in transportation or selected related fields.

Eligibility This program is open to currently-enrolled college students who are majoring in transportation, traffic management, or a related business field. Applicants must be residing in the eastern sector of the country. Along with their application, they must submit a 1-page statement on their educational and career goals. Selection is based on academic ability, professional interest, financial need, and character.

Financial data Stipends range from $500 to $2,000. Payment is made directly to the college.

Duration 1 year.

Number awarded 4 each year.

Deadline March of each year.

[112]
EDITH LOIS WILSON 4-H SCHOLARSHIP

Amarillo Area Foundation
Attn: Scholarship Coordinator
801 South Fillmore, Suite 700
Amarillo, TX 79101
(806) 376-4521   Fax: (806) 373-3656
E-mail: laquita@aaf-hf.org
Web: www.aaf-hf.org/scholarships.html

Purpose To provide financial assistance to high school seniors in specified areas of Texas who are 4-H members and interested in studying fields related to home economics in college.

Eligibility This program is open to graduating seniors at high schools in District 1 of the Texas Association of Extension Home Economists. Applicants must have completed at least 3 years of 4-H club work, have participated in home economics-related projects each year, and rank in the upper 25% of their graduating class. They must be planning to attend and accredited college or university in Texas and major in an area related to human science, including (but not limited to) food and nutrition/dietetics; family and consumer science education; restaurant, hotel, and institutional management; family financial planning; interior and/or fashion design; merchandising; early childhood; human development; or family studies. Financial need is considered in the selection process.

Financial data The stipend is $500.

Duration 1 year; nonrenewable.

Number awarded 1 or more each year.

Deadline February of each year.

[113]
EDNA A. LAUTERBACH SCHOLARSHIP

Community Foundation for the Capital Region
Attn: Scholarship Coordinator
Executive Park Drive
Albany, NY 12203
(518) 446-9638   Fax: (518) 446-9708
E-mail: info@cfcr.org
Web: www.cfcr.org/scholarships/scholarships.htm

Purpose To provide financial assistance to nurses in New York who are interested in taking business-related courses in college or graduate school.

Eligibility This program is open to nurses in New York (registered and licensed practical nurses) who 1) plan to or are engaged in running a business related to health care and 2) want to take business-related courses in college or pursue other appropriate training. Applicants must demonstrate that the proposed classes/training will improve their ability to run a business. Financial need is considered in the selection process.

Financial data The amount awarded varies each year.

Additional information This program was established in the memory of a former president of Competent Care, Inc. and American Care, Inc.

Duration 1 year.

Number awarded Varies each year.

Deadline July of each year.

[114]
EDUCATIONAL FOUNDATION COLLEGE/UNIVERSITY SCHOLARSHIPS

Colorado Society of Certified Public Accountants
Attn: CSCPA Educational Foundation
7979 East Tufts Avenue, Suite 500
Denver, CO 80237-2845
(303) 741-8613   Toll-free: (800) 523-9082 (within CO)
Fax: (303) 773-6344   E-mail: gmantz@cocpa.org
Web: www.cocpa.org/student_faculty/scholarships.asp

Purpose To provide financial assistance to undergraduate and graduate students in Colorado who are studying accounting.

Eligibility This program is open to undergraduate and graduate students at colleges and universities in Colorado who have completed at least 8 semester hours of accounting courses (including at least 1 intermediate accounting class) and have a GPA, both overall and in accounting, of at least 3.0. Selection is based first on scholastic achievement and second on financial need.

Financial data The stipend is $1,000. Funds are paid directly to the recipient's school to be used for books, tuition, room, board, fees, and expenses.

Duration 1 year; recipients may reapply.

Number awarded 20 each year.

Deadline June of each year for fall semester or quarter; November of each year for winter quarter or spring semester.

[115]
EDUCATIONAL FOUNDATION HIGH SCHOOL SCHOLARSHIPS

Colorado Society of Certified Public Accountants
Attn: CSCPA Educational Foundation
7979 East Tufts Avenue, Suite 500
Denver, CO 80237-2845
(303) 741-8613   Toll-free: (800) 523-9082 (within CO)
Fax: (303) 773-6344   E-mail: gmantz@cocpa.org
Web: www.cocpa.org/student_faculty/scholarships.asp

Purpose To provide financial assistance to high school seniors in Colorado who plan to study accounting in college.

Eligibility This program is open to seniors graduating from Colorado high schools who have a GPA of at least 3.0. Applicants must be planning to attend a college in Colorado with an accredited program in accounting. Selection is based on scholastic achievement.

Financial data The stipend is $1,000.

Duration 1 year; nonrenewable.

Number awarded 8 to 10 each year.

Deadline February of each year.

[116]
EDWARD W. O'CONNELL MEMORIAL SCHOLARSHIP

WISS & Company, LLP
Attn: O'Connell Memorial Scholarship Fund, Inc.
354 Eisenhower Parkway
Livingston, NJ 07039

Purpose To provide financial assistance to high school seniors in New Jersey who are planning to major in accounting in college.

Eligibility Eligible to apply are New Jersey high school seniors who have a GPA of 3.0 or higher, have lived in the state for at least 2 years, have been accepted at a college or university in New Jersey as a full-time or part-time student, and intend to declare a major in accounting in college. Applicants must submit 2 letters of recommendation, an official high school transcript, and an acceptance letter from a New Jersey college or university. Immediate family of WISS employees, clients, and employees of clients are not eligible to apply.

Financial data A stipend is awarded (amount not specified).

Duration 1 year.

Deadline April of each year.

[117]
EFWA WOMEN IN TRANSITION ACCOUNTING SCHOLARSHIP

Educational Foundation for Women in Accounting
Attn: Foundation Administrator
P.O. Box 1925
Southeastern, PA 19399-1925
(610) 407-9229   Fax: (610) 644-3713
E-mail: info@efwa.org
Web: www.efwa.org/scholarships.htm

Purpose To provide financial support to women who have become the sole support of their family and wish to work on an undergraduate accounting degree.

Eligibility This program is open to women who, either through divorce of death of a spouse, have become the sole source of support for themselves and their family. They must wish to work on a degree in accounting as a means to gainful employment. Women who are single parents as a result of other circumstances are also considered. Applicants should be incoming or current freshmen, or they may be returning to school with sufficient credits to qualify for freshman status. Selection is based on aptitude for accounting, commitment to the goal of working on a degree in accounting (including evidence of continued commitment after receiving this award), clear evidence that the candidate has established goals and a plan for achieving those goals, and financial need.

Financial data The stipend is $4,000 per year.

Duration 1 year; may be renewed 3 additional years if the recipient completes at least 12 hours each semester.

Additional information This program, established in 1990, was formerly called the Displaced Homemaker's Scholarship.

Number awarded 1 each year.

Deadline April of each year.

[118]
ELDON REINKE SCHOLARSHIP

North Dakota Society of CPAs
Attn: North Dakota Society of CPAs Foundation
2701 South Columbia Road
Grand Forks, ND 58201
(701) 775-7100   Toll-free: (877) 637-2727
Fax: (701) 775-7430   E-mail: mail@ndscpa.org
Web: www.ndscpa.org/societyfoundation.htm

Purpose To provide financial assistance to college students in North Dakota who are majoring in accounting.

Eligibility This program is open to accounting majors who are second semester juniors or higher. Applicants must be attending 1 of the following schools: University of North Dakota, Minnesota State University at Moorhead, North Dakota State University, Minot State University, University of Mary, Jamestown College, Dickinson State College, or Concordia College. The award rotates among those 8 schools. Selection is based on academic performance.

Financial data The stipend is $500.

Duration 1 year.

Additional information This program was established in 2001.

Number awarded 1 each year.

[119]
EMPIRE STATE POTATO GROWERS SCHOLARSHIPS

Empire State Potato Growers, Inc.
Attn: Scholarship Fund
P.O. Box 566
Stanley, NY 14561
(585) 526-5356   Toll-free: (877) 697-7837
Fax: (585) 526-6576
E-mail: mwickham@empirepotatogrowers.com
Web: www.empirepotatogrowers.com/scholarship.htm

Purpose To provide financial assistance to residents of New York majoring in a field related to agriculture (including agricultural economics) at a college or university in the state.

Eligibility This program is open to undergraduate students at colleges and universities in New York who are residents of the state. Applicants must be majoring in fields related to agriculture, such as agricultural engineering, agronomy, crop and soil sciences, entomology, food sciences, horticulture, plant pathology, or agricultural economics. Along with their application, they must submit a 100-word essay on their career goals and a 200-word essay on how their goals and ambitions qualify them for this scholarship. Selection is based on academic achievement and leadership abilities; financial need is not considered.

Financial data The stipend is $500 per year.

Duration 1 year; may be renewed up to 3 additional years provided the recipient maintains a GPA of 2.7 or higher and full-time enrollment.

Number awarded 1 or more each year.

Deadline January of each year.

[120]
ENID HALL GRISWOLD MEMORIAL SCHOLARSHIP

National Society Daughters of the American Revolution
Attn: Scholarship Committee
1776 D Street, N.W.
Washington, DC 20006-5392
(202) 628-1776
Web: www.dar.org/natsociety/edout_scholar.html

Purpose To provide financial assistance to upper-division college students majoring in selected social science fields.

Eligibility Eligible to apply for these scholarships are undergraduate students entering their junior or senior year with a major in political science, history, government, or economics. Applicants must be sponsored by a local chapter of the Daughters of the American Revolution (DAR). Selection is based on academic excellence, commitment to the field of study, and financial need. U.S. citizenship is required.

Financial data The stipend is $1,000.

Duration 1 year; nonrenewable.

Additional information Information is also available from Cindy B. Findley, DAR Scholarship Committee Chair, 4929 Warfield Drive, Greensboro, NC 27406-8338, (336) 674-5777, E-mail: cfindley@bellsouth.net. Requests for applications must be accompanied by a self-addressed stamped envelope.

Number awarded Varies each year.

Deadline February of each year.

[121]
ENVIRONMENTAL MANAGEMENT SCHOLARSHIP

Hispanic Scholarship Fund Institute
1001 Connecticut Avenue, N.W., Suite 632
Washington, DC 20036
(202) 296-0009   Fax: (202) 296-3633
E-mail: info@hsfi.org
Web: www.hsfi.org/sch_energy.html

Purpose To provide financial assistance to Hispanic undergraduate students majoring in designated business, engineering, and science fields related to the U.S. Department of Energy (DOE) goals of environmental restoration and waste management.

Eligibility This program is open to U.S. citizens and permanent residents of Hispanic background who have completed at least 12 undergraduate credits with a GPA of 2.8 or higher. Applicants must be interested in preparing for a career supportive of the DOE goals of environmental restoration and waste management. Eligible academic majors are in the fields of business (management and system analysis), engineering (agricultural, chemical, civil, electrical, environmental, industrial, mechanical, metallurgical, nuclear, and petroleum), and science (applied math/physics, chemistry, computer science, ecology, environmental, epidemiology, geology, health physics, hydrology, radiochemistry, radio-ecology, and toxicology). Along with their application, they must submit a 2-page essay on why a career in public service interests them, how their academic major connects with their stated DOE career goal, why the DOE should invest in them through this program, and how they believe the DOE will benefit from this investment. Selection is based on academic achievement, financial need, and demonstrated commitment to a career in public service.

Financial data The stipend is $3,000 per year for 4-year university students or $2,000 per year for community college students.

Duration 1 year.

Additional information This program, which began in 1990, is sponsored by DOE's Office of Environmental Management. Recipients must enroll full time at a college or university in the United States.

Number awarded Varies each year.

Deadline February of each year.

[122]
ERNEST LEE GILBERT MEMORIAL SCHOLARSHIP

Vermont Student Assistance Corporation
Champlain Mill
Attn: Scholarship Programs
P.O. Box 2000
Winooski, VT 05404-2601
(802) 654-3798   Toll-free: (800) 642-3177
Fax: (802) 654-3765   TDD: (802) 654-3766
TDD: (800) 281-3341 (within VT) E-mail: info@vsac.org
Web: www.vsac.org

Purpose To provide financial assistance for college to residents of Vermont who are interested in preparing for a career in the construction industry.

Eligibility This scholarship is available to high school seniors, high school graduates, and currently-enrolled college students who are residents of Vermont. Applicants must be enrolled or planning to enroll in an academic, vocational, technical, or advanced training program in business or other fields related to the construction industry. Selection is based on participation in extracurricular activities and/or community service, academic achievement, financial need, a letter of recommendation, and required essays.

Financial data The stipend is either $1,000 or $500.

Duration 1 year.

Additional information The Vermont Subcontractors Association, Inc. established this program in 2001.

Number awarded Either 1 scholarship at $1,000 or 2 scholarships at $500 each year.

Deadline April of each year.

[123]
ERNST & YOUNG LLP MINORITY LEADERSHIP AWARDS

New Jersey Society of Certified Public Accountants
Attn: Student Programs Coordinator
425 Eagle Rock Avenue, Suite 100
Roseland, NJ 07068-1723
(973) 226-4494, ext. 209   Fax: (973) 226-7425
E-mail: njscpa@njscpa.org
Web: www.njscpa.org

Purpose To provide financial assistance to minority undergraduates in New Jersey who are preparing for a career as a certified public accountant.

Eligibility This program is open to African American, Asian, Hispanic, and Native American residents of New Jersey who are attending a college or university in the state. Applicants must be sophomores who are majoring or concentrating in accounting and have completed at least 3 credits in accounting courses. Along with their application, they must submit a letter of recommendation from an accounting professor, an official transcript indicating a GPA of 3.2 or higher, a resume, and an essay of 250 to 500 words on what motivated them to choose accounting as a career choice.

Financial data The stipend is $5,000.

Duration 1 year.

Additional information This program is sponsored by Ernst & Young.

Number awarded 2 each year.

Deadline January of each year.

[124]
ERNST & YOUNG SCHOLARSHIP PROGRAM

Hispanic College Fund
Attn: National Director
1717 Pennsylvania Avenue, N.W., Suite 460
Washington, D.C. 20006
(202) 296-5400   Toll-free: (800) 644-4223
Fax: (202) 296-3774
E-mail: hispaniccollegefund@earthlink.net
Web: www.hispanicfund.org

Purpose To provide financial assistance to Hispanic American undergraduate students who are interested in preparing for a career in accounting.

Eligibility This program is open to U.S. citizens of Hispanic background (at least 1 grandparent must be 100% Hispanic) who are entering their sophomore or junior year of college. Applicants must be working on a bachelor's degree in accounting or a related field and have a cumulative GPA of 3.0 or higher. They must be enrolled in a college or university in the 50 states or Puerto Rico as a full-time student. Financial need is considered in the selection process.

Financial data Stipends range from $500 to $5,000, depending on the need of the recipient, and average approximately $3,000. Funds are paid directly to the recipient's college or university to help cover tuition and fees.

Duration 1 year; recipients may reapply.

Additional information This program is sponsored by Ernst & Young. All applications must be submitted online; no paper applications are available.

Number awarded Varies each year.

Deadline April of each year.

[125]
EXECUTIVE WOMEN INTERNATIONAL SCHOLARSHIP PROGRAM

Executive Women International
Attn: Scholarship Coordinator
515 South 700 East, Suite 2A
Salt Lake City, UT 84102
(801) 355-2800   Toll-free: (888) EWI-1229
Fax: (801) 355-2852   E-mail: ewi@executivewomen.org
Web: www.executivewomen.org

Purpose To recognize and reward high school juniors with outstanding business and leadership potential.

Eligibility High school juniors attending public, private, and parochial schools located in Executive Women International (EWI) chapter cities are eligible to compete for this scholarship, if they are interested in majoring in business at a 4-year college or university. Because this program targets business students, those planning careers in medicine, law, art, social welfare, political science, or related fields are not eligible to compete. Each high school within the territorial boundaries of a participating EWI chapter may submit the name of 1 junior class student for the local competition. Students are required to submit a notebook (which includes a student application, autobiographical essay, and a list of honors and awards) to their EWI chapter. A sponsoring teacher is also required to submit an endorsement, a transcript of the student's grades, and 1 personal reference. Competing students are interviewed by local judges. Winners then submit their notebooks for competition on the district level. Notebooks and videotaped interviews of the 15 district winners are reviewed by the semifinals' judges and 3 winners (plus 2 alternates) are selected as winners. The winners and their sponsoring teachers receive an all-expense paid trip to the EWI annual meeting, where they compete for first- , second- , and third-place awards. Selection is based on scholastic achievement, honors and awards, ability to work well with others, citizenship, leadership qualities, proven dependability and responsibility, communication skills, and extracurricular activities.

Financial data Stipends are $10,000 for the first-place winner, $6,000 for the second-place winner, $4,000 for the third-place winner, and $2,000 for finalists. These funds are paid to the winners' colleges. Local and district winners also receive scholarships (generally under $2,000). A total of $150,000 is distributed through this program each year.

Duration The scholarship funds are disbursed over a period of no more than 5 years.

Number awarded 6 national winners are selected each year.

Deadline Applications must be received by local chapters by the end of March so they can select their winners by mid-April. Districts complete their judging by mid-May. The final judging is completed by mid-July.

[126]
F. GRANT WAITE, CPA, MEMORIAL SCHOLARSHIP

Massachusetts Society of Certified Public Accountants
Attn: MSCPA Educational Foundation
105 Chauncy Street, Tenth Floor
Boston, MA 02111
(617) 556-4000   Toll-free: (800) 392-6145
Fax: (617) 556-4126
E-mail: biannoni@MSCPAonline.org
Web: www.cpatrack.com/financial_aid/scholarship.php

Purpose To provide financial assistance to college juniors majoring in accounting at a Massachusetts college or university.

Eligibility This program is open to Massachusetts residents who have completed their sophomore year and are majoring in accounting at a college or university in the state. Applicants must be enrolled in school on a full-time basis. They must demonstrate superior academic standing, financial need, and an intention to seek a career in a public accounting firm in Massachusetts. Special consideration is given to married students with children.

Financial data The stipend is $1,000.

Duration 1 year.

Additional information This program is supported, in part, by the firm of Vitale Caturano & Company CPAs PC

Number awarded 1 each year.

[127]
FARM CREDIT BANK OF TEXAS SCHOLARSHIPS

Texas FFA Association
614 East 12th Street
Austin, TX 78701
(512) 480-8045   Fax: (512) 472-0555
E-mail: txffa@texasffa.org
Web: www.texasffa.org/ffa/tfa-scho.html

Purpose To provide financial assistance to high school senior members of FFA in Texas who plan to study a field related to agricultural or life sciences (including agribusiness) at a college or university in the state.

Eligibility This program is open to high school seniors in Texas who are FFA members and have been members at least 2 of the 3 previous years. Applicants must be planning to major in a field related to the agricultural or life sciences at a college or university in Texas. They must have completed at least 5 semesters of instruction in agriculture and/or agribusiness during high school and scored at least 950 on the SAT or 20 on the ACT. U.S. citizenship and ranking in the top half

of their graduating class are also required. Selection is based on class rank (16 points), SAT or ACT scores (14 points), academic achievement in agricultural science and career related instruction (10 points), FFA achievements (30 points), financial need (10 points), and an interview (25 points).

Financial data The stipend is $2,000.

Duration 1 year.

Additional information The list of approved majors includes plant and soil sciences (agronomy, botany, clothing and textiles, floriculture, horticulture, plant science, soil science); natural and environmental sciences (aquaculture, atmospheric science, bioenvironmental science, entomology, forestry, fisheries, mariculture, marine biology, meteorology, range science, soil and water conservation, and wildlife science); human and animal sciences (animal science, dairy science, food and nutrition, food science, food technology, poultry science, preveterinary medicine, scientific nutrition, and zoology); support curriculums (agricultural development, agricultural business, agricultural economics, agricultural education, agricultural engineering, agricultural journalism, agricultural science, agricultural services, agricultural systems, biomedical engineering, chemical engineering, food engineering, land use and planning, landscape architecture, and recreation and parks); and basic sciences (biochemistry, biology, biomedical science, biotechnology, chemistry, genetics, microbiology, and pharmacology). Students may not apply for both 4-H and FFA scholarships.

Number awarded 4 each year.

[128]
FASTLINE PUBLICATIONS SCHOLARSHIPS

National FFA Organization
Attn: Scholarship Office
6060 FFA Drive
P.O. Box 68960
Indianapolis, IN 46268-0960
(317) 802-4321   Fax: (317) 802-5321
E-mail: scholarships@ffa.org
Web: www.ffa.org

Purpose To provide financial assistance to FFA members from designated states who are interested in studying agricultural business management.

Eligibility This program is open to members who are graduating high school seniors planning to enroll full time in college. Applicants must be interested in working on a degree in agricultural business management and demonstrate interest in managing a farm. They must be planning to be students at 1) 4-year colleges and residents of the following states: Alabama, Arkansas, Georgia, Illinois, Indiana, Iowa, Kansas, Kentucky, Missouri, Nebraska, New York, North Carolina, Ohio, Oklahoma, Pennsylvania, Tennessee, or Texas; or 2) 2-year colleges and vocational schools and residents of the following states: Alabama, Georgia, Kansas, Missouri, New York, Ohio, Pennsylvania, or Texas. Selection is based on academic achievement (10 points for GPA, 10 points for SAT or ACT score, 10 points for class rank), leadership in FFA activities (30 points), leadership in community activities (10 points), and participation in the Supervised Agricultural Experience (SAE) program (30 points). U.S. citizenship is required.

Financial data The stipend is $1,000 per year. Funds are paid directly to the recipient.

Duration 1 year; nonrenewable.

Additional information Funding for these scholarships is provided by Fastline Publications.

Number awarded 21 each year: 1 each to 4-year students who are residents of 12 designated states (Arkansas, Illinois, Indiana, Iowa, Kansas, Kentucky, Missouri, Nebraska, Ohio, Oklahoma, Tennessee, and Texas); 1 to a 4-year student who is a resident of New York or Pennsylvania; 1 to a 4-year student who is a resident of Georgia or Alabama; 1 to a year-year student who is a resident of North Carolina or South Carolina; 1 each to 2-year students who are residents of 4 designated states (Kansas, Missouri, Ohio, and Texas); 1 to a 2-year student who is a resident of Alabama or Georgia; and 1 to a 2-year student who is a resident of New York or Pennsylvania.

Deadline February of each year.

[129]
FFA SAN ANTONIO LIVESTOCK EXPOSITION SCHOLARSHIPS

Texas FFA Association
614 East 12th Street
Austin, TX 78701
(512) 480-8045   Fax: (512) 472-0555
E-mail: txffa@texasffa.org
Web: www.texasffa.org/ffa/tfa-scho.html

Purpose To provide financial assistance to high school senior members of FFA in Texas who plan to study a field related to agricultural or life sciences (including agricultural economics) at a college or university in the state.

Eligibility This program is open to high school seniors in Texas who are FFA members and have been members at least 2 of the 3 previous years. Applicants must be planning to major in a field related to the agricultural or life sciences at a college or university in Texas. They must have completed at least 5 semesters of instruction in agriculture and/or agribusiness during high school and scored at least 950 on the SAT or 20 on the ACT. U.S. citizenship and ranking in the top half of their graduating class are also required. Selection is based on class rank (16 points), SAT or ACT scores (14 points), academic achievement in agricultural science and career related instruction (10 points), FFA achievements (30 points), financial need (10 points), and an interview (25 points).

Financial data Stipends are either $3,750 or $2,500 per year.

Duration 4 years.

Additional information The list of approved majors includes plant and soil sciences (agronomy, botany, clothing and textiles, floriculture, horticulture, plant science, soil science); natural and environmental sciences (aquaculture, atmospheric science, bioenvironmental science, entomology, forestry, fisheries, mariculture, marine biology, meteorology, range science, soil and water conservation, and wildlife science); human and animal sciences (animal science, dairy science, food and nutrition, food science, food technology, poultry science, preveterinary medicine, scientific nutrition, and zoology); support curriculums (agricultural development, agricultural business, agricultural economics, agricultural education, agricultural engineering, agricultural journalism, agricultural science, agricultural services, agricultural systems, biomedical engineering, chemical engineering, food engineering, land use and planning, landscape architecture, and recreation and parks); and basic sciences (biochemistry, biology, biomedical science, biotechnology, chemistry, genetics,

microbiology, and pharmacology). Funding for this program is provided by the San Antonio Livestock Exposition. Students may not apply for both 4-H and FFA scholarships.

Number awarded 13 each year: 4 at $3,750 and 9 at $2,500.

[130]
FFA/BURLINGTON NORTHERN SANTA FE CORPORATION SCHOLARSHIPS

National FFA Organization
Attn: Scholarship Office
6060 FFA Drive
P.O. Box 68960
Indianapolis, IN 46268-0960
(317) 802-4321   Fax: (317) 802-5321
E-mail: scholarships@ffa.org
Web: www.ffa.org

Purpose To provide financial assistance to FFA members from selected states interested in studying field related to agribusiness in college.

Eligibility This program is open to members who are graduating high school seniors planning to enroll full time in college. Applicants must be residents of California, Illinois, Iowa, Kansas, Minnesota, Montana, Nebraska, North Dakota, South Dakota, or Texas planning to work on a 4-year degree in the following areas of agriculture: business management, finance, economics, sales, and marketing. They must have a GPA of 3.0 or higher. Selection is based on academic achievement (10 points for GPA, 10 points for SAT or ACT score, 10 points for class rank), leadership in FFA activities (30 points), leadership in community activities (10 points), and participation in the Supervised Agricultural Experience (SAE) program (30 points). U.S. citizenship is required.

Financial data The stipend is $1,250 per year. Funds are paid directly to the recipient.

Duration 1 year; may be renewed up to 3 additional years provided the recipient maintains a GPA of 3.0 or higher.

Additional information Funding for these scholarships is provided by the Burlington Northern Santa Fe Foundation.

Number awarded 10 each year.

Deadline February of each year.

[131]
FINANCIAL WOMEN INTERNATIONAL OF HAWAII SCHOLARSHIP

Hawai'i Community Foundation
Attn: Scholarship Department
1164 Bishop Street, Suite 800
Honolulu, HI 96813
(808) 537-6333   Toll-free: (888) 731-3863
Fax: (808) 521-6286
E-mail: scholarships@hcf-hawaii.org
Web: www.hawaiicommunityfoundation.org

Purpose To provide financial assistance to women in Hawaii who are studying business on the upper-division or graduate school level.

Eligibility This program is open to Hawaii residents who are majoring in business or a business-related field as a junior, senior, or graduate student. They must be able to demonstrate academic achievement (GPA of 3.5 or higher), good moral character, and financial need. Applications must be accompanied by a short statement indicating reasons for attending college, planned course of study, and career goals.

Financial data The amounts of the awards depend on the availability of funds and the need of the recipient; recently, stipends averaged $800.

Duration 1 year.

Additional information This program was established in 1998.

Number awarded Varies each year; recently, 2 of these scholarships were awarded.

Deadline February of each year.

[132]
FISHER BROADCASTING SCHOLARSHIPS FOR MINORITIES

Fisher Communications
Attn: Minority Scholarship
100 Fourth Avenue North, Suite 440
Seattle, WA 98109
(206) 404-7000   Fax: (206) 404-6037
E-mail: Info@fsci.com
Web: www.fsci.com/x100.xml

Purpose To provide financial assistance to minority college students in selected states who are interested in preparing for a career in broadcasting, marketing, or journalism.

Eligibility This program is open to students of non-white origin who are U.S. citizens, have a GPA of 2.5 or higher, and are at least sophomores enrolled in 1) a broadcasting, marketing, or journalism curriculum leading to a bachelor's degree at an accredited 4-year college or university; 2) a broadcast curriculum at an accredited community college, transferable to a 4-year baccalaureate degree program; or 3) a broadcast curriculum at an accredited vocational/technical school. Applicants must be either 1) residents of Washington, Oregon, Idaho, or Montana; or 2) attending a school in those states. They must submit an essay that explains their financial need, education and career goals, and school activities; a copy of their college transcript; and 2 letters of recommendation. Selection is based on need, academic achievement, and personal qualities.

Financial data A stipend is awarded (amount not specified).

Duration 1 year; recipients may reapply.

Additional information This program began in 1987.

Number awarded Several each year.

Deadline April of each year.

[133]
FLORIDA BANKERS EDUCATIONAL FOUNDATION GRANTS

Florida Bankers Association
Attn: Florida Bankers Educational Foundation
1001 Thomasville Road, Suite 201
P.O. Box 1360
Tallahassee, FL 32302-1360
(850) 224-2265, ext. 139   Fax: (850) 224-2423
E-mail: lnewton@flbankers.net
Web: www.floridabankers.com

Purpose To provide financial assistance to undergraduate and graduate students who are interested in preparing for a career in Florida banking.

Eligibility This program is open to undergraduate and graduate students who have at least 5 years of full-time experience working in Florida banking. Applicants must be Florida residents, registered at 1 of 27 participating colleges or universities in the state, and taking banking-related classes. They must have a GPA of 2.5 or higher. Along with their application, they must submit 2 letters of recommendation from their place of employment: 1 from the bank president or other high-level employee and 1 from an immediate supervisor. Selection is based on interest in Florida banking, scholastic achievement, aptitude, ability, leadership, personality, and character.

Financial data The amount of assistance is based on the number of semester hours the student has remaining until graduation. The maximum award is $1,500 per year for the freshman and sophomore years, $2,000 per year for the junior and senior years, and $5,000 as a graduate student.

Duration Up to 4 years as an undergraduate and another 2 years as a graduate student.

Additional information Recipients must maintain a 2.5 GPA and take at least 12 credit hours per calendar year.

Number awarded Several each year.

Deadline February, May, August, or November of each year.

[134]
FLORIDA ETHICS IN BUSINESS MATCHING SCHOLARSHIPS

Florida Independent College Fund
929 North Spring Garden Avenue, Suite 165
DeLand, FL 32720-0981
(386) 734-2745   Fax: (386) 734-0839
E-mail: Scholarships@ficf.org
Web: www.ficf.org

Purpose To provide financial assistance to students working on a degree in business at designated private colleges and universities in Florida.

Eligibility This program is open to residents of Florida who are attending an private college or university in the state that is a member of the Independent Colleges and Universities of Florida (ICUF). Preference is given to students majoring in business.

Financial data The maximum stipend is $2,600. Funds may be matched on a 1:1 basis by ICUF institutions.

Duration 1 year.

Additional information The Florida Independent College Fund (FICF) was established in 1956 and merged with the ICUF in 1996. It provides financial assistance to students at the 27 independent colleges and universities that are members of the ICUF.

Number awarded Each of the 27 institutions receives 1 of these scholarships, which it may award as a lump sum to 1 student or distribute to several students.

Deadline November of each year.

[135]
FLORIDA INSTITUTE OF CPAS SCHOLARSHIPS

Florida Institute of CPAs Educational Foundation, Inc.
Attn: FICPA Educational Foundation
325 West College Avenue
P.O. Box 5437
Tallahassee, FL 32314
(850) 224-2727, ext. 200
Toll-free: (800) 342-3197, ext. 200
Fax: (850) 222-8190
Web: www.ficpa.org

Purpose To provide financial assistance to upper-division students in Florida who are majoring in accounting.

Eligibility Eligible to apply for this support are Florida residents who are fourth- or fifth-year accounting students enrolled full time in an accounting program at a Florida college or university. A faculty member in the accounting department of their college must nominate them. Applicants should be planning to sit for the CPA exam and indicate a desire to work in Florida. Selection is based on financial need, educational achievement, and demonstrated professional, social, and charitable activities.

Financial data Stipends range from $1,000 to $1,250.

Duration 1 year; recipients may reapply for 1 additional year of support.

Number awarded Varies each year; recently, a total of 114 scholarships were awarded, including 52 worth $65,000 by the Educational Foundation, 58 worth $60,500 by various chapters of the association, 3 Walter Friedly Memorial Scholarships worth $3,426, and 1 Paychex Entrepreneur Scholarship worth $1,000.

[136]
FLORIDA ROCK INDUSTRIES INTERNSHIP PROGRAM

Florida Independent College Fund
929 North Spring Garden Avenue, Suite 165
DeLand, FL 32720-0981
(386) 734-2745   Fax: (386) 734-0839
E-mail: Scholarships@ficf.org
Web: www.ficf.org

Purpose To provide financial assistance and work experience to business and engineering students at designated private colleges and universities in Florida who are interested in a career in the construction materials business.

Eligibility This program is open to students majoring in business or engineering at 24 designated independent colleges or universities in Florida. Applicants must be entering their junior year and have a GPA of 3.0 or higher. They must be able to demonstrate an interest in the construction materials business.

Financial data The stipend is $7,000 per year. A paid internship is also provided.

Duration The stipend is provided for the junior and senior years of college. The internship is provided for the summer between the junior and senior years.

Additional information This program is sponsored by Florida Rock Industries, Inc. For a list of the 24 eligible institutions, contact the Florida Independent College Fund.

Number awarded 1 each year.

Deadline April of each year.

[137]
FOOD MARKETING INSTITUTE SCHOLARSHIPS

DECA
1908 Association Drive
Reston, VA 20191-1594
(703) 860-5000   Fax: (703) 860-4013
E-mail: decainc@aol.com
Web: www.deca.org/scholarships/index.html

Purpose To provide financial assistance to DECA members who are women or minorities and interested in attending college to prepare for a marketing career.

Eligibility This program is open to DECA members who are women or minorities interested in working full time on a 2-year or 4-year degree in marketing, business, or marketing education. Applicants must be able to demonstrate evidence of DECA activities, supermarket industry experience, academic achievement, leadership ability, and community service involvement. Selection is based on merit, not financial need.

Financial data The stipend is $1,000.

Duration 1 year.

Additional information This program is sponsored by the Food Marketing Institute.

Number awarded 5 each year.

Deadline February of each year.

[138]
FORTUNE BRANDS SCHOLARS PROGRAM

United Negro College Fund
Attn: Corporate Scholars Program
P.O. Box 1435
Alexandria, VA 22313-9998
Toll-free: (866) 671-7237   E-mail: internship@uncf.org
Web: www.uncf.org/internships/index.asp

Purpose To provide financial assistance and work experience to minority juniors majoring in fields related to business and law students interested in an internship at corporate headquarters of Fortune Brands.

Eligibility This program is open to juniors and first- and second-year law students who are members of minority groups. Applicants must have a GPA of 3.0 or higher and an undergraduate major in accounting, finance, human resources, information systems, information technology, or marketing. They must be attending a designated college, university, or law school and be interested in an internship at Fortune Brands corporate headquarters in Lincolnshire, Illinois. Along with their application, they must submit a resume, 2 letters of recommendation, and official transcripts.

Financial data The program provides a paid internship and (based on successful internship performance) a $7,500 scholarship.

Duration 8 to 10 weeks for the internship; 1 year for the scholarship.

Additional information Eligible undergraduate institutions are Florida A&M University, Florida State University, Hampton University, Howard University, Morehouse College, North Carolina A&T State University, Northwestern University, Spelman College, University of Chicago, and University of Wisconsin. Participating law schools are those at Howard University, Northwestern University, University of Chicago, and University of Wisconsin.

Number awarded Varies each year.

Deadline February of each year.

[139]
FRANK D. VISCEGLIA MEMORIAL SCHOLARSHIP

Boy Scouts of America
Patriots' Path Council 358
Attn: Dennis Kohl, Scout Executive
222 Columbia Turnpike
Florham Park, NJ 07932
(973) 361-1800   Fax: (973) 361-1954

Purpose To provide financial assistance for college to Eagle Scouts in New Jersey who have shown an interest in the balance between the economy and the environment.

Eligibility This program is open to Eagle Scouts who are residents of New Jersey. Preference is given to Scouts 1) whose Eagle service projects are related to the environment and/or the economy and 2) whose career goals are in development-related fields and/or who intend to major in related fields. Applicants must have been accepted to, have applied for, or plan to attend an accredited 4-year college. Selection is based on Scouting record, other Scout activities, a description of the Eagle Scout project, and an essay of 250 words or less on the applicant's philosophy on the future of the world's environment.

Financial data The stipend is $1,000.

Duration 1 year.

Additional information This program is underwritten by the Association for Commercial Real Estate, formerly the National Association of Industrial and Office Parks.

Number awarded 1 each year.

Deadline May of each year.

[140]
FRANK L. GREATHOUSE GOVERNMENT ACCOUNTING SCHOLARSHIP

Government Finance Officers Association
Attn: Scholarship Committee
203 North LaSalle Street, Suite 2700
Chicago, IL 60601-1210
(312) 977-9700   Fax: (312) 977-4806
Web: www.gfoa.org/services/scholarships.shtml

Purpose To provide financial assistance to undergraduate students who are preparing for a career in public accounting.

Eligibility This program is open to full-time seniors in college who are enrolled in an accounting program and preparing for a career in state and local government finance. Applicants must be citizens or permanent residents of the United States or Canada and able to provide a letter of recommendation

from the dean of their academic program. Selection is based on career plans, academic record, plan of study, letters of recommendation, and GPA. Financial need is not considered.

Financial data The award is $3,500.

Duration 1 year.

Number awarded 1 each year.

Deadline February of each year.

[141]
FRED LUSTER, SR. EDUCATION FOUNDATION COLLEGE SCHOLARSHIPS

American Health and Beauty Aid Institute
Attn: Fred Luster, Sr. Education Foundation
401 North Michigan Avenue
Chicago, IL 60611
(312) 644-6610   Fax: (312) 321-5194
E-mail: ahbai@sba.com
Web: www.proudlady.org/scholar/scholar.html

Purpose To provide financial assistance to high school seniors interested in studying chemistry, engineering, or business in college.

Eligibility This program is open to high school seniors planning to attend a 4-year college to major in business, chemistry, or engineering. Applicants must have a GPA of 3.0 or higher and provide verification of their family income. Selection is based on academic achievement, school activities, and extracurricular activities.

Financial data Stipends are $500 or $250.

Duration 1 year.

Additional information The American Health and Beauty Aid Institute (AHBAI) is a trade association representing Black-owned companies that manufacture ethnic hair care and beauty related products featuring the Proud Lady Symbol. It established the Fred Luster, Sr. Education Foundation in 1991.

Number awarded Varies each year. Since it was established, the foundation has awarded more than $200,000 in scholarships.

Deadline February of each year.

[142]
FUKUNAGA SCHOLARSHIP

Fukunaga Scholarship Foundation
Attn: Scholarship Administrator
900 Fort Street Mall, Suite 600
P.O. Box 2788
Honolulu, HI 96803-2788
(808) 521-6511, ext. 286   Fax: (808) 523-3937
E-mail: sandyw@servco.com
Web: www.servco.com/scholarship

Purpose To provide financial assistance to Hawaii residents who are interested in majoring in business in college.

Eligibility This program is open to Hawaii residents who are graduating from high school or already enrolled in a 4-year college or university. Applicants must be majoring or planning to major in business administration. They should have at least a 3.0 GPA and plan to return to or remain in Hawaii or the Pacific Islands region. Selection is based on academic achievement; interest in business; participation, leadership, and responsibility in school activities and community service; and financial need.

Financial data The stipend is $2,500 per year.

Duration Up to 4 years for high school seniors; up to the remainder of the approved undergraduate program for recipients currently in college.

Additional information To maintain eligibility, recipients must enroll in school full time and maintain at least a 3.0 GPA.

Number awarded 12 to 16 each year.

Deadline February of each year.

[143]
G.A. MAVON MEMORIAL SCHOLARSHIP

Professional Independent Insurance Agents of Illinois
Attn: College Scholarship Program
4360 Wabash Avenue
Springfield, IL 62707
(217) 793-6660   Toll-free: (800) 628-6436
Fax: (217) 793-6744   E-mail: admin@piiai.org
Web: www.piiai.org/youngagents/scholarship.htm

Purpose To provide financial assistance to upper-division students from Illinois who are majoring in business and have an interest in insurance.

Eligibility This program is open to residents of Illinois who are full-time juniors or seniors in college. Applicants must be enrolled in a business degree program with an interest in insurance. They must have a letter of recommendation from a current or retired member of the Professional Independent Insurance Agents of Illinois. Along with their application, they must submit an essay (500 words or less) on the contribution the insurance industry provides to society. Financial need is not considered in the selection process.

Financial data The stipend is $2,000, payable in 2 equal installments. Funds are paid directly to the recipient's school.

Duration 1 year.

Number awarded 1 each year.

Deadline June of each year.

[144]
GALLUP SCHOLARSHIP

Nebraska DECA
301 Centennial Mall South
P.O. Box 94987
Lincoln, NE 68509-4987
(402) 471-4803   Fax: (402) 471-8850
E-mail: scholarships@nedeca.org
Web: www.nedeca.org

Purpose To provide financial assistance to Nebraska DECA members who are interested in majoring in selected fields in college.

Eligibility This program is open to members of Nebraska DECA who plan to major in teaching, marketing, psychology, statistics, or computer science in college. Applicants must have a GPA of 3.5 or higher. They must submit an official high school and/or college transcript, standardized test scores, a list of DECA activities and accomplishments, a completed application form, and 3 letters of recommendation. Financial need is not considered in the selection process.

Financial data The stipend is $500.

Duration 1 year.

Number awarded 1 each year.

Deadline January of each year.

[145]
GAP FOUNDATION SCHOLARSHIP

United Negro College Fund
Attn: Scholarships and Grants Department
8260 Willow Oaks Corporate Drive
P.O. Box 10444
Fairfax, VA 22031-8044
(703) 205-3466   Toll-free: (800) 331-2244
Fax: (703) 205-3574
Web: www.uncf.org/scholarships/index.asp

Purpose To provide financial assistance to students majoring in business or design at colleges and universities that are members of the United Negro College Fund (UNCF).

Eligibility This program is open to students enrolled in business, fashion design, or retailing at UNCF-member institutions. Applicants must have a GPA of 2.5 or higher and be able to demonstrate financial need.

Financial data The maximum stipend is $10,000.

Duration 1 year.

Additional information This program is sponsored by the GAP Foundation.

Number awarded 1 or more each year.

[146]
GENE SWACKHAMER AG ECONOMICS/AG BUSINESS GRANT

Alpha Gamma Rho Fraternity
Attn: Educational Foundation of AGR
10101 North Ambassador Drive
Kansas City, MO 64153-1395
(816) 891-9200   Fax: (816) 891-9401
E-mail: agr@AlphaGammaRho.org
Web: www.agrs.org

Purpose To provide financial assistance to members of Alpha Gamma Rho Fraternity (a national agricultural fraternity) who are majoring in agribusiness in college.

Eligibility This program is open to undergraduate members of the fraternity who are majoring in agricultural economics, agribusiness, resource management, or a closely-related field of study. Brothers living in the chapter house (where applicable) are given priority in the selection process.

Financial data The stipend is $1,000.

Duration 1 year.

Number awarded 1 each year.

Deadline April of each year.

[147]
GENERAL ELECTRIC FUND/LEAGUE OF UNITED LATIN AMERICAN CITIZENS SCHOLARSHIPS

League of United Latin American Citizens
Attn: LULAC National Education Service Centers
2000 L Street, N.W., Suite 610
Washington, DC 20036
(202) 833-6130   Fax: (202) 833-6135
E-mail: LNESCAward@aol.com
Web: www.lulac.org/Programs/Scholar.html

Purpose To provide financial assistance to minority students who are studying engineering or business in college.

Eligibility Eligible to apply are minority students who will be enrolled as college sophomores pursuing full-time studies in a program leading to a baccalaureate degree in engineering or business at colleges or universities in the United States approved by the League of United Latin American Citizens (LULAC) and General Electric. They must have a GPA of 3.25 or higher and be U.S. citizens or legal residents. Selection is based on academic performance, likelihood of preparing for a career in business or engineering, performance in business or engineering subjects, writing ability, extracurricular activities, and community involvement.

Financial data The stipends are $5,000 per year. The funds are to be used to pay for tuition, required fees, room and board, and required educational materials and books. The funds are sent directly to the college or university and deposited in the scholarship recipient's name.

Duration 1 year; may be renewed if the recipient maintains a GPA of 3.0 or higher.

Additional information Funding for this program is provided by the General Electric Fund. All requests for applications or information must include a self-addressed stamped envelope.

Number awarded 2 each year.

Deadline July of each year.

[148]
GENERATION III SCHOLARSHIP

Delaware Community Foundation
Attn: Executive Vice President
100 West 10th Street, Suite 115
P.O. Box 1636
Wilmington, DE 19899
(302) 504-5222   Fax: (302) 571-1553
E-mail: rgentsch@delcf.org
Web: www.delcf.org

Purpose To provide financial assistance to high school seniors in Delaware who are interested in studying business or construction at selected colleges in the state.

Eligibility This program is open to graduating high school seniors who reside in Delaware, have a GPA of 2.5 or higher, and are interested in studying business or construction-related fields in college. They must plan to work on a 2-year or 4-year degree at 1 of the following colleges: University of Delaware, Delaware State University, Delaware Technical and Community College, Goldey Beacom College, or Wesley College. Selection is based on academic achievement, financial need, and chosen field of study.

Financial data The stipend is $1,000 per year.

Duration 1 year, renewable.

Additional information This scholarship was established in 1998. Information is also available from Nikki Donelson, EDiS Company, 110 South Poplar Street, Wilmington, DE 19801, (302) 421-5700.

Number awarded At least 1 each year.

Deadline April of each year.

[149]
GEORGE A. NIELSEN PUBLIC INVESTOR SCHOLARSHIP

Government Finance Officers Association
Attn: Scholarship Committee
203 North LaSalle Street, Suite 2700
Chicago, IL 60601-1210
(312) 977-9700   Fax: (312) 977-4806
Web: www.gfoa.org/services/scholarships.shtml

Purpose To provide financial assistance to public employees who are undergraduate and graduate students and have research or career interests in the investment of public funds.

Eligibility This program is open to employees (for at least 1 year) of a local government or other public entity who are enrolled or planning to enroll in an undergraduate or graduate program in public administration, finance, business administration, or a related field. Applicants must be citizens or permanent residents of the United States or Canada and able to provide a letter of recommendation from their employer. They must have a research or career interest in the efficient and productive investment of public funds. Financial need is not considered in the selection process.

Financial data The stipend is $5,000 or $2,500.

Duration 1 year.

Additional information Funds for this program are provided by George A. Nielsen LLP.

Number awarded Each year, either 1 scholarship at $5,000 or 2 at $2,500 are awarded.

Deadline February of each year.

[150]
GEORGE PULAKOS SCHOLARSHIP

New Mexico Society of Certified Public Accountants
Attn: Scholarships in Accounting
1650 University N.E., Suite 450
Albuquerque, NM 87102-1733
(505) 246-1699   Toll-free: (800) 926-2522
Fax: (505) 246-1686   E-mail: nmcpa@nmcpa.org
Web: www.nmcpa.org

Purpose To provide financial assistance to accounting students at New Mexico universities and colleges.

Eligibility This program is open to full-time students at New Mexico colleges and universities who have completed 12 semester hours in accounting, are currently enrolled in 6 or more accounting hours, have completed 75 hours overall, and have a cumulative GPA of 3.0 or higher. Selection is based on academic achievement, extracurricular activities, career objectives and goals in accounting, and financial need.

Financial data A stipend is awarded (amount not specified).

Duration 1 year; may be renewed 1 additional year.

Additional information This program was established in 1999.

Number awarded   1 each year.

Deadline   September of each year.

[151]
GEORGIA AFFILIATE SCHOLARSHIP

American Woman's Society of Certified Public
    Accountants-Georgia Affiliate
c/o Amy Knowles-Jones, President
Internal Audit Department
222 Piedmont Avenue, N.E.
Atlanta, GA 30308-3306
(404) 653-1242   Fax: (404) 653-1575
E-mail: aknowles-jones@oxfordinc.com
Web: www.awscpa.org

Purpose   To provide financial assistance to women who are working on an undergraduate degree in accounting at a college or university in Georgia.

Eligibility   This program is open to women who are enrolled in a Georgia college or university. Applicants must have completed or be currently enrolled in a course in intermediate accounting II.

Financial data   The stipend is $1,000.

Duration   1 year.

Number awarded   1 each year.

[152]
GEORGIA GOVERNMENT FINANCE OFFICERS ASSOCIATION SCHOLARSHIP

Georgia Government Finance Officers Association
Attn: Scholarship Selection Committee
P.O. Box 6473
Athens, GA 30604-6473
(706) 542-8162   Fax: (706) 542-9856
E-mail: ggfoa@cviog.uga.edu
Web: www.ggfoa.org/Scholarships/scholarships.htm

Purpose   To provide financial assistance to undergraduate or graduate students in Georgia who are preparing for a career in public finance.

Eligibility   This program is open to undergraduate or graduate students who are preparing for a career in public finance and are currently enrolled or accepted (for graduate school) as full-time students at a college or university in Georgia. Applicants must have a GPA of 3.0 or higher. Along with their application, they must submit a letter of recommendation from the head of the applicable program (e.g., public administration, accounting, finance, business) and a 2-page statement describing their proposed career plans and plan of study. Preference is given to members of the Georgia Government Finance Officers Association (GGFOA) and employees of GGFOA governmental entities who are eligible for in-state tuition.

Financial data   The stipend is $3,000.

Duration   1 year.

Number awarded   2 each year.

Deadline   June of each year.

[153]
GEORGIA SOCIETY OF CPAS SCHOLARSHIP PROGRAM

Georgia Society of CPAs
Attn: Educational Foundation
3353 Peachtree Road, N.E., Suite 400
Atlanta, GA 30326-1414
(404) 231-8676   Toll-free: (800) 330-8889, ext. 2943
Fax: (404) 237-1291   E-mail: gscpaweb@gscpa.org
Web: www.gscpa.org

Purpose   To provide financial assistance to upper-division and graduate students who are majoring in accounting in Georgia.

Eligibility   This program is open to residents of Georgia who have demonstrated a commitment to a career in accounting. Applicants must be 1) rising junior or senior undergraduate accounting majors, or 2) graduate students enrolled in a master's degree in accounting or a business administration program. They must be enrolled in an accredited public or private college or university in Georgia with a GPA of 3.0 or higher either overall or in their accounting courses. Along with their application, they must submit documentation of financial need, transcripts, a resume, and a 250-word essay on their personal career goals and how this scholarship will help them attain those goals.

Financial data   A stipend is awarded (amount not specified).

Duration   1 year.

Additional information   This program includes the following named scholarships: the Time + Plus Scholarship, the Robert H. Lange Memorial Scholarship, the Julius M. Johnson Memorial Scholarship, and the Paychex Entrepreneur Scholarship.

Number awarded   Varies each year; recently, 36 of these scholarships were awarded.

Deadline   April of each year.

[154]
GILLETTE/NATIONAL URBAN LEAGUE SCHOLARSHIP FOR MINORITY STUDENTS

National Urban League
Attn: Scholarship Coordinator
120 Wall Street
New York, NY 10005
(212) 558-5300   Toll-free: (888) 839-0467
Fax: (212) 344-5332   E-mail: info@nul.org
Web: www.nul.org/caaa/scholarship/gillette_schol.html

Purpose   To provide financial assistance to minority students who are interested in completing their college education in designated areas of business and engineering.

Eligibility   Eligible to apply are minority students who are pursuing full-time studies leading to a bachelor's degree at an accredited institution of higher learning. They must be juniors or third-year students at the time the scholarship award begins, have a GPA of 3.0 or higher, be U.S. citizens or permanent residents or have a student visa, be able to demonstrate financial need, and be majoring in business-related fields (e.g., accounting, business administration, economics, engineering, finance, human resource management, ITS, manufacturing operations, marketing, MIS, public relations). Applications must be endorsed by an Urban League affiliate.

Financial data The stipend is $2,500 per year. Funds must be used for tuition, room, board, and the purchase of required educational materials and books.

Duration 2 years.

Number awarded Approximately 5 each year.

Deadline January of each year.

[155]
GMP MEMORIAL SCHOLARSHIPS

Glass, Molders, Pottery, Plastics and Allied Workers
    International Union
Attn: Memorial Scholarship Program
608 East Baltimore Pike
P.O. Box 607
Media, PA 19063
(610) 565-5051   Fax: (610) 565-0983
E-mail: gmpiu@ix.netcom.com
Web: www.gmpiu.org

Purpose To provide financial assistance to the children of members of the Glass, Molders, Pottery, Plastics and Allied Workers International Union (GMP) who are interested in attending college.

Eligibility All children, stepchildren, and adopted children of GMP members who rank in the top quarter of their high school senior class are eligible to apply. Children of deceased members are also eligible, if the deceased parent was a dues-paying member at the time of death. Similarly, children of retired members may apply, if the parent member has retained retirement status. Children of officers and employees of GMP, however, are ineligible. Recipients are free to select any accredited school in the United States or Canada and any regular program of college studies, although GMP hopes that recipients will consider majoring in ceramic engineering, industrial relations, or other fields of interest to the trade union movement. Selection is based on SAT or ACT scores, extra-curricular activities, leadership qualities, high school recommendations, and the student's own statements.

Financial data The stipend is $4,000 per year. Funds are sent to the recipient's school and may be used to pay for tuition, fees, room, board, books, or other appropriate educational expenses.

Duration 1 year; may be renewed for up to 3 additional years, if satisfactory academic progress is made.

Number awarded 8 each year.

Deadline October of each year.

[156]
GORDON SCHEER SCHOLARSHIP

Colorado Society of Certified Public Accountants
Attn: CSCPA Educational Foundation
7979 East Tufts Avenue, Suite 500
Denver, CO 80237-2845
(303) 741-8613   Toll-free: (800) 523-9082 (within CO)
Fax: (303) 773-6344   E-mail: gmantz@cocpa.org
Web: www.cocpa.org/student_faculty/scholarships.asp

Purpose To provide financial assistance to undergraduate and graduate students in Colorado who are studying accounting.

Eligibility This program is open to undergraduate and graduate students at colleges and universities in Colorado who

have completed at least 1 intermediate accounting class and have a GPA, both overall and in accounting, of at least 3.5. Selection is based on scholastic achievement.

Financial data The stipend is $1,250. Funds are paid directly to the recipient's school to be used for books, tuition, room, board, fees, and expenses.

Duration 1 year; recipients may reapply.

Number awarded 1 each year.

Deadline June of each year.

[157]
GRACE BYRNE UNDERGRADUATE
SCHOLARSHIP

Women's Transportation Seminar-Puget Sound Chapter
c/o Lorelei Mesic, Scholarship Co-Chair
W&H Pacific
3350 Monte Villa Parkway
Bothell, WA 98021-8972
(425) 951-4872   Fax: (425) 951-4808
E-mail: lmesic@whpacific.com
Web: www.wtspugetsound.org/nscholarships.html

Purpose To provide financial assistance to women undergraduate students from Washington working on a degree related to transportation.

Eligibility This program is open to women who are residents of Washington, studying at a college in the state, or working as an intern in the state. Applicants must be currently enrolled in an undergraduate degree program in a transportation-related field, such as engineering, planning, finance, or logistics. They must have a GPA of 3.0 or higher and plans to prepare for a career in a transportation-related field. Minority candidates are encouraged to apply. Along with their application, they must submit a 500-word statement about their career goals after graduation and why they think they should receive this scholarship award. Selection is based on that statement, academic record, and transportation-related activities or job skills. Financial need is not considered.

Financial data The stipend is $1,500.

Duration 1 year.

Additional information The winner is also nominated for scholarships offered by the national organization of the Women's Transportation Seminar.

Number awarded 1 each year.

Deadline October of each year.

[158]
GREAT FALLS ADVERTISING FEDERATION
COMMUNICATION/MARKETING SCHOLARSHIP

Great Falls Advertising Federation
Attn: Advertising Scholarship Committee
P.O. Box 634
Great Falls, MT 59403
(406) 761-6454   Toll-free: (800) 803-3351
Fax: (406) 453-1128   E-mail: gfaf@gfaf.com
Web: www.gfaf.com/scholarships_adv.html

Purpose To provide financial assistance to high school seniors in Montana interested in preparing for a career related to advertising.

Eligibility This program is open to residents of Montana who are high school seniors planning to attend a college or university. Applicants must be interested in preparing for a career in advertising, communication, electronic media, graphic design, marketing, or a related field. They must submit a letter describing how they will use the scholarship; a resume highlighting their work experience, extracurricular activities, honors, and awards; at least 2 letters of recommendation; and a marketing plan based on either an existing business or product or an imaginary business or product.

Financial data The stipend is $2,000.

Duration 1 year.

Additional information This program began in 1983.

Number awarded 1 each year.

Deadline February of each year.

[159]
GREDE FOUNDRIES COLLEGE-TO-WORK SCHOLARSHIP

Wisconsin Foundation for Independent Colleges, Inc.
735 North Water Street, Suite 800
Milwaukee, WI 53202-4100
(414) 273-5980   Fax: (414) 273-5995
E-mail: info@wficweb.org
Web: www.wficweb.org/documents/coll_work.htm

Purpose To provide financial assistance and work experience to students at designated private colleges in Wisconsin who are interested in preparing for a career in a field related to business or engineering.

Eligibility This program is open to full-time sophomores, juniors, and seniors at the following independent colleges in Wisconsin: Lakeland College, Milwaukee School of Engineering, Mount Mary College, and Wisconsin Lutheran College. Applicants must be preparing for a career in accounting, human resources, sales, production control, quality control, computer science, or metallurgical, mechanical, or metallurgical engineering. They must have a GPA of 2.0 or higher and be interested in an internship with Grede Foundries. Along with their application, they must submit a 1-page autobiography, transcripts, a list of campus involvement and academic honors, a resume including 3 references, and 2 letters of recommendation.

Financial data The scholarship stipend is $1,500. The internship is paid hourly.

Duration 1 year for the scholarship; 10 weeks during the summer for the internship.

Additional information This program is sponsored by Grede Foundries, Inc. Internships are available at the following locations: Iron Mountain, Michigan; Reedsburg, Wisconsin; and Milwaukee, Wisconsin.

Number awarded 1 each year.

Deadline January of each year.

[160]
GUS SWANSON COMMUNICATIONS SCHOLARSHIP PROGRAM

Swanson Russell Associates
1222 P Street
Lincoln, NE 68508
(402) 437-6411   Fax: (402) 437-6401
E-mail: nathano@sramarketing.com
Web: www.sramarketing.com/press/scholarship.cfm

Purpose To provide financial assistance to residents of Nebraska interested in studying a field related to communications at a college in the state.

Eligibility This program is open to Nebraska residents who are either high school seniors planning to enroll or college students already enrolled at an institution in the state with at least sophomore standing. Applicants must be studying or planning to major in a field related to communications: advertising, marketing, communications studies, mass communications, public relations, journalism, graphic design, desktop publishing, or associated areas. Along with their application, they must submit a marketing essay based on a current international, national, regional, or local advertising campaign. High school seniors must have a GPA of 3.25 or higher; college students must have a GPA of 3.0 or higher.

Financial data Stipends are $500 for high school seniors or $1,000 for students already enrolled in college.

Duration 1 year.

Number awarded 2 each year: 1 to a high school senior and 1 to a college student.

Deadline March of each year.

[161]
GWSCPA SCHOLARSHIP

Greater Washington Society of CPAs
1828 L Street, N.W., Suite 900
Washington, DC 20036
(202) 204-8014   Fax: (202) 204-8015
E-mail: info@gwscpa.org
Web: www.gwscpa.org/2PScholarship.htm

Purpose To provide financial assistance to accounting majors at several universities in the Washington, D.C. area.

Eligibility Rising seniors who are majoring in accounting are eligible to be nominated for this award if they are attending of the following schools in the Washington, D.C. area: American University, Catholic University, Gallaudet University, George Washington University, Georgetown University, Howard University, Southeastern University, Strayer University, or the University of the District of Columbia. Each university may submit 2 nominations; 1 winner per school is then selected.

Financial data The stipend is $2,000.

Duration 1 year; nonrenewable.

Additional information The scholarship fund was established in 1963. Since its inception, it has awarded more than $175,000 to accounting students.

Number awarded 9 each year: 1 at each of the participating schools.

[162]
HABJ SCHOLARSHIP PROGRAM

Houston Association of Black Journalists
Attn: Scholarship Selection Committee
P.O. Box 565
Houston, TX 77001-0565
(281) 920-2284   Fax: (713) 335-9128
E-mail: info@habj.org
Web: www.habj.org

Purpose To provide financial assistance to African American college students who are interested in preparing for a career in journalism (including marketing).

Eligibility This program is open to African Americans attending an accredited 4-year institution or community college at the sophomore, junior, or senior level. Applicants must have a GPA of 2.5 or higher and be majoring in radio, television, film, broadcasting, print journalism, photography, online journalism, marketing, or public relations. They must include a 1-page essay on the topic, "How Does Technology Influence the Media?" Selection is based on academic achievement, letters of recommendation, extracurricular activities, and community involvement.

Financial data A stipend is awarded (amount not specified). Funds are paid directly to the recipient's college or university.

Duration 1 year.

Additional information These scholarships are issued in the names of George McElroy and Leroy Patterson.

Number awarded Varies each year; recently, 4 of these scholarships were awarded.

Deadline May of each year.

[163]
HARRY A. APPLEGATE SCHOLARSHIP AWARD

DECA
1908 Association Drive
Reston, VA 20191-1594
(703) 860-5000   Fax: (703) 860-4013
E-mail: decainc@aol.com
Web: www.deca.org/scholarships/index.html

Purpose To provide financial assistance to DECA members interested in working on a college degree in marketing, entrepreneurship, or management.

Eligibility This program is open to DECA members in either the high school or Delta Epsilon Chi (collegiate) division. Applicants must intend to work full time on a 2- or 4-year degree in marketing, entrepreneurship, or management. Complete applications are to be submitted to the state advisor. Each state is allocated a number of applications it may forward to the national organization. Selection is based on DECA involvement, leadership ability, community service, and grades. The program is merit-based, but applicants may include a statement in support of financial need and it will be reviewed.

Financial data The stipend is $1,000. Funds are paid directly to the recipient's college or university.

Duration 1 year.

Number awarded Varies each year; recently, 18 of these scholarships were awarded.

Deadline Each state sets its own deadline, usually in January.

[164]
HARRY S. TRUMAN SCHOLARSHIP PROGRAM

Harry S. Truman Scholarship Foundation
Attn: Executive Secretary
712 Jackson Place, N.W.
Washington, DC 20006
(202) 395-4831   Fax: (202) 395-6995
E-mail: office@truman.gov
Web: www.truman.gov

Purpose To provide financial assistance to undergraduate students who have outstanding leadership potential, plan to prepare for a career in government or other public service, and wish to attend graduate school in the United States or abroad to prepare themselves for a public service career.

Eligibility Students must be nominated to be considered for this program. Nominees must be full-time students with junior standing at a 4-year institution, committed to a career in government or public service, in the upper quarter of their class, and U.S. citizens or nationals. Each participating institution may nominate up to 4 candidates (and up to 3 additional students who completed their first 2 years at a community college); community colleges and other 2-year institutions may nominate former students who are enrolled as full-time students with junior-level academic standing at accredited 4-year institutions. Selection is based on extent and quality of community service and government involvement, academic performance, leadership record, suitability of the nominee's proposed program of study for a career in public service, and writing and analytical skills. Priority is given to candidates who plan to enroll in a graduate program that specifically trains them for a career in public service, including government at any level, uniformed services, public interest organizations, nongovernmental research and/or educational organizations, public and private schools, and public service oriented non-profit organizations. The fields of study may include agriculture, biology, engineering, environmental management, physical and social sciences, and technology policy, as well as such traditional fields as economics, education, government, history, international relations, law, nonprofit management, political science, public administration, public health, and public policy. Interviews are required.

Financial data The scholarship provides up to $26,000: up to $2,000 for the senior year of undergraduate education and as much as $24,000 for graduate studies. All scholars are eligible to receive up to $12,000 for the first year of graduate study. They are eligible to receive up to $12,000 for their final year of graduate study if they provide assurance that they will enter public service immediately upon graduation or completion of a judicial clerkship after graduation.

Duration 1 year of undergraduate study and up to 3 years of graduate study, as long as the recipient maintains satisfactory academic performance.

Additional information Recipients may attend graduate school in the United States or in foreign countries.

Number awarded 75 to 80 each year: a) 1 "state" scholarship is available to a qualified resident nominee in each of the 50 states, the District of Columbia, Puerto Rico, and (considered as a single entity) Guam, the Virgin Islands, American Samoa, and the Commonwealth of the Northern Mariana Islands; and b) up to 30 at-large scholars.

Deadline February of each year.

[165]
HELENA CHEMICAL COMPANY SCHOLARSHIPS

National FFA Organization
Attn: Scholarship Office
6060 FFA Drive
P.O. Box 68960
Indianapolis, IN 46268-0960
(317) 802-4321   Fax: (317) 802-5321
E-mail: scholarships@ffa.org
Web: www.ffa.org

Purpose To provide financial assistance to FFA members from specified states who are interested in studying agricultural economics or agribusiness in college.

Eligibility This program is open to members who are graduating high school seniors planning to enroll full time in college. Applicants must be residents of Alabama, Arkansas, Florida, Georgia, Louisiana, Mississippi, North Carolina, South Carolina, or Tennessee interested in working on a 4-year degree in agricultural economics or agribusiness. They must have a GPA of 2.5 or higher and be able to demonstrate financial need. Selection is based on academic achievement (10 points for GPA, 10 points for SAT or ACT score, 10 points for class rank), leadership in FFA activities (30 points), leadership in community activities (10 points), and participation in the Supervised Agricultural Experience (SAE) program (30 points). U.S. citizenship is required.

Financial data The stipend is $1,000. Funds are paid directly to the recipient.

Duration 1 year; may be renewed up to 3 additional years provided the recipient maintains full-time enrollment and a GPA of 2.5 or higher.

Additional information Funding for these scholarships is provided by Helena Chemical Company.

Number awarded 1 each year.

Deadline February of each year.

[166]
HENRY A. ZUBERANO SCHOLARSHIPS

Hawai'i Community Foundation
Attn: Scholarship Department
1164 Bishop Street, Suite 800
Honolulu, HI 96813
(808) 537-6333   Toll-free: (888) 731-3863
Fax: (808) 521-6286
E-mail: scholarships@hcf-hawaii.org
Web: www.hawaiicommunityfoundation.org

Purpose To provide financial assistance to Hawaii residents who are studying fields related to public service as undergraduates.

Eligibility This program is open to Hawaii residents who are working on an undergraduate degree. Applicants must be majoring in political science, international relations, international business, or public administration. They must be able to demonstrate academic achievement (GPA of 2.7 or higher), good moral character, and financial need.

Financial data The amounts of the awards depend on the availability of funds and the need of the recipient; recently, stipends averaged $2,000.

Duration 1 year.

Number awarded Varies each year; recently, 10 of these scholarships were awarded.

Deadline February of each year.

[167]
HERMAN J. NEAL SCHOLARSHIP PROGRAM

Illinois CPA Society
Attn: Director, CPAsPI and CPA Endowment Fund of
    Illinois
550 West Jackson, Suite 900
Chicago, Il 60661-5716
(312) 993-0407, ext. 227   Toll-free: (800) 993-0407
Fax: (312) 993-9954
Web: www.icpas.org/icpas/endowment/programs.asp

Purpose To provide financial assistance to African American students undertaking their fifth year of course work to complete the educational requirements to sit for the CPA examination in Illinois.

Eligibility This program is open to African American residents of Illinois who are attending a college or university in the state and planning to sit for the CPA examination in Illinois within 3 years of the application date. Applicants must have at least a 3.0 GPA and be able to demonstrate financial need or special circumstances; the society is especially interested in assisting students who, because of limited options or opportunities, may not have alternative means of support. Selection is based on both academic achievement and financial need.

Financial data The maximum stipend is $4,000.

Duration 1 year (fifth year for accounting students planning to become a CPA).

Additional information The scholarship does not cover the cost of CPA examination review courses. Recipients may not receive a full graduate assistantship, fellowship, or scholarship from a college or university, participate in a full-tuition reimbursement cooperative education or internship program, or participate in an employee full-tuition reimbursement program during the scholarship period.

Number awarded 1 each year.

Deadline May of each year.

[168]
HERMAN LERDAL SCHOLARSHIP

South Dakota Bankers Foundation
109 West Missouri Avenue
P.O. Box 1081
Pierre, SD 57501-1081
(605) 224-1653   Fax: (605) 224-7835
Web: www.sdba.com/about/scholarships.asp

Purpose To provide financial assistance to students at South Dakota colleges or universities who are preparing for a career in banking or finance.

Eligibility This program is open to juniors at colleges or universities in South Dakota who are working on a business-related degree in preparation for a career in banking or finance. Applicants must have at least a 3.0 GPA. To apply, they must submit a completed application, a statement on their career interests, a description of their special talents and leadership abilities, a statement on obstacles they have overcome, and 3 letters of recommendation. Financial need is not considered in the selection process.

Financial data The stipend is $1,000.

Duration 1 year.
Number awarded 1 each year.
Deadline March of each year.

[169]
HILTON HOTELS CORPORATION SCHOLARSHIPS

DECA
1908 Association Drive
Reston, VA 20191-1594
(703) 860-5000   Fax: (703) 860-4013
E-mail: decainc@aol.com
Web: www.deca.org/scholarships/index.html

Purpose To provide financial assistance for college to DECA members interested in the hospitality industry.

Eligibility This program is open to DECA members who are interested in working full time on a 2-year or 4-year degree in marketing, business, or marketing education. Applicants must be able to demonstrate evidence of DECA activities, academic achievement, leadership ability, and experience working for Hilton Hotels or in the hospitality industry. Students whose parents work for Hilton are also eligible. Selection is based on merit, not financial need.

Financial data The stipend is $1,000.

Duration 1 year.

Additional information This program is sponsored by Hilton Hotels Corporation.

Number awarded Up to 5 each year.

Deadline February of each year.

[170]
HIMSS FOUNDATION SCHOLARSHIPS

Healthcare Information and Management Systems
  Society
Attn: HIMSS Foundation Scholarship Program
  Coordinator
230 East Ohio Street, Suite 500
Chicago, IL 60611-3269
(312) 664-4467   Fax: (312) 664-6143
Web: www.himss.org/asp/scholarships.asp

Purpose To provide financial assistance to upper-division or graduate student members of the Healthcare Information and Management Systems Society (HIMSS) who are interested in the field of health care information and management systems.

Eligibility This program is open to student members of the society, although an application for membership, including dues, may accompany the scholarship application. Applicants must be upper-division or graduate students enrolled in an accredited program designed to prepare them for a career in health care information or management systems, which may include industrial engineering, health care informatics, operations research, computer science and information systems, mathematics, and quantitative programs in business administration and hospital administration. Selection is based on academic achievement and demonstration of leadership potential, including communication skills and participation in society activity.

Financial data The stipend is $5,000. The award includes an all-expense paid trip to the annual HIMSS conference and exhibition.

Duration 1 year.

Additional information This program was established in 1986 for undergraduate and master's degree students. The first Ph.D. scholarship was awarded in 2002.

Number awarded 3 each year: 1 to an undergraduate student, 1 to a master's degree student, and 1 to a Ph.D. candidate.

Deadline October of each year.

[171]
H.I.S. PROGRAM

Hispanic College Fund
Attn: National Director
1717 Pennsylvania Avenue, N.W., Suite 460
Washington, D.C. 20006
Toll-free: (800) 644-4223   Fax: (202) 296-3774
E-mail: hispaniccollegefund@earthlink.net
Web: www.hispanicfund.org

Purpose To provide financial assistance and summer work experience to Hispanic American undergraduate students who are interested in preparing for a career in telecommunications.

Eligibility This program is open to U.S. citizens of Hispanic background (at least 1 grandparent must be 100% Hispanic) who are entering their freshman, sophomore, junior, or senior year of college. Applicants must be working on a bachelor's degree in accounting, business administration, computer science, economics, engineering specialties, finance, information systems, management, or other relevant technology or business fields. They must have an interest in telecommunications, have a cumulative GPA of 3.0 or higher, and be available to complete at least 2 consecutive summer internships before graduating from college. Financial need is considered in the selection process.

Financial data Stipends range from $500 to $5,000, depending on need and academic achievement. Funds are paid directly to the recipient's college or university to help cover tuition and fees.

Duration 1 year; recipients may reapply.

Additional information This program is a joint venture of the Hispanic College Fund (which provides scholarships), INROADS (which provides monthly coaching, leadership development, community service, and mentorship), and Sprint (which provides 10- to 12-week paid summer internships). All applications must be submitted online; no paper applications are available.

Number awarded Varies each year.

Deadline April of each year.

[172]
HISPANIC DESIGNERS GENERAL SCHOLARSHIPS

Hispanic Designers, Inc.
Attn: National Hispanic Education and Communications
    Projects
1101 30th Street, N.W., Suite 500
Washington, DC 20007
(202) 337-9636   Fax: (202) 337-9635
E-mail: HispDesign@aol.com
Web: www.hispanicdesigners.org

Purpose To provide financial assistance to Hispanic students enrolled in fashion design schools and majoring in selected fields, including merchandising and marketing.

Eligibility This program is open to students who are Hispanic or of Hispanic descent enrolled in accredited fashion design schools or other accredited institutions for a degree or certified program in fashion design, fashion merchandising, illustration, jewelry design, interior design, apparel manufacturing or management, marketing management, merchandising communications, theater costume design, or special event/fashion show production. Applicants must have documented evidence of extracurricular activities in the field of fashion through an internship or work training program, a GPA of 3.0 or higher, and financial need. U.S. citizenship or permanent resident status is required.

Financial data Stipends range from $500 to $2,500 per year; awards are paid directly to the recipient's school.

Duration 1 year.

Additional information No telephone inquiries are accepted.

Number awarded Varies each year; recently, 34 scholarships were awarded.

Deadline August of each year.

[173]
HISPANIC SCHOLARSHIP FUND/FORD MOTOR COMPANY CORPORATE SCHOLARSHIP PROGRAM

Hispanic Scholarship Fund
Attn: Selection Committee
55 Second Street, Suite 1500
San Francisco, CA 94105
Toll-free: (877) HSF-INFO   Fax: (415) 808-2302
E-mail: specialprograms@hsf.net
Web: www.hsf.net/scholarship/Special.htm

Purpose To provide financial assistance to Hispanic college juniors who are majoring in business, computer science, or engineering.

Eligibility This program is open to U.S. citizens and permanent residents who are of Hispanic heritage (each parent half Hispanic or 1 parent fully Hispanic). Applicants must be juniors attending a U.S. accredited college or university on a full-time basis and majoring in business, computer science, or engineering with a GPA of 3.0 or higher. As part of the application process, they must submit a 2-page essay that addresses the following topics: their Hispanic heritage and family background, personal and academic achievements, academic plans and career goals, efforts toward making a difference in their community, and financial need.

Financial data Stipends range up to $15,000 per year, depending on the unmet financial need of the recipient.

Duration 1 year; may be renewed up to 2 additional years if the recipient continues to meet eligibility requirements.

Additional information This program is sponsored by Ford Motor Company, which may also offer a summer internship to recipients.

Number awarded Varies each year.

Deadline March of each year.

[174]
HOMESTEAD CAPITAL HOUSING SCHOLARSHIP

Oregon Student Assistance Commission
Attn: Grants and Scholarships Division
1500 Valley River Drive, Suite 100
Eugene, OR 97401-2146
(541) 687-7395   Toll-free: (800) 452-8807, ext. 7395
Fax: (541) 687-7419
E-mail: awardinfo@mercury.osac.state.or.us
Web: www.osac.state.or.us

Purpose To provide financial assistance to graduates of Oregon high schools majoring in fields related to housing and community development at a college in Oregon or Washington.

Eligibility This program is open to graduates of high schools in Oregon who are entering at least their junior year at a 4-year college in Oregon or Washington. Applicants must have a cumulative GPA of 2.75 or higher and be majoring in accounting, architecture, community development, construction management, finance, real estate, or engineering (structural, civil, or environmental). Along with their application, they must submit an essay on how this scholarship and their applied discipline will contribute to affordable housing and community development.

Financial data Scholarship amounts vary, depending upon the needs of the recipient.

Duration 1 year.

Number awarded Varies each year.

Deadline February of each year.

[175]
HOWARD GREENE SCHOLARSHIP

Rhode Island Society of Certified Public Accountants
45 Royal Little Drive
Providence, RI 02904
(401) 331-5720   Fax: (401) 454-5780
E-mail: rchurch@riscpa.org
Web: www.riscpa.org/student.php

Purpose To provide financial assistance to students in Rhode Island who are majoring in accounting.

Eligibility This program is open to residents of Rhode Island who are enrolled in college and have expressed an interest in public accounting during their undergraduate years. Applicants must be U.S. citizens who have a GPA of 3.0 or higher. Selection is based on demonstrated potential to become a valued member of the public accounting profession. Finalists are interviewed.

Financial data The stipend is $2,000.

Duration 1 year.

Number awarded 1 each year.

Deadline April of each year.

[176]
HRA-NCA ACADEMIC SCHOLARSHIPS

Human Resource Association of the National Capital
  Area
Attn: Chair, College Relations
P.O. Box 7503
Arlington, VA 22207
(703) 241-0229   Fax: (703) 532-9473
E-mail: info@hra-nca.org
Web: hra-nca.org/studentservices.asp

Purpose To provide financial assistance to students working on an undergraduate or graduate degree in human resources at colleges and universities in the Washington, D.C. metropolitan area.

Eligibility This program is open to undergraduate and graduate students working on a degree in human resources or a related field at a college or university in the Washington, D.C. metropolitan area. Applicants must have completed at least half of their degree program and have at least a full semester remaining. Selection is based on academic performance and commitment to human resources as demonstrated by participation in a student chapter of the Society for Human Resource Management (SHRM), an internship, or relevant work experience or community service.

Financial data The stipend is $1,500.

Duration 1 year.

Additional information The Human Resource Association of the National Capital Area (HRA-NCA) is the local affiliate of SHRM.

Number awarded 2 each year.

Deadline Applications are generally due in spring of each year.

[177]
HSCPA SCHOLARSHIPS

Hawaii Society of Certified Public Accountants
900 Fort Street Mall, Suite 850
P.O. Box 1754
Honolulu, HI 98606
(808) 537-9475   Fax: (808) 537-3520
E-mail: info@hscpa.org
Web: www.hscpa.org

Purpose To provide financial assistance to accounting students in Hawaii.

Eligibility This program is open to residents of Hawaii currently enrolled at a college or university in the state. Applicants must be majoring or concentrating in accounting and be planning to take the C.P.A. examination. They must have completed intermediate accounting and have a GPA of 3.0 or higher.

Financial data Stipends range from $300 to $1,500.

Duration 1 year.

Number awarded Varies each year; recently, 4 of these scholarships were awarded.

[178]
HUMANE STUDIES FELLOWSHIPS

Institute for Humane Studies at George Mason University
3301 North Fairfax Drive, Suite 440
Arlington, VA 22201-4432
(703) 993-4880   Toll-free: (800) 697-8799
Fax: (703) 993-4890   E-mail: ihs@gmu.edu
Web: www.TheIHS.org

Purpose To provide financial assistance to undergraduate and graduate students in the United States or abroad who intend to pursue "intellectual careers" and have demonstrated an interest in classical liberal principles.

Eligibility This program is open to students who will be full-time college juniors, seniors, or graduate students planning academic or other intellectual careers, including law, public policy, and journalism. Applicants must have a clearly demonstrated interest in the classical liberal/libertarian tradition of individual rights and market economics. Applications from students outside the United States or studying abroad receive equal consideration. Selection is based on academic or professional performance, relevance of work to the advancement of a free society, and potential for success.

Financial data The maximum stipend is $12,000.

Duration 1 year; may be renewed upon reapplication.

Additional information As defined by the sponsor, the core principles of the classical liberal/libertarian tradition include the recognition of individual rights and the dignity and worth of each individual; protection of these rights through the institutions of private property, contract, the rule of law, and freely evolved intermediary institutions; voluntarism in all human relations, including the unhampered market mechanism in economic affairs; and the goals of free trade, free migration, and peace. This program began in 1983 as Claude R. Lambe Fellowships. The application fee is $25.

Number awarded Approximately 100 each year.

Deadline December of each year.

[179]
ICI EDUCATIONAL FOUNDATION SCHOLARSHIP PROGRAM

Hispanic College Fund
Attn: National Director
1717 Pennsylvania Avenue, N.W., Suite 460
Washington, D.C. 20006
(202) 296-5400   Toll-free: (800) 644-4223
Fax: (202) 296-3774
E-mail: hispaniccollegefund@earthlink.net
Web: www.hispanicfund.org

Purpose To provide financial assistance to Hispanic American undergraduate students who are interested in preparing for a career in business, computer science, or engineering.

Eligibility This program is open to U.S. citizens of Hispanic background (at least 1 grandparent must be 100% Hispanic) who are entering their freshman, sophomore, junior, or senior year of college. Applicants must be working on a bachelor's or associate degree in business, computer science, or a business-related major and have a cumulative GPA of 3.0 or higher. They must be applying to or enrolled in a college or university in the 50 states or Puerto Rico as a full-time student. Financial need is considered in the selection process.

Financial data Stipends range from $500 to $5,000, depending on the need of the recipient, and average approximately $3,000. Funds are paid directly to the recipient's college or university to help cover tuition and fees.

Duration 1 year; recipients may reapply.

Additional information This program is sponsored by the ICI Educational Foundation. All applications must be submitted online; no paper applications are available.

Number awarded Varies each year.

Deadline April of each year.

[180]
IDAHO STATE BROADCASTERS ASSOCIATION SCHOLARSHIPS

Idaho State Broadcasters Association
270 North 27th Street, Suite B
Boise, ID 83702-4741
(208) 345-3072   Fax: (208) 343-8946
E-mail: isba@rmci.net
Web: www.idahobroadcasters.org/scholarships.aspx

Purpose To provide financial assistance to students at Idaho colleges and universities who are preparing for a career in the broadcasting field.

Eligibility This program is open to full-time students at Idaho schools who are preparing for a career in broadcasting, including business administration, sales, journalism, and engineering. Applicants must have a GPA of at least 2.0 for the first 2 years of school or 2.5 for the last 2 years. Along with their application, they must submit a letter of recommendation from the general manager of a broadcasting state that is a member of the Idaho State Broadcasters Association and a 1-page essay describing their career plans and why they want the scholarship. Applications are encouraged from a wide and diverse student population. The Wayne C. Cornils Scholarship is reserved for a less advantaged applicant.

Financial data The stipend for the general scholarships is $1,000. The stipend of the Wayne C. Cornils Scholarship depends on the need of the recipient.

Duration 1 year.

Number awarded 3 each year: 2 general scholarships and the Cornils Scholarship.

Deadline March of each year.

[181]
IDDBA SCHOLARSHIP

International Dairy-Deli-Bakery Association
Attn: Scholarship Committee
313 Price Place, Suite 202
P.O. Box 5528
Madison, WI 53705-0528
(608) 238-7908   Fax: (608) 238-6330
E-mail: iddba@iddba.org
Web: www.iddba.org

Purpose To provide financial assistance for undergraduate or graduate study to students interested in a career in the food industry who are employed in a supermarket dairy, deli, or bakery department (or related companies).

Eligibility This program is open to high school seniors, college students, vocational/technical students, and graduate students. Applicants must be currently employed in a super-

market dairy, deli, or bakery department or be employed by a company that services those departments (e.g., food manufacturers, brokers, or wholesalers). They must be majoring in a food-related field, e.g., culinary arts, baking/pastry arts, food science, business, or marketing. Employees of restaurants, retail bakeries, bakery-cafes, or other food service establishments not associated with a supermarket are not eligible. While a GPA of 2.5 or higher is required, this may be waived for first-time applicants. Selection is based on academic achievement, work experience, and a statement of career goals and/or how their degree will be beneficial to their job. Financial need is not considered.

Financial data Stipends range from $250 to $1,000. Funds are paid jointly to the recipient and the recipient's school. If the award exceeds tuition fees, the excess may be used for other educational expenses.

Duration 1 year; recipients may reapply.

Number awarded Varies each year; a total of $75,000 is available for this program annually.

Deadline Applications must be submitted prior to the end of March, June, September, or December of each year.

[182]
ILLINOIS CPA SOCIETY ACCOUNTING SCHOLARSHIP PROGRAM

Illinois CPA Society
Attn: Director, CPAsPI and CPA Endowment Fund of
    Illinois
550 West Jackson, Suite 900
Chicago, Il 60661-5716
(312) 993-0407, ext. 227   Toll-free: (800) 993-0407
Fax: (312) 993-9954
Web: www.icpas.org/icpas/endowment/programs.asp

Purpose To provide financial assistance to Illinois students undertaking their fifth year of course work to complete the educational requirements to sit for the CPA examination in Illinois.

Eligibility This program is open to residents of Illinois who are attending a college or university in the state and planning to sit for the CPA examination in Illinois within 3 years of the application date. Applicants must have at least a 3.0 GPA and be able to demonstrate financial need or special circumstances; the society is especially interested in assisting students who, because of limited options or opportunities, may not have alternative means of support. Selection is based on both academic achievement and financial need.

Financial data The maximum stipend is $4,000.

Duration 1 year (fifth year for accounting students planning to become a CPA).

Additional information This program was established in 1998. In addition to the general scholarships, the following named scholarships are available: the Arthur R. Wyatt Accounting Scholarship Program which provides stipends of $4,000 to students at the University of Illinois at Urbana-Champaign, the Kenneth J. Hull and Jacqueline M. Hull Scholarship for students at Southern Illinois University at Carbondale, and the Needles/Snow/Wish Scholarship of $2,500 for students at DePaul University. The scholarship does not cover the cost of CPA examination review courses. Recipients may not receive a full graduate assistantship, fellowship, or scholarship from a college or university, participate in a full-tuition reimbursement cooperative education or internship program, or participate in an employee full-tuition reimbursement program during the scholarship period.

Number awarded Varies each year; recently, 7 of these scholarships were awarded.

Deadline May of each year.

[183]
ILLINOIS REAL ESTATE EDUCATIONAL FOUNDATION ACADEMIC SCHOLARSHIPS

Illinois Association of Realtors
Attn: Illinois Real Estate Educational Foundation
3180 Adloff Lane, Suite 400
P.O. Box 19451
Springfield, IL 62794-9451
(217) 529-2600   E-mail: IARaccess@iar.org
Web: www.illinoisrealtor.org/iar/about/scholarships.htm

Purpose To provide financial assistance to Illinois residents who are preparing for a career in real estate.

Eligibility Applicants must be U.S. citizens and Illinois residents who are attending a college or university in the state on a full-time basis and working on a degree with an emphasis in real estate. They must have completed at least 30 credits. As part of the application process, students must submit copies of their transcripts and letters of recommendation and reference. Selection is based on academic record, economic need, references and recommendations, and career plans in the field of real estate or an allied field (e.g., construction, land use planning, mortgage banking, property management, real estate appraising, real estate assessing, real estate brokerage, real estate development, real estate investment counseling, real estate law, and real estate syndication). Finalists are interviewed.

Financial data The stipend is $1,000.

Duration 1 year.

Number awarded 1 or more each year.

Deadline March of each year.

[184]
IMA MEMORIAL EDUCATION FUND SCHOLARSHIPS

Institute of Management Accountants
Attn: Committee on Students
10 Paragon Drive
Montvale, NJ 07645-1760
(201) 573-9000   Toll-free: (800) 638-4427, ext. 1543
Fax: (201) 573-8438   E-mail: students@imanet.org
Web: www.imanet.org

Purpose To provide financial assistance to student members of the Institute of Management Accountants (IMA) who are interested in preparing for a career in a field related to management accounting.

Eligibility This program is open to undergraduate and graduate student IMA members who have a GPA of 2.8 or higher. Applicants must be preparing for a career in management accounting, financial management, or information technology. They must submit a 2-page statement on their reasons for applying for the scholarship, reasons that they deserve the award, specific contributions to the IMA, ideas on how they will promote awareness and increase membership and certifi-

cation within IMA, and their career goals and objectives. Selection is based on that statement, academic merit, IMA participation, the quality of the presentation, a resume, and letters of recommendation.

Financial data Stipends range from $1,000 to $2,500 per year.

Duration 1 year.

Additional information Up to 30 finalists in each category (including the scholarship winners) receive a scholarship to take 5 parts of the Certified Management Accountant (CMA) and/or Certified in Financial Management (CFM) examination within a year of graduation.

Number awarded Varies each year.

Deadline February of each year.

[185]
INTERNATIONAL PUBLIC MANAGEMENT ASSOCIATION FOR HUMAN RESOURCES SCHOLARSHIP

International Public Management Association for Human
  Resources
Attn: Fellowship Committee
1617 Duke Street
Alexandria, VA 22314
(703) 549-7100   Fax: (703) 684-0948
Web: www.ipma-hr.org

Purpose To provide financial assistance for college to children of members of the International Public Management Association for Human Resources (IPMA-HR), especially those interested in majoring in human resources or public administration.

Eligibility This program is open to students who are enrolled or planning to enroll at an accredited college or university. At least 1 parent or legal guardian must have been an IPMA-HR member for at least the previous 3 years. Preference is given to applicants in human resources or public administration. Applicants must submit a list of activities and awards, a statement of goals and objectives, high school and undergraduate transcripts, and (for entering freshmen) a copy of their college acceptance letter. Financial need is not considered in the selection process.

Financial data The stipend is $1,000 per year.

Duration 1 year.

Number awarded 1 or more each year.

Deadline May of each year.

[186]
INVESTING IN THE FUTURE SCHOLARSHIP

Charles and Agnes Kazarian Eternal
  Foundation/ChurchArmenia.com
Attn: Educational Scholarships
30 Kennedy Plaza, Second Floor
Providence, RI 02903
E-mail: info@churcharmenia.com
Web: www.churcharmenia.com/scholarship1.html

Purpose To provide financial assistance to outstanding undergraduate or graduate students of Armenian descent who are preparing for a career in finance, business, medicine, or research.

Eligibility Applicants must be of Armenian descent and accepted to or qualified for highly competitive undergraduate or graduate degree programs focusing on finance, medicine, business, or research. They must submit a completed application form, official academic transcripts, 3-page personal statement, and up to 3 letters of recommendation. Selection is based on academic record, financial need, and future ability to make an investment or return to the Armenian community.

Financial data The stipend is $10,000.

Duration 1 year.

Number awarded 1 or more each year.

[187]
IRWA SCHOLARSHIPS

International Right of Way Association—New England
Chapter 16
c/o Norman Twaddel
Portland Water District
P.O. Box 3553
Portland, ME 04104-3553
(207) 774-5961, ext. 3057　　　　Fax: (207) 761-8307
E-mail: twaddel@pwd.org

Purpose To provide financial assistance to high school seniors in New England who are interested in studying right-of-way issues in college.

Eligibility This program is open to high school seniors who reside in Maine, New Hampshire, Vermont, Massachusetts, or Rhode Island. They must be planning to attend an accredited postsecondary institution in the fall and to major in a field that will prepare them for a career in the right-of-way profession (e.g., business, civil engineering, communications, economics, environmental engineering, international relations, or law). Applicants must have a GPA of 3.0 or higher and be able to demonstrate financial need.

Financial data The stipend ranges from $300 to $500 each year.

Duration 1 year.

Number awarded Up to 4 each year.

Deadline March of each year.

[188]
JAMES A. TURNER, JR. MEMORIAL SCHOLARSHIP

American Welding Society
Attn: AWS Foundation, Inc.
550 N.W. LeJeune Road
Miami, FL 33126
(305) 445-6628　　　Toll-free: (800) 443-9353, ext. 461
Fax: (305) 443-7559　　　　E-mail: found@aws.org
Web: www.aws.org/foundation/turner.html

Purpose To provide financial assistance to college students interested in a management career related to welding.

Eligibility This program is open to full-time undergraduate students who are working on a 4-year bachelor's degree in business that will lead to a management career in welding store operations or a welding distributorship. Applicants must be U.S. citizens who are currently employed for at least 10 hours a week at a welding distributorship. Financial need is not required.

Financial data The stipend is $3,000.

Duration 1 year; recipients may reapply.

Number awarded 1 each year.

Deadline January of each year.

[189]
JANE M. KLAUSMAN CPS, CPP-T, PRP SCHOLARSHIP

International Association of Administrative Professionals-
New York State Division
c/o Lorraine Engenito CAP
210-50 41st Avenue, 5-J
Bayside, NY 11361
(516) 949-7550
Web: www.geocities.com/nystatedivision

Purpose To provide financial assistance to residents of New York who are enrolled or planning to enroll in a degree or diploma program in administrative/office technology or business education.

Eligibility This program is open to New York residents who are 1) high school seniors planning to enroll in an accredited community college or university; 2) students currently enrolled in an accredited community college or university; 3) students currently enrolled in an accredited junior or senior college of business or business school; or 4) students not above the junior year in an accredited 4-year college or university. Applicants must be working on or planning to work on a degree or diploma in the field of administrative/office technology or business education. Along with their application, they must submit a 1-page letter explaining their reasons for preparing for a career as an administrative professional, a 1-page letter describing their need for financial assistance, and a 1-page letter of reference from their school advisor.

Financial data The stipend is $500. Funds are paid directly to the recipient's college, university, community college, technical school, junior or senior college of business, or business school.

Duration 1 year.

Number awarded 1 or more each year.

Deadline April of each year.

[190]
JANE M. KLAUSMAN WOMEN IN BUSINESS SCHOLARSHIPS

Zonta International
557 West Randolph Street
Chicago, IL 60661-2206
(312) 930-5848　　　　Fax: (312) 930-0951
E-mail: Zontafdtn@zonta.org
Web: www.zonta.org

Purpose To provide financial assistance to women working on an undergraduate degree in business.

Eligibility This program is open to women who are currently enrolled in the second or third year of a business-related undergraduate degree program at a college or university anywhere in the world. Applicants first enter at the club level, and then advance to district and international levels. Selection is based on academic record, demonstrated intent to complete a program in business, achievement in business-related subjects, 2 letters of recommendation, and a 500-word statement on academic program and professional goals (including the relevance of academic program to a career in business and how this scholarship will help reach that objective).

Financial data Each winner at the U.S. district level receives a $400 scholarship; the international winners receive a $4,000 scholarship.

Duration 1 year.

Additional information This program began in the 1998-2000 biennium.

Number awarded Several U.S. district winner and 5 international winners each year.

Deadline Clubs set their own deadlines but must submit their winners to the district governor by May of each year.

[191]
JEDIDIAH ZABROSKY SCHOLARSHIP

Vermont Student Assistance Corporation
Champlain Mill
Attn: Scholarship Programs
P.O. Box 2000
Winooski, VT 05404-2601
(802) 654-3798   Toll-free: (800) 642-3177
Fax: (802) 654-3765   TDD: (802) 654-3766
TDD: (800) 281-3341 (within VT)   E-mail: info@vsac.org
Web: www.vsac.org

Purpose To provide financial assistance to Vermont residents who are studying business or education at a college in the state.

Eligibility This scholarship is available to residents of Vermont who currently attend a public college in the state. Applicants must be working on a 2-year or 4-year degree in business or education and be employed at least 10 hours per week. Selection is based on academic achievement (GPA of 2.5 or higher), school and community involvement, letters of recommendation, required essays, and financial need.

Financial data The stipend is $2,000.

Duration 1 year.

Additional information This program was established in 2002.

Number awarded 1 each year.

Deadline April of each year.

[192]
JERRY BARTOW SCHOLARSHIP FUND

National Urban League
Attn: Scholarship Coordinator
120 Wall Street
New York, NY 10005
(212) 558-5300   Toll-free: (888) 839-0467
Fax: (212) 344-5332   E-mail: info@nul.org
Web: www.nul.org

Purpose To provide financial assistance to undergraduate students at Historically Black Colleges and Universities (HBCUs) that are participating in the Black Executive Exchange Program (BEEP).

Eligibility This program is open to African American sophomores, juniors, and seniors at HBCUs that are participating in the BEEP. Applicants must be majoring in business, management, technology, and/or education.

Financial data The stipend is $1,500 per year.

Duration 1 year.

Additional information This program was established in 1997 by ITT Hartford Insurance Company. Recipients are required to attend the annual BEEP conference to accept the award. Travel and hotel arrangements are provided by BEEP.

Number awarded 2 each year.

Deadline January of each year.

[193]
JIM BOB NORMAN MEMORIAL SCHOLARSHIP

Texas FFA Association
614 East 12th Street
Austin, TX 78701
(512) 480-8045   Fax: (512) 472-0555
E-mail: txffa@texasffa.org
Web: www.texasffa.org/ffa/tfa-scho.html

Purpose To provide financial assistance to high school senior members of FFA in Texas who plan to study a field related to agricultural (including agribusiness) or life sciences at a college or university in the state.

Eligibility This program is open to high school seniors in Texas who are FFA members and have been members at least 2 of the 3 previous years. Applicants must be planning to major in a field related to the agricultural or life sciences at a college or university in Texas. They must have completed at least 5 semesters of instruction in agriculture and/or agribusiness during high school and scored at least 950 on the SAT or 20 on the ACT. U.S. citizenship and ranking in the top half of their graduating class are also required. Selection is based on class rank (16 points), SAT or ACT scores (14 points), academic achievement in agricultural science and career related instruction (10 points), FFA achievements (30 points), financial need (10 points), and an interview (25 points).

Financial data The stipend is $2,000 per year.

Duration 4 years.

Additional information The list of approved majors includes plant and soil sciences (agronomy, botany, clothing and textiles, floriculture, horticulture, plant science, soil science); natural and environmental sciences (aquaculture, atmospheric science, bioenvironmental science, entomology, forestry, fisheries, mariculture, marine biology, meteorology, range science, soil and water conservation, and wildlife science); human and animal sciences (animal science, dairy science, food and nutrition, food science, food technology, poultry science, preveterinary medicine, scientific nutrition, and zoology); support curriculums (agricultural development, agricultural business, agricultural economics, agricultural education, agricultural engineering, agricultural journalism, agricultural science, agricultural services, agricultural systems, biomedical engineering, chemical engineering, food engineering, land use and planning, landscape architecture, and recreation and parks); and basic sciences (biochemistry, biology, biomedical science, biotechnology, chemistry, genetics, microbiology, and pharmacology). Students may not apply for both 4-H and FFA scholarships.

Number awarded 1 each year.

[194]
JIM SHELENHAMER MEMORIAL SCHOLARSHIP

Missouri DECA
Attn: Missouri State DECA Advisor
P.O. Box 480
Jefferson City, MO 65102-0480
(573) 751-4367   Fax: (573) 751-4361
E-mail: julie.lyman@dese.mo.gov
Web: www.modeca.org/d_scholarships.htm

Purpose To provide financial assistance to high school seniors who have served as Missouri DECA state officers and are interested in studying marketing or management in college.

Eligibility This program is open to high school seniors who are past or present Missouri DECA state action team members. Applicants must be interested in attending an accredited 2- or 4-year postsecondary institution to continue their study of marketing and/or management. Selection is based on leadership record, involvement in DECA and other organizations, career plans, volunteer services, academic record, and letters of recommendation.

Financial data The stipend is $1,000.

Duration 1 year; nonrenewable.

Number awarded 1 each year.

Deadline February of each year.

[195]
JOHN CULVER WOODDY SCHOLARSHIPS

Actuarial Foundation
Attn: Actuarial Education and Research Fund Committee
475 North Martingale Road, Suite 800
Schaumburg, IL 60173-2226
(847) 706-3565   Fax: (847) 706-3599
E-mail: sbaker@soa.org
Web: www.aerf.org/awards.html

Purpose To provide financial assistance to undergraduate students who are preparing for a career in actuarial science.

Eligibility Eligible to be nominated are undergraduate students who will have senior standing in the semester after receiving the scholarship. Applicants must rank in the top quartile of their class and have successfully completed 1 actuarial examination. Each university may nominate only 1 student. Preference is given to candidates who have demonstrated leadership potential by participating in extracurricular activities. Financial need is not considered in the selection process.

Financial data The stipend is $2,000 per academic year.

Duration 1 year.

Additional information This program was established in 1996.

Number awarded 4 each year.

Deadline June of each year.

[196]
JOHN SWAIN SCHOLARSHIP

Direct Marketing Association of Washington
Attn: Educational Foundation
801 Roeder Road, Suite 575
Silver Spring, MD 20910
(301) 427-0050   Fax: (301) 565-9791
E-mail: dmaw@hqstaff.com
Web: www.dmaw.org

Purpose To provide financial assistance to upper-division college students in Washington, D.C., Maryland, and Virginia who have an interest in direct marketing.

Eligibility All applicants must meet the following requirements: be a junior or senior in college; be enrolled in a college or university in Washington, D.C., Virginia, or Maryland; have at least a 3.0 GPA, and have an interest in direct marketing.

Financial data The stipend is $3,000.

Duration 1 year.

Number awarded 1 each year.

Deadline April of each year.

[197]
JOHNSONVILLE SAUSAGE COLLEGE-TO-WORK SCHOLARSHIP

Wisconsin Foundation for Independent Colleges, Inc.
735 North Water Street, Suite 800
Milwaukee, WI 53202-4100
(414) 273-5980   Fax: (414) 273-5995
E-mail: info@wficweb.org
Web: www.wficweb.org/documents/coll_work.htm

Purpose To provide financial assistance and work experience to college seniors in Wisconsin who are enrolled at private colleges and universities in the state and preparing for a career in supply chain management.

Eligibility This program is open to seniors who are enrolled full time at 1 of the 20 independent colleges or universities in Wisconsin. Preference is given to residents of Sheboygan County, but others are invited to apply. Applicants must be interested in preparing for a career in supply chain management, industrial or manufacturing engineering, or industrial technology. They must have earned a GPA of 3.0 or higher and be interested in an internship at Johnsonville Sausage in Sheboygan, Wisconsin. Along with their application, they must submit a 1-page autobiography, transcripts, a list of campus involvement and academic honors, a resume including 3 references, and 2 letters of recommendation.

Financial data The stipends are $3,500 for the scholarship and $1,500 for the internship.

Duration 1 year for the scholarship; 10 weeks for the internship.

Additional information The participating schools are Alverno College, Beloit College, Cardinal Stritch University, Carroll College, Carthage College, Concordia University of Wisconsin, Edgewood College, Lakeland College, Lawrence University, Marian College, Marquette University, Milwaukee Institute of Art & Design, Milwaukee School of Engineering, Mount Mary College, Northland College, Ripon College, St. Norbert College, Silver Lake College, Viterbo University, and Wisconsin Lutheran College. This program is sponsored by Johnsonville Sausage, LLC.

Number awarded 2 each year.

Deadline January of each year.

[198]
JUAN EUGENE RAMOS SCHOLARSHIP

Hispanic Designers, Inc.
Attn: National Hispanic Education and Communications
   Projects
1101 30th Street, N.W., Suite 500
Washington, DC 20007
(202) 337-9636   Fax: (202) 337-9635
E-mail: HispDesign@aol.com
Web: www.hispanicdesigners.org

Purpose To provide financial assistance to Hispanic students enrolled in a fashion design school who are preparing for a career in marketing.

Eligibility Applicants must be Hispanic or of Hispanic descent, be able to demonstrate financial need, be U.S. citizens or residents, have participated in an internship or work training program in the field of fashion, and have a GPA of 3.0 or higher. They must be enrolled in an accredited postsecondary institution and studying for a degree or certified program that incorporates the importance of marketing and merchandising in fashion design.

Financial data The stipend is $5,000 per year; awards are paid directly to the institution.

Duration 1 year.

Additional information This program was established in 1995. No telephone inquiries are accepted.

Number awarded 1 each year.

Deadline August of each year.

[199]
JULIAN AND JAN HESTER MEMORIAL SCHOLARSHIPS

Community Bankers Association of Georgia
1900 The Exchange, Suite 600
Atlanta, GA 30339-2022
(770) 541-4490   Fax: (770) 541-4496
E-mail: info@cbaofga.com
Web: www.cbaofga.com/programs.htm

Purpose To provide financial assistance to high school seniors in Georgia who are interested in preparing for a career in banking.

Eligibility This program is open to high school seniors in Georgia who are planning to attend a college, university, or trade school in the state. They must be interested in preparing for a career in community banking. Selection is based solely on merit; family financial need is not considered.

Financial data The stipend is $1,000.

Duration 1 year; nonrenewable.

Number awarded At least 4 each year.

Deadline March of each year.

[200]
JUNIOR ACHIEVEMENT OF MAINE SCHOLARSHIP

Junior Achievement of Maine, Inc.
Attn: Scholarship Committee
90 Bridge Street, Suite 120
Westbrook, ME 04092-2952
(207) 591-9005   Fax: (207) 591-9007
E-mail: program@jamaine.org
Web: maine.ja.org/programs_volunteer.html

Purpose To provide financial assistance for college to high school seniors and college students in Maine who have participated in Junior Achievement.

Eligibility This program is open to high school seniors in Maine who have participated in a Junior Achievement program (including JA Company Program, JA Economics, JA TITAN, and JA Personal Finance) or taught a JA class in an elementary school. Applicants must also have applied to a 2-year, 4-year, or community college. Also eligible are college students currently enrolled at a 2-year, 4-year, or community college who have taught a JA program in the elementary or middle grades. Selection is based on academic accomplishments (GPA of 2.5 or higher), participation in the program, and short answers to 3 questions: what influence has Junior Achievement had on you and your future plans, why do you feel it is important to continue your education at the collegiate level, and where do you see yourself in 10 years?

Financial data The stipend is $1,000.

Duration 1 year.

Number awarded 1 each year.

Deadline March of each year.

[201]
KANSAS JUNIOR LIVESTOCK ASSOCIATION SCHOLARSHIPS

Kansas Livestock Association
Attn: Kansas Livestock Foundation
6031 S.W. 37th Street
Topeka, KS 66614-5129
(785) 273-5115   Fax: (785) 273-3399
E-mail: kla@kla.org
Web: www.kla.org/scholarapp.htm

Purpose To provide financial assistance to members of the Kansas Junior Livestock Association (KJLA) who are or will be majoring in a field related to agriculture (including agricultural economics).

Eligibility Eligible to apply for this program are KJLA members who are entering or returning to a junior or senior college in Kansas. Applicants must be majoring or planning to major in a field related to agriculture (e.g., agricultural economics, agronomy, animal science). Selection is based on academic achievement (20 points), personal livestock enterprises (25 points), 4H/FFA/KJLA activities and leadership (30 points), school activities and honors (30 points), other activities and leadership (25 points), work experience (25 points), significant honors or recognition (25 points), and career plans (20 points).

Financial data The stipend is $500. Funds are paid directly to the recipient in 2 equal installments at the beginning of each semester, upon proof of enrollment.

Duration 1 year.

Additional information This program is offered by the Kansas Junior Livestock Association in conjunction with the Kansas Livestock Foundation.

Number awarded 2 each year.

Deadline April of each year.

[202]
KARL CHRISTMAN MEMORIAL SCHOLARSHIPS

New Mexico Society of Certified Public Accountants
Attn: Scholarships in Accounting
1650 University N.E., Suite 450
Albuquerque, NM 87102-1733
(505) 246-1699   Toll-free: (800) 926-2522
Fax: (505) 246-1686   E-mail: nmcpa@nmcpa.org
Web: www.nmcpa.org

Purpose To provide financial assistance to accounting students at New Mexico universities and colleges.

Eligibility This program is open to full-time students at New Mexico colleges and universities who have completed 12 semester hours in accounting, are currently enrolled in 6 or more accounting hours, have completed 75 hours overall, and have a cumulative GPA of 3.0 or higher. Selection is based on academic achievement, extracurricular activities, career objectives and goals in accounting, and financial need.

Financial data The stipend is $1,000.

Duration 1 year; may be renewed 1 additional year.

Number awarded 3 each year.

Deadline September of each year.

[203]
KATHLEEN M. PEABODY, CPA, MEMORIAL SCHOLARSHIP

Massachusetts Society of Certified Public Accountants
Attn: MSCPA Educational Foundation
105 Chauncy Street, Tenth Floor
Boston, MA 02111
(617) 556-4000   Toll-free: (800) 392-6145
Fax: (617) 556-4126
E-mail: biannoni@MSCPAonline.org
Web: www.cpatrack.com/financial_aid/scholarship.php

Purpose To provide financial assistance to college juniors majoring in accounting at a Massachusetts college or university.

Eligibility This program is open to Massachusetts residents who have completed their sophomore year and are majoring in accounting at a college or university in the state. Applicants must be enrolled in school on a full-time basis. They must demonstrate superior academic standing, financial need, and an intention to seek a career in a public accounting firm.

Financial data The stipend is $1,000.

Duration 1 year.

Additional information This program is sponsored by Wolf & Company, PC.

Number awarded 1 each year.

[204]
KATHRYN BEICH SCHOLARSHIP

Missouri DECA
Attn: Missouri State DECA Advisor
P.O. Box 480
Jefferson City, MO 65102-0480
(573) 751-4367   Fax: (573) 751-4361
E-mail: julie.lyman@dese.mo.gov
Web: www.modeca.org/d_scholarships.htm

Purpose To provide financial assistance to high school seniors who are members of Missouri DECA interested in studying marketing or management in college.

Eligibility This program is open to high school seniors who are members of Missouri DECA enrolled in a marketing education or cooperative occupational education program. Applicants must have been an active member of a DECA chapter that has participated in a state-approved Kathryn Beich fundraising project during the school year. They must be interested in attending an accredited 2- or 4-year postsecondary institution to continue their study of marketing and/or management. Selection is based on leadership record, involvement in DECA and other organizations, career plans, volunteer services, academic record, and letters of recommendation.

Financial data The stipend is $750.

Duration 1 year; nonrenewable.

Number awarded 1 each year.

Deadline February of each year.

[205]
KC AD CLUB FOUNDATION SCHOLARSHIPS

Advertising Club of Kansas City
Attn: Ad Club Foundation
1625 Oak Street, Suite 240
Kansas City, MO 64108
(816) 822-0300   Fax: (816) 822-1840
E-mail: rachel@kcadclub.com
Web: www.kcadclub.com/Foundation.asp

Purpose To provide financial assistance to college students in any state who are interested in preparing for an advertising career in the Kansas City area.

Eligibility This program is open to students entering their junior or senior year of college and majoring in a sequence related to the marketing, advertising, communications, or graphic arts industry. The sponsor does not require that applicants reside or attend school in any specified area, but it does select recipients on the basis of merit and their potential contribution to the advertising industry in the Kansas City area. It does not consider financial need. Selected applicants are invited to Kansas City for an interview.

Financial data The stipend is $750 per semester.

Duration 1 year; junior-year recipients may reapply if they remain in the required field of study, maintain a GPA established by their university, and make satisfactory progress toward a degree.

Additional information Other benefits for recipients include support and counsel of a mentor from the membership of the Advertising Club of Kansas City, membership in the club while in school, invitations to attend all regular program activities of the club at no cost while in school, all mailings of the club, and membership in the American Advertising Federation.

Number awarded 1 or more each year.

Deadline January of each year.

[206]
KEITH PAYNE MEMORIAL SCHOLARSHIP

Professional Independent Insurance Agents of Illinois
Attn: College Scholarship Program
4360 Wabash Avenue
Springfield, IL 62707
(217) 793-6660   Toll-free: (800) 628-6436
Fax: (217) 793-6744   E-mail: admin@piiai.org
Web: www.piiai.org/youngagents/scholarship.htm

Purpose To provide financial assistance to upper-division students from Illinois who are majoring in business and have an interest in insurance.

Eligibility This program is open to residents of Illinois who are full-time juniors or seniors in college. Applicants must be enrolled in a business degree program with an interest in insurance. They must have a letter of recommendation from a current or retired member of the Professional Independent Insurance Agents of Illinois. Along with their application, they must submit an essay (500 words or less) on the contribution the insurance industry provides to society. Financial need is not considered in the selection process.

Financial data The stipend is $1,000, payable in 2 equal installments. Funds are paid directly to the recipient's school.

Duration 1 year.

Number awarded 1 each year.

Deadline June of each year.

[207]
KEMPER SCHOLARS GRANT PROGRAM

James S. Kemper Foundation
One Kemper Drive
Long Grove, IL 60049-0001
(312) 332-3114
Web: www.jskemper.org/kemper_scholar_pgm.htm

Purpose To provide financial assistance and work experience to freshmen at selected colleges and universities who are interested in preparing for a career in business.

Eligibility This program is open to students enrolled as freshmen at 1 of 19 participating colleges and universities. Applicants must be interested in preparing for a career in business and must demonstrate enough "maturity, imagination and intelligence" to learn from the program, which includes participation in a full-time summer work program with Kemper Insurance Companies.

Financial data All scholars receive a stipend of at least $3,000 per year (regardless of financial need). Scholars who demonstrate financial need may receive up to $8,000 per year. During the summer work experience, scholars receive standard compensation.

Duration 3 years, as long as the scholar maintains a GPA of 3.0 or higher each academic term.

Additional information The 19 participating schools are Beloit College (Beloit, Wisconsin), Brigham Young University (Provo, Utah), Drake University (Des Moines, Iowa), Howard University (Washington, D.C.), Illinois State University (Normal, Illinois), Knox College (Galesburg, Illinois), Lake Forest College (Lake Forest, Illinois), LaSalle University (Philadelphia, Penn-

sylvania), Loyola University (Chicago, Illinois), Millikin University (Decatur, Illinois), Northern Illinois University (DeKalb, Illinois), Rochester Institute of Technology (Rochester, New York), University of North Florida (Jacksonville, Florida), University of the Pacific (Stockton, California), University of Wisconsin at Whitewater, Valparaiso University (Valparaiso, Indiana), Washington University (St. Louis, Missouri), Washington and Lee University (Lexington, Virginia), and Wake Forest University (Winston-Salem, North Carolina). Summer assignments are within Kemper companies throughout the United States. For at least 1 of the summers, usually after the junior year, the assignment is at the home office in Long Grove, Illinois.

Number awarded 60 to 70 each year.

Deadline Deadlines vary at each institution.

[208]
KENT MCDANIEL MEMORIAL SCHOLARSHIP

Missouri DECA
Attn: Missouri State DECA Advisor
P.O. Box 480
Jefferson City, MO 65102-0480
(573) 751-4367   Fax: (573) 751-4361
E-mail: julie.lyman@dese.mo.gov
Web: www.modeca.org/d_scholarships.htm

Purpose To provide financial assistance to high school seniors who are members of Missouri DECA and have been involved in marketing and cooperative education.

Eligibility This program is open to high school seniors who are members of Missouri DECA and have been enrolled in a marketing education or cooperative occupational education program. Applicants must be interested in attending an accredited 2- or 4-year postsecondary institution to continue their study of marketing, management, marketing education, or a related program. They must submit an essay on how involvement in DECA and marketing and cooperative education has made a difference in their life. Selection is based on the essay, a letter of recommendation from their DECA advisor, DECA involvement, school and community activities, and volunteer services.

Financial data The stipend is $1,000.

Duration 1 year; nonrenewable.

Number awarded 1 each year.

Deadline February of each year.

[209]
KENTUCKY SOCIETY OF CERTIFIED PUBLIC ACCOUNTANTS COLLEGE SCHOLARSHIPS

Kentucky Society of Certified Public Accountants
Attn: Educational Foundation
1735 Alliant Avenue
Louisville, KY 40299-6326
(502) 266-5272   Toll-free: (800) 292-1754 (within KY)
Fax: (502) 261-9512   E-mail: kycpa@kycpa.org
Web: www.kycpa.org

Purpose To provide financial assistance to students in Kentucky who are interested in majoring in accounting in college.

Eligibility Eligible to apply are students who are currently enrolled as a sophomore or above in a Kentucky college or university. Applicants must have an overall GPA of at least

2.75 and an accounting GPA of at least 3.0. They must have completed the "principles of accounting" course and must be currently enrolled in or have completed intermediate accounting. Along with their application, they must submit a 500-word essay on their career goals, reasons for choosing accounting, and financial need. Selection is based on the essay, scholastic achievement, and leadership qualities. At least 1 scholarship is reserved for a student member of the Kentucky Society of Certified Public Accountants.

Financial data The stipend is $1,000.

Duration 1 year.

Additional information This program was established in 1988. Winners are presented at the society's spring awards banquet.

Number awarded Varies each year.

Deadline January of each year.

[210]
KENTUCKY SOCIETY OF CERTIFIED PUBLIC ACCOUNTANTS SCHOLARSHIPS FOR HIGH SCHOOL SENIORS

Kentucky Society of Certified Public Accountants
Attn: Educational Foundation
1735 Alliant Avenue
Louisville, KY 40299-6326
(502) 266-5272   Toll-free: (800) 292-1754 (within KY)
Fax: (502) 261-9512   E-mail: kycpa@kycpa.org
Web: www.kycpa.org

Purpose To provide financial assistance to high school seniors in Kentucky who are interested in majoring in accounting in college.

Eligibility This program is open to seniors graduating from high schools in Kentucky and planning to attend a college or university in the state to major in accounting. Applicants must have a GPA of 2.75 or higher overall and 3.0 or higher in any accounting classes they may have taken. Candidates are judged by 2 different sets of criteria. For 1 set, selection is based on overall academic record and interest in becoming a certified public accountant; financial need may be considered when judging between equally qualified candidates. For the other set, selection is based on financial need and interest in becoming a certified public accountant; overall academic record may be considered when judging between equally qualified candidates.

Financial data The stipend is $500; funds are sent directly to the recipient's school and must be used to pay for tuition and other educational expenses.

Duration 1 year.

Additional information Recipients must attend school in Kentucky.

Number awarded 10 each year: 5 in each of the sets of judging criteria.

Deadline February of each year.

[211]
KERRI KEITH MEMORIAL SCHOLARSHIP

Alpha Omicron Pi Foundation
Attn: Scholarship Committee
5390 Virginia Way
P.O. Box 395
Brentwood, TN 37024-0395
(615) 370-0920   Fax: (615) 370-4424
E-mail: foundation@alphaomicronpi.org
Web: www.aoiifoundation.org

Purpose To provide financial assistance for college to members of Alpha Omicron Pi, especially those from Georgia majoring in actuarial science or a related field.

Eligibility This program is open to collegiate members of Alpha Omicron Pi who wish to continue their undergraduate education. First preference is given to full-time juniors and seniors at Gamma Sigma chapter who have a GPA of 3.0 or higher, especially those who are majoring in actuarial science or a related field; second preference is given to members in Georgia. Applicants must submit 50-word essays on the following topics: 1) the circumstances that have created their need for this scholarship, and 2) their immediate and long-term life objectives. Selection is based on academic excellence, dedication to serving the community and Alpha Omicron Pi, and financial need.

Financial data A stipend is awarded (amount not specified).

Duration 1 year.

Number awarded 1 each year.

Deadline February of each year.

[212]
KIRBY MCDONALD EDUCATION ENDOWMENT SCHOLARSHIP FUND

Cook Inlet Region, Inc.
Attn: CIRI Foundation
2600 Cordova Street, Suite 206
Anchorage, AK 99503
(907) 263-5582   Toll-free: (800) 764-3382
Fax: (907) 263-5588   E-mail: tcf@ciri.com
Web: www.ciri.com/tcf/designated.html

Purpose To provide financial assistance for undergraduate or graduate studies to Alaska Natives who are original enrollees to Cook Inlet Region, Inc. (CIRI) and their lineal descendants.

Eligibility This program is open to Alaska Native enrollees under the Alaska Native Claims Settlement Act (ANCSA) of 1971 and the lineal descendants of Cook Inlet Region, Inc. There are no Alaska residency requirements or age limitations. Applicants must be accepted or enrolled full time in a 4-year undergraduate or a graduate degree program. Preference is given to students in the culinary arts, business administration, or engineering. They must have a GPA of 2.5 or higher. Selection is based on academic achievement, rigor of course work or degree program, quality of a statement of purpose, student financial contribution, financial need, grade level, previous work performance, education and community activities, letters of recommendation, seriousness of purpose, and practicality of educational and professional goals.

Financial data The stipend is $9,000 per year, $7,000 per year, or $2,000 per semester, depending on GPA.

Duration 1 year (2 semesters).

Additional information This program was established in 1991. Recipients must attend school on a full-time basis.

Deadline May of each year.

[213]
KITTREDGE CODDINGTON MEMORIAL SCHOLARSHIP

Vermont Student Assistance Corporation
Champlain Mill
Attn: Scholarship Programs
P.O. Box 2000
Winooski, VT 05404-2601
(802) 654-3798   Toll-free: (800) 642-3177
Fax: (802) 654-3765   TDD: (802) 654-3766
TDD: (800) 281-3341 (within VT) E-mail: info@vsac.org
Web: www.vsac.org

Purpose To provide financial assistance to high school seniors in Vermont who are interested in working on a degree in business.

Eligibility This scholarship is available to the residents of Vermont who are seniors in high school. Applicants must be planning to enroll in a 2-year or 4-year postsecondary degree program in business or a related field. Males and females compete separately. Selection is based on required essays and letters of recommendation.

Financial data The stipend is $500.

Duration 1 year; nonrenewable.

Additional information This program was established by the Vermont Chamber of Commerce in 1989.

Number awarded 2 each year: 1 is set aside for a female and 1 for a male.

Deadline April of each year.

[214]
KLF SCHOLARSHIP

Kansas Livestock Association
Attn: Kansas Livestock Foundation
6031 S.W. 37th Street
Topeka, KS 66614-5129
(785) 273-5115   Fax: (785) 273-3399
E-mail: kla@kla.org
Web: www.kla.org/scholarapp.htm

Purpose To provide financial assistance to Kansas residents who are or will be majoring in a field related to agriculture.

Eligibility Eligible to apply for this program are Kansas residents who are entering or returning to a junior or senior college in the state. Applicants must be majoring or planning to major in a field related to agriculture (e.g., agricultural economics, agronomy, animal science). Selection is based on academic achievement (20 points), personal livestock enterprises (25 points), 4H/FFA/KJLA activities and leadership (30 points), school activities and honors (30 points), other activities and leadership (25 points), work experience (25 points), significant honors or recognition (25 points), and career plans (20 points). Preference is given to students planning to be involved full time in production agriculture after graduation.

Financial data The stipend is $1,000. Funds are paid directly to the recipient in 2 equal installments at the beginning of each semester, upon proof of enrollment.

Duration 1 year.

Additional information This program is sponsored by the Kansas Livestock Foundation (KLF).

Number awarded 1 each year.

Deadline April of each year.

[215]
KNIGHT RIDDER HBCU SCHOLARSHIPS

Knight Ridder, Inc.
Attn: Office of Diversity
50 West San Fernando Street, Suite 1200
San Jose, CA 95113
(408) 938-7734   Fax: (408) 938-7755
Web: www.kri.com/working/interns.html

Purpose To provide financial assistance and work experience to students at selected Historically Black Colleges and Universities (HBCUs) who are studying advertising, business, or journalism.

Eligibility This program is open to students at selected HBCUs who are entering their junior year. Applicants must be majoring in advertising, business, or journalism.

Financial data The stipend is $2,500 per year. Recipients also work as an intern at a Knight Ridder newspaper during the summer after their junior year and receive a salary according to the newspaper's normal scale.

Duration 1 year; may be renewed for 1 additional year, if the recipient maintains a GPA of 3.0 or higher.

Additional information The participating HBCUs are Howard University, Florida A&M University, Morehouse College, and Spelman College. Further information is available from the placement office at those institutions.

Number awarded Varies each year.

[216]
KSCPA COLLEGE SCHOLARSHIPS

Kansas Society of Certified Public Accountants
Attn: Educational Foundation
1080 S.W. Wanamaker Road, Suite 200
P.O. Box 4291
Topeka, KS 66604-0291
(785) 272-4366   Toll-free: (800) 222-0452 (within KS)
Fax: (785) 262-4468   E-mail: kscpa@kscpa.org
Web: www.kscpa.org/scholarship.cfm

Purpose To provide financial assistance to college students in Kansas who are majoring in accounting.

Eligibility This program is open to upper-division students at each of the 6 regent institutions in Kansas and at Washburn University. Applicants must be studying accounting.

Financial data The stipend is $1,250.

Duration 1 year.

Number awarded 7 each year: 1 at each of the participating institutions.

Deadline June of each year.

[217]
KSCPA HIGH SCHOOL SCHOLARSHIPS

Kansas Society of Certified Public Accountants
Attn: Educational Foundation
1080 S.W. Wanamaker Road, Suite 200
P.O. Box 4291
Topeka, KS 66604-0291
(785) 272-4366   Toll-free: (800) 222-0452 (within KS)
Fax: (785) 262-4468   E-mail: kscpa@kscpa.org
Web: www.kscpa.org/scholarship.cfm

Purpose To provide financial assistance for college to high school seniors in Kansas who plan to major in accounting.

Eligibility This program is open to high school seniors who will be entering a Kansas college or university the following academic year. Applicants must be planning to study accounting. Selection is based on ACT or SAT scores.

Financial data Stipends are $1,000, $600, $500, $400, or $200.

Duration 1 year.

Number awarded 9 each year: 1 each at $1,000, $600, $500, and $400, plus 5 at $200.

Deadline Test scores must be submitted by March of each year; applications are due in April.

[218]
KSCPA INDEPENDENT COLLEGE SCHOLARSHIP

Kansas Society of Certified Public Accountants
Attn: Educational Foundation
1080 S.W. Wanamaker Road, Suite 200
P.O. Box 4291
Topeka, KS 66604-0291
(785) 272-4366   Toll-free: (800) 222-0452 (within KS)
Fax: (785) 262-4468   E-mail: kscpa@kscpa.org
Web: www.kscpa.org/scholarship.cfm

Purpose To provide financial assistance to students in Kansas who are majoring in accounting at independent colleges.

Eligibility This program is open to juniors who are majoring in accounting at independent colleges in Kansas. Each college may nominate 1 candidate.

Financial data The stipend is $1,250.

Duration 1 year.

Number awarded 1 each year.

Deadline April of each year.

[219]
LAGRANT FOUNDATION SCHOLARSHIPS

LAGRANT FOUNDATION
555 South Flower Street, Suite 700
Los Angeles, CA 90071-2423
(323) 469-8680   Fax: (323) 469-8683
Web: www.lagrantfoundation.org

Purpose To provide financial assistance to minority high school seniors or college students who are interested in majoring in advertising, public relations, or marketing.

Eligibility This program is open to African Americans, Asian Pacific Americans, Hispanics, or Native Americans who are full-time students at a 4-year accredited institution or high school seniors planning to attend a 4-year accredited institu-
tion on a full-time basis. Applicants must have a GPA of 2.5 or higher and be majoring or planning to major in advertising, marketing, or public relations. They must submit 1) a 1- to 2-page essay outlining their career goals; what steps they will take to increase ethnic representation in the fields of advertising, marketing, and public relations; and the role of an advertising, marketing, or public relations practitioner; 2) a paragraph explaining how they are financing or planning to finance their education and why they need financial assistance; 3) a paragraph explaining the high school, college, and/or community activities in which they are involved; 4) a brief paragraph describing any honors and awards they have received; 5) if they are currently employed, a paragraph indicating the hours worked each week, responsibilities, and if the job will be kept while attending school; 6) a resume; and 7) an official transcript. Applicants majoring in public relations must write an essay on the importance and relevance of the Arthur W. Page Society Prniciples.

Financial data The stipend is $5,000 per year.

Duration 1 year.

Number awarded 10 each year.

Deadline March of each year.

[220]
LANDS' END 21 CLUB SCHOLARSHIP PROGRAM

Wisconsin Foundation for Independent Colleges, Inc.
735 North Water Street, Suite 800
Milwaukee, WI 53202-4100
(414) 273-5980   Fax: (414) 273-5995
E-mail: info@wficweb.org
Web: www.wficweb.org/documents/schinfo.htm

Purpose To provide financial assistance to students from Wisconsin who are majoring in selected business-related fields at private colleges in the state.

Eligibility This program is open to students enrolled full time at the 20 independent colleges or universities in Wisconsin and majoring in business, economics, communications, or computer science. Applicants must have earned a GPA of 3.0 or higher. Preference is given to residents of the following Wisconsin counties: Adams, Columbia, Dane, Grant, Iowa, Juneau, Lafayette, Marathon, Portage, Richland, Sauk, Shawano, Waushara, and Wood.

Financial data The stipend is $1,000.

Duration 1 year.

Additional information The participating schools are Alverno College, Beloit College, Cardinal Stritch University, Carroll College, Carthage College, Concordia University of Wisconsin, Edgewood College, Lakeland College, Lawrence University, Marian College, Marquette University, Milwaukee Institute of Art & Design, Milwaukee School of Engineering, Mount Mary College, Northland College, Ripon College, St. Norbert College, Silver Lake College, Viterbo University, and Wisconsin Lutheran College.

Number awarded 20 each year: 1 at each of the participating colleges and universities.

Deadline March of each year.

[221]
LAWRENCE "LARRY" FRAZIER MEMORIAL SCHOLARSHIP

Lincoln Community Foundation
215 Centennial Mall South, Suite 200
Lincoln, NE 68508
(402) 474-2345   Fax: (402) 476-8532
E-mail: lcf@lcf.org
Web: www.lcf.org

Purpose To provide financial assistance to residents of Nebraska who are interested in studying designated fields in college.

Eligibility This program is open to residents of Nebraska who are graduating or have graduated from a high school in the state. Preference is given to applicants who intend to prepare for a career in the field of aviation, insurance, or law. They must attend a 2- or 4-year college or university in Nebraska as a full-time student. Preference is also given to applicants who have experience in debate and who participated in Boy Scouts or Girl Scouts as youth. Selection is based on academic achievement in high school, potential to excel in college, and financial need.

Financial data A stipend is awarded (amount not specified).

Duration 1 year.

Additional information This program is supported by the Nebraska Chapter of the Charter Property Casualty Underwriters Society, c/o Mark Clymer, Allied Insurance, P.O. Box 80758, Lincoln, NE 68501.

Number awarded 1 each year.

Deadline April of each year.

[222]
LCPA EDUCATIONAL FOUNDATION SCHOLARSHIPS

Society of Louisiana Certified Public Accountants
Attn: LCPA Education Foundation
2400 Veterans Boulevard, Suite 500
Kenner, LA 70062-4739
(504) 464-1040   Toll-free: (800) 288-5272
Fax: (504) 469-7930
Web: www.lcpa.org/LCPAScholarships.html

Purpose To provide financial assistance to currently-enrolled college students in Louisiana who are interested in becoming certified public accountants.

Eligibility This program is open to Louisiana residents who are currently enrolled full time in an accounting program at a 4-year college or university in Louisiana. Applicants must have completed at least 4 semesters by the fall of the academic year in which the application is filed and have a GPA of 2.5 or higher. Along with their application, they must submit a 2-page essay on their perception of the CPA's role on the job and in the community, including how they plan to contribute to the profession and to the community.

Financial data Stipends range from $500 to $1,000.

Duration 1 year.

Additional information Individual chapters of the society also offer scholarships. The Baton Rouge Chapter awards $1,000 scholarships to students at in-town colleges and universities. Central Louisiana Chapter awards approximately $500 to students at Louisiana College, Northwestern State University, and Louisiana State University at Alexandria. Lafayette Chapter gives $1,000 to a student at the University of Southwestern Louisiana. Lake Charles Chapter contributes $1,000 to student scholarships at McNeese State. Northeast Chapter grants scholarships between $250 and $1,000 to students at Northeastern Louisiana University, Louisiana Tech, and Grambling State. Shreveport Chapter offers 2 or 3 scholarships (approximately $1,500) to local students. South Central Chapter awards a $250 scholarship to a student at Nicholls State University.

Number awarded Varies each year; recently, 13 of these scholarships were awarded: 1 at $1,000, 2 at $800, and 10 at $500.

[223]
LEADERSHIP FOUNDATION UNDERGRADUATE SCHOLARSHIPS

Delta Sigma Pi
Attn: Leadership Foundation
330 South Campus Avenue
P.O. Box 230
Oxford, OH 45056-0230
(513) 523-1907, ext. 230   Fax: (513) 523-7292
E-mail: foundation@dspnet.org
Web: www.dspnet.org

Purpose To provide financial assistance for college to undergraduate brothers of Delta Sigma Pi, a business education honor society.

Eligibility This program is open to currently-enrolled undergraduate students who are majoring in business and are members in good standing of the fraternity. Applicants must have at least 1 full semester or quarter of undergraduate studies remaining. Selection is based on academic achievement, financial need, fraternal service, letters of recommendation, service activities, and overall presentation of the required materials.

Financial data The stipend is either $1,250 or $500.

Duration 1 year; recipients may reapply.

Number awarded 10 each year: 2 at $1,250 and 8 at $500.

Deadline June of each year.

[224]
LEAP SCHOLARSHIPS

Missouri Society of Certified Public Accountants
Attn: LEAP Program
275 North Lindbergh Boulevard, Suite 10
P.O. Box 419042
St. Louis, MO 63141-9042
(314) 997-7966   Toll-free: (800) 264-7966 (within MO)
Fax: (314) 997-2592   E-mail: scholarships@mocpa.org
Web: www.mocpa.org/leap/index.html

Purpose To provide financial assistance to residents of Missouri who are majoring or planning to major in accounting at colleges and universities in the state.

Eligibility This program is open to residents of Missouri who are high school seniors or college students majoring or planning to major in accounting as a full-time student at a college or university in the state. Applicants must submit a 500-word essay on what inspired them to become a CPA. Selection is based on the essay, academic achievement, and demonstrated leadership potential. Financial need is not considered.

Financial data The stipend is $1,000 per year.

Duration 1 year.

Additional information These scholarships are offered through the sponsor's Lead and Enhance the Accounting Profession (LEAP) program, established in 2001.

Number awarded 20 each year: 10 for high school seniors and 10 for current college students.

Deadline January of each year.

[225]
LEE ENTERPRISES COLLEGE-TO-WORK SCHOLARSHIP

Wisconsin Foundation for Independent Colleges, Inc.
735 North Water Street, Suite 800
Milwaukee, WI 53202-4100
(414) 273-5980   Fax: (414) 273-5995
E-mail: info@wficweb.org
Web: www.wficweb.org/documents/coll_work.htm

Purpose To provide financial assistance and work experience to minority students majoring in fields related to business or news at private colleges in Wisconsin.

Eligibility This program is open to full-time minority sophomores, juniors, and seniors at the 20 independent colleges and universities in Wisconsin. Applicants may be majoring in any liberal arts field, but they must be preparing for a career in accounting, information technology, computers, graphic design, sales, marketing, news reporting, or communications. They must have a GPA of 3.0 or higher and be interested in an internship at 1 of the 3 Lee newspapers in the state: the *Wisconsin State Journal,* the *La Crosse Tribune,* or the *Racine Journal Times.* Along with their application, they must submit a 1-page autobiography, transcripts, a list of campus involvement and academic honors, a resume including 3 references, and 2 letters of recommendation.

Financial data The stipends are $3,500 for the scholarship and $1,500 for the internship.

Duration 1 year for the scholarship; 10 weeks for the internship.

Additional information The participating schools are Alverno College, Beloit College, Cardinal Stritch University, Carroll College, Carthage College, Concordia University of Wisconsin, Edgewood College, Lakeland College, Lawrence University, Marian College, Marquette University, Milwaukee Institute of Art & Design, Milwaukee School of Engineering, Mount Mary College, Northland College, Ripon College, St. Norbert College, Silver Lake College, Viterbo University, and Wisconsin Lutheran College. This program is sponsored by Lee Enterprises/Madison Newspapers, Inc.

Number awarded 3 each year.

Deadline January of each year.

[226]
LEGACY SCHOLARSHIPS

Legacy, Inc.
P.O. Box 3813
Montgomery, AL 36109
(334) 270-5921   Toll-free: (800) 240-5115 (within AL)
Fax: (334) 270-5527
Web: www.legacyenved.org/fund/fund_college.htm

Purpose To provide financial assistance to upper-division and graduate students in Alabama who are interested in preparing for an environmentally-related career.

Eligibility Open to upper-division (juniors and seniors) and graduate students who reside in Alabama, are enrolled in a college or university in the state, and are planning to prepare for an environmentally-related career. Given the interdisciplinary nature of environmental education, it is not a requirement that all applicants have an environmental title attached to their major; some examples of career fields that have been funded in the past include: business, education, government, law, medicine, public relations, and geography. Finalists are interviewed.

Financial data Undergraduates receive up to $1,500; graduate students receive up to $2,000.

Duration 1 year,

Additional information Legacy's scholarship funds are made available, in part, from proceeds derived from the sale of Alabama's "Protect Our Environment" license tag.

Number awarded 20 each year: 10 to undergraduates, 4 to master's degree students, and 6 to doctoral students.

Deadline May of each year.

[227]
LEONARD R. BRICE UNDERGRADUATE LEADERSHIP AWARD

Society for Human Resource Management
Attn: Student Program Manager
1800 Duke Street
Alexandria, VA 22314-3499
(703) 535-6084   Toll-free: (800) 283-SHRM
Fax: (703) 739-0399   TDD: (703) 548-6999
E-mail: SHRMStudent@shrm.org
Web: www.shrm.org/students/ags_published

Purpose To recognize, financially, the leadership skills of undergraduate student members of the Society for Human Resource Management (SHRM).

Eligibility This program is open to full-time undergraduate students who have completed their sophomore year, have maintained a GPA of 2.0 or higher, and are national student members of the society. Selection is based on leadership ability as demonstrated in an SHRM student chapter, commitment to the human resources profession, scholastic average and standing, and additional leadership activities (such as service to a campus organization and/or a community or charitable organization).

Financial data The award includes a $1,000 honorarium, a commemorative plaque, and complimentary registration to the society's annual conference and exposition.

Duration The award is offered annually.

Number awarded 1 each year.

Deadline February of each year.

[228]
LESTER B. KESTERSON SCHOLARSHIP

Missouri DECA
Attn: Missouri State DECA Advisor
P.O. Box 480
Jefferson City, MO 65102-0480
(573) 751-4367   Fax: (573) 751-4361
E-mail: julie.lyman@dese.mo.gov
Web: www.modeca.org/d_scholarships.htm

Purpose To provide financial assistance to high school seniors who are members of Missouri DECA interested in studying marketing or management in college.

Eligibility This program is open to high school seniors who are members of Missouri DECA enrolled in a marketing education or cooperative occupational education program. Applicants must be interested in attending an accredited 2- or 4-year postsecondary institution to continue their study of marketing and/or management. They must have attended the state Career Development Conference as a competitive events participant. Selection is based on leadership record, involvement in DECA and other organizations, career plans, volunteer services, academic record, and letters of recommendation.

Financial data The stipend is $1,000.

Duration 1 year; nonrenewable.

Number awarded Up to 3 each year.

Deadline February of each year.

[229]
LIBERTY MUTUAL SCHOLARSHIPS

United Negro College Fund
Attn: Scholarships and Grants Department
8260 Willow Oaks Corporate Drive
P.O. Box 10444
Fairfax, VA 22031-8044
(703) 205-3466   Toll-free: (800) 331-2244
Fax: (703) 205-3574
Web: www.uncf.org/scholarships/index.asp

Purpose To provide financial assistance to juniors from selected states who are majoring in fields related to business at colleges and universities that are members of the United Negro College Fund (UNCF).

Eligibility This program is open to first-semester juniors enrolled full time at UNCF-member institutions and majoring in actuarial science, business, finance, or other business-related fields. Applicants must be residents of California, Florida, Georgia, Massachusetts, New Hampshire, New Jersey, New York, Pennsylvania, Texas, or Wisconsin. They must have a GPA of 3.4 or higher and be able to demonstrate financial need. Along with their application, they must submit an essay that explains why they have chosen their current course of study, which of the courses that they have taken have been the most compelling and why, an experience in which they exceeded their own expectations, other experiences (outside of course work and employment experience) they wish to share, how they envision using their skills and course work at Liberty Mutual, and what this scholarship would mean to them both academically and financially.

Financial data The stipend is $5,000.

Duration 1 year; renewable until graduation.

Additional information This program is supported by Liberty Mutual.

Number awarded 3 each year.

Deadline December of each year.

[230]
LOTUS YEE CHEIGH SCHOLARSHIP

American Society of Women Accountants-Honolulu
    Chapter
c/o Grace Morioka
1600 Kapiolani Boulevard, Suite 1010
Honolulu, HI 96814
(808) 949-3522   Fax: (808) 949-4522
Web: community.hei.com/aswa/scholarship.html

Purpose To provide financial assistance to accounting students from Hawaii.

Eligibility This program is open to part- and full-time students from Hawaii working on a bachelor's degree in accounting. Applicants must have completed at least 60 semester hours with a GPA of 2.7 or higher. They are not required to be a member of the American Society of Women Accountants. Selection is based on a statement of career goals, communication skills, GPA, and financial need and circumstances.

Financial data The stipend is $1,000.

Duration 1 year.

Number awarded 1 each year.

Deadline March of each year.

[231]
LOUIS AND FANNIE SAGER MEMORIAL SCHOLARSHIP

National Society of Accountants
Attn: NSA Scholarship Foundation
1010 North Fairfax Street
Alexandria, VA 22314-1574
(703) 549-6400, ext. 1312
Toll-free: (800) 966-6679, ext. 1312
Fax: (703) 549-2512   E-mail: snoell@nsacct.org
Web: www.nsacct.org

Purpose To provide financial assistance to undergraduate students in accounting from Virginia.

Eligibility This program is open to graduates of Virginia public high schools who are enrolled as an undergraduate at a Virginia college or university. Applicants must be majoring in accounting and have a GPA of 3.0 or higher. They must submit a letter of intent outlining their reasons for seeking the award, their intended career objective, and how this scholarship award would be used to accomplish that objective. Selection is based on academic attainment, demonstrated leadership ability, and financial need.

Financial data The stipend ranges from $500 to $1,000 per year.

Duration 1 year.

Number awarded 1 each year.

Deadline March of each year.

[232]
LOUISE MORITZ MOLITORIS LEADERSHIP AWARD

Women's Transportation Seminar
Attn: National Headquarters
1666 K Street, N.W., Suite 1100
Washington, DC 20006
(202) 496-4340   Fax: (202) 496-4349
E-mail: wts@wtsnational.org
Web: www.wtsnational.org

Purpose To provide financial assistance to undergraduate women interested in a career in transportation.

Eligibility This program is open to women who are working on an undergraduate degree in transportation or a transportation-related field (e.g., transportation engineering, planning, finance, or logistics). Applicants must have at least a 3.0 GPA and be interested in a career in transportation. They must submit a 500-word statement about their career goals after graduation and why they think they should receive the scholarship award; their statement should specifically address the issue of leadership. Applications must be submitted first to a local chapter; the chapters forward selected applications for consideration on the national level. Minority candidates are encouraged to apply. Selection is based on transportation involvement and goals, job skills, academic record, and leadership potential; financial need is not considered.

Financial data The stipend is $3,000.

Duration 1 year.

Number awarded 1 each year.

Deadline Applications must be submitted by November to a local WTS chapter.

[233]
MACDONALD SCHOLARSHIP

Maine Society of CPAs
Attn: Executive Director
153 U.S. Route 1, Suite 8
Scarborough, ME 04074-9053
(207) 883-6090   Toll-free: (800) 660-2721 (within ME)
Fax: (207) 883-6211   E-mail: wwhiting@mecpa.org
Web: www.mecpa.org

Purpose To provide financial assistance to students in Maine majoring in accounting.

Eligibility This program is open to college students majoring in accounting in Maine. Applicants must have a GPA of 3.0 or higher, be able to demonstrate writing skills, and have participated in community activities. Selection is based on academic achievement, writing skills, extracurricular activities, work experience, career goals, and financial need.

Financial data The stipend is $1,000.

Duration 1 year.

Number awarded 1 each year.

[234]
MAINE STATE CHAMBER OF COMMERCE SCHOLARSHIPS

Maine Education Services
Attn: MES Foundation
One City Center, 11th Floor
Portland, ME 04101
(207) 791-3600   Toll-free: (800) 922-6352
Fax: (207) 791-3616   E-mail: info@mesfoundation.com
Web: www.mesfoundation.com

Purpose To provide financial assistance for a college-level technical, education, or business program to residents of Maine.

Eligibility This program is open to residents of Maine who are 1) high school seniors planning to work on a technical associate degree at a 2-year college; 2) high school seniors planning to work on a business-related bachelor's degree at a 4-year college or university; and 3) adult learners planning to attend a 2-year college to work on a degree in a business- or education-related field (those applicants must meet federal financial aid criteria for independent student status, i.e., be 24 years of age or older, or be married, or have legal dependents other than a spouse, or be an orphan or ward of the court, or be a veteran of the U.S. armed forces). Preference is given to applicants planning to attend college in Maine. Selection is based on academic achievement, employment and community activities, a letter of recommendation from a high school or community official, an essay describing challenges that businesses face in Maine, and financial need.

Financial data The stipend is $1,500.

Duration 1 year.

Number awarded 3 each year: 1 to a high school senior pursuing a technical degree at a 2-year college, 1 to a high school senior pursuing a business degree at a 4-year institution, and 1 to an adult learner working on a 2-year degree in business or education.

Deadline April of each year.

[235]
MALCOLM BALDRIGE SCHOLARSHIPS

Connecticut Community Foundation
81 West Main Street, Fourth Floor
Waterbury, CT 06702-1216
(203) 753-1315   Fax: (203) 756-3054
E-mail: info@conncf.org
Web: www.conncf.org

Purpose To provide financial assistance for college to residents of Connecticut interested in a career in foreign trade or manufacturing.

Eligibility This program is open to residents of Connecticut who are attending or entering their freshmen year at a college or university in the state. Applicants must be interested in majoring in international business or manufacturing. U.S. citizenship is required. Selection is based on academic achievement, financial need, and (for students studying international business) accomplishment in foreign language study.

Financial data Stipends range from $1,000 to $4,000 per year.

Duration 1 year; renewable.

Number awarded 1 to 3 each year.

Deadline February of each year.

[236]
MALT-O-MEAL COMPANY SCHOLARSHIP
National FFA Organization
Attn: Scholarship Office
6060 FFA Drive
P.O. Box 68960
Indianapolis, IN 46268-0960
(317) 802-4321   Fax: (317) 802-5321
E-mail: scholarships@ffa.org
Web: www.ffa.org

Purpose To provide financial assistance to FFA members from Minnesota interested in studying food-related fields at a college or university in the state.

Eligibility This program is open to members who are graduating high school seniors planning to enroll full time in college. Applicants must be residents of Minnesota interested in working on a 2- or 4-year degree in agriculture, food science, food technology, or business at a college or university in the state. Selection is based on academic achievement (10 points for GPA, 10 points for SAT or ACT score, 10 points for class rank), leadership in FFA activities (30 points), leadership in community activities (10 points), and participation in the Supervised Agricultural Experience (SAE) program (30 points). U.S. citizenship is required.

Financial data The stipend is $1,000 per year. Funds are paid directly to the recipient.

Duration 1 year; nonrenewable.

Additional information Funding for this scholarship is provided by Malt-O-Meal Company.

Number awarded 2 each year.

Deadline February of each year.

[237]
MARINE CORPS STAFF NONCOMMISSIONED OFFICERS DEGREE COMPLETION PROGRAM
U.S. Marine Corps
Manpower and Reserve Affairs (MMEA-85)
3280 Russell Road
Quantico, VA 22134-5103
(703) 784-9264   Fax: (703) 784-9843
Web: www.usmc.mil

Purpose To allow selected noncommissioned Marine Corps officers to earn a bachelor's degree in selected field by pursuing full-time college study while continuing to receive their regular pay and allowances.

Eligibility Eligible to participate in this program are regular active-duty Marines, especially in the grades of staff sergeant and gunnery sergeant. Applicants must have completed at least 2 years of postsecondary study and have been accepted by an accredited degree-granting college or university in a program offered to all matriculating students; enrollment in a multiple major program designed for adults returning to school does not qualify. The program recently was limited to the following majors: accounting, business administration with an emphasis on accounting or financial management, education, environmental safety, environmental health management, hazardous material and waste control, music, occupational safety, psychology, safety education, safety management, and waste management.

Financial data Noncommissioned officers selected to participate in this program receive their regular Marine Corps pay while attending college or university on a full-time basis. Tuition, matriculation fees, and other expenses (such as books) must be paid by the recipient through personal funds, in-service Montgomery GI Bill benefits, student loans, or other non-Marine Corps means.

Duration Up to the equivalent of 2 academic years.

Additional information Applicants must agree to extend/reenlist for a period of 4 years beyond completion of this program.

Number awarded Varies each year; recently, 11 Marines were selected to participate in this program.

Deadline April of each year.

[238]
MARION MACCARRELL SCOTT SCHOLARSHIP
Hawai'i Community Foundation
Attn: Scholarship Department
1164 Bishop Street, Suite 800
Honolulu, HI 96813
(808) 537-6333   Toll-free: (888) 731-3863
Fax: (808) 521-6286
E-mail: scholarships@hcf-hawaii.org
Web: www.hawaiicommunityfoundation.org

Purpose To provide financial assistance to residents of Hawaii for undergraduate or graduate studies in fields related to achieving world cooperation and international understanding.

Eligibility This program is open to graduates of public high schools in Hawaii. They must plan to attend school as full-time students (on the undergraduate or graduate level) on the mainland, majoring in history, government, political science, anthropology, economics, geography, international relations, law, psychology, philosophy, or sociology. They must be residents of the state of Hawaii, able to demonstrate financial need, interested in attending an accredited 2- or 4- year college or university, and able to demonstrate academic achievement (GPA of 2.8 or higher). Along with their application, they must submit an essay on their commitment to world peace that includes their learning experiences (courses, clubs, community activities, or travel) related to achieving world peace and international understanding and explaining how their experiences have enhanced their ability to achieve those goals.

Financial data The amounts of the awards depend on the availability of funds and the need of the recipient; recently, stipends averaged $2,097.

Duration 1 year.

Number awarded Varies each year; recently, 233 of these scholarships were awarded.

Deadline February of each year.

[239]
MARK MILLER AWARD

National Association of Black Accountants
Attn: Director, Center for Advancement of Minority
    Accountants
7249-A Hanover Parkway
Greenbelt, MD 20770
(301) 474-NABA, ext. 114   Fax: (301) 474-3114
E-mail: cquinn@nabainc.org
Web: www.nabainc.org

Purpose To provide financial assistance to student members of the National Association of Black Accountants (NABA) who are working on an undergraduate or graduate degree in a field related to accounting.

Eligibility This program is open to NABA members who are members of ethnic minority groups enrolled full time as 1) an undergraduate freshman, sophomore, junior, or first-semester senior majoring in accounting, business, or finance; or 2) a graduate student working on a master's degree in accounting. Applicants must have a GPA of 2.0 or higher in their major and 2.5 or higher overall. Selection is based on grades, financial need, and a 500-word autobiography that discusses career objectives, leadership abilities, community activities, and involvement in NABA.

Financial data The stipend is $1,000 per year.

Duration 1 year.

Number awarded 1 each year.

Deadline December of each year.

[240]
MARRIOTT INTERNATIONAL SCHOLARSHIPS

DECA
1908 Association Drive
Reston, VA 20191-1594
(703) 860-5000   Fax: (703) 860-4013
E-mail: decainc@aol.com
Web: www.deca.org/scholarships/index.html

Purpose To provide financial assistance for college to DECA members interested in the hospitality industry.

Eligibility This program is open to DECA members who are interested in working full time on a 2-year or 4-year degree in marketing, business, or marketing education. Applicants must be able to demonstrate evidence of DECA activities, academic achievement, leadership ability, and interest or experience in the hospitality industry. Selection is based on merit, not financial need.

Financial data The stipend is $1,000.

Duration 1 year.

Additional information This program is sponsored by Marriott International, Inc.

Number awarded Up to 6 each year.

Deadline February of each year.

[241]
MARY C. RAWLINS SCHOLARSHIP

Connecticut Association of Affirmative Action
    Professionals
P.O. Box 260412
Hartford, CT 06126
(860) 270-8025

Purpose To provide financial assistance to Connecticut residents who are attending a community college in the state and planning on a career in human resources management or a related field.

Eligibility This program is open to Connecticut residents attending a community college in the state. Applicants must be interested in preparing for a career in human resources management, criminal justice, business law, or human services. Applicants must have a GPA of 2.5 or higher, have completed at least 12 credit hours, and be able to document financial need. As part of the application process, students must submit a personal statement, 2 letters of recommendation, a transcript, proof of enrollment, and an essay.

Financial data Stipends range from $500 to $1,000. Funds are sent directly to the recipient's institution.

Duration 1 year; nonrenewable.

Number awarded 1 to 2 each year.

Deadline May of each year.

[242]
MARY CRAIG SCHOLARSHIP FUND

American Society of Women Accountants-Billings Big
    Sky Chapter
820 Division Street
Billings, MT 59101
Web: www.imt.net/~aswa

Purpose To provide financial assistance to students working on a bachelor's or master's degree in accounting at a college or university in Montana.

Eligibility This program is open to students working on a bachelor's or master's degree in accounting at an accredited Montana college or university. Applicants must have completed at least 60 semester hours. Selection is based on career goals, communication skills, GPA, personal circumstances, and financial need. Membership in the American Society of Women Accountants is not required.

Financial data The stipend is $1,500.

Duration 1 year.

Additional information Information is also available from Jane Crowder, (406) 248-2990, E-mail: jane_bowl@yahoo.com.

Number awarded 1 each year.

Deadline March of each year.

[243]
MARY M. FRAIJO SCHOLARSHIPS

American Society of Women Accountants-Inland
  Northwest Chapter
Attn: Leslie Miller
P.O. Box 3202
Spokane, WA 99220-3202
(509) 444-6832   E-mail: editor@aswa4.org
Web: www.aswa4.org/appform.htm

Purpose To provide financial assistance to women from the Inland Northwest area (Washington and Idaho) who are interested in working on an undergraduate or graduate degree in accounting.

Eligibility This program is open to women whose primary residence is Washington or Idaho. Applicants must be either 1) part-time or full-time students working on a bachelor's or master's degree in accounting who have completed a minimum of 60 semester hours with a declared accounting major; or 2) students enrolled in a formal 2-year accounting program at a community college, junior college, or accredited trade school who have completed the first year of the accounting program. Membership in the American Society of Women Accountants is not required. Selection is based on a statement of career goals, communication skills, financial needs and circumstances, GPA, and personal circumstances.

Financial data The amount of the award depends on the availability of funds.

Duration 1 year; may reapply.

Number awarded 3 or 4 each year.

Deadline March of each year.

[244]
MARYLAND ASSOCIATION OF CERTIFIED PUBLIC ACCOUNTANTS SCHOLARSHIP PROGRAM

Maryland Association of Certified Public Accountants
Attn: MACPA Educational Foundation
901 Dulaney Valley Road, Suite 710
Towson, MD 21204-2683
(410) 296-6250   Toll-free: (800) 782-2036
Fax: (410) 296-8713   E-mail: info@macpa.org
Web: www.macpa.org

Purpose To provide financial assistance to residents of Maryland working on an undergraduate or graduate degree in accounting.

Eligibility This program is open to Maryland residents attending a college or university in the state and taking enough undergraduate or graduate courses to qualify as a full-time student at their school. Applicants must have completed at least 60 total credit hours at the time of the award, including at least 6 hours in accounting courses. They must have a GPA of 3.0 or higher and be able to demonstrate financial need. U.S. citizenship is required.

Financial data Stipends are at least $1,000. The exact amount of the award depends upon the recipient's financial need.

Duration 1 year; may be renewed until completion of the 150-hour requirement and eligibility for sitting for the C.P.A. examination in Maryland. Renewal requires continued full-time enrollment and a GPA of 3.0 or higher.

Number awarded Several each year.

Deadline April of each year.

[245]
MARYLAND LEGION AUXILIARY CHILDREN AND YOUTH FUND SCHOLARSHIP

American Legion Auxiliary
Attn: Department of Maryland
1589 Sulphur Spring Road, Suite 105
Baltimore, MD 21227
(410) 242-9519   Fax: (410) 242-9553
E-mail: anna@alamd.org

Purpose To provide financial assistance for college to the daughters of veterans who are Maryland residents and wish to study arts, sciences, business, public administration, education, or a medical field.

Eligibility Eligible for this scholarship are Maryland senior high girls with veteran parents who wish to study arts, sciences, business, public administration, education, or a medical field other than nursing at a college or university in Maryland. Preference is given to children of members of the American Legion or American Legion Auxiliary. Selection is based on character (30%), Americanism (20%), leadership (10%), scholarship (20%), and financial need (20%).

Financial data The stipend is $2,000.

Duration 1 year; may be renewed up to 3 additional years.

Number awarded 1 each year.

Deadline April of each year.

[246]
MBA SCHOLARSHIP PROGRAM

Montana Broadcasters Association
HC 70 Box 98
Bonner, MT 59823
(406) 244-4622   Fax: (406) 244-5518
E-mail: mba@mtbroadcasters.org
Web: www.mtbroadcasters.org/scholarships.phtml

Purpose To provide financial assistance to college students in Montana who are preparing for a career in the broadcasting industry.

Eligibility This program consists of the following scholarships: 1) the Joe Durso Memorial Scholarship for a student at the University of Montana at Missoula who is entering the senior year with a major in radio-television or broadcast journalism; 2) the Directors' Scholarship at Montana State University at Bozeman for a student majoring in media and theater arts; 3) the Engineers' Scholarship for a second-year student at the UM College of Technology at Helena who is working on a degree in broadcast engineering; 4) the Great Falls Broadcasters Association Scholarship for a student who has graduated from a high school in north central Montana (Cascade, Meagher, Judith Basin, Fergus, Chouteau, Teton, Pondera, Glacier, Toole, Liberty, Hill, Blaine, Phillips, or Valley counties) and is enrolled in at least the second year in radio-television at any public or private Montana college or university; and 5) the Billings Broadcasters Association Scholarships for residents of Montana or Wyoming who are preparing for careers in the broadcast industry at Montana State University at Billings by majoring in such fields as promotions, public relations, graphic design, information technology, marketing, or other related areas. Applicants must submit a 1 page statement summarizing their professional abilities, career goals, and extracurricular activities; 2 letters of recommendation; and their most recent transcript.

Financial data Stipends are awarded for all scholarships; the stipend for the Billings Broadcasters Association Scholarships is $1,000 per year.

Duration 1 year.

Additional information The Montana Broadcasters Association (MBA) funds 3 of these scholarships directly. It provides matching funding to the Great Falls Broadcasters Association and the Billings Broadcasters Association for the other 2 scholarships.

Number awarded 6 each year: 2 of the Billings Broadcasters Association Scholarships and 1 of each of the other scholarships.

Deadline March of each year.

[247]
MBIA/WILLIAM O. BAILEY SCHOLARS PROGRAM

United Negro College Fund
Attn: Scholarships and Grants Department
8260 Willow Oaks Corporate Drive
P.O. Box 10444
Fairfax, VA 22031-8044
(703) 205-3466   Toll-free: (800) 331-2244
Fax: (703) 205-3574
Web: www.uncf.org/scholarships/index.asp

Purpose To provide financial assistance to juniors from New York, New Jersey, and Connecticut at colleges and universities that are members of the United Negro College Fund (UNCF) who are majoring in finance or business.

Eligibility This program is open to juniors at UNCF-member colleges and universities who are majoring in finance or business and commit to take between 18 and 24 credit hours. Applicants must be residents of New York, New Jersey, or Connecticut. They must have a GPA of 3.0 or higher and be able to demonstrate financial need.

Financial data Full tuition scholarships are awarded.

Duration 1 year; may be renewed.

Additional information Recipients may be offered a summer internship at Municipal Bond Investors Assurance (MBIA) Corporation.

Number awarded 2 each year.

Deadline November of each year.

[248]
M.E. FRANKS SCHOLARSHIP

International Association of Food Industry Suppliers
Attn: IAFIS Foundation
1451 Dolley Madison Boulevard
McLean, VA 22101-3850
(703) 761-2600   Fax: (703) 761-4334
E-mail: info@iafis.org
Web: www.iafis.org

Purpose To provide financial assistance to outstanding undergraduate and graduate students who are interested in working on a degree in a field related to food science, dairy foods, or agribusiness.

Eligibility This program is open to students working on a degree in dairy foods, food science, food technology, food marketing, agricultural economics, or agricultural business management on the undergraduate or graduate school level. Undergraduate students must be entering their junior or senior year. Graduate students must be working on a master's or Ph.D. degree. U.S. or Canadian citizenship is required. Applicants in food science departments must provide evidence that they will enroll in at least 1 specialized course in the processing, chemistry, or microbiology of milk or dairy products and 1 additional course with an emphasis in dairy processing, dairy product sensory evaluation, chemistry, or microbiology. Students in dairy science departments must provide evidence of enrollment in a dairy foods option or specialization. Completed applications should be submitted to the applicant's department head/chairperson, who then forwards them on to the foundation office. Selection is based on academic performance; commitment to a career in the food industry; and evidence of leadership ability, character, initiative and integrity. Graduate students are also evaluated on their statement of purpose for their master's or Ph.D. thesis proposal. Age, sex, race, and financial need are not considered in the selection process.

Financial data The stipend is $3,000 per year. Funds are paid directly to the recipient.

Duration 1 year; nonrenewable.

Additional information This program is administered by the International Association of Food Industry Suppliers on behalf of the Dairy Recognition and Education Foundation, which provides the funding. Recipients must enroll in school full time.

Number awarded Up to 8 each year: 4 to undergraduates and up to 4 to graduate students.

Deadline November of each year.

[249]
MELVILLE H. COHEE STUDENT LEADER CONSERVATION SCHOLARSHIPS

Soil and Water Conservation Society
945 S.W. Ankeny Road
Ankeny, IA 50021-9764
(515) 289-2331   Toll-free: (800) THE SOIL
Fax: (515) 289-1227   E-mail: swcs@swcs.org
Web: www.swcs.org/t_membership_scholar.htm

Purpose To provide financial assistance to student officers of the Soil and Water Conservation Society (SWCS) who are interested in working on undergraduate or graduate studies with a focus on natural resource conservation.

Eligibility Applicants must have been members of the society for more than 1 year, have served for 1 academic year or longer as a student chapter officer for a chapter with at least 15 members, have earned a GPA of 3.0 or higher, be in school at least half time, not be an employee or immediate family member of the scholarship selection committee, and be in the junior or senior year of undergraduate study or the first or second year of graduate study in conservation or resource-related fields (such as agricultural economics, soils, planned land use management, forestry, wildlife biology, agricultural engineering, hydrology, rural sociology, agronomy, or water management) or related environmental protection or resource management fields at an accredited college or university. Financial need is not considered in the selection process.

Financial data The stipend is $1,000.

Duration 1 year.

Additional information This scholarship may not be combined with other SWCS scholarships or internships.

Number awarded 2 each year.

Deadline February of each year.

[250]
METRO NEW YORK CHAPTER UNDERGRADUATE SCHOLARSHIP AWARD

National Black MBA Association-New York Chapter
P.O. Box 8138
New York, NY 10116
(212) 439-5100
Web: www.nyblackmba.org/html/studentrel.asp

Purpose To provide financial assistance for college to minority students from New York majoring in business or management.

Eligibility This program is open to minority students who are residents of New York and either high school seniors or full-time undergraduate students working on a bachelor's degree in business or management. Applicants must submit a 2-page essay on a topic that changes annually but recently was "What are the major benefits that a large corporation seeks by expanding its business internationally?" Special consideration is given to applicants who have participated in the sponsor's Leaders of Tomorrow program. Financial need is not considered in the selection process.

Financial data A stipend is awarded (amount not specified).

Duration 1 year.

Number awarded 1 or more each year.

Deadline September of each year.

[251]
MICHIGAN ACCOUNTANCY FOUNDATION FIFTH/GRADUATE YEAR STUDENT SCHOLARSHIPS

Michigan Association of Certified Public Accountants
Attn: Michigan Accountancy Foundation
5480 Corporate Drive, Suite 200
P.O. Box 5068
Troy, MI 48007-5068
(248) 267-3700   Toll-free: (888) 877-4CPE
Fax: (248) 267-3737   E-mail: maf@michcpa.org
Web: www.michcpa.org/maf/scholarships.asp

Purpose To provide financial assistance to students at Michigan colleges and universities who are working on a degree in accounting.

Eligibility This program is open to U.S. citizens enrolled full time at accredited Michigan colleges and universities with a declared concentration in accounting. Applicants must have completed at least 50% of their school's requirements toward completion of their junior year. They must intend to or have successfully passed the Michigan C.P.A. examination and intend to practice public accounting in the state. Along with their application, they must submit a statement about their educational and career aspirations, including on- and off-campus activities, professional goals, current professional accomplishments, and a summary of personal and profes-

sional activities (including community involvement). Documentation of financial need may also be included.

Financial data The stipend is $4,000 per year.

Duration 1 year; may be renewed for the fifth or graduate year of study, provided that all requirements continue to be met and that funding is available.

Number awarded Varies each year; recently, 15 of these scholarships were awarded.

Deadline January of each year.

[252]
MICHIGAN PRESS ASSOCIATION FOUNDATION HIGH SCHOOL MATCH SCHOLARSHIPS

Michigan Press Association
Attn: MPA Foundation
827 North Washington Avenue
Lansing, MI 48906-5199
(517) 372-2424   Fax: (517) 372-2429
E-mail: mpa@michiganpress.org
Web: www.michiganpress.org/foundation.shtml

Purpose To provide financial assistance for college to high school seniors in Michigan who agree to work as an intern at a newspaper during the summer following graduation.

Eligibility This program is open to seniors graduating from high schools in Michigan who are interested in a paid summer internship with a newspaper that is a member of the Michigan Press Association (MPA). Candidates may be interested in an internship in writing, photography, advertising, circulation, or marketing. They must be nominated by their high school journalism advisor. If they obtain an internship, they qualify to receive this scholarship to attend a 4-year college or university or a community college.

Financial data The stipend is $2,000; that includes $1,000 provided by the newspaper that hires the student as an intern plus $1,000 from the Michigan Press Association (MPA) Foundation.

Duration Scholarships are for 1 year.

Additional information Information is also available from Janet Mendler, P.O. Box 230, Howell, MI 48844-0230, (517) 552-2811, E-mail: jmendler@ht.homecomm.net.

Number awarded Varies each year; recently, 13 of these scholarships were awarded.

Deadline December of each year.

[253]
MID-ATLANTIC CHAPTER SCHOLARSHIPS

Society of Satellite Professionals International
Attn: Scholarship Program
New York Information Technology Center
55 Broad Street, 14th Floor
New York, NY 10004
(212) 809-5199   Fax: (212) 825-0075
E-mail: sspi@sspi.org
Web: www.sspi.org/html/scholarship.html

Purpose To provide financial assistance to students in designated mid-Atlantic states who are interested in working on an undergraduate or graduate degree in satellite-related disciplines (including business).

Eligibility This program is open to high school seniors, college undergraduates, and graduate students majoring or planning to major in fields related to satellite technologies, policies, or applications. Fields of study in the past have included broadcasting, business, distance learning, energy, government, imaging, meteorology, navigation, remote sensing, space law, and telecommunications. Applicants must be attending or planning to attend school in Delaware, the District of Columbia, Maryland, Virginia, or West Virginia. Selection is based on academic and leadership achievement, commitment to pursue educational and career opportunities in the satellite communications industry, potential for significant contribution to that industry, a personal statement of 500 to 750 words on their interest in satellite communications and why they deserve the award, and a creative work (such as a research report, essay, article, videotape, artwork, computer program, or scale model of an antenna or spacecraft design) that reflects the applicant's interests and talents. Financial need is not considered.

Financial data The stipend is $4,000.

Duration 1 year.

Number awarded 1 to 3 each year.

Deadline May of each year.

[254]
MINNESOTA SPACE GRANT CONSORTIUM SCHOLARSHIPS AND FELLOWSHIPS

Minnesota Space Grant Consortium
c/o University of Minnesota
Department of Aerospace Engineering and Mechanics
107 Akerman Hall
110 Union Street S.E.
Minneapolis, MN 55455
(612) 626-9295   Fax: (612) 626-1558
E-mail: mnsgc@aem.umn.edu
Web: www.aem.umn.edu

Purpose To provide financial assistance for space-related studies (including economics) to undergraduate and graduate students in Minnesota.

Eligibility This program is open to graduate and undergraduate full-time students at institutions that are affiliates of the Minnesota Space Grant Consortium. U.S. citizenship and a GPA of 3.2 or higher are required. Eligible fields of study include the physical sciences (astronomy, astrophysics, chemistry, computer science, mathematics, physics, planetary geoscience, and planetary science), life sciences (biology, biochemistry, botany, health science/nutrition, medicine, molecular/cellular biology, and zoology), social sciences (anthropology, architecture, art, economics, education, history, philosophy, political science/public policy, and psychology), earth sciences (atmospheric science, climatology/meteorology, environmental science, geography, geology, geophysics, and oceanography), and engineering (agricultural, aeronautical, aerospace, architectural, bioengineering, chemical, civil, computer, electrical, electronic, environmental, industrial, materials science, mechanical, mining, nuclear, petroleum, engineering science, and engineering mechanics). The Minnesota Space Grant Consortium is a component of the U.S. National Aeronautics and Space Administration (NASA) Space Grant program, which encourages participation by women, underrepresented minorities, and persons with disabilities.

Financial data This program awards approximately $125,000 in undergraduate scholarships and $25,000 in grad-

uate fellowships each year. The amounts of the awards are set by each of the participating institutions, which augment funding from this program with institutional resources.

Duration 1 year; renewable.

Additional information This program is funded by NASA. The member institutions are: Augsburg College, Bethel College, Bemidji State University, College of St. Catherine, Carleton College, Concordia College, Fond du Lac Community College, Itasca Community College, Leech Lake Tribal College, Macalaster College, Normandale Community College, Southwest State University, University of Minnesota at Duluth, University of Minnesota at Twin Cities, and University of St. Thomas.

Number awarded 8 to 12 undergraduate scholarships and 2 to 3 graduate fellowships are awarded each year.

Deadline March of each year.

[255]
MINORITIES IN GOVERNMENT FINANCE SCHOLARSHIP

Government Finance Officers Association
Attn: Scholarship Committee
203 North LaSalle Street, Suite 2700
Chicago, IL 60601-1210
(312) 977-9700   Fax: (312) 977-4806
Web: www.gfoa.org/services/scholarships.shtml

Purpose To provide financial assistance to minority undergraduate and graduate students who are preparing for a career in state and local government finance.

Eligibility This program is open to upper-division undergraduate and graduate students who are enrolled in a full-time program and preparing for a career in public finance. Applicants must be members of a minority group, citizens or permanent residents of the United States or Canada, and able to provide a letter of recommendation from the dean of their school. Selection is based on career plans, academic record, plan of study, letters of recommendation, and GPA. Financial need is not considered.

Financial data The stipend is $5,000.

Duration 1 year.

Additional information Funding for this program is provided by Fidelity Investments Tax-Exempt Services Company.

Number awarded 1 or more each year.

Deadline February of each year.

[256]
MISS AMERICA COMPETITION AWARDS

Miss America Pageant
Attn: Scholarship Department
Two Miss America Way, Suite 1000
Atlantic City, NJ 08401
(609) 345-7571, ext. 27   Toll-free: (800) 282-MISS
Fax: (609) 347-6079   E-mail: info@missamerica.org
Web: www.missamerica.org

Purpose To provide educational scholarships to participants in the Miss America Pageant on local, state, and national levels.

Eligibility To enter an official Miss America Preliminary Pageant, candidates must meet certain basic requirements and agree to abide by all the rules of the local, state, and national Miss America Pageants. Among the qualifications required are that the applicant be female, between the ages of 17 and 24, a resident of the town or state in which they first compete, in good health, of good moral character, and a citizen of the United States. A complete list of all eligibility requirements is available from each local and state pageant. A number of special awards are also presented to national contestants: the Active International Scholarship for Business and Marketing is presented to the highest scoring contestant who lists business, marketing, or a related business career as a stated ambition; the Bernie Wayne Performing Arts Award is presented to the contestant with the highest talent score among those women with performing arts as a stated ambition; the Eleanor (Big Mama) Andrews Scholarship is presented to the non-finalist contestant with the highest talent score among those women with performing arts as a stated ambition; the Charles and Theresa Brown Scholarships are presented to Miss America, the 4 runners-up, Miss Alaska, Miss Hawaii, Miss Illinois, and Miss Ohio; and the Quality of Life Awards are presented to the 3 contestants who demonstrate the most outstanding commitment to enhancing the quality of life for others through volunteerism and community service.

Financial data More than $45 million in cash and tuition assistance is awarded annually at the local, state, and national Miss America Pageants. At the national level, a total of $455,000 is awarded: Miss America receives $50,000 in scholarship money, the first runner-up $40,000, second runner-up $30,000, third runner-up $25,000, fourth runner-up $20,000, semifinalists $10,000 each, finalists $6,000 each, and national contestants $5,000 each. Among the preliminary winners, those for community achievement in interview receive $5,000, those for artistic expression in talent receive $4,000, those for on-stage knowledge and awareness receive $3,000, those for presence and poise in evening wear receive $2,000, and those for lifestyle and fitness in swimsuit receive $2,000. In addition, the overall knowledge and community achievement in interview winner receives $5,000, the overall artistic expression in talent winner receives $4,000, and the overall elegance and lifestyle winner (including both evening wear and swimsuit) receives $3,000. Of the special awards presented to national contestants, the Active International Scholarship for Business and Marketing is $3,000; the Bernie Wayne Performing Arts Award is $2,500; the Charles and Theresa Brown Scholarships are $2,500 each; and the Quality of Life Awards are $6,000 for first place, $400 for second, and $3,000 for third.

Duration The pageants are held every year.

Additional information The Miss America Pageant has been awarding scholarships since 1945. Scholarships are to be used for tuition, room, board, supplies, and other college expenses. Use of the scholarships must begin within 4 years from the date of the award (5 years if the recipient is Miss America) unless a reasonable extension is requested and granted. Training under the scholarship should be continuous and completed within 10 years from the date the scholarship is activated; otherwise, the balance of the scholarship may be canceled without further notice.

Deadline Varies, depending upon the date of local pageants leading to the state and national finals.

Number awarded At the national level, 52 contestants (1 from each state, the District of Columbia, and the Virgin Islands) share the awards.

[257]
MISSISSIPPI SOCIETY OF CERTIFIED PUBLIC ACCOUNTANTS UNDERGRADUATE SCHOLARSHIP

Mississippi Society of Certified Public Accountants
Attn: MSCPA Awards, Education and Scholarships
    Committee
Highland Village, Suite 246
P.O. Box 16630
Jackson, MS 39236
(601) 366-3473   Toll-free: (800) 772-1099 (within MS)
Fax: (601) 981-6-79   E-mail: mail@ms-cpa.org
Web: www.ms-cpa.org

Purpose To provide financial assistance to upper-division students majoring in accounting at designated 4-year institutions in Mississippi.

Eligibility This program is open to residents of Mississippi who have completed or are completing their junior year of college, are majoring in accounting, have completed at least 6 hours of accounting courses above the principles or introductory level, and are attending 1 of the following schools in Mississippi: Alcorn State University, Belhaven College, Delta State University, Jackson State University, Millsaps College, Mississippi College, Mississippi State University, Mississippi University for Women, Mississippi Valley State University, University of Mississippi, University of Southern Mississippi, or William Carey College. They must be nominated by their academic institution. Nominees must submit a completed application form, transcripts (GPA of 3.0 or higher both overall and in accounting classes), and a 1-page essay explaining why they plan a career in public accounting. Selection is based on the essay, academic excellence, recommendations, financial need, and campus involvement.

Financial data The stipend is $1,000. Checks are made payable to the recipient's school.

Duration 1 year.

Number awarded 1 each year.

Deadline June of each year.

[258]
MISSOURI DECA MARKETING EDUCATION TEACHER HALL OF FAME SCHOLARSHIP

Missouri DECA
Attn: Missouri State DECA Advisor
P.O. Box 480
Jefferson City, MO 65102-0480
(573) 751-4367   Fax: (573) 751-4361
E-mail: julie.lyman@dese.mo.gov
Web: www.modeca.org/d_scholarships.htm

Purpose To provide financial assistance to high school senior members of Missouri DECA who are interested in preparing for a career as a marketing education teacher-coordinator.

Eligibility This program is open to members of Missouri DECA who are high school seniors planning to attend college to prepare for a career as a marketing education teacher-coordinator. Applicants must submit official high school transcripts, 3 letters of recommendation, and a brief essay on their interest in teaching marketing education. Selection is based on DECA involvement; educational, civic, community, and leadership activities; scholastic ability as indicated by transcripts and SAT or ACT scores; and letters of recommendation.

Financial data The stipend is $500.

Duration 1 year; nonrenewable.

Number awarded 1 or more each year.

Deadline February of each year.

[259]
MISSOURI DECA MARKETING EDUCATION TEACHER PROFESSIONAL SCHOLARSHIP

Missouri DECA
Attn: Missouri State DECA Advisor
P.O. Box 480
Jefferson City, MO 65102-0480
(573) 751-4367   Fax: (573) 751-4361
E-mail: julie.lyman@dese.mo.gov
Web: www.modeca.org/d_scholarships.htm

Purpose To provide financial assistance to upper-division college students in Missouri who are interested in preparing for a career as a marketing education teacher-coordinator in the state.

Eligibility This program is open to college students in Missouri who are at least juniors and have been accepted into a marketing education teacher-coordinator program with the intent to prepare for a career as a marketing education teacher-coordinator in Missouri. Applicants must meet the requirements to enroll in their institution's marketing education core courses. They must submit a brief essay on their interest in teaching marketing education. Selection is based on educational, civic, community, and leadership activities; scholastic ability as based on college transcripts and SAT or ACT scores; commitment to education as a profession; and letters of recommendation.

Financial data The stipend is $500.

Duration 1 year; nonrenewable.

Number awarded 1 or more each year.

Deadline February of each year.

[260]
MISSOURI INSURANCE EDUCATION FOUNDATION COLLEGE SCHOLARSHIPS

Missouri Insurance Education Foundation
Attn: Scholarship Administrator
P.O. Box 1654
Jefferson City, MO 65102
(573) 893-4234   E-mail: miis@midamerica.net
Web: www.mief.org/collegeapp.htm

Purpose To provide financial assistance to upper-division students from Missouri who are working on a degree in insurance at a college or university in the state.

Eligibility This program is open to juniors and seniors majoring in insurance or a related area at a Missouri college or university. Applicants must be enrolled full time, have a GPA of 2.5 or higher, and be residents of Missouri. Preference is given to students who can demonstrate financial need. Finalists may be interviewed. The top-ranked applicant receives the C. Lawrence Leggett Scholarship.

Financial data Stipends are $2,000 or $1,500.

Duration 1 year.

Additional information This program was established in 1991.

Number awarded 6 each year: 1 at $2,000 (the C. Lawrence Leggett Scholarship) and 5 at $1,500.

Deadline March of each year.

[261]
MISSOURI INSURANCE EDUCATION FOUNDATION HIGH SCHOOL SCHOLARSHIPS

Missouri Insurance Education Foundation
Attn: Scholarship Administrator
P.O. Box 1654
Jefferson City, MO 65102
(573) 893-4234   E-mail: miis@midamerica.net
Web: www.mief.org/collegeapp.htm

Purpose To provide financial assistance to high school seniors from Missouri who plan to major in insurance or a related field at a college or university in the state.

Eligibility This program is open to seniors graduating from high schools in Missouri who plan to attend a college or university in the state. Applicants must be planning to major in insurance, risk management, or actuarial science as a full-time student. Selection is based on academic achievement, participation in school and outside activities and organizations, honors and awards, and work experience; financial need is not considered.

Financial data The stipend is $1,000.

Duration 1 year.

Additional information This program was established in 1991.

Number awarded 4 each year.

Deadline March of each year.

[262]
MNCPA SCHOLARSHIP PROGRAM

Minnesota Society of Certified Public Accountants
1650 West 82nd Street, Suite 600
Bloomington, MN 55431-1458
(952) 831-2707   Toll-free: (800) 331-4288
Fax: (952) 831-7875
Web: www.mncpa.org

Purpose To provide financial assistance to upper-division students in Minnesota who are majoring in accounting.

Eligibility This program is open to Minnesota residents who are at least sophomores, are majoring in accounting, have a GPA of 3.0 or higher, and are attending 1 of the following colleges or universities in the state: University of Minnesota, University of St. Thomas, St. Cloud State University, College of St. Catherine, College of St. Benedict, Bethel College, Minnesota State University at Mankato, University of Minnesota at Duluth, St. John's University, Winona State University, Metropolitan State University, Bemidji State University, Augsburg College, Gustavus Adolphus College, Concordia College at Moorhead, and Northwestern College. Recipients are selected by the individual schools on the basis of academic record, extracurricular activities, and honors and awards.

Financial data The stipend is $1,000.

Duration 1 year.

Additional information Recipients are also given a 1-year student membership in the society and a CPA mentorship opportunity.

Number awarded Each year, 25 scholarships are awarded. Of these, the number of scholarships given at each of the participating schools depends on the number of students from that school who passed the CPA exam during the previous year.

[263]
MONTANA MEAT PROCESSORS ASSOCIATION SCHOLARSHIP

Montana 4-H Foundation
c/o Montana State University
211 Taylor Hall
P.O. Box 173580
Bozeman, MT 59717
(406) 994-5911   Fax: (406) 994-5417
E-mail: 4hfdn@montana.edu
Web: www.giveto4hkids.org

Purpose To provide financial assistance to members of 4-H and FFA in Montana who are interested in studying a field related to meat science in college.

Eligibility This program is open to seniors and graduates of Montana high schools who are entering college for the first time. Applicants must have been members of 4-H or FFA within the last 4 years and participated in such activities as livestock and meat judging, carcass evaluation, or a livestock project related to meat. They must be planning to attend a 4-year college or university to major in agribusiness, agricultural communications, agriculture and/or extension education, animal science, business, food science, home economics, or meat science. Along with their application, they must submit an essay on their honors and activities (especially those related to their 4-H and FFA involvement); a letter of recommendation from a Montana Meat Processors Association member plant; and a letter of recommendation from a 4-H leader, FFA advisor, or county extension agent.

Financial data The stipend is $500.

Duration 1 year.

Additional information This program is sponsored by the Montana Meat Processors Association.

Number awarded 1 each year.

Deadline April of each year.

[264]
MONTANA SOCIETY OF CERTIFIED PUBLIC ACCOUNTANTS SCHOLARSHIPS

Montana Society of Certified Public Accountants
Attn: Education Endowment
33 South Last Chance Gulch, Suite 2 B
Helena, MT 59601
(406) 442-7301   Fax: (406) 443-7278
E-mail: mscpa@crom.net
Web: www.mscpa.org

Purpose To provide financial assistance to upper-division and graduate students majoring in accounting or related fields in Montana.

Eligibility Eligible for this support are juniors and graduate students who are majoring in accounting, business, or finance

at the following 4-year institutions in Montana: University of Montana, Montana State University, Montana State University at Billings, and Carroll College. Applicants must have a GPA of 2.75 or higher overall and 3.0 or higher in business courses. Preference is given to student members of the Montana Society of Certified Public Accountants (MSCPA).

Financial data The stipend is $1,000.

Duration 1 year.

Additional information This program includes the Anthony Gerharz Scholarship for a student at Montana State University at Billings and the Scott Brownlee Memorial Scholarship for a student at Carroll College.

Number awarded 4 each year: 1 at each of the participating institutions.

[265]
MONTANA WOMEN IN TRANSITION SCHOLARSHIP

American Society of Women Accountants-Billings Big
   Sky Chapter
820 Division Street
Billings, MT 59101
Web: www.imt.net/~aswa

Purpose To provide financial assistance to women in Montana who are returning to school to work on an undergraduate degree in accounting.

Eligibility This program is open to women in Montana who are incoming freshmen, currently enrolled, or returning to school with sufficient credits to qualify for freshman status. Applicants must be women who, either through divorce or death of a spouse, have become the sole source of support for themselves and their family and wish to work on a degree in accounting as a means to gainful employment. Selection is based on commitment to the goal of working on a degree in accounting, including evidence of continued commitment after receiving this award; aptitude for accounting and business; clear evidence that the candidate has established goals and a plan for achieving those goals, both personal and professional; and financial need.

Financial data The stipend is $1,500.

Duration 1 year.

Additional information Information is also available from Jane Crowder, (406) 248-2990, E-mail: jane_bowl@yahoo.com.

Number awarded 1 each year.

Deadline March of each year.

[266]
MORGAN STANLEY SCHOLARSHIP/INTERNSHIP

United Negro College Fund
Attn: Scholarships and Grants Department
8260 Willow Oaks Corporate Drive
P.O. Box 10444
Fairfax, VA 22031-8044
(703) 205-3466   Toll-free: (800) 331-2244
Fax: (703) 205-3574
Web: www.uncf.org/scholarships/index.asp

Purpose To provide financial assistance and work experience to students who are majoring in banking or finance at a college or university that is a member of the United Negro College Fund.

Eligibility This program is open to students majoring in banking or finance at UNCF-member institutions. Applicants must have a GPA of 2.5 or higher and be able to demonstrate financial need.

Financial data The maximum stipend is $10,000. The program includes a summer internship at Morgan Stanley.

Duration 1 year.

Number awarded 1 or more each year.

[267]
MORGAN STANLEY/AMERICAN INDIAN COLLEGE FUND SCHOLARSHIP

American Indian College Fund
Attn: Scholarship Department
8333 Greenwood Boulevard
Denver, CO 80221
(303) 426-8900   Toll-free: (800) 776-FUND
Fax: (303) 426-1200   E-mail: info@collegefund.org
Web: www.collegefund.org/Morgan_Stanley.shtml

Purpose To provide financial assistance to American Indian students who are preparing for a career in the financial services field.

Eligibility Eligible to apply are American Indians or Alaska Natives who are currently enrolled in a 4-year degree program at an accredited college or university in the United States and are interested in exploring career options in the financial services industry. Applicants must be able to demonstrate exceptional academic achievement (at least a 3.0 GPA), as well as leadership, service, and commitment to the American Indian community. To apply, they must submit a completed application form, official college transcripts, personal essays (500 words or less), 2 letters of recommendation, tribal enrollment information, and a color photograph.

Financial data The stipend is $10,000 per year.

Duration 1 year.

Additional information This scholarship is sponsored by Morgan Stanley, in partnership with the American Indian College Fund.

Number awarded 5 each year.

Deadline April of each year.

[268]
M&T BANK SCHOLARSHIP PROGRAM

Hispanic College Fund
Attn: National Director
1717 Pennsylvania Avenue, N.W., Suite 460
Washington, D.C. 20006
(202) 296-5400   Toll-free: (800) 644-4223
Fax: (202) 296-3774 E-mail: hcf-info@hispanicfund.org
Web: www.hispanicfund.org

Purpose To provide financial assistance to Hispanic American undergraduate students from Maryland, New York, Virginia, and Pennsylvania who are interested in preparing for a career in business, computer science, or engineering.

Eligibility This program is open to U.S. citizens of Hispanic background (at least 1 grandparent must be 100% Hispanic) who are entering their freshman, sophomore, junior, or senior year of college. Applicants must be residents of Maryland,

New York, Virginia, or Pennsylvania. They must be working on a bachelor's degree in business, computer science, engineering, or a business-related major and have a cumulative GPA of 3.0 or higher. They must be applying to or enrolled in a college or university in the 50 states or Puerto Rico as a full-time student. Financial need is considered in the selection process.

Financial data Stipends range from $500 to $5,000, depending on the need of the recipient, and average approximately $3,000. Funds are paid directly to the recipient's college or university to help cover tuition and fees.

Duration 1 year; recipients may reapply.

Additional information This program is sponsored by M&T Bank and administered by the Hispanic College Fund (HCF). All applications must be submitted online; no paper applications are available.

Number awarded Varies each year.

Deadline April of each year.

[269]
NABA CORPORATE SCHOLARSHIPS

National Association of Black Accountants
Attn: Director, Center for Advancement of Minority
    Accountants
7249-A Hanover Parkway
Greenbelt, MD 20770
(301) 474-NABA, ext. 114   Fax: (301) 474-3114
E-mail: cquinn@nabainc.org
Web: www.nabainc.org

Purpose To provide financial assistance to student members of the National Association of Black Accountants (NABA) who are working on an undergraduate or graduate degree in a field related to accounting.

Eligibility This program is open to NABA members who are members of ethnic minority groups enrolled full time as 1) an undergraduate freshman, sophomore, junior, or first-semester senior majoring in accounting, business, or finance; or 2) a graduate student working on a master's degree in accounting. Applicants must have a GPA of 3.5 or higher in their major and 3.3 or higher overall. Selection is based on grades, financial need, and a 500-word autobiography that discusses career objectives, leadership abilities, community activities, and involvement in NABA.

Financial data Stipends range from $1,000 to $5,000 per year.

Duration 1 year.

Number awarded Varies each year.

Deadline December of each year.

[270]
NAIW EDUCATION FOUNDATION COLLEGE SCHOLARSHIPS

National Association of Insurance Women
Attn: NAIW Education Foundation
5310 East 31st Street, Suite 302
Tulsa, OK 74135
(918) 622-1816   Toll-free: (866) 349-1816
Fax: (918) 622-1821
E-mail: foundation@naiwfoundation.org
Web: www.naiwfoundation.org/college.htm

Purpose To provide financial assistance to college and graduate students working on a degree in insurance and risk management.

Eligibility This program is open to candidates for a bachelor's degree or higher with a major or minor in insurance, risk management, or actuarial science. Applicants must 1) be completing or have completed their second year of college; 2) have an overall GPA of 3.0 or higher; 3) have successfully completed at least 2 insurance or risk management-related courses; and 4) not be receiving full reimbursement for the cost of tuition, books, or other educational expenses from their employer or any other outside source. Selection is based on academic record and honors, extracurricular and personal activities, work experience, 3 letters of recommendation, and a 500-word essay on career path and goals.

Financial data Stipends range from $1,000 to $4,000 per year; funds are paid jointly to the institution and to the student.

Duration 1 year.

Additional information The National Association of Insurance Women established the NAIW Educational Foundation in 1993. It provides financial assistance to both men and women interested in careers in the insurance industry.

Number awarded Varies each year; recently, 15 of these scholarships were awarded.

Deadline February each year.

[271]
NATIONAL ASSOCIATION OF BLACK ACCOUNTANTS NATIONAL SCHOLARSHIP

National Association of Black Accountants
Attn: Director, Center for Advancement of Minority
   Accountants
7249-A Hanover Parkway
Greenbelt, MD 20770
(301) 474-NABA, ext. 114   Fax: (301) 474-3114
E-mail: cquinn@nabainc.org
Web: www.nabainc.org

Purpose To provide financial assistance to student members of the National Association of Black Accountants (NABA) who are working on an undergraduate or graduate degree in a field related to accounting.

Eligibility This program is open to NABA members who are members of ethnic minority groups enrolled full time as 1) an undergraduate freshman, sophomore, junior, or first-semester senior majoring in accounting, business, or finance; or 2) a graduate student working on a master's degree in accounting. Applicants must have a GPA of 3.5 or higher in their major and 3.3 or higher overall. Selection is based on grades, financial need, and a 500 word autobiography that discusses

career objectives, leadership abilities, community activities, and involvement in NABA.

Financial data The stipend ranges from $3,000 to $6,000 per year.

Duration 1 year.

Number awarded 1 each year.

Deadline December of each year.

[272]
NATIONAL BLACK MBA ASSOCIATION UNDERGRADUATE SCHOLARSHIP PROGRAM

National Black MBA Association
180 North Michigan Avenue, Suite 1400
Chicago, IL 60601
(312) 236-2622, ext. 8086   Fax: (312) 236-4131
E-mail: scholarship@nbmbaa.org
Web: www.nbmbaa.org

Purpose To provide financial assistance to African American students interested in working on an undergraduate business degree.

Eligibility This program is open to African American students who wish to work on an undergraduate degree in a field related to business. Applicants must submit a completed application, high school or undergraduate transcripts, and an essay on a topic that changes annually. Selection is based on GPA, extracurricular activities, and quality of the essay.

Financial data The stipend is $1,000.

Duration 1 year.

Additional information This program is funded by the national office of the National Black MBA Association (NBMBAA), which develops the application and selects the essay topics. It is administered by local chapters, which select the winners. Applications must be submitted to local chapters; for the name and address of a contact person at each chapter, write to the association. Recipients must attend college on a full-time basis.

Number awarded Each year, each NBMBAA chapter selects 1 recipient. Currently, there are 31 chapters in the United States.

Deadline Each chapter determines its deadline date; most are in the spring.

[273]
NATIONAL DAIRY SHRINE/DMI MILK MARKETING SCHOLARSHIPS

National Dairy Shrine
Attn: Office of Executive Director
1224 Alton Darby Creek Road
Columbus, OH 43228-9792
(614) 878-5333   Fax: (614) 870-2622
E-mail: shrine@cobaselect.com
Web: www.dairyshrine.org/students.asp

Purpose To encourage college students enrolled in a dairy science program and to prepare for careers in the marketing of dairy products.

Eligibility Applicants must be college sophomores, juniors, or seniors who have a cumulative GPA of 2.5 or higher. They must be majoring in dairy science, animal science, agricultural economics, agricultural communications, agricultural education, general agriculture, or food and nutrition. Selection is based on student organizational activities (15%), other organizations and activities (10%), academic standing and course work associated with marketing (25%), honors and awards (10%), marketing experiences (10%), and reasons for interest in dairy product marketing, including plans for the future (30%).

Financial data Stipends are $1,000 or $500.

Duration 1 year.

Additional information This program, which began in 1976, is jointly sponsored by the National Dairy Shrine and Dairy Management Inc. (DMI).

Number awarded 11 each year; 1 at $1,500 and 10 at $500 each.

Deadline March of each year.

[274]
NDPRB UNDERGRADUATE SCHOLARSHIP PROGRAM

Dairy Management Inc.
O'Hare International Center
10255 West Higgins Road, Suite 900
Rosemont, IL 60018-5616
(847) 803-2000   Fax: (847) 803-2077
E-mail: marykateg@rosedmi.com
Web: www.dairyinfo.com

Purpose To provide financial assistance to undergraduate students in fields related to dairy science.

Eligibility This program is open to sophomore, junior, and senior undergraduate students enrolled in college and university programs that emphasize dairy. Eligible majors include agricultural education, business, communications and/or public relations, economics, food science, journalism, marketing, and nutrition. Fields related to production (e.g., animal science) are not eligible. Selection is based on academic performance; apparent commitment to a career in dairy; involvement in extracurricular activities, especially those relating to dairy; and evidence of leadership ability, initiative, character, and integrity. The applicant who is judged most outstanding is awarded the James H. Loper Memorial Scholarship.

Financial data Stipends are $2,500 or $1,500.

Duration 1 year; may be renewed.

Additional information Dairy Management Inc. manages this program on behalf of the National Dairy Promotion and Research Board (NDPRB).

Number awarded 20 each year: the James H. Loper Memorial Scholarship at $2,500 and 19 other scholarships at $1,500.

Deadline May of each year.

[275]
NDTA SCOTT-ST. LOUIS SCHOLASTIC AWARDS

National Defense Transportation Association-Scott-St. Louis Chapter
Attn: Scholarship Committee
P.O. Box 25486
Scott Air Force Base, IL 62225-0486
Web: www.ndtascottstlouis.org/scholarships.htm

Purpose To provide financial assistance for college to students from designated midwestern states interested in preparing for a career in business, transportation, logistics, or physical distribution.

Eligibility This program is open to students interested in preparing for a career in business, transportation, logistics, or physical distribution. High school applicants must be residents of Missouri or Illinois. College students must be enrolled full time at an accredited institution in Colorado, Iowa, Illinois, Indiana, Kansas, Michigan, Minnesota, Missouri, Montana, Nebraska, North Dakota, South Dakota, Wisconsin, or Wyoming. They may be enrolled in any field of study, but priority is given to applicants majoring in business, logistics, physical distribution, or transportation. High school seniors and college students who are the immediate family of members of the Scott-St. Louis chapter of the National Defense Transportation Association (NDTA) are also eligible; they may reside in any state. All applicants must submit an essay, up to 800 words in length, on how their chosen field of study and future career may someday be supported by or contribute to an improve transportation and logistics. Selection is based on the essay, transcripts, SAT/ACT scores (not required for college students), and 2 letters of recommendation. An interview may be requested.

Financial data The stipend is $2,500. Funds are sent directly to the recipient's college or university as payment for tuition, books, fees, and college-sponsored room and board.

Duration 1 year.

Additional information Information is also available from Michael A. Carnes, 926 Thornbury Place, O'Fallon, IL 62269-6810, (618) 550-8608, E-mail: carnes74@charter.net. The award for the highest-ranked applicant overall is designated the Major General John Stanford Memorial Scholarship. The award for the Scott-St. Louis NDTA member dependent is designated the Colonel Robert A. Miles, Jr. Memorial Scholarship.

Number awarded 6 each year: 4 for high seniors, 1 for a college student, and 1 for an immediate relative of an active member of the Scott-St. Louis NDTA chapter.

Deadline February of each year.

[276]
NEBRASKA SOCIETY OF CERTIFIED PUBLIC ACCOUNTANTS SCHOLARSHIPS

Nebraska Society of Certified Public Accountants
Attn: Foundation
635 South 14th Street, Suite 330
Lincoln, NE 68508
(402) 476-8482   Toll-free: (800) 642-6178
Fax: (402) 476-8731   E-mail: nebrscpa@inetnebr.com
Web: www.nescpa.com

Purpose To provide financial assistance to upper-division accounting students at colleges and universities in Nebraska.

Eligibility This program is open to students who are majoring in accounting and have completed their junior year at a Nebraska college or university. Applicants must have the interest and capabilities of becoming a successful C.P.A., be considering such a career in Nebraska, and be planning to take the C.P.A. examination. They must be nominated by accounting faculty members. Institutions having fifth-year accounting (150-hour) programs may also nominate up to 2 students for scholarships specifically designated for such students. Selection is based on scholarship, leadership, and character; the highest scholastic average is not necessarily required.

Financial data Stipends range from $750 to $2,500. Scholarships for fifth-year students are at least $1,500.

Duration March of each year.

Additional information This program includes the following named awards: the Arnold L. Magnuson Scholarship, the James R. Greisch Scholarship, the Delmar A. Lienemann, Sr. Scholarship, the Nancy J. Stara Scholarship, and the Irving R. Dana III Scholarship. Scholarships for fifth-year students include the Aureus Financial Scholarship (funded by Aureus Financial of Lincoln and Omaha) and the J. Edmunds Miller Scholarship.

Number awarded Varies each year; recently, 50 of these scholarships (including 16 fifth-year scholarships) were awarded.

Deadline March of each year.

[277]
NEED-BASED SCHOLARSHIPS FOR ACCOUNTING MAJORS

Washington Society of Certified Public Accountants
Attn: Scholarship Committee
902 140th Avenue N.E.
Bellevue, WA 98005-3480
(425) 644-4800 Toll-free: (800) 272-8273 (within WA)
Fax: (425) 562-8853
E-mail: memberservices@wscpa.org
Web: www.wscpa.org

Purpose To provide financial assistance to undergraduate students in Washington who are majoring in accounting and can demonstrate financial need.

Eligibility This program is open to accounting majors in Washington who have completed their sophomore year at an accredited 4-year institution or 2 terms at a 2-year institution. Preference is given to residents of Washington. Applicants must be U.S. citizens or have applied for citizenship and have a GPA of 3.0 or higher. Along with their application, they must submit essays on 1) what sparked their interest in working on a degree in accounting and what excites them about the profession; 2) their career goals; 3) their involvement in an extracurricular activity, organization, or community service experience and how it affected their life; and 4) why they should be awarded a scholarship. Selection is based on the essays, academic achievement, campus and/or community activities, work history, 2 letters of recommendation, probability of success in obtaining a CPA license, and financial need.

Financial data The stipend is $3,500 per year. Funds may be used to pay for tuition only.

Duration 1 year; nonrenewable.

Number awarded 11 each year.

Deadline April of each year.

[278]
NEHRA FUTURE STARS IN HR SCHOLARSHIPS

Northeast Human Resources Association
Attn: Scholarship Awards
One Washington Street, Suite 101
Wellesley, MA 02481
(781) 235-2900 Fax: (781) 237-8745
E-mail: info@nehra.com
Web: www.nehra.com/scholarships.php

Purpose To provide financial assistance to undergraduate and graduate students at colleges and universities in New England who are preparing for a career in human resources.

Eligibility This program is open to full-time undergraduate and graduate students at accredited colleges and universities in New England. Applicants must have completed at least 1 course related to human resources and have a GPA of 3.0 or higher. Along with their application, they must submit 2 essays: 1) why they are interested in becoming a human resources professional; and 2) what qualities they believe are critical to the success of a human resources professional, which of those they currently possess, and how they intend to acquire the others. Selection is based on interest in becoming a human resources professional, academic success, leadership skills, and participation in non-academic activities. The applicant who is judged most outstanding receives the John D. Erdlen Scholarship Award.

Financial data Stipends are $3,000 or $2,500 per year.

Duration 1 year; may be renewed.

Additional information The sponsor is an affiliate of the Society for Human Resource Management (SHRM).

Number awarded 4 each year: 1 at $3,000 (the John D. Erdlen Scholarship Award) and 3 at $2,500.

Deadline March of each year

[279]
NEW ENGLAND GAS ENVIRONMENTAL SCHOLARSHIPS

New England Gas Company
Attn: Manager of Community Relations
100 Weybosset Street
Providence, RI 02903
(401) 574-2062 E-mail: malbanese@negasco.com
Web: www.negasco.com/about/scholarship.php

Purpose To provide financial assistance to college students from the service area of New England Gas Company who are interested in a career in environmental management or research.

Eligibility Applicants must live in a household or other residential facility served by the company. They must be full-time students who are 1) entering their sophomore, junior, or senior year of a bachelor's degree program at an accredited U.S. college or university, and 2) preparing for a career in environmental management or research. Along with their application, they must submit a 3-page description of their career goals and a brief explanation of their financial need and how this scholarship will benefit or make a difference to them in the pursuit of their goal to protect or study the environment.

Financial data The stipend is $2,000 per year.

Duration 1 year; may be renewed up to 2 additional years.

Additional information The New England Gas Company was established in 2000 when it absorbed the Providence Gas

Company, which had established this program in 1989, and several other small gas utilities serving Rhode Island and southeastern Massachusetts. It serves 33 of the 39 towns and cities in Rhode Island as well as the Massachusetts communities of Fall River, North Attleboro, Plainville, Somerset, Swansea, and Westport.

Number awarded 2 each year.

Deadline March of each year.

[280]
NEW HAMPSHIRE SOCIETY OF CERTIFIED PUBLIC ACCOUNTANTS SCHOLARSHIP PROGRAM

New Hampshire Society of Certified Public Accountants
Attn: Financial Careers Committee
1750 Elm Street, Suite 403
Manchester, NH 03104
(603) 622-1999   Fax: (603) 626-0204
E-mail: info@nhscpa.org
Web: nhscpa.org/student.htm

Purpose To provide financial assistance to undergraduate and graduate students in New Hampshire who are preparing for a career as a certified public accountant.

Eligibility This program is open to residents of New Hampshire who are 1) entering their junior or senior year in an accounting or business program at an accredited 4-year college or university or 2) full-time graduate students in an accredited master's degree program in accounting or business. A recommendation or appraisal from the person in charge of the applicant's accounting program must be included in the application package. Selection is based on academic record, not financial need, although if academic measures between 2 or more students are the same, financial need may be considered secondarily.

Financial data A stipend is awarded (amount not specified).

Duration 1 year.

Number awarded 2 or more each year.

Deadline October of each year.

[281]
NEW HAMPSHIRE/VERMONT CHAPTER HFMA CONTINUING EDUCATION SCHOLARSHIP

Healthcare Financial Management Association-New
   Hampshire/Vermont Chapter
c/o Jeffrey D. Walla, Scholarship Committee
Berry, Dunn, McNeil & Parker
46 Centerra Parkway, Suite 210
Lebanon, NH 03766
(603) 653-0015   Fax: (603) 640-6195
Web: www.nhvthfma.org

Purpose To provide financial assistance to members of the New Hampshire/Vermont chapter of the Healthcare Financial Management Association (HFMA) who are working on a degree in health care financial management.

Eligibility This program is open to chapter members who are enrolled in a bachelor's or master's program at an accredited college or university in the field of health care finance or administration. Applicants must have accumulated at least 40 founders award points. They may only apply for 1 course per

college term. Along with their application, they must submit a description of their financial need, the benefit they will receive by attending the course, their desire to further their education, and anything else they feel is important. The program in which they wish to enroll may be located in any state.

Financial data The maximum stipend is $1,000. Funds are paid directly to the school.

Duration Funding is provided for 1 course; recipients may apply for support for 1 additional course if they earn a GPA of 3.0 or higher for the first course.

Number awarded 2 each year.

Deadline October or May of each year.

[282]
NEW HOLLAND CREDIT COMPANY SCHOLARSHIPS

National FFA Organization
Attn: Scholarship Office
6060 FFA Drive
P.O. Box 68960
Indianapolis, IN 46268-0960
(317) 802-4321   Fax: (317) 802-5321
E-mail: scholarships@ffa.org
Web: www.ffa.org

Purpose To provide financial assistance to FFA members who are interested in studying an agribusiness field in college.

Eligibility This program is open to members who are either graduating high school seniors planning to enroll in college or students already enrolled in college. Applicants must be interested in working full time on a 4-year degree in agricultural management, finance, marketing, or sales. They must have a GPA of 3.5 or higher. Preference is given to applicants with a study emphasis in economics or finance. Selection is based on academic achievement (10 points for GPA, 10 points for SAT or ACT score, 10 points for class rank), leadership in FFA activities (30 points), leadership in community activities (10 points), and participation in the Supervised Agricultural Experience (SAE) program (30 points). U.S. citizenship is required.

Financial data The stipend is $3,500. Funds are paid directly to the recipient.

Duration 1 year; nonrenewable.

Additional information Funding for these scholarships is provided by New Holland Credit Company, a subsidiary of CNH Capital. Recipients are provided with information regarding possible summer internships at CNH Capital.

Number awarded 5 each year.

Deadline February of each year.

[283]
NEW JERSEY DECA STATE SCHOLARSHIPS

New Jersey DECA
c/o Gene Adams, State Advisor
Goucester County Institute of Technology
1360 Tanyard Road
Sewell, NJ 08080
(856) 468-1445, ext. 2200   Fax: (856) 468-1035
E-mail: cadams@gcit.org
Web: www.njdeca.org

Purpose To provide financial assistance to New Jersey high school seniors who are DECA members planning to study marketing, management, merchandising, or marketing education in college.

Eligibility This program is open to DECA members who are seniors graduating from high schools in New Jersey. Applicants must be planning to attend a 2-year or 4-year institution to major in marketing, management, merchandising, or marketing education. Selection is based on participation in DECA and other activities, individual character, and financial need.

Financial data Stipends are $1,000, $750, or $500.

Duration 1 year.

Number awarded Varies each year.

[284]
NEW JERSEY HFMA MEMBER SCHOLARSHIP

Healthcare Financial Management Association-New
 Jersey Chapter
c/o Gabrielle Parseghian, Scholarship Committee Chair
P.O. Box 6422
Bridgewater, NJ 08807
(732) 583-7428   Fax: (732) 583-7428
E-mail: gabbyparseghian@yahoo.com
Web: www.hfmanj.org

Purpose To provide financial assistance to members of the New Jersey Chapter of the Healthcare Financial Management Association (HFMA) and their families who are interested in working on a degree related to health care administration.

Eligibility Applicants must have been a member of the chapter for at least 2 years or the spouse or dependent of a 2-year member. They must be enrolled in an accredited college, university, nursing school, or other allied health professional school. Preference is given to applicants working on a degree in finance, accounting, health care administration, or a field of study related to health care. Along with their application, they must submit an essay describing their educational and professional goals and the role of this scholarship in helping achieve those. Selection is based on the essay, merit, academic achievement, civic and professional activities, course of study, and content of the application. Financial need is not considered.

Financial data A total of $3,000 is available for this program each year.

Duration 1 year.

Number awarded Varies each year; recently, the sponsor offered 2 scholarships at $1,500 each.

Deadline March of each year.

[285]
NEW JERSEY MARKETING EDUCATION SCHOLARSHIPS

New Jersey DECA
c/o Gene Adams, State Advisor
Goucester County Institute of Technology
1360 Tanyard Road
Sewell, NJ 08080
(856) 468-1445, ext. 2200   Fax: (856) 468-1035
E-mail: cadams@gcit.org
Web: www.njdeca.org

Purpose To provide financial assistance to high school seniors from New Jersey who are DECA members planning to study marketing, management, merchandising, or marketing education in college.

Eligibility This program is open to DECA members who are seniors graduating from high schools in New Jersey. Applicants must be planning to attend a 2-year or 4-year institution to major in marketing, management, merchandising, or marketing education. They must submit a copy of their high school transcript, a letter of recommendation, a 250-word essay on "What marketing education has done for me," and documentation of financial need.

Financial data The stipend is $500.

Duration 1 year.

Additional information This program offers scholarships to students in 3 different regions: central New Jersey, northern New Jersey, and southern New Jersey.

Number awarded Several each year.

Deadline January of each year.

[286]
NEW JERSEY SOCIETY OF CERTIFIED PUBLIC ACCOUNTANTS COLLEGE SCHOLARSHIP PROGRAM

New Jersey Society of Certified Public Accountants
Attn: Student Programs Coordinator
425 Eagle Rock Avenue, Suite 100
Roseland, NJ 07068-1723
(973) 226-4494, ext. 209   Fax: (973) 226-7425
E-mail: njscpa@njscpa.org
Web: www.njscpa.org

Purpose To provide financial assistance to upper-division and graduate students in New Jersey who are preparing for a career as a certified public accountant.

Eligibility This program is open to residents of New Jersey who are attending a college or university in the state. Applicants must be 1) juniors who are majoring or concentrating in accounting; or 2) graduate students entering an accounting-related program. Students may apply directly or be nominated by the accounting department chair at their college. Selection is based on academic achievement (GPA of 3.0 or higher).

Financial data Stipends range from $500 to $4,000.

Duration 1 year. Each student may receive only 1 undergraduate and 1 graduate scholarship during their academic career.

Number awarded Varies each year. Recently, 46 of these scholarships were awarded: 1 at $4,000, 35 at $3,000, 3 at $2,000, 2 at $1,000, 3 at $750, and 2 at $500.

Deadline January of each year.

[287]
NEW MEXICO BROADCASTERS ASSOCIATION SCHOLARSHIPS

New Mexico Broadcasters Association
Attn: Scholarship Program
8014 Menaul, N.W.
Albuquerque, NM 87110
(505) 881-4444   Toll-free: (800) 622-2414
Fax: (505) 881-5353
Web: www.nmba.org

Purpose To provide financial assistance to undergraduate students in New Mexico who are preparing for a career in the broadcasting industry.

Eligibility This program is open to residents of New Mexico who are entering their sophomore, junior, or senior year at an accredited college, vocational institution, or university in the state. Applicants must be preparing for a career in the broadcast industry, including news, announcing, sales, accounting, management, engineering, traffic and billing, promotion, community affairs, programming, production, or other aspects of the industry. They must submit brief statements on their work experience at a broadcast facility and why they want to prepare for a career in the field. Race, gender, age, and financial need are not considered in the selection process. Nontraditional and reentry students are encouraged to apply.

Financial data The maximum stipend is $2,500 per year. Funds are paid directly to the student to help pay the cost of tuition, books, supplies and fees.

Duration 1 year.

Additional information Recipients must secure an internship with a New Mexico broadcast facility.

Number awarded Up to 10 each year.

Deadline April of each year.

[288]
NEW MEXICO SOCIETY OF CPAS SCHOLARSHIPS

New Mexico Society of Certified Public Accountants
Attn: Scholarships in Accounting
1650 University N.E., Suite 450
Albuquerque, NM 87102-1733
(505) 246-1699   Toll-free: (800) 926-2522
Fax: (505) 246-1686   E-mail: nmcpa@nmcpa.org
Web: www.nmcpa.org

Purpose To provide financial assistance to accounting students at New Mexico universities and colleges.

Eligibility This program is open to full-time students at New Mexico colleges and universities who have completed 12 semester hours in accounting, are currently enrolled in 6 or more accounting hours, have completed 75 hours overall, and have a cumulative GPA of 3.0 or higher. Selection is based on academic achievement, extracurricular activities, career objectives and goals in accounting, and financial need.

Financial data The stipend is $750.

Duration 1 year; may be renewed 1 additional year.

Number awarded Varies each year.

Deadline September of each year.

[289]
NEW YORK BEEF PRODUCERS' ASSOCIATION SCHOLARSHIP

New York Beef Producers' Association
3 Second Street
Camden, NY 13316
(315) 245-3386
Web: www.tjbailey.com/nybpa

Purpose To provide financial assistance to college students from New York who are preparing for a career in the cattle industry.

Eligibility This program is open to residents of New York who are currently enrolled in an accredited 2-year or 4-year agricultural college. Applicants must be majoring in a field of study related to agriculture (e.g., animal and/or crop science, business, economics, communications, agricultural engineering) and planning a career related to the beef industry. Along with their application, they must submit an essay that covers the following: 1) their experience and interest in the beef industry; 2) their involvement in agricultural-related activities, including organizations (community, school, 4-H), events, awards, and leadership positions; 3) their future intentions and career plans as they relate to the beef industry; and 4) how they view the future of the beef industry. Selection is based primarily on involvement in the beef industry and future plans. Financial need is not considered.

Financial data The stipend is $1,000.

Duration 1 year.

Number awarded 1 each year.

Deadline December of each year.

[290]
NEW YORK EXCELLENCE IN ACCOUNTING SCHOLARSHIP

New York State Society of Certified Public Accountants
Attn: Foundation for Accounting Education
530 Fifth Avenue, Fifth Floor
New York, NY 10036-5101
(212) 719-8379   Toll-free: (800) 633-6320
Fax: (212) 719-3364   E-mail: jlewis@nysscpa.org
Web: www.nysscpa.org/scholarship/scholarship.htm

Purpose To provide financial assistance to residents of New York who are majoring in accounting at a college or university in the state.

Eligibility Applicants must be residents of New York and either U.S. citizens or permanent residents. They must be entering the third or fourth year of a 4-year or 5-year degree program in accounting at a New York college or university and have a GPA of 3.0 or higher. Students who already hold a bachelor's degree and are working on a master's degree in accounting are not eligible. Applications, on behalf of students, are accepted only when forwarded from the applicant's institution. Financial need is considered in the selection process.

Financial data The stipend is $1,500 for full-time students and $750 for part-time students. Payment is made co-payable to the student and the school.

Duration 1 year; may be renewed for 1 additional year for students working on a 4-year bachelor's degree or 2 additional years for students in a "150-hour" 5-year program.

Number awarded Varies each year; recently, the society awarded more than $111,000 in new scholarships and renewals.

Deadline March of each year.

[291]
NEW YORK STATE AFL-CIO SCHOLARSHIP

New York State AFL-CIO
Attn: Education Director
100 South Swan Street
Albany, NY 12210-1939
(518) 436-8516   Fax: (518) 436-8470
E-mail: gduesberg@nysaflcio.org
Web: www.nysaflcio.org

Purpose To provide financial assistance for education in labor relations to children of union members in New York.

Eligibility Eligible are graduating high school seniors whose parent or guardian is a member of a union affiliated with the New York State AFL-CIO. Applicants must intend to prepare for a career in labor relations or a labor-related interest in another field (history, economics, law, political science, sociology, or journalism) at an accredited institution of higher education in New York. Selection is based on a letter of recommendation from a teacher or counselor, official transcripts, SAT scores, and an essay of 400 to 500 words on a topic that changes annually; recently, the topic was "How Unions Help All Workers." Finalists are interviewed.

Financial data The stipend is $2,000 per year.

Duration 4 years.

Additional information Information is also available from New York State AFL-CIO Scholarship Committee, c/o Dr. Lois Gray, Cornell University, ILR School, 16 East 34th Street, Fourth Floor, New York, NY 10016. This scholarship was established in 1988.

Number awarded 1 each year.

Deadline April of each year.

[292]
NEXT GENERATION OF PUBLIC SERVANTS SCHOLARSHIP

Hispanic Scholarship Fund Institute
1001 Connecticut Avenue, N.W., Suite 632
Washington, DC 20036
(202) 296-0009   Fax: (202) 296-3633
E-mail: info@hsfi.org
Web: www.hsfi.org/sch_nextgen.html

Purpose To provide financial assistance to Hispanic and other students majoring in designated business, engineering, social science, and science fields who are interested in employment with the U.S. Department of Energy (DOE).

Eligibility This program is open to U.S. citizens enrolled full time as sophomores with a GPA of 2.8 or higher. Applicants must be interested in preparing for a career with the DOE in an energy-related field. Eligible academic majors are in the fields of business (accounting, business administration, finance, and management), engineering (biomedical, chemical, civil, computer, electrical, environmental, industrial, materials, mechanical, metallurgical, nuclear, and petroleum), social science (economics, organizational psychology, political science, and sociology), and science (biological sciences,

computer science, geology, information technology, mathematics, microbiology, and physics). They must be willing to participate in co-ops with the DOE. Along with their application, they must submit a 2-page essay on why a career in public service interests them, how their academic major connects with their stated DOE career goal, why the DOE should invest in them through this program, and how they believe the DOE will benefit from this investment. Selection is based on academic achievement, financial need, demonstrated commitment to public service, and interest in federal employment with the DOE.

Financial data The stipend is $3,000 per year.

Duration 1 year; may be renewed up to 2 additional years if the recipient maintains full-time enrollment and a GPA of 2.8 or higher.

Additional information This program, sponsored by DOE's Office of Economic Impact and Diversity, is administered by the Hispanic Scholarship Fund Institute as part of its effort to increase Hispanic participation in federal service.

Number awarded Varies each year.

Deadline February of each year.

[293]
NFIB FREE ENTERPRISE SCHOLARS PROGRAM

National Federation of Independent Business
Attn: NFIB Education Foundation
1020 F Street, N.W., Suite 200
Washington, DC 20004
(202) 554-9000   Toll-free: (800) NFIB-NOW
E-mail: aaron.taylor@nfib.org
Web: www.nfibeducationfoundation.org

Purpose To provide financial assistance for college to high school seniors who are interested in private enterprise and entrepreneurship.

Eligibility This program is open to graduating high school seniors who plan to enter their freshman year at an accredited 2-year college, 4-year college or university, or vocational/technical institute. Students must be nominated by a member of the National Federation of Independent Business (NFIB). Nominees must meet or exceed academic standards, using standardized test scores (ACT/SAT), class rank, and GPA as indicators. They must answer a short, personal question defining their entrepreneurial efforts and compose another essay of 500 words or less about the importance of free enterprise. Selection is based on those essays, involvement in extracurricular and/or community activities, and special recognition or honors.

Financial data The stipend is $1,000.

Duration 1 year; nonrenewable.

Additional information These scholarships were first awarded in 2003.

Number awarded At least 100 each year.

Deadline March of each year.

[294]
NIB GRANT M. MACK MEMORIAL SCHOLARSHIP

American Council of the Blind
Attn: Coordinator, Scholarship Program
1155 15th Street, N.W., Suite 1004
Washington, DC 20005
(202) 467-5081   Toll-free: (800) 424-8666
Fax: (202) 467-5085   E-mail: info@acb.org
Web: www.acb.org

Purpose To provide financial assistance to students who are blind and working on an undergraduate or graduate degree in business or management.

Eligibility All legally blind persons who are majoring in business or management (undergraduate or graduate) and are U.S. citizens or resident aliens are eligible to apply. In addition to letters of recommendation and copies of academic transcripts, applications must include an autobiographical sketch. A cumulative GPA of 3.3 or higher is generally required. Selection is based on demonstrated academic record, involvement in extracurricular and civic activities, and academic objectives. The severity of the applicant's visual impairment and his/her study methods are also taken into account.

Financial data The stipend is $2,000. In addition, the winner receives a $1,000 cash scholarship from the Kurzweil Foundation and, if appropriate, a Kurzweil-1000 Reading System.

Duration 1 year.

Additional information This scholarship is sponsored by National Industries for the Blind (NIB) in honor of a dedicated leader of the American Council of the Blind. Scholarship winners are expected to be present at the council's annual conference; the council will cover all reasonable expenses connected with convention attendance.

Number awarded 1 each year.

Deadline February of each year.

[295]
NORFOLK SOUTHERN FOUNDATION SCHOLARSHIPS

National FFA Organization
Attn: Scholarship Office
6060 FFA Drive
P.O. Box 68960
Indianapolis, IN 46268-0960
(317) 802-4321   Fax: (317) 802-5321
E-mail: scholarships@ffa.org
Web: www.ffa.org

Purpose To provide financial assistance to current or former FFA members who are interested in studying a field related to agriculture (including management and merchandising) at a college or university in designated states.

Eligibility This program is open to members who are either graduating high school seniors planning to enroll in college or students already enrolled in college. Applicants must be interested in working full time on a 4-year degree in agricultural and forestry production, communication, education, engineering, finance, management, marketing, merchandising, sales, or agricultural science. They must be planning to attend a college or university in Alabama, Delaware, Georgia, Illinois, Indiana, Louisiana, Maryland, Michigan, Missouri, New York,

North Carolina, Ohio, Pennsylvania, South Carolina, Tennessee, or Virginia. Selection is based on academic achievement (10 points for GPA, 10 points for SAT or ACT score, 10 points for class rank), leadership in FFA activities (30 points), leadership in community activities (10 points), and participation in the Supervised Agricultural Experience (SAE) program (30 points). U.S. citizenship is required.

Financial data The stipend is $1,000. Funds are paid directly to the recipient.

Duration 1 year; nonrenewable.

Additional information Funding for these scholarships is provided by the Norfolk Southern Foundation.

Number awarded 3 each year.

Deadline February of each year.

[296]
NORTH CAROLINA CPA FOUNDATION SCHOLARSHIPS

North Carolina Association of Certified Public
     Accountants
Attn: North Carolina CPA Foundation, Inc.
3100 Gateway Centre Boulevard
P.O. Box 80188
Raleigh, NC 27623-0188
(919) 469-1040, ext. 133   Toll-free: (800) 722-2836
Fax: (919) 469-3959   E-mail: vpironio@ncacpa.org
Web: www.ncacpa.org

Purpose To provide financial assistance to students majoring in accounting at colleges and universities in North Carolina.

Eligibility This program is open to North Carolina residents. Applicants must have completed at least 1 upper-division accounting program, must have completed at least 4 semesters, and must be majoring in accounting at a North Carolina college or university. They must be sponsored by 2 accounting faculty members and they must submit an essay on what they believe the C.P.A. of the 21st century will be like. Selection is based equally on GPA (3.0 or higher), extracurricular activities, awards or honors received, essay content, and essay grammar.

Financial data Stipends range from $1,000 to $5,000.

Duration 1 year.

Number awarded Varies each year. Recently, 29 of these scholarships were awarded.

Deadline January of each year.

[297]
NORTH CAROLINA SOCIETY OF ACCOUNTANTS SCHOLARSHIP

North Carolina Society of Accountants Scholarship
     Foundation
P.O. Box 10387
Raleigh, NC 27605
(919) 834-1072   Fax: (919) 821-3072
Web: www.ncsainc.org/schfnd.htm

Purpose To provide financial assistance to residents of North Carolina who are working on an accounting degree at a college or university in the state.

Eligibility This program is open to residents of North Carolina who are enrolled at an accredited college or university in the state in an accounting program with 6 or more credits per semester and planning to work in the accounting field after graduation. Applicants must submit a recent photograph, a completed application form, 2 letters of reference, a letter of intent, an official transcript, and a copy of their or their parents' most recent income tax return.

Financial data The stipend is $500.

Duration 1 year.

Additional information This program began in 1970.

Number awarded 1 or more each year.

Deadline April of each year.

[298]
NSA ANNUAL SCHOLARSHIP AWARDS

National Society of Accountants
Attn: NSA Scholarship Foundation
1010 North Fairfax Street
Alexandria, VA 22314-1574
(703) 549-6400, ext. 1312
Toll-free: (800) 966-6679, ext. 1312
Fax: (703) 549-2512   E-mail: snoell@nsacct.org
Web: www.nsacct.org

Purpose To provide financial assistance to undergraduate students majoring in accounting.

Eligibility This program is open to undergraduate students enrolled on a full-time basis in an accounting degree program at an accredited 2-year or 4-year college or university with a GPA of 3.0 or better. Students in 2-year colleges may apply during their first year or during their second year if transferring to a 4-year institution, provided they have committed themselves to a major in accounting throughout the remainder of their college career; students in 4-year colleges may apply for a scholarship for their second, third, or fourth year of studies, provided they have committed themselves to a major in accounting through the remainder of their college career. Only U.S. or Canadian citizens attending a U.S. accredited business school, college, or university may apply. Selection is based on academic attainment, demonstrated leadership ability, and financial need.

Financial data The stipend is approximately $500 per year for students entering their second year of studies or approximately $1,000 per year for students entering the third or fourth year.

Duration 1 year.

Additional information The outstanding student in this competition, designated the Charles H. Earp Memorial Scholar, receives an additional stipend of $200 and an appropriate plaque.

Number awarded Approximately 40 each year.

Deadline March of each year.

[299]
NYWICI FOUNDATION SCHOLARSHIPS

New York Women in Communications, Inc.
Attn: NYWICI Foundation
355 Lexington Avenue, 17th Floor
New York, NY 10017-6603
(212) 297-2133   Fax: (212) 370-9047
E-mail: nywicipr@nywici.org
Web: www.nywici.org/foundation.scholarships.html

Purpose To provide financial assistance for college or graduate school to residents of designated eastern states who are interested in preparing for a career in the communications profession.

Eligibility This program is open to 1) seniors graduating from high schools in the state of New York; 2) undergraduate students who are permanent residents of New York, New Jersey, Connecticut, or Pennsylvania; 3) graduate students who are permanent residents of New York, New Jersey, Connecticut, or Pennsylvania; and 4) current members of New York Women in Communications, Inc. (NYWICI) who are returning to school. Applicants must be majoring in a communications-related major (advertising, broadcasting, communications, journalism, marketing, new media, or public relations) and have a GPA of 3.5 or higher in their major and 3.0 overall. Along with their application, they must submit a resume that includes school and extracurricular activities, significant achievements, academic honors and awards, and community service work; a statement of their future goals in the communications profession; a 300- to 500-word personal essay describing how events in their lives have inspired them to achieve success and overcome difficulty in the face of any financial and/or other obstacles; 2 letters of recommendation; and an official transcript.

Financial data The maximum stipend is $10,000.

Duration 1 year.

Number awarded 1 or more each year.

Deadline January of each year.

[300]
OHIO SOCIETY OF CPAS CHAPTER SCHOLARSHIPS

Ohio Society of Certified Public Accountants
535 Metro Place
P.O. Box 1810
Dublin, OH 43017
(614) 764-2727   Toll-free: (800) 686-2727
E-mail: oscpa@ohio-cpa.com
Web: www.ohioscpa.com

Purpose To provide financial assistance to students at Ohio colleges and universities who are majoring in accounting.

Eligibility This program is open to students majoring in accounting at Ohio colleges and universities who are nominated by their department. Applicants must be attending an institution that is located in a section of the state with a chapter of the sponsoring organization that offers a scholarship. Winners of chapter scholarships are then invited to participate in Scholarship Day at the state organization's offices and take part in an interview process. Based on those interviews, a state grand prize winner is selected.

Financial data Chapters provide each recipient with a stipend of $500, which is matched by the state organization. The state prize is $3,000.

Duration 1 year.

Number awarded Varies each year.

[301]
OHIO STATE CLAIMS ASSOCIATION SCHOLARSHIPS

Griffith Foundation for Insurance Education
172 East State Street, Suite 305A
Columbus, OH 43215-4321
(614) 341-2392   Fax: (614) 442-0402
E-mail: griffithfoundation@attglobal.net
Web: www.griffithfoundation.org

Purpose To provide financial assistance to children of members of Ohio State Claims Association (OSCA) affiliated organizations who agree to take at least 1 course in risk management and insurance in college.

Eligibility This program in open to the children, stepchildren, and adopted children of members of an affiliated organization of OSCA. Applicants must be either high school seniors who have been accepted and intend to enroll in an accredited college or university in the United States working on an undergraduate degree or full-time students already enrolled. They must commit to take 1 course in risk management and insurance or submit evidence that they have already taken such a course. Selection is based on academic achievement, extracurricular activities and honors, work experience, 3 letters of recommendation, and financial need.

Financial data Stipends up to $2,500 per year are provided.

Duration 1 year; renewable.

Additional information Information is also available from the OSCA Scholarship Chair, Edward A. Borocz, c/o Admiral Adjusting Company, P.O. Box 360227, Strongsville, OH 44136, (440) 572-7700, E-mail: Eborocz@aol.com.

Number awarded 1 or more each year.

Deadline April of each year.

[302]
O.J. BOOKER SCHOLARSHIP AWARD

Healthcare Financial Management Association-Georgia
    Chapter
c/o Judy King Williams, Awards Chair
McKesson Information Solutions
5995 Windward Parkway
Alpharetta, GA 30005
(404) 338-3749   Fax: (404) 338-6101
E-mail: JudyKing.Williams@mcKesson, com
Web: www.georgiahfma.org/scholarships.asp

Purpose To provide financial assistance to members of the Georgia chapter of the Healthcare Financial Management Association (HFMA) who are planning to enter the health care financial management industry.

Eligibility This program is open to student members of the HFMA Georgia chapter who are nominated by a chapter member. Letters of nomination should include the place of employment, degree of program being pursued, and reason for nomination. Nominees must be enrolled full time in a pro-

gram to prepare for a career in the health care financial management industry.

Financial data The stipend is $1,500.

Duration 1 year.

Additional information This program was established in 1987.

Number awarded 1 each year.

[303]
OKLAHOMA SOCIETY OF CERTIFIED PUBLIC ACCOUNTANTS SCHOLARSHIP

Oklahoma Society of Certified Public Accountants
Attn: OSCPA Educational Foundation
1900 N.W. Expressway Street, Suite 910
Oklahoma City, OK 73118-1898
(405) 841-3800, ext. 3829
Toll-free: (800) 522-8261 (within OK)
Fax: (405) 841-3801   E-mail: dmeyer@oscpa.com
Web: www.oscpa.com

Purpose To provide financial assistance to upper-division students working on a bachelor's degree in accounting in Oklahoma.

Eligibility This program is open to juniors and seniors who are nominated by a 4-year or 5-year accounting program at an Oklahoma college or university. Nominees must have successfully completed at least 12 hours of accounting, including 6 hours of intermediate accounting, and 60 hours of general college credit. As part of the application process, nominees must submit a resume, a transcript, standardized test scores, and 3 letters of reference.

Financial data The stipend is at least $500.

Duration 1 year.

Number awarded Varies each year; recently, 17 of these scholarships were awarded.

Deadline April of each year.

[304]
OMAHA CHAPTER SCHOLARSHIPS

American Society of Women Accountants-Omaha
    Chapter
c/o Beth Byrne, Scholarship Committee
823 Auburn Lane
Papillion, NE 68046
Web: www.geocities.com/aswaomaha/scholarships.htm

Purpose To provide financial assistance to accounting students in Nebraska.

Eligibility This program is open to part- and full-time students working on a bachelor's or master's degree in accounting at a college or university in Nebraska. Applicants must have completed at least 60 semester hours. They are not required to be a member of the American Society of Women Accountants. Selection is based on academic achievement, extracurricular activities and honors, a statement of career goals and objectives, letters of recommendation, and financial need.

Financial data A total of $2,000 is available for this program each year.

Duration 1 year.

Additional information The highest ranked recipient is entered into the national competition for scholarships that range from $1,500 to $4,500.

Number awarded Varies each year; recently, 3 of these scholarships were awarded.

Deadline January of each year.

[305]
ORACLE/UNCF INTERNSHIP AND SCHOLARSHIP PROGRAM

United Negro College Fund
Attn: Corporate Scholars Program
P.O. Box 1435
Alexandria, VA 22313-9998
Toll-free: (866) 671-7237   E-mail: internship@uncf.org
Web: www.uncf.org/internships/index.asp

Purpose To provide financial assistance and work experience to students majoring in business-related fields at colleges and universities that are members of the United Negro College Fund (UNCF) and at other Historically Black Colleges and Universities (HBCUs).

Eligibility This program is open to second-semester juniors and seniors who are enrolled full time at UNCF-member institutions and other HBCUs. Applicants must be majoring in accounting, business administration, computer engineering, computer science, finance, human resources, management information systems, or marketing and have a GPA of 3.0 or higher. They must be interested in a summer internship at Oracle Corporation facilities at Redwood Shores, California or Reston, Virginia. Along with their application, they must submit a 1-page personal statement describing their career interests and goals, a current resume, a letter of recommendation, official transcripts, and a financial need statement.

Financial data This program provides a round-trip transportation to Redwood Shores or Reston, local transportation while working at the internship site, housing accommodations at the internship location, a monthly internship salary of $4,000, and (upon successful completion of the internship) a scholarship of $10,000.

Duration 8 weeks for the internships; 1 year for the scholarships.

Additional information This program, established in 2002, is sponsored by Oracle.

Number awarded Varies each year.

Deadline March of each year.

[306]
OREGON ASSOCIATION OF INDEPENDENT ACCOUNTANTS SCHOLARSHIPS

Oregon Association of Independent Accountants
Attn: OAIA Scholarship Foundation
1804 N.E. 43rd Avenue
Portland, OR 97231
(503) 282-7247
Web: www.oaia.net/scholarship.html

Purpose To provide financial assistance to Oregon residents interested in majoring in accounting in college.

Eligibility This program is open to Oregon residents who are enrolled in or accepted by an accredited school in the state for the study of accounting. Applicants must intend to

carry a minimum of 12 credit hours. Along with their application, they must submit an essay on why they have chosen to study and prepare for a career in accounting. Selection is based on financial need, scholastic achievement, personal qualifications, and professional promise.

Financial data Stipends range from $1,000 to $2,000. Checks are made payable to the recipient and the recipient's college. Funds may be used for tuition, fees, books, or other academic expenses during the year.

Duration 1 year; renewable.

Additional information The Scholarship Foundation is sponsored by the Oregon Association of Independent Accountants (formerly the Oregon Association of Public Accountants). Recipients may attend a college, university, or community college. They are given an honorary 1-year student membership in the Oregon Association of Independent Accountants.

Deadline March of each year.

[307]
OREGON STATE FISCAL ASSOCIATION SCHOLARSHIP

Oregon Student Assistance Commission
Attn: Grants and Scholarships Division
1500 Valley River Drive, Suite 100
Eugene, OR 97401-2146
(541) 687-7395   Toll-free: (800) 452-8807, ext. 7395
Fax: (541) 687-7419
E-mail: awardinfo@mercury.osac.state.or.us
Web: www.osac.state.or.us

Purpose To provide financial assistance for college or graduate school to members of the Oregon State Fiscal Association and their children.

Eligibility This program is open to members of the association and their children who are enrolled or planning to enroll at a college or university in Oregon as an undergraduate or graduate student. Members must study public administration, finance, economics, or related fields, but they may enroll part time. Children may enroll in any program of study, but they must be full-time students.

Financial data Scholarship amounts vary, depending upon the needs of the recipient.

Duration 1 year.

Number awarded Varies each year.

Deadline February of each year.

[308]
OSCAR AND ROSETTA FISH FUND

Hawai'i Community Foundation
Attn: Scholarship Department
1164 Bishop Street, Suite 800
Honolulu, HI 96813
(808) 537-6333   Toll-free: (888) 731-3863
Fax: (808) 521-6286
E-mail: scholarships@hcf-hawaii.org
Web: www.hawaiicommunityfoundation.org

Purpose To provide financial assistance to Hawaii residents who are interested in studying business at 1 of the campuses of the University of Hawaii.

Eligibility This program is open to Hawaii residents who are interested in studying business on the undergraduate or graduate school level at any campus of the University of Hawaii except Manoa. Applicants must be able to demonstrate academic achievement (GPA of 2.7 or higher), good moral character, and financial need. In addition to filling out the standard application form, applicants must write a short statement indicating their reasons for attending college, their planned course of study, and their career goals.

Financial data The amounts of the awards depend on the availability of funds and the need of the recipient; recently, stipends averaged $2,000.

Duration 1 year.

Additional information This program was established in 1999. Recipients must be full-time students.

Number awarded Varies each year; recently, 27 of these scholarships were awarded.

Deadline February of each year.

[309]
OSCPA EDUCATIONAL FOUNDATION COLLEGE SCHOLARSHIPS

Oregon Society of Certified Public Accountants
Attn: OSCPA Educational Foundation
10206 S.W. Laurel Street
Beaverton, OR 97005-3209
(503) 641-7200   Toll-free: (800) 255-1470, ext. 29
Fax: (503) 626-2942   E-mail: oscpa@orcpa.org
Web: www.orcpa.org

Purpose To provide financial assistance to undergraduate and graduate students in Oregon who are working on a degree in accounting.

Eligibility This program is open to Oregon college and university students who are working full time on an undergraduate or master's degree in accounting. Applicants must have a GPA of 3.2 or higher in accounting/business classes and overall. Along with their application, they must submit 3 letters of recommendation and a recent transcript. Selection is based on scholastic ability and interest in the accounting profession.

Financial data For graduate students and undergraduates enrolled in or transferring to 4-year colleges and universities, stipends range from $1,000 to $3,000. For students enrolled in community colleges, the stipend is $500.

Duration 1 year.

Number awarded Varies each year.

Deadline February of each year.

[310]
OSCPA EDUCATIONAL FOUNDATION HIGH SCHOOL SCHOLARSHIPS

Oregon Society of Certified Public Accountants
Attn: OSCPA Educational Foundation
10206 S.W. Laurel Street
Beaverton, OR 97005-3209
(503) 641-7200   Toll-free: (800) 255-1470, ext. 29
Fax: (503) 626-2942   E-mail: oscpa@orcpa.org
Web: www.orcpa.org

Purpose To provide financial assistance to high school seniors in Oregon who are interested in studying accounting in college.

Eligibility This program is open to seniors at high schools in Oregon who are interested in studying accounting at a college or university in the state. Applicants must have a GPA of 3.5 or higher and be planning to enroll full time. Along with their application, they must submit 3 letters of recommendation and their high school transcript. Selection is based on scholastic ability and interest in the accounting profession.

Financial data For students planning to attend a 4-year college or university, the stipend is $1,000. For students planning to attend a community college, the stipend is $500.

Duration 1 year.

Number awarded Varies each year.

Deadline February of each year.

[311]
OTIS SPUNKMEYER STUDENT SCHOLARSHIPS

DECA
1908 Association Drive
Reston, VA 20191-1594
(703) 860-5000   Fax: (703) 860-4013
E-mail: decainc@aol.com
Web: www.deca.org/scholarships/index.html

Purpose To provide financial assistance to DECA members interested in studying business in college.

Eligibility This program is open to DECA members who are interested in working full time on a 2-year or 4-year degree in marketing, business, or marketing education. Applicants must be able to demonstrate evidence of DECA activities, academic achievement, leadership ability, and community service involvement. Selection is based on merit, not financial need.

Financial data The stipend is $1,000.

Duration 1 year.

Additional information This program is sponsored by Otis Spunkmeyer, Inc.

Number awarded 15 each year.

Deadline February of each year.

[312]
PATRICIA ASIP SCHOLARSHIP FOR MARKETING AND PROMOTION

Hispanic Designers, Inc.
Attn: National Hispanic Education and Communications
   Projects
1101 30th Street, N.W., Suite 500
Washington, DC 20007
(202) 337-9636   Fax: (202) 337-9635
E-mail: HispDesign@aol.com
Web: www.hispanicdesigners.org

Purpose To provide financial assistance to Hispanic students enrolled in fashion design schools who are interested in preparing for a career in marketing and promotion.

Eligibility Applicants must be Hispanic or of Hispanic descent, be able to demonstrate financial need, be U.S. citizens or residents, have participated in an internship or work training program in the field of fashion, and have a GPA of 3.0 or higher. They must be enrolled in an accredited postsecondary institution studying for a degree or in certified programs in fashion design or a related field. Selection is based on the presentation of a merchandising strategy for a ready-to-wear collection targeting the U.S. Hispanic market; the presentation must include samples of advertising in English and Spanish, description of the target customer, price range, type of store and department in which the collection would be carried, a press kit on the designer and the collection, a design hang tag for garments in the collection, and a design label or logo for the collection.

Financial data The stipend is $5,000 per year; awards are paid directly to the recipient's institution.

Duration 1 year.

Additional information This program was established in 1998 to honor Patricia V. Asip, who coordinated the Hispanic Designers Model Search for her employer, JCPenney Company, Inc. No telephone inquiries are accepted.

Number awarded 1 each year.

Deadline August of each year.

[313]
PAUL HAGELBARGER MEMORIAL SCHOLARSHIP

Alaska Society of Certified Public Accountants
341 West Tudor Road, Suite 105
Anchorage, AK 99503
(907) 562-4334   Toll-free: (800) 478-4334
Fax: (907) 562-4025
Web: www.akcpa.org/scholarships.htm

Purpose To provide financial assistance to upper-division and graduate students at colleges and universities in Alaska who are preparing for a career in public accounting.

Eligibility This program is open to juniors, seniors, and graduate students majoring in accounting at 4-year colleges and universities in Alaska. Applicants must submit brief essays on their educational goals, career goals, and financial need. Selection is based on academic achievement, intent to prepare for a career in public accounting in Alaska, and financial need.

Financial data The stipend is at least $2,000.

Duration 1 year.

Additional information This program was established in 1964.

Number awarded 1 or more each year.

Deadline November of each year.

[314]
PAYCHEX INC. ENTREPRENEUR SCHOLARSHIP

Massachusetts Society of Certified Public Accountants
Attn: MSCPA Educational Foundation
105 Chauncy Street, Tenth Floor
Boston, MA 02111
(617) 556-4000   Toll-free: (800) 392-6145
Fax: (617) 556-4126
E-mail: biannoni@MSCPAonline.org
Web: www.cpatrack.com/financial_aid/scholarship.php

Purpose To provide financial assistance to residents of Massachusetts working on a degree in accounting at a college or university in the state.

Eligibility This program is open to Massachusetts residents enrolled full time at a college or university in the state with a cumulative GPA of 3.0 or higher. Applicants must be entering their junior year and be able to demonstrate both financial need and a commitment to preparing for a career as a certified public accountant.

Financial data The stipend is $1,000.

Duration 1 year.

Number awarded 1 each year.

[315]
PBI MEDIA SCHOLARSHIP

Society of Satellite Professionals International
Attn: Scholarship Program
New York Information Technology Center
55 Broad Street, 14th Floor
New York, NY 10004
(212) 809-5199   Fax: (212) 825-0075
E-mail: sspi@sspi.org
Web: www.sspi.org/html/scholarship.html

Purpose To provide financial assistance to students interested in majoring in satellite-related disciplines (including business) in college or graduate school.

Eligibility This program is open to high school seniors, college undergraduates, and graduate students majoring or planning to major in fields related to satellite technologies, policies, or applications. Fields of study in the past have included broadcasting, business, distance learning, energy, government, imaging, meteorology, navigation, remote sensing, space law, and telecommunications. Applicants may be from any country. Selection is based on academic and leadership achievement, commitment to pursue educational and career opportunities in the satellite communications industry, potential for significant contribution to that industry, a personal statement of 500 to 750 words on interest in satellite communications and why they deserve the award, and a creative work (such as a research report, essay, article, videotape, artwork, computer program, or scale model of an antenna or spacecraft design) that reflects the applicant's interests and talents. This award recognizes innovative work in the satellite field that emphasizes the commercial and/or humanitarian aspects of new technologies and services. It is conferred on the applicant who best analyzes the entrepreneurial possibilities of new satellite services, technologies, or applications from a profit-driven or public service-oriented perspective. Financial need is not considered.

Financial data The stipend is $2,000.

Duration 1 year.

Number awarded 1 each year.

Deadline May of each year.

[316]
PEGGY JACQUES MEMORIAL SCHOLARSHIP

Epsilon Sigma Alpha
Attn: ESA Foundation Assistant Scholarship Director
P.O. Box 270517
Fort Collins, CO 80527
(970) 223-2824   Fax: (970) 223-4456
Web: www.esaintl.com/esaf

Purpose To provide financial assistance for college to students from Michigan planning to study business.

Eligibility This program is open to residents of Michigan who are either 1) graduating high school seniors in the top 25% of their class or with minimum scores of 20 on the ACT or 950 on the SAT, or 2) students already enrolled in college with a GPA of 3.0 or higher. Students enrolled for training in a technical school or returning to school after an absence are also eligible. Applicants must be planning to study business. Selection is based on character (25%), leadership (25%), service (20%), financial need (15%), and scholastic ability (15%).

Financial data The stipend is $500.

Duration 1 year; may be renewed.

Additional information Epsilon Sigma Alpha (ESA) is a women's service organization, but scholarships are available to both men and women. Information is also available from Kathy Loyd, Scholarship Director, 1222 N.W. 651, Blairstown, MO 64726, (660) 747-2216, Fax: (660) 747-0807, E-mail: kloyd@iland.net. Completed applications must be submitted to the ESA State Counselor who verifies the information before forwarding them to the scholarship director. A $5 processing fee is required.

Number awarded 1 each year.

Deadline January of each year.

[317]
PENNSYLVANIA SOCIETY OF PUBLIC ACCOUNTANTS SCHOLARSHIPS

Pennsylvania Society of Public Accountants
Attn: Executive Office
20 Erford Road, Suite 200A
Lemoyne, PA 17043
(717) 234-4129   Toll-free: (800) 270-3352
Fax: (717) 234-9556   E-mail: info@pspa-state.org
Web: www.pspa-state.org/scholarships.html

Purpose To provide financial assistance to accounting majors in Pennsylvania.

Eligibility This program is open to Pennsylvania residents who have completed at least 3 semesters at a college or university in the state with a major in accounting and a GPA of 3.0 or higher. Selection is based primarily on academic merit. Student activities, leadership positions, and financial need may also be considered in the selection process.

Financial data The stipend is $1,000 per year.

Duration 1 year.

Number awarded 3 each year.

Deadline May of each year.

[318]
PETER A. DECOURSEY MEMORIAL AWARD

Junior Achievement of Delaware, Inc.
522 South Walnut Street
Wilmington, DE 19801-5230
(302) 654-4510   Toll-free: (866) JA-TODAY
Fax: (302) 654-0783
Web: delaware.ja.org/programs_evaluations.html

Purpose To provide financial assistance for college to high school seniors who have made an outstanding contribution to Junior Achievement (JA) in Delaware.

Eligibility This program is open to high school seniors who are members of JA in Delaware. Finalists are interviewed. Selection is based on leadership and ability to motivate others.

Financial data The stipend is $1,000.

Duration 1 year.

Additional information Junior Achievement of Delaware serves the state of Delaware, Salem County in New Jersey, and Cecil County in Maryland. This program is administered by the Delaware Community Foundation, 100 West 10th Street, Suite 115, P.O. Box 1636, Wilmington, DE 19899-1636, (302) 504-5222, Fax: (302) 571-1553.

Number awarded 1 each year.

Deadline April of each year.

[319]
PFIZER/UNCF CORPORATE SCHOLARS PROGRAM

United Negro College Fund
Attn: Corporate Scholars Program
P.O. Box 1435
Alexandria, VA 22313-9998
Toll-free: (866) 671-7237   E-mail: internship@uncf.org
Web: www.uncf.org/internships/index.asp

Purpose To provide financial assistance and work experience to minority undergraduate and graduate students majoring in designated fields and interested in an internship at a Pfizer facility.

Eligibility This program is open to sophomores, juniors, graduate students, and first-year law students who are African American, Hispanic American, Asian/Pacific Islander American, or American Indian/Alaskan Native. Applicants must have a GPA of 3.0 or higher and be enrolled at an institution that is a member of the United Negro College Fund (UNCF) or at another targeted college or university. They must be working on 1) a bachelor's degree in animal science, business, chemistry (organic or analytical), human resources, logistics, microbiology, organizational development, operations management, pre-veterinary medicine, or supply chain management; 2) a master's degree in chemistry (organic or analytical), finance, human resources, or organizational development; or 3) a law degree. Eligibility is limited to U.S. citizens, permanent residents, asylees, refugees, and lawful temporary residents. Along with their application, they must submit a 1-page essay about themselves and their career goals, including information about their interest in Pfizer (the program's sponsor), their personal background, and any particular challenges they have faced.

Financial data The program provides an internship stipend of up to $5,000, housing accommodations near Pfizer Corporate facilities, and (based on successful internship performance) a $15,000 scholarship.

Duration 8 to 10 weeks for the internship; 1 year for the scholarship.

Additional information Opportunities for first-year law students include the summer internship only.

Number awarded Varies each year.

Deadline January of each year.

[320]
PHILIP MORRIS SCHOLARS
Virginia Foundation for Independent Colleges
Attn: Director of Development
8010 Ridge Road, Suite B
Richmond, VA 23229
(804) 288-6609   Toll-free: (800) 230-6757
Fax: (804) 282-4635   E-mail: sgro@vfic.org
Web: www.vfic.org

Purpose To provide financial assistance to high school seniors who are entering a college or university that is a member of the Virginia Foundation for Independent Colleges (VFIC).

Eligibility This program is open to high school seniors who have been accepted at 1 of the 15 VFIC member institutions. Applicants majoring in biology, business, chemistry, computer science, economics, engineering, or physics are especially encouraged to apply. Selection is based on merit.

Financial data The stipend is $10,000 per year.

Duration 1 year. May be renewed up to 3 additional years if the recipient maintains a GPA of 3.0 or higher and a record of good citizenship and conduct.

Additional information Funding for this program, established in 2001, is provided by Philip Morris, USA. The 15 member institutions are Bridgewater College, Emory and Henry College, Hampden-Sydney College, Hollins University, Lynchburg College, Mary Baldwin College, Marymount University, Randolph-Macon College, Randolph-Macon Woman's College, Roanoke College, Shenandoah University, Sweet Briar College, University of Richmond, Virginia Wesleyan College, and Washington and Lee University.

Number awarded 5 each year.

Deadline December of each year.

[321]
PICPA SOPHOMORE SCHOLARSHIPS
Pennsylvania Institute of Certified Public Accountants
Attn: Careers in Accounting Team
1650 Arch Street, 17th Floor
Philadelphia, PA 19103-2099
(215) 496-9272   Toll-free: (888) CPA-2001 (within PA)
Fax: (215) 496-9212   E-mail: schools@picpa.org
Web: www.cpazone.org/scholar/sophomor.asp

Purpose To provide financial assistance to Pennsylvania sophomores majoring in accounting.

Eligibility To qualify for this scholarship, an applicant must be a full-time sophomore at a 4-year college or university in Pennsylvania and be nominated by the accounting department chair at that school. Nominees are evaluated on the basis of academic record, SAT scores, intent to become a CPA and practice in Pennsylvania, need, faculty recommendation, work ethic, reasons for career choice, qualities of leadership, and the student's resume.

Financial data Stipends are either $3,000, $1,500, or $1,000.

Duration 1 year; most may be renewed for up to 2 additional years.

Additional information This program includes the Joseph Taricani Memorial Scholarship, a 1-time award of $1,000.

Number awarded 18 each year: 5 at $3,000, 12 at $1,500, and 1 at $1,000.

Deadline March of each year.

[322]
PIKES PEAK CHAPTER SCHOLARSHIP PROGRAM
Institute of Management Accountants-Pikes Peak Chapter
Attn: Scholarship Selection Committee
P.O. Box 752
Colorado Springs, CO 80901-0752
(719) 637-8539
E-mail: scholarships@pikespeakima.org
Web: www.pikespeakima.org

Purpose To provide financial assistance to undergraduate and graduate students interested in preparing for a career in management accounting or financial management.

Eligibility This program is open to students who are 1) attending a 2-year college in business administration or accounting and planning to continue their education in a 4- or 5-year management accounting or financial management program; 2) attending a 4-year undergraduate institution in business administration, accounting, or finance; or 3) working on a graduate degree with a declared major in management accounting or financial management or have majored in management accounting or financial management as an undergraduate. Applicants must be members of the Institute of Management Accountants (IMA) studying in the United States or Puerto Rico at a regionally-accredited institution. Selection is based on academic merit, quality of the application presentation, demonstrated community leadership, and potential for success in expressed career goals in a financial management position.

Financial data The stipend is $500.

Duration 1 academic year; nonrenewable.

Number awarded 1 each year.

Deadline January of each year.

[323]
POST SCHOLARSHIP
American Association of Airport Executives-Northeast Chapter
c/o Richard J. Williams, Executive Secretary
P.O. Box 8
West Milford, NJ 07480-0008
(973) 728-6760   Fax: (973) 728-6760
Web: www.necaaae.org/postnec.htm

Purpose To provide financial assistance to upper-division students majoring in aviation management.

Eligibility This program is open to juniors and seniors in colleges and universities who are majoring in aviation management. Preference is given to those with a permanent residence in the northeast region. Student preparing for a career as commercial pilots are not eligible. Applicants must indicate how they will benefit from the grant and provide documentation of financial need.

Financial data The stipend is $1,000.

Duration 1 year.

Additional information The northeast region covers Connecticut, Delaware, Maine, Maryland, Massachusetts, New Hampshire, New Jersey, New York, Pennsylvania, Rhode

Island, Vermont, Washington D.C., and the Canadian provinces of New Brunswick, Newfoundland, Nova Scotia, Prince Edward Island, and Quebec.

Number awarded 4 each year.

Deadline February of each year.

[324]
PRINCIPAL FINANCIAL GROUP SCHOLARSHIP

United Negro College Fund
Attn: Scholarships and Grants Department
8260 Willow Oaks Corporate Drive
P.O. Box 10444
Fairfax, VA 22031-8044
(703) 205-3466   Toll-free: (800) 331-2244
Fax: (703) 205-3574
Web: www.uncf.org/scholarships/index.asp

Purpose To provide financial assistance to students from Iowa who are majoring in selected fields at colleges and universities that are members of the United Negro College Fund (UNCF).

Eligibility This program is open to residents of Iowa who are majoring in business, finance, information systems, or the liberal arts at UNCF-member institutions. Applicants must be enrolled full time and have a GPA of 3.0 or higher. Selection is based on academic achievement, work experience, writing skills, community involvement, extracurricular school activities and leadership, academic and personal references, and financial need.

Financial data The stipend depends on the need of the recipient, to a maximum of $12,000 per year.

Duration 1 year; may be renewed until completion of an undergraduate degree (up to 3 years) provided the recipient maintains a GPA of 3.0 or higher.

Additional information Funds for this scholarship are provided by the Principal Financial Group, Inc.

Number awarded 1 or more each year.

Deadline February of each year.

[325]
PUBLIC SERVICE SCHOLARSHIPS

Hispanic Scholarship Fund Institute
1001 Connecticut Avenue, N.W., Suite 632
Washington, DC 20036
(202) 296-0009   Fax: (202) 296-3633
E-mail: info@hsfi.org
Web: www.hsfi.org/sch_pss.html

Purpose To provide financial assistance to undergraduate and graduate students interested in preparing for a career in a field of interest to the U.S. Department of Agriculture (USDA), including business administration.

Eligibility This program is open to 1) full-time undergraduates and 2) master's degree students (who may be enrolled part time) at accredited institutions in the United States. Applicants must be U.S. citizens or permanent residents majoring in a field of interest to the USDA: accounting, agribusiness, agriculture, business administration, civil engineering, computer science, economics, finance, food sciences, information technology, management, mathematics, nutrition, soil science, or statistics. They must have a GPA of 2.75 or higher and a strong interest in a career in public service with the

USDA. Along with their application, they must submit a 2-page essay on why a career in public service interests them, how their academic major connects with their stated USDA career goal, why the USDA should invest in them through this program, and how they believe the USDA will benefit from this investment. Selection is based mainly on academic achievement, commitment to public service, and interest in federal employment with the USDA, but financial need is also considered.

Financial data The program provides recipients with full payment of tuition and fees, employment with USDA (including employee benefits), a fully-equipped personal computer, and networking opportunities.

Duration 1 year; may be renewed.

Additional information After graduation, recipients must be prepared to work for USDA for 1 year for each year of educational assistance they receive. For a list of the USDA agencies, the academic majors in which they are interested, and the locations where they offer employment, contact the sponsor or see the web site.

Number awarded Approximately 30 each year.

Deadline April of each year.

[326]
PWC MINORITY SCHOLARS PROGRAM

PricewaterhouseCoopers LLP
Attn: Office of Diversity & WorkLife Quality
1177 Avenue of the Americas
New York, NY 10036
(646) 471-4000   Fax: (646) 471-3188
Web: www.pwcglobal.com

Purpose To provide financial assistance to underrepresented minority undergraduate students interested in preparing for a career in public accounting.

Eligibility This program is open to African American, Native American, and Hispanic American students entering their sophomore or junior year of college. Applicants must have a GPA of 3.3 or higher, be able to demonstrate interpersonal skills and leadership ability, and intend to prepare for a career in public accounting (audit, tax, or forensic accounting). They must be attending 1 of the 31 colleges and universities that are part of the PricewaterhouseCoopers (PwC) Priority School Network and must be legally authorized to work in the United States. Finalists are interviewed in person by a PwC partner, manager or recruiter.

Financial data The stipend is $3,000 per year.

Duration 1 year; may be renewed if the recipient maintains a GPA of 3.3 or higher.

Additional information Recipients also participate in the annual Minorities in Business Leadership Conference (held in New York City), are considered for an internship position with PwC, and engage in a mentoring program. This program began in 1990.

Number awarded 60 each year.

Deadline January of each year.

[327]
RALPH AND VALERIE THOMAS SCHOLARSHIP

National Association of Black Accountants
Attn: Director, Center for Advancement of Minority
   Accountants
7249-A Hanover Parkway
Greenbelt, MD 20770
(301) 474-NABA, ext. 114   Fax: (301) 474-3114
E-mail: cquinn@nabainc.org
Web: www.nabainc.org

Purpose To provide financial assistance to student members of the National Association of Black Accountants (NABA) who are working on an undergraduate or graduate degree in a field related to accounting.

Eligibility This program is open to NABA members who are members of ethnic minority groups enrolled full time as 1) an undergraduate freshman, sophomore, junior, or first-semester senior majoring in accounting, business, or finance; or 2) a graduate student working on a master's degree in accounting. Applicants must have a GPA of 3.5 or higher in their major and 3.3 or higher overall. Selection is based on grades, financial need, and a 500-word autobiography that discusses career objectives, leadership abilities, community activities, and involvement in NABA.

Financial data The stipend is $1,000 per year.

Duration 1 year.

Number awarded 1 each year.

Deadline December of each year.

[328]
RAY FOLEY MEMORIAL SCHOLARSHIP PROGRAM

American Wholesale Marketers Association
Attn: Distributors Education Foundation
2750 Prosperity Avenue, Suite 530
Fairfax, VA 22031
(703) 208-3358   Toll-free: (800) 482-2962
Fax: (703) 573-5738   E-mail: info@awmanet.org
Web: www.awmanet.org/edu/edu-schol.html

Purpose To provide financial assistance to undergraduate or graduate students who are employed by or related to an employee of a member of the American Wholesale Marketers Association (AWMA) and working on a degree in business.

Eligibility This program is open to full-time undergraduate and graduate students working on a degree in a business course of study (accounting or business administration) at an accredited college or university. Applicants must be employed by an AWMA wholesaler distributor member or be an immediate family member (spouse, child, stepchild) of an employee of an AWMA wholesaler distributor member. They must be able to demonstrate interest in a career in distribution of candy, tobacco, and convenience products. Selection is based on academic merit and career interest in the candy/tobacco/convenience-products wholesale industry.

Financial data The scholarships are $5,000 per year. Funds are paid directly to the college or university to cover tuition, on-campus room and board, and other direct costs; any remaining funds are paid to the student for reimbursement of school-related expenses, when appropriate receipts are available.

Duration 1 year; nonrenewable.

Additional information The American Wholesale Marketers Association (AWMA) resulted from the 1991 merger of the National Association of Tobacco Distributors (NATD) and the National Candy Wholesalers Association (NCWA). This scholarship was established in memory of Ray Foley, the late executive vice president of the NCWA.

Number awarded 2 each year.

Deadline May of each year.

[329]
RAYMOND H. TROTT SCHOLARSHIP FOR BANKING

Rhode Island Foundation
Attn: Scholarship Coordinator
One Union Station
Providence, RI 02903
(401) 274-4564   Fax: (401) 331-8085
E-mail: libbym@rifoundation.org
Web: www.rifoundation.org

Purpose To provide financial assistance to Rhode Island undergraduates of color interested in preparing for a career in banking.

Eligibility This program is open to minority residents of Rhode Island who are entering their senior year in college. Applicants must plan to prepare for a career in banking and be able to demonstrate financial need. Along with their application, they must submit an essay (up to 300 words) on the impact they would like to have on the banking industry.

Financial data The stipend is $1,000.

Duration 1 year; nonrenewable.

Additional information This program was established in 1980.

Number awarded 1 each year.

Deadline June of each year.

[330]
RICHARD P.COVERT, PH.D., FHIMSS SCHOLARSHIP

Healthcare Information and Management Systems
   Society
Attn: HIMSS Foundation Scholarship Program
   Coordinator
230 East Ohio Street, Suite 500
Chicago, IL 60611-3269
(312) 664-4467   Fax: (312) 664-6143
Web: www.himss.org/asp/scholarships.asp

Purpose To provide financial assistance to student members of the Healthcare Information and Management Systems Society (HIMSS) who are working on a degree in management engineering.

Eligibility This program is open to student members of the society, although an application for membership, including dues, may accompany the scholarship application. Applicants must be upper-division or graduate students working on a degree in management engineering. Selection is based on academic achievement and demonstration of leadership potential, including communication skills and participation in society activity.

Financial data The stipend is $5,000. The award includes an all-expense paid trip to the annual HIMSS conference and exhibition.

Duration 1 year.

Additional information This program was established in 2004.

Number awarded 1 each year.

Deadline October of each year.

[331]
RITCHIE-JENNINGS MEMORIAL SCHOLARSHIPS PROGRAM

Association of Certified Fraud Examiners
Attn: Scholarship Program
The Gregor Building
716 West Avenue
Austin, TX 78701-2727
(512) 478-9070   Toll-free: (800) 245-3321
Fax: (512) 478-9297   E-mail: scholarships@cfenet.com
Web: www.cfenet.com/services/scholarships.asp

Purpose To provide financial assistance to undergraduate and graduate students working on an accounting or criminal justice degree.

Eligibility This program is open to students working full time on an undergraduate or graduate degree in accounting or criminal justice. Applicants must submit a short essay on why they deserve the award and how fraud awareness will affect their professional career development. Selection is based on the essay, academic achievement, and several letters of recommendation (including at least 1 from a certified fraud examiner).

Financial data The stipend is $1,000.

Duration 1 year.

Additional information This program was established in 1995 and given its current name in 1998.

Number awarded 15 each year.

Deadline May of each year.

[332]
ROBERT E. COOK SCHOLARSHIP FUND

Illinois Association of Realtors
Attn: Illinois Real Estate Educational Foundation
3180 Adloff Lane, Suite 400
P.O. Box 19451
Springfield, IL 62794-9451
(217) 529-2600   E-mail: IARaccess@iar.org
Web: www.illinoisrealtor.org/iar/about/scholarships.htm

Purpose To provide financial assistance to Illinois residents who are interested in pursuing further education for a career in association management.

Eligibility This program is open to Illinois residents who 1) are an executive officer of a local real estate board or association; 2) have expressed an interest in becoming a local real estate board or association executive officer; or 3) are currently employed by a local real estate board or association and are interested in preparing for a career in association management. Applicants must be interested in furthering their education at a junior college, college, or university by pursuing a course of study that relates to the field of association management. They may also be interested in participating in asso-

ciation management training programs sponsored by such organizations as the National Association of Realtors, the United States Chamber of Commerce, or the American Society of Association Executives. Selection is based on the applicant's indication of interest in preparing or continuing to prepare for a career in association management, letters of recommendation, and the plan for use of the scholarship.

Financial data Awards up to $500 are available.

Duration 1 year.

Number awarded Varies each year.

Deadline February of each year.

[333]
ROBERT H. THOMAS SCHOLARSHIP FUND

Healthcare Financial Management Association-Virginia
  Chapter
c/o Herbert D. Harvey, Scholarship Committee Chair
Obici Health System
2800 Godwin Boulevard
Suffolk, VA 23435
(757) 934-4642   E-mail: hharvey@obici.com
Web: www.vahfma.org

Purpose To provide financial assistance to members of the Virginia chapter of the Healthcare Financial Management Association (HFMA) who are interested in a program of continuing education.

Eligibility This program is open to HFMA members in Virginia who are interested in working on an advanced degree, completing a certification program, taking undergraduate courses, or engaging in other educational activities to enhance their career. Selection is based primarily on a 2-page essay that describes their academic goals, how the scholarship will help them achieve those goals, and how they expect their career to be improved.

Financial data The stipend is $1,000.

Duration 1 year.

Number awarded 1 each year.

Deadline April of each year.

[334]
ROGER BUCHHOLZ MEMORIAL SCHOLARSHIPS

Wisconsin Institute of Certified Public Accountants
Attn: WICPA Educational Foundation
235 North Executive Drive, Suite 200
P.O. Box 1010
Brookfield, WI 53008-1010
(414) 785-0445
Toll-free: (800) 772-6939 (within WI and MN)
Fax: (414) 785-0838   E-mail: Tammy@wicpa.org
Web: www.wicpa.org

Purpose To provide financial assistance to college juniors in Wisconsin working on a degree in finance.

Eligibility This program is open to juniors majoring in finance at designated universities in Wisconsin. Applicants must submit an essay describing their career objectives.

Financial data The stipend is $2,500 per year.

Duration 1 year.

Additional information This program is supported by the Milwaukee chapter of Financial Executives International

Number awarded Varies each year; recently, 2 of these scholarships were awarded.
Deadline February of each year.

[335]
ROY & HARRIET ROBINSON SCHOLARSHIP

Professional Independent Insurance Agents of Illinois
Attn: College Scholarship Program
4360 Wabash Avenue
Springfield, IL 62707
(217) 793-6660   Toll-free: (800) 628-6436
Fax: (217) 793-6744   E-mail: admin@piiai.org
Web: www.piiai.org/youngagents/scholarship.htm

Purpose To provide financial assistance to upper-division students from Illinois who are majoring in business and have an interest in insurance.

Eligibility This program is open to residents of Illinois who are full-time juniors or seniors in college. Applicants must be enrolled in a business degree program with an interest in insurance. They must have a letter of recommendation from a current or retired member of the Professional Independent Insurance Agents of Illinois. Along with their application, they must submit an essay (500 words or less) on the contribution the insurance industry provides to society. Financial need is not considered in the selection process.

Financial data The stipend is $1,000, payable in 2 equal installments. Funds are paid directly to the recipient's school.

Duration 1 year.

Number awarded 1 each year.

Deadline June of each year.

[336]
RYAN MOTT MEMORIAL SCHOLARSHIP

Texas FFA Association
614 East 12th Street
Austin, TX 78701
(512) 480-8045   Fax: (512) 472-0555
E-mail: txffa@texasffa.org
Web: www.texasffa.org/ffa/tfa-scho.html

Purpose To provide financial assistance to high school seniors in Texas who are FFA members and interested in majoring in agriculture or life sciences in college.

Eligibility This program is open to high school seniors in Texas who are FFA members and have been members at least 2 of the 3 previous years. Applicants must demonstrate personal qualities of kindness, courtesy, hard work, and dedication to FFA. They should also possess strong leadership and communication skills that they use on an individual basis as well as in team situations. Their proposed major at a Texas college or university should be in the agricultural or life sciences. Scores on ACT or SAT tests are not considered; selection is based on FFA activities (15 points); FFA awards (5 points); FFA offices (5 points); school activities, awards, and/or offices (10 points); community activities, awards, and/or offices (10 points); work experience (5 points); need for the scholarship (15 points); a 150-word paragraph explaining why awarding the applicant would be a wise investment (15 points), and 3 letters of recommendation (15 points).

Financial data The stipend is $1,000.

Duration 1 year.

Additional information The list of approved majors includes plant and soil sciences (agronomy, botany, clothing and textiles, floriculture, horticulture, plant science, soil science); natural and environmental sciences (aquaculture, atmospheric science, bioenvironmental science, entomology, forestry, fisheries, mariculture, marine biology, meteorology, range science, soil and water conservation, and wildlife science); human and animal sciences (animal science, dairy science, food and nutrition, food science, food technology, poultry science, preveterinary medicine, scientific nutrition, and zoology); support curriculums (agricultural development, agricultural business, agricultural economics, agricultural education, agricultural engineering, agricultural journalism, agricultural science, agricultural services, agricultural systems, biomedical engineering, chemical engineering, food engineering, land use and planning, landscape architecture, and recreation and parks); and basic sciences (biochemistry, biology, biomedical science, biotechnology, chemistry, genetics, microbiology, and pharmacology). This program was established in 1998 to honor Ryan Mott, an FFA student leader who died of cancer that year. Students may not apply for both 4-H and FFA scholarships.

Number awarded 1 each year.

[337]
SALLIE MAE FUND FIRST IN MY FAMILY SCHOLARSHIP PROGRAM

Hispanic College Fund
Attn: National Director
1717 Pennsylvania Avenue, N.W., Suite 460
Washington, D.C. 20006
Toll-free: (800) 644-4223   Fax: (202) 296-3774
E-mail: hispaniccollegefund@earthlink.net
Web: www.hispanicfund.org

Purpose To provide financial assistance to Hispanic American undergraduate students who are the first in their family to attend college and are majoring in business, computer science, or engineering.

Eligibility This program is open to U.S. citizens of Hispanic background (at least 1 grandparent must be 100% Hispanic) who are entering their freshman, sophomore, junior, or senior year of college and are the first member of their family to attend college. Applicants must be working on a bachelor's degree in business, computer science, engineering, or a business-related major and have a cumulative GPA of 3.0 or higher. They must be applying to or enrolled in a college or university in the 50 states or Puerto Rico as a full-time student. Financial need is considered in the selection process.

Financial data Stipends range from $1,000 to $5,000, depending on the need of the recipient. Funds are paid directly to the recipient's college or university to help cover tuition and fees.

Duration 1 year; recipients may reapply.

Additional information This program is sponsored by the Sallie Mae Community Foundation for the National Capital Region and the Sallie Mae Fund. All applications must be submitted online; no paper applications are available.

Number awarded Varies each year; recently, 155 of these scholarships were awarded.

Deadline April of each year.

[338]
SAMMAMISH VALLEY CHAPTER ACCOUNTING SCHOLARSHIPS

Washington Society of Certified Public Accountants
Attn: Scholarship Committee
902 140th Avenue N.E.
Bellevue, WA 98005-3480
(425) 644-4800   Toll-free: (800) 272-8273 (within WA)
Fax: (425) 562-8853
E-mail: memberservices@wscpa.org
Web: www.wscpa.org

Purpose To provide financial assistance to currently-enrolled college students in Washington who are majoring in accounting.

Eligibility This program is open to vocational and transfer accounting students who have completed at least 2 quarters of accounting at the time of application and who plan to complete their education in Washington. They must intend to attend an accredited 2-year or 4-year institution in Washington state. U.S. citizenship is required. Selection is based on academic achievement (GPA of 3.0 or higher), campus and/or community activities, preparation for an accounting career, work history, financial need, a personal statement that includes their career goals and interests and how they anticipate that the accounting curriculum will enhance their career objectives, and 2 letters of recommendation.

Financial data The stipend is $750 per year.

Duration 1 year; may be renewed up to 3 additional years.

Additional information This program is sponsored by the Sammamish Valley Chapter of the Washington Society of CPAs.

Number awarded Up to 3 each year.

Deadline April of each year.

[339]
SCHOLARSHIPS FOR MINORITY ACCOUNTING STUDENTS

American Institute of Certified Public Accountants
Attn: Academic and Career Development Division
1211 Avenue of the Americas
New York, NY 10036-8775
(212) 596-6223   Fax: (212) 596-6292
E-mail: educat@aicpa.org
Web: www.aicpa.org

Purpose To provide financial assistance to underrepresented minorities interested in studying accounting at the undergraduate or graduate school level.

Eligibility Undergraduate applicants must be minority students who are enrolled full time, have completed at least 30 semester hours of college work (including at least 6 semester hours in accounting), be majoring in accounting with an overall GPA of 3.3 or higher, and be U.S. citizens or permanent residents. Minority students who are interested in a graduate degree must be 1) in the final year of a 5-year accounting program; 2) an undergraduate accounting major currently accepted or enrolled in a master's-level accounting, business administration, finance, or taxation program; or 3) any undergraduate major currently accepted in a master's-level accounting program. Selection is based primarily on merit (academic and personal achievement); financial need is evaluated as a secondary criteria. For purposes of this program,

the American Institute of Certified Public Accountants (AICPA) considers minority students to be those of Black, Native American/Alaskan Native, Pacific Island, or Hispanic ethnic origin.

Financial data The maximum stipend is $5,000 per year.

Duration 1 year; may be renewed, if recipients are making satisfactory progress toward graduation.

Additional information These scholarships are granted by the institute's Minority Educational Initiatives Committee.

Number awarded Varies each year; recently, 187 students received funding through this program.

Deadline June of each year.

[340]
SEALASKA HERITAGE INSTITUTE 7(I) SCHOLARSHIPS

Sealaska Corporation
Attn: Sealaska Heritage Institute
One Sealaska Plaza, Suite 201
Juneau, AK 99801-1249
(907) 586-9177   Toll-free: (888) 311-4992
Fax: (907) 586-9293
E-mail: scholarship@sealaska.com
Web: www.sealaskaheritage.org

Purpose To provide financial assistance for undergraduate or graduate study to Native Alaskans who have a connection to Sealaska Corporation and are majoring in designated fields.

Eligibility This program is open to 1) Alaska Natives who are enrolled to Sealaska Corporation, and 2) Native lineal descendants of Alaska Natives enrolled to Sealaska Corporation, whether or not the applicant owns Sealaska Corporation stock. Applicants must be enrolled or accepted for enrollment as full-time undergraduate or graduate students. Along with their application, they must submit 2 essays: 1) their personal history and educational goals, and 2) their past history of and expected contributions to the Alaska Native community. Financial need is also considered in the selection process. The following areas of study qualify for these awards: natural resources (environmental sciences, engineering, conservation biology, fisheries, geology, marine science/biology, forestry, wildlife management, and mining technology); business administration (accounting, finance, marketing, international business, international commerce and trade, management of information systems, human resources management, economics, computer information systems, and industrial management); and other special fields (cadastral surveys, chemistry, equipment/machinery operators, industrial safety specialists, occupational health specialists, plastics engineers, trade specialists, physics, mathematics, and marine trades and occupations).

Financial data The amount of the award depends on the availability of funds, the number of qualified applicants, class standing, and cumulative GPA.

Duration 1 year; may be renewed up to 5 years for a bachelor's degree, up to 3 years for a master's degree, up to 2 years for a doctorate, or up to 3 years for vocational study. The maximum total support is limited to 9 years. Renewal depends on recipients' maintaining full-time enrollment and a GPA of 2.5 or higher.

Additional information Funding for this program is provided from Alaska Native Claims Settlement Act (ANSCA) Section 7(i) revenue sharing provisions.

Number awarded Varies each year.

Deadline February of each year.

[341]
SEATTLE CHAPTER SCHOLARSHIPS

American Society of Women Accountants-Seattle
  Chapter
c/o Anne Macnab
800 Fifth Avenue, Suite 101
Seattle, WA 98104-3191
E-mail: scholarship@aswaseattle.com
Web: www.aswaseattle.com/scholarships.htm

Purpose To provide financial assistance to students working on a bachelor's or master's degree in accounting at a college or university in Washington.

Eligibility This program is open to part-time and full-time students working on an associate, bachelor's, or master's degree in accounting at a college or university in Washington. Applicants must have completed at least 30 semester hours and have maintained a GPA of at least 2.5 overall and 3.0 in accounting. Membership in the American Society of Women Accountants is not required. Selection is based on career goals, communication skills, GPA, personal circumstances, and financial need.

Financial data The amounts of the awards vary. Recently, a total of $12,000 was available for this program. Funds are paid directly to the recipient's school.

Duration 1 year.

Number awarded April of each year.

Deadline Varies each year.

[342]
SEATTLE PROFESSIONAL CHAPTER SCHOLARSHIPS

Association for Women in Communications-Seattle
  Professional Chapter
Attn: Scholarship Chair
1319 Dexter Avenue North, Number 370
Seattle, WA 98109
(206) 654-2929   Fax: (206) 285-5220
E-mail: awcseattle@qwest.net
Web: www.seattleawc.org/scholarships.html

Purpose To provide financial assistance to upper-division and graduate students in Washington who are preparing for a career in the communications industry.

Eligibility This program is open to Washington state residents who are enrolled at a 4-year college or university in the state as a junior, senior, or graduate student (sophomores at 2-year colleges applying to a 4-year institution are also eligible). Applicants must be majoring, or planning to major, in a communications program, including print and broadcast journalism, television and radio production, film, advertising, public relations, marketing, graphic design, multimedia design, photography or technical communication. Selection is based on demonstrated excellence in communications; contributions made to communications on campus and in the community; scholastic achievement; financial need; and writing sam

ples from journalism, advertising, public relations, or broadcasting.

Financial data The stipend is $1,500. Funds are paid directly to the recipient's school and must be used for tuition and fees.

Duration 1 year.

Number awarded 2 each year.

Deadline February of each year.

[343]
SENTRY INSURANCE 20 CLUB SCHOLARSHIPS

Wisconsin Foundation for Independent Colleges, Inc.
735 North Water Street, Suite 800
Milwaukee, WI 53202-4100
(414) 273-5980   Fax: (414) 273-5995
E-mail: info@wficweb.org
Web: www.wficweb.org/documents/schinfo.htm

Purpose To provide financial assistance to freshmen majoring in selected fields at private colleges in Wisconsin.

Eligibility This program is open to full-time students at the 20 independent colleges or universities in Wisconsin. Applicants must be majoring in 1 of the following fields: business, economics, mathematics, management information systems, industrial design, communication design, or interior architecture and design. They must have earned a GPA of 3.3 or higher.

Financial data The stipend is $1,000.

Duration 1 year.

Additional information The participating schools are Alverno College, Beloit College, Cardinal Stritch University, Carroll College, Carthage College, Concordia University of Wisconsin, Edgewood College, Lakeland College, Lawrence University, Marian College, Marquette University, Milwaukee Institute of Art & Design, Milwaukee School of Engineering, Mount Mary College, Northland College, Ripon College, St. Norbert College, Silver Lake College, Viterbo University, and Wisconsin Lutheran College.

Number awarded 20 each year: 1 at each of the participating schools.

Deadline March of each year.

[344]
SHARON D. BANKS MEMORIAL UNDERGRADUATE SCHOLARSHIP

Women's Transportation Seminar
Attn: National Headquarters
1666 K Street, N.W., Suite 1100
Washington, DC 20006
(202) 496-4340   Fax: (202) 496-4349
E-mail: wts@wtsnational.org
Web: www.wtsnational.org

Purpose To provide financial assistance to undergraduate women interested in a career in transportation.

Eligibility This program is open to women who are working on an undergraduate degree in transportation or a transportation-related field (e.g., transportation engineering, planning, finance, or logistics). Applicants must have at least a 3.0 GPA and be interested in a career in transportation. They must submit a 500-word statement about their career goals after graduation and why they think they should receive the scholarship award. Applications must be submitted first to a local chapter; the chapters forward selected applications for consideration on the national level. Minority candidates are encouraged to apply. Selection is based on transportation involvement and goals, job skills, and academic record; financial need is not considered.

Financial data The stipend is $3,000.

Duration 1 year.

Additional information This program was established in 1992.

Number awarded 1 each year.

Deadline Applications must be submitted by November to a local WTS chapter.

[345]
SHRM FOUNDATION REGIONAL ACADEMIC SCHOLARSHIPS

Society for Human Resource Management
Attn: Member Chapter Relations Department
1800 Duke Street
Alexandria, VA 22314-3499
(703) 548-3440   Toll-free: (800) 283-SHRM
Fax: (703) 535-6490   TDD: (703) 548-6999
E-mail: shrm@shrm.org
Web: www.shrm.org/students/ags_published

Purpose To provide financial assistance to regular (nonstudent) members of the Society for Human Resource Management (SHRM) who are interested in pursuing an an undergraduate or graduate degree in human resource management while working full time.

Eligibility This program is open to national professional, general, and association members of the society who are employed full time in human resources and working on either an undergraduate or graduate degree in the field at an accredited institution of higher learning, either through correspondence, online, and/or classroom learning. Applicants must submit a 1-page essay in which they discuss their contribution to the human resource profession to date, their future goals as a human resources professional, how this scholarship will help to achieve those goals, and their financial need. Selection is based on human resource work experience and involvement (50%), volunteer activity (20%), financial need (20%), and letters of reference (10%).

Financial data The stipend is $3,000.

Duration 1 year.

Number awarded 5 each year: 1 in each of the society's 5 regions.

Deadline April of each year.

[346]
SHRM FOUNDATION UNDERGRADUATE SCHOLARSHIPS

Society for Human Resource Management
Attn: Foundation Administrator
1800 Duke Street
Alexandria, VA 22314-3499
(703) 535-6020   Toll-free: (800) 283-SHRM
Fax: (703) 535-6490   TDD: (703) 548-6999
E-mail: speyton@shrm.org
Web: www.shrm.org/students/ags_published

Purpose To provide financial assistance for college to undergraduate student members of the Society for Human Resource Management (SHRM).

Eligibility This program is open to undergraduate student members of the society. Applicants must have completed at least 55 semester hours of course work in a human relations major or human relations emphasis area (including at least 1 human relations management course) and have an overall GPA of 3.0 or higher.

Financial data The stipend is $2,500.

Duration 1 year.

Number awarded 2 each year.

Deadline October of each year.

[347]
SIGMA IOTA EPSILON UNDERGRADUATE SCHOLARSHIPS

Sigma Iota Epsilon
c/o Colorado State University
Management Department
324 Rockwell Hall
Fort Collins, CO 80523-1275
(970) 491-7200   Fax: (970) 491-3522
E-mail: brenda.ogden@colostate.edu
Web: www.sienational.com

Purpose To provide financial assistance to undergraduate student members of Sigma Iota Epsilon (SIE), the national honorary and professional management fraternity.

Eligibility This program is open to active undergraduate student members. Applicants must submit a brief description of their career objectives. Selection is based on scholastic, fraternity, and other extracurricular achievements.

Financial data Stipends are $1,000 or $500.

Number awarded Each year, 5 scholarships for $1,000 are awarded; the number of $500 awards varies each year, but has been 2 in recent years.

Deadline May of each year.

[348]
SMITH BARNEY WOMEN IN BUSINESS SCHOLARSHIPS

Nevada Women's Fund
770 Smithridge Drive, Suite 300
Reno, NV 89502
(702) 786-2335   Fax: (702) 786-8152
E-mail: info@nevadawomensfund.com
Web: www.nevadawomensfund.com/scholarships

Purpose   To provide funding to women in Nevada who are interested in working on an undergraduate or graduate education.

Eligibility   This program is open to women who are working on or planning to work on an academic degree or vocational training on the undergraduate or graduate level. Preference is given to northern Nevada residents and those attending northern Nevada institutions. Selection is based on academic achievement, financial need, work experience, community involvement, other life experiences, family responsibilities, and the applicant's plan after completing study. Women of all ages are eligible. An interview may be required.

Financial data   Stipends are $1,000 or $500. A total of $6,000 is available for these scholarships each year.

Duration   1 year; may be renewed.

Number awarded   Varies each year. Recently, 7 of these scholarships were awarded: 5 at $1,000 and 2 at $500.

Deadline   February of each year.

[349]
SOCIETY OF ACTUARIES SCHOLARSHIPS FOR MINORITY STUDENTS

Society of Actuaries
Attn: Minority Scholarship Coordinator
475 North Martingale Road, Suite 800
Schaumburg, IL 60173-2226
(847) 706-3509   Fax: (847) 706-3599
E-mail: cleathe@soa.org
Web: www.beanactuary.org/minority/scholarship.cfm

Purpose   To provide financial assistance to underrepresented minority undergraduate students who are interested in preparing for an actuarial career.

Eligibility   This program is open to African Americans, Hispanics, and Native North Americans who are Canadian or U.S. citizens or have a permanent resident visa. Before applying for this program, students should have taken either the SAT or the ACT. Applicants must be admitted to a college or university offering either a program in actuarial science or courses that will prepare them for an actuarial career. Selection is based on financial need, academic achievement, demonstrated mathematical ability, and understanding of and interest in an actuarial career.

Financial data   The amount of the award depends on the need and merit of the recipient. There is no limit to the size of the scholarship. Recipients are awarded an additional $500 for each actuarial examination they have passed.

Duration   1 year; may be renewed.

Additional information   This program is jointly sponsored by the Society of Actuaries and the Casualty Actuarial Society.

Number awarded   There is no limit to the number of scholarships awarded.

Deadline   April of each year.

[350]
SOCIETY OF AUTOMOTIVE ANALYSTS SCHOLARSHIP

Society of Automotive Analysts
Attn: Scholarships
3300 Washtenaw Avenue, Suite 220
Ann Arbor, MI 48104-4200
(734) 677-3518   Fax: (734) 677-2407
E-mail: cybersaa@cybersaa.org
Web: www.cybersaa.org/scholarship_info.html

Purpose   To provide financial assistance to undergraduate students preparing for a career in an analytic field related to the automotive industry.

Eligibility   Eligible to apply for this scholarship are full-time undergraduate students who are majoring in business, economics, finance, marketing, or management. Applicants must have at least a 3.0 GPA and demonstrate interest in automotive analysis. Along with their application, they must submit a 1-page essay explaining their interest in the automotive industry and 1 letter of reference.

Financial data   The stipend is $1,500. Funds are paid to the recipient's school.

Duration   1 year; nonrenewable.

Number awarded   1 or more each year.

Deadline   May of each year.

[351]
SOUTH CAROLINA ASSOCIATION OF CPA'S SCHOLARSHIP PROGRAM

South Carolina Association of Certified Public
   Accountants
Attn: Educational Fund, Inc.
570 Chris Drive
West Columbia, SC 29169
(803) 791-4181   Toll-free: (888) 557-4814
Fax: (803) 791-4196
Web: www.scacpa.org

Purpose   To provide financial assistance to upper-division and graduate students majoring in accounting in South Carolina.

Eligibility   This program is open to South Carolina residents who are majoring in accounting at a college or university in the state. Applicants must be juniors, seniors, or graduate students with a GPA of 3.25 or higher overall and 3.5 or higher in accounting. They must submit their college transcripts, a listing of awards and other scholarships, 2 letters of reference, a resume, a 250-word essay on their personal career goals, and certification of their accounting major. Financial need is not considered in the selection process.

Financial data   Stipends range from $500 to $1,500. Funds are paid to the recipient's school.

Duration   1 year.

Number awarded   Varies each year.

Deadline   June of each year.

[352]
SOUTH CAROLINA TAX COUNCIL SCHOLARSHIP

South Carolina Tax Council
Attn: Scholarship Committee
P.O. Box 887
Lancaster, SC 29721
(803) 283-9988   Fax: (803) 286-8928
Web: www.sctaxcouncil.org/scholarship.htm

Purpose To provide financial assistance to South Carolina residents who are majoring in accounting or taxation in college.

Eligibility This program is open to South Carolina residents who are majoring in accounting or taxation as either a rising senior at a 4-year college or a rising second-year student at a 2-year college. Applicants have have a GPA of 3.0 or higher both in accounting and overall. They must submit a completed application form, certification of their class standing, a listing of their other scholarships and awards, 2 letters of reference, a resume, and an essay on their personal career goals (up to 250 words).

Financial data Stipends range from $500 to $1,000.

Duration 1 year.

Additional information Information is also available from Ray Partain, 1309 North Boulevard, Anderson, SC 29621, (864) 224-4775, Fax: (864) 231-6558.

Number awarded Varies each year.

Deadline May of each year.

[353]
SOUTH DAKOTA CPA SOCIETY SCHOLARSHIPS

South Dakota CPA Society
Attn: Executive Director
1000 North West Avenue, Suite 100
P.O. Box 1798
Sioux Falls, SD 57101-1798
(605) 334-3848   Fax: (605) 334-8595
E-mail: lcoome@iw.net
Web: www.sdcpa.org

Purpose To provide financial assistance to upper-division students in South Dakota who are majoring in accounting.

Eligibility This program is open to accounting majors in South Dakota who have completed at least 90 credit hours. Applicants must have an excellent academic record, leadership potential, an interest in the profession of public accountancy, and a record of extracurricular activities. They must submit a completed application form, an official transcript, a brief statement of career goals and objectives, a list of awards and extracurricular activities, and information on work experience. Financial need is not considered in the selection process.

Financial data The amount of the awards depends on the availability of funds and the number of qualified applicants.

Duration 1 year; recipients may reapply.

Number awarded Varies each year; recently, 9 accounting students received $6,250 in these scholarships.

Deadline April of each year.

[354]
SOUTH DAKOTA RETAILERS ASSOCIATION SCHOLARSHIPS

South Dakota Retailers Association
P.O. Box 638
Pierre, SD 57501
(605) 224-5050   Toll-free: (800) 658-5545
Fax: (605) 224-2059   E-mail: dleslie@sdra.org
Web: www.sdra.org

Purpose To provide financial assistance to South Dakota residents who are interested in preparing for a career in retailing.

Eligibility This program is open to residents of South Dakota who are interested in a career in a retail field. Applicants must have graduated from a South Dakota high school or be enrolled in a vocational school, college, or university in the state. Full-time enrollment is required. Selection is not based solely on financial need or on outstanding scholarship.

Financial data Stipends range from $500 to $1,000.

Duration 1 year.

Additional information Examples of eligible fields include, but are not limited to, agribusiness, apparel merchandising, auto mechanics, automotive technology, business administration, business management, computer science, culinary arts, commercial baking, diesel mechanics, electrical maintenance, heating and ventilation, hotel and restaurant management, landscape design, pharmacy, printing industries, refrigeration, sales and marketing management, and tourism industry management.

Number awarded Varies each year; recently, 6 of these scholarships were awarded.

Deadline March of each year.

[355]
SOUTHWESTERN EXPOSITION FFA SCHOLARSHIPS

Texas FFA Association
614 East 12th Street
Austin, TX 78701
(512) 480-8045   Fax: (512) 472-0555
E-mail: txffa@texasffa.org
Web: www.texasffa.org/ffa/tfa-scho.html

Purpose To provide financial assistance to high school senior members of FFA in Texas who plan to study a field related to agricultural or life sciences (including agricultural economics and agribusiness) at a college or university in the state.

Eligibility This program is open to high school seniors in Texas who are FFA members and have been members at least 2 of the 3 previous years. Applicants must be planning to major in a field related to the agricultural or life sciences at a college or university in Texas. They must have completed at least 5 semesters of instruction in agriculture and/or agribusiness during high school and scored at least 950 on the SAT or 20 on the ACT. U.S. citizenship and ranking in the top half of their graduating class are also required. Selection is based on class rank (16 points), SAT or ACT scores (14 points), academic achievement in agricultural science and career related instruction (10 points), FFA achievements (30 points), financial need (10 points), and an interview (25 points).

Financial data The stipend is $1,000 per year.

Duration 4 years.

Additional information The list of approved majors includes plant and soil sciences (agronomy, botany, clothing and textiles, floriculture, horticulture, plant science, soil science); natural and environmental sciences (aquaculture, atmospheric science, bioenvironmental science, entomology, forestry, fisheries, mariculture, marine biology, meteorology, range science, soil and water conservation, and wildlife science); human and animal sciences (animal science, dairy science, food and nutrition, food science, food technology, poultry science, preveterinary medicine, scientific nutrition, and zoology); support curriculums (agricultural development, agricultural business, agricultural economics, agricultural education, agricultural engineering, agricultural journalism, agricultural science, agricultural services, agricultural systems, biomedical engineering, chemical engineering, food engineering, land use and planning, landscape architecture, and recreation and parks); and basic sciences (biochemistry, biology, biomedical science, biotechnology, chemistry, genetics, microbiology, and pharmacology).

Additional information Funding for this program is provided by the Southwestern Exposition and Livestock Show presented by the Fort Worth Stock Show Syndicate. Students may not apply for both 4-H and FFA scholarships.

Number awarded 2 each year.

[356]
SPACE SYSTEMS/LORAL SCHOLARSHIP

Society of Satellite Professionals International
Attn: Scholarship Program
New York Information Technology Center
55 Broad Street, 14th Floor
New York, NY 10004
(212) 809-5199   Fax: (212) 825-0075
E-mail: sspi@sspi.org
Web: www.sspi.org/html/scholarship.html

Purpose To provide financial assistance to women interested in majoring in satellite-related disciplines (including business) in college or graduate school.

Eligibility This program is open to high school seniors, college undergraduates, and graduate students majoring or planning to major in fields related to satellite technologies, policies, or applications. Fields of study in the past have included broadcasting, business, distance learning, energy, government, imaging, meteorology, navigation, remote sensing, space law, and telecommunications. Applicants must be women born and living in the United States. Selection is based on academic and leadership achievement, commitment to pursue educational and career opportunities in the satellite communications industry, potential for significant contribution to that industry, a personal statement of 500 to 750 words on interest in satellite communications and why they deserve the award, and a creative work (such as a research report, essay, article, videotape, artwork, computer program, or scale model of an antenna or spacecraft design) that reflects the applicant's interests and talents. Financial need is not considered.

Financial data The stipend ranges from $2,000 to $5,000.

Duration 1 year.

Number awarded 1 each year.

Deadline May of each year.

[357]
STANLEY H. STEARMAN SCHOLARSHIP AWARD

National Society of Accountants
Attn: NSA Scholarship Foundation
1010 North Fairfax Street
Alexandria, VA 22314-1574
(703) 549-6400, ext. 1312
Toll-free: (800) 966-6679, ext. 1312
Fax: (703) 549-2512   E-mail: snoell@nsacct.org
Web: www.nsacct.org

Purpose To provide funding for the undergraduate and graduate study of accounting to relatives of active or deceased members of the National Society of Accountants.

Eligibility Both undergraduate and graduate students may apply for this award. They must be working on a degree in accounting, have a GPA of 3.0 or higher, be enrolled full time at an accredited college or university, and be the relative (spouse, son, daughter, grandchild, niece, nephew, or son- or daughter-in-law) of an active National Society of Accountants' member or deceased member. Applicants must submit a letter of intent outlining their reasons for seeking the award, their intended career objective, and how this scholarship award would be used to accomplish that objective. Selection is based on academic attainment, demonstrated leadership ability, and financial need.

Financial data The stipend is $2,000 per year.

Duration Up to 3 years.

Number awarded 1 each year.

Deadline March of each year.

[358]
STATE FARM ACTUARIAL INTERNSHIP PROGRAM

State Farm Insurance Companies
Attn: Corporate Resume Scanning Unit, ASC P-3
Three State Farm Plaza
Bloomington, IL 61791-0001
Fax: (309) 735-3422
Web: www.statefarm.com/careers/jobs/intern.htm

Purpose To provide work experience and financial assistance to students entering their senior year of college with a major in mathematics, actuarial science, or statistics.

Eligibility This program is open to students majoring in mathematics, actuarial science, or statistics with a GPA of 3.0 or higher. Preference is given to students who have completed at least 1 actuarial examination. Applicants must be interested in working for State Farm Insurance Company during the summer prior to their senior year of college. They must have strong communication skills, analytical skills, and computer skills.

Financial data Interns are paid a stipend for the summer that is higher for those who have completed an actuarial examination. A relocation allowance may be available. Students who complete a summer internship successfully are awarded a stipend of up to $12,500 as tuition assistance for their senior year and the offer of full-time employment with State Farm after graduation.

Duration The internship is for 10 weeks, from May through August of each year. Tuition assistance is for 1 year.

Additional information   Interns work in designated departments within State Farm's corporate headquarters in Bloomington, Illinois.

Number awarded   Varies each year.

[359]
STUART CAMERON AND MARGARET MCLEOD MEMORIAL SCHOLARSHIP

Institute of Management Accountants
Attn: Committee on Students
10 Paragon Drive
Montvale, NJ 07645-1760
(201) 573-9000   Toll-free: (800) 638-4427, ext. 1543
Fax: (201) 573-8438   E-mail: students@imanet.org
Web: www.imanet.org

Purpose   To provide financial assistance to undergraduate or graduate student members of the Institute of Management Accountants (IMA) who are interested in preparing for a career in management accounting or financial management.

Eligibility   This program is open to undergraduate and graduate student IMA members who have a GPA of 2.8 or higher. Applicants must be preparing for a career in management accounting, financial management, or information technology. They must submit a 2-page statement on their reasons for applying for the scholarship, reasons that they deserve the award, specific contributions to the IMA, ideas on how they will promote awareness and increase membership and certification within IMA, and their career goals and objectives. Selection is based on that statement, academic merit, IMA participation, quality of the presentation, a resume, and letters of recommendation.

Financial data   The stipend is $5,000.

Duration   1 year.

Additional information   The recipient is required to participate in the parent chapter, at the council level, or at the national level.

Number awarded   1 each year.

Deadline   February of each year.

[360]
SUPPLY CORPS OPTION OF THE SEAMAN TO ADMIRAL-21 PROGRAM

U.S. Navy
Attn: Chief of Naval Education and Training
N79A5 (STA-21)
250 Dallas Street
Pensacola, FL 32508-5220
(850) 452-9422   Toll-free: (800) NAV-ROTC
Fax: (850) 452-2486   E-mail: sta21@cnet.navy.mil
Web: www.sta-21.navy.mil

Purpose   To allow outstanding enlisted Navy personnel to complete a bachelor's degree and receive a commission in the Supply Corps.

Eligibility   This program is open to U.S. citizens who are currently serving on active duty in the U.S. Navy or Naval Reserve, including Training and Administration of the Reserves (TAR), Selected Reserves (SELRES), and Navy Reservists on active duty except for those on active for training (ACDUTRA). Applicants must be high school graduates (or GED recipients) who are able to complete requirements for a baccalaureate degree in a business, engineering, or mathematics related field in 36 months or less. When they complete their degree requirements, they must be younger than 35 years of age. They must have taken the SAT or ACT test within the past 2 years and achieved a score of 1000 or higher on the SAT (including at least 500 on the math portion and 500 on the verbal portion) or 41 or higher on the ACT (including at least 21 on the math portion and 20 on the English portion).

Financial data   Awardees continue to receive their regular Navy pay and allowances while they attend college on a full-time basis. They also receive reimbursement for tuition, fees, and books up to $10,000 per year. If base housing is available, they are eligible to live there. Participants are not eligible to receive benefits under the Navy's Tuition Assistance Program (TA), the Montgomery GI Bill (MGIB), or the Veterans Educational Assistance Program (VEAP).

Duration   Selectees are supported for up to 36 months of full-time, year-round study or completion of a bachelor's degree, as long as they maintain a GPA of 2.5 or higher.

Additional information   This program was established in 2001 as a replacement for the Seaman to Admiral Program (established in 1994), the Enlisted Commissioning Program, and other specialized programs for sailors to earn a commission. Upon acceptance into the program, selectees attend the Naval Science Institute (NSI) in Newport, Rhode Island for an 8-week program in the fundamental core concepts of being a naval officer (navigation, engineering, weapons, military history and justice, etc.). They then enter a college or university with an NROTC unit or affiliation and pursue full-time study for a bachelor's degree. They become members of and drill with the NROTC unit. When they complete their degree, they are commissioned as ensigns in the United States Naval Reserve and assigned to initial training as an officer in the Supply Corps. After commissioning, 5 years of active service are required.

Number awarded   Varies each year.

Deadline   July of each year.

[361]
SUTHERLAND/PURDY SCHOLARSHIP

Phi Upsilon Omicron
Attn: Educational Foundation
P.O. Box 329
Fairmont, WV 26555-0329
(304) 368-0612   E-mail: rickards@access.mountain.net
Web: ianrwww.unl.edu/phiu

Purpose   To provide financial assistance to undergraduate student members of Phi Upsilon Omicron, a national honor society in family and consumer sciences.

Eligibility   This program is open to members of the society who are working on a bachelor's degree in family and consumer sciences or a related area. Preference is given to majors in clothing and textiles or a related area, such as apparel design or fashion merchandising. Applicants must have held a leadership position in their chapter of the society and have a GPA of 3.0 or higher. Selection is based on scholastic record, participation in society and other collegiate activities, statement of professional aims and goals, professional services, and recommendations.

Financial data   The stipend is $650.

Duration   1 year.

Number awarded 1 each year.

Deadline January of each year.

[362]
TDC SCHOLARSHIP

National Association of Black Accountants
Attn: Director, Center for Advancement of Minority
  Accountants
7249-A Hanover Parkway
Greenbelt, MD 20770
(301) 474-NABA, ext. 114   Fax: (301) 474-3114
E-mail: cquinn@nabainc.org
Web: www.nabainc.org

Purpose To provide financial assistance to student members of the National Association of Black Accountants (NABA) who are working on an undergraduate or graduate degree in a field related to accounting.

Eligibility This program is open to NABA members who are members of ethnic minority groups enrolled full time as 1) an undergraduate freshman, sophomore, junior, or first-semester senior majoring in accounting, business, or finance; or 2) a graduate student working on a master's degree in accounting. Applicants must have a GPA of 2.0 or higher in their major and 2.5 or higher overall. Selection is based on grades, financial need, and a 500-word autobiography that discusses career objectives, leadership abilities, community activities, and involvement in NABA.

Financial data The stipend is $1,000 per year.

Duration 1 year.

Number awarded 1 each year.

Deadline December of each year.

[363]
TENNESSEE SOCIETY OF CPAS STUDENT SCHOLARSHIPS

Tennessee Society of CPAs
Attn: Educational and Memorial Foundation
201 Powell Place
Brentwood, TN 37027
(615) 377-3825   Toll-free: (800) 762-0272
Fax: (615) 377-3904   E-mail: crhea@tscpa.com
Web: www.tscpa.com

Purpose To provide financial assistance to college students in Tennessee who are majoring in accounting.

Eligibility This program is open to legal residents of Tennessee who are majoring in accounting at a college or university in the state. Applicants must have completed introductory courses in accounting. Selection is based on academic achievement, professor recommendation, leadership skills, and financial need.

Financial data Stipends range from $250 to $1,000. Up to $100,000 is distributed annually.

Duration 1 year.

Additional information The highest ranked applicant receives an award designated the Paul L. Royston Scholarship Award.

Number awarded Varies each year; recently, 101 of these scholarships were awarded.

[364]
TEXAS AGRICULTURAL EDUCATION FUND SCHOLARSHIPS

Texas FFA Association
614 East 12th Street
Austin, TX 78701
(512) 480-8045   Fax: (512) 472-0555
E-mail: txffa@texasffa.org
Web: www.texasffa.org/ffa/tfa-scho.html

Purpose To provide financial assistance to high school senior members of FFA in Texas who plan to study a field related to agricultural or life sciences (including agricultural economics and business) at a college or university in the state.

Eligibility This program is open to high school seniors in Texas who are FFA members and have been members at least 2 of the 3 previous years. Applicants must be planning to major in a field related to the agricultural or life sciences at a college or university in Texas. They must have completed at least 5 semesters of instruction in agriculture and/or agribusiness during high school and scored at least 950 on the SAT or 20 on the ACT. U.S. citizenship and ranking in the top half of their graduating class are also required. Selection is based on class rank (16 points), SAT or ACT scores (14 points), academic achievement in agricultural science and career related instruction (10 points), FFA achievements (30 points), financial need (10 points), and an interview (25 points).

Financial data The stipend is $2,000.

Duration 1 year.

Additional information The list of approved majors includes plant and soil sciences (agronomy, botany, clothing and textiles, floriculture, horticulture, plant science, soil science); natural and environmental sciences (aquaculture, atmospheric science, bioenvironmental science, entomology, forestry, fisheries, mariculture, marine biology, meteorology, range science, soil and water conservation, and wildlife science); human and animal sciences (animal science, dairy science, food and nutrition, food science, food technology, poultry science, preveterinary medicine, scientific nutrition, and zoology); support curriculums (agricultural development, agricultural business, agricultural economics, agricultural education, agricultural engineering, agricultural journalism, agricultural science, agricultural services, agricultural systems, biomedical engineering, chemical engineering, food engineering, land use and planning, landscape architecture, and recreation and parks); and basic sciences (biochemistry, biology, biomedical science, biotechnology, chemistry, genetics, microbiology, and pharmacology). Students may not apply for both 4-H and FFA scholarships.

Number awarded 1 each year.

[365]
TEXAS FIFTH-YEAR ACCOUNTING STUDENT SCHOLARSHIP PROGRAM

Texas Higher Education Coordinating Board
Attn: Grants and Special Programs
1200 East Anderson Lane
P.O. Box 12788, Capitol Station
Austin, TX 78711-2788
(512) 427-6101   Toll-free: (800) 242-3062
Fax: (512) 427-6127
E-mail: grantinfo@thecb.state.tx.us
Web: www.collegefortexans.com

Purpose To provide financial assistance to accounting students attending college in Texas.

Eligibility This program is open to both residents and non-residents of Texas. Applicants must be enrolled at least half time and have completed at least 120 hours of college course work, including at least 15 semester credit hours of accounting. They may not have already taken the CPA exam, but they must plan to take it in Texas and be willing to sign a written statement confirming their intent to take the written examination conducted by the Texas State Board of Public Accountancy to become a certified public accountant. Selection is based on financial need and scholastic ability and performance.

Financial data The maximum stipend is $3,000.

Duration 1 year.

Additional information Information and application forms may be obtained from the director of financial aid at the public college or university in Texas the applicant attends. This program began in 1996. Study must be conducted in Texas; funds cannot be used to support attendance at an out-of-state institution.

Number awarded Varies each year; recently, 336 of these scholarships were awarded.

[366]
TEXAS 4-H OPPORTUNITY ASSOCIATE DEGREE/TECHNICAL CERTIFICATION SCHOLARSHIPS

Texas 4-H Foundation
Attn: Executive Director
Texas A&M University
7606 Eastmark Drive, Suite 101
Box 4-H
College Station, TX 77843-2473
(979) 845-1213   Fax: (979) 845-6495
E-mail: p-pearce@tamu.edu
Web: texas4-h.tamu.edu/foundation/schol.html

Purpose To provide financial assistance to 4-H members in Texas who plan to work on an associate degree or technical certificate in selected science or social science fields at an institution in the state.

Eligibility This program is open to graduating seniors at high schools in Texas who have been actively participating in 4-H and plan to attend an institution in the state to work on an associate degree or technical certificate in an approved major. Applicants must have passed all sections of the TAAS/TASP/TAKS test. Some scholarships require applicants to demonstrate financial need; selection for those awards is based on GPA (15%), 4-H experience (60%), financial need

(20%), and a personal interview (5%). For other scholarships, selection is based on GPA (15%), 4-H experience (80%), and a personal interview (5%).

Financial data Scholarships range from $500 to $15,000, depending on the contributions from various donors.

Duration 1 year.

Additional information The approved majors and courses of study include accounting associate, aircraft pilot training technology, applied graphic design technology, aquaculture technology, auctioneering services, automotive body/collision technology, automotive technology, aviation maintenance technology, aviation technology, biomedical equipment technology, biotechnology, business/office administration, caption reporting proficiency, carpentry, chemical laboratory technology, child development, commercial art and advertising, computer aided design and drafting, computer information systems, computer maintenance technology, computer network administration/technology, computer science technology, construction management and technology, court/realtime reporting, criminal justice, dental assistant, dental hygiene, diagnostic medical sonography, diesel and heavy equipment technology, dietary management, digital imaging technology, digital media design, drafting and design technology, echocardiology technology, e-commerce technology, educational assistant, electrical technology, electronics engineering technology, emergency medical services, environmental health and safety technology, farrier technology, fire science, food service/culinary arts, GIS/GPS technology, golf course and landscape management, HVAC technology, histology technology, horticulture technology, hotel and restaurant management, industrial maintenance and engineering technology, information management/technology, instrument and control technology, interpretation preparation program/deaf, invasive cardiovascular technology, logistics technology, machining technology, marketing, meat technology, mechanical engineering technology, media communications and information technology, medical assistant, medical data specialist, medical laboratory technology, mental health associate, mortuary science, music, nuclear medicine, nursing (associate degree and vocational), occupational therapy assistant, paralegal/legal assistant, pharmacy technology, phlebotomy, physical therapist assistant, plastics technology, process technology, radiation therapy, radiography, radio-television, ranch and feedlot operations, real estate, respiratory care, semiconductor manufacturing, surgical technology, telecommunications technology, travel/exposition/meeting management, veterinary technology, video technology, and welding technology. Students who apply to the Texas FFA Association or the Texas chapter of Family, Career and Community Leaders of America (FCCLA) for a scholarship will have their 4-H application voided.

Number awarded Varies each year; recently, Texas 4-H awarded 156 scholarships with a total value of more than $1,000,000.

Deadline Students submit their applications to their county extension office, which must forward them to the district extension office by February of each year.

[367]
TEXAS-LOUISIANA DIVISION SCHOLARSHIPS

International Association of Administrative Professionals-
  Texas-Louisiana Division
c/o Barbara Wyatt CAP, President
2909 Greenwood Lane
Tyler, TX 75701-3735
Web: www.iaap-txla.org

Purpose To provide financial assistance to members of the Texas-Louisiana Division of the International Association of Administrative Professionals (IAAP) and their immediate family who are working on a business degree.

Eligibility This program is open to IAAP members and their immediate family in Texas and Louisiana who have completed at least 18 semester credit hours toward a business degree. Applicants must be taking at least 6 hours per semester and have a GPA of 3.0 or higher. Selection is based on educational objectives, financial need, character, and scholarship.

Financial data The stipend is $500.

Duration 1 year.

Number awarded 6 each year.

Deadline January of each year.

[368]
THEODORE W. BATTERMAN FOUNDATION COLLEGE-TO-WORK SCHOLARSHIPS

Wisconsin Foundation for Independent Colleges, Inc.
735 North Water Street, Suite 800
Milwaukee, WI 53202-4100
(414) 273-5980   Fax: (414) 273-5995
E-mail: info@wficweb.org
Web: www.wficweb.org/documents/coll_work.htm

Purpose To provide financial assistance and work experience at nonprofit organizations to students at private colleges in Wisconsin.

Eligibility This program is open to full-time students at the 20 independent colleges and universities in Wisconsin. Applicants must be interested in working at designated nonprofit organizations in Jefferson and Rock counties. Each organization designates preferred areas of study, but all liberal arts majors are invited to apply.

Financial data The stipends are $3,500 for the scholarship and $1,500 for the internship.

Duration 1 year for the scholarship; 10 weeks for the internship.

Additional information The participating schools are Alverno College, Beloit College, Cardinal Stritch University, Carroll College, Carthage College, Concordia University of Wisconsin, Edgewood College, Lakeland College, Lawrence University, Marian College, Marquette University, Milwaukee Institute of Art & Design, Milwaukee School of Engineering, Mount Mary College, Northland College, Ripon College, St. Norbert College, Silver Lake College, Viterbo University, and Wisconsin Lutheran College. This program is sponsored by the Theodore W. Batterman Foundation. The following nonprofits (with their preferred areas of study) are currently participating in the program: Alzheimer's Support Center of Janesville (a combination of social work or psychology with business and/or marketing); Community Foundation of Southern Wisconsin in Janesville (nonprofit management, business administration, marketing, communications, or graphic

design); Council for the Performing Arts of Jefferson (marketing, arts administration, management, communication, or education); Hedberg Public Library of Janesville (an education major who enjoys working with children of all ages); Milton Historical Society (African American studies, American history, business, education, history, museum science); Opportunities, Inc. of Fort Atkinson (public relations, printmaking, recreation, human resources, marketing, social sciences, special education, manufacturing, criminal justice); and YWCA of Rock County in Janesville (social work, psychology, sociology, and pre-law).

Number awarded 7 each year.

Deadline January of each year.

[369]
THOMAS F. SEAY SCHOLARSHIP

Illinois Association of Realtors
Attn: Illinois Real Estate Educational Foundation
3180 Adloff Lane, Suite 400
P.O. Box 19451
Springfield, IL 62794-9451
(217) 529-2600   E-mail: IARaccess@iar.org
Web: www.illinoisrealtor.org/iar/about/scholarships.htm

Purpose To provide financial assistance to Illinois residents who are preparing for a career in real estate.

Eligibility Applicants must be U.S. citizens and Illinois residents who are attending a college or university in any state on a full-time basis and working on a degree with an emphasis in real estate. They must have completed at least 30 credits with a GPA of at least 3.5 on a 5.0 scale. As part of the application process, students must submit copies of their transcripts and letters of recommendation and reference. Selection is based on academic record, economic need, references and recommendations, and career plans in the field of real estate or an allied field (e.g., construction, land use planning, mortgage banking, property management, real estate appraising, real estate assessing, real estate brokerage, real estate development, real estate investment counseling, real estate law, and real estate syndication). Finalists are interviewed.

Financial data The stipend is $2,000.

Duration 1 year.

Number awarded 1 each year.

Deadline March of each year.

[370]
TLMI SCHOLARSHIP PROGRAM

Tag and Label Manufacturers Institute, Inc.
40 Shurman Boulevard, Suite 295
Naperville, IL 60563
(630) 357-9222   Toll-free: (800) 533-8564
Fax: (630) 357-0192   E-mail: office@tlmi.com
Web: www.tlmi.com/board-committee/scholarship.htm

Purpose To provide financial assistance to third- and fourth-year college students who are preparing for a career in the tag and label manufacturing industry.

Eligibility This program is open to juniors and seniors who are attending school on a full-time basis and preparing for a career in the tag and label manufacturing industry. This includes students majoring in management, production, graphic arts, sales and marketing, and graphic design. Applicants must have a GPA of 3.0 or higher. They must submit references from 3 persons who are not members of their families and a 1-page personal statement describing their financial circumstances, career and/or educational goals, employment experience, and reasons why they should be selected for the award. A personal interview may be required. Selection is based on that statement, academic achievement, demonstrated interest in entering the industry, and an interview.

Financial data   The stipend is $5,000. Funds are sent to the recipient's school and paid in 2 equal installments.

Duration   1 year; may be renewed for 1 additional year, provided the recipient maintains a GPA of 3.0 or higher.

Additional information   In addition to the scholarships, internships may be offered to applicants.

Number awarded   6 each year.

Deadline   March of each year.

[371]
TOMMY RAMEY SCHOLARSHIP

Tommy Ramey Foundation
Attn: Scholarship Committee
1052 Highland Colony Parkway, Suite 125
Ridgeland, MS 39157
E-mail: admin@tommyrameyscholarship.org
Web: www.tommyrameyscholarship.org

Purpose   To provide financial assistance to college students who reside in Mississippi and are majoring in either 1) marketing or a related field or 2) culinary arts or a related field.

Eligibility   This program is open to Mississippi residents who are full-time students at an accredited postsecondary institution, have at least a 2.5 GPA, and are enrolled in either 1) marketing or a related field (business, advertising, communications, public relations, journalism, graphic design) or 2) culinary arts or a related field (travel or tourism, hotel or restaurant management, food production). Applicants must submit a list of student activities and a 500-word essay on either "My favorite TV commercial" (marketing students) or "My favorite meal" (culinary students). Selection is based more on personal merit than on academic record.

Financial data   The stipend is $2,500 per semester.

Duration   1 semester; recipients may reapply.

Number awarded   2 each semester.

Deadline   January of each year for the fall term; September of each year for the spring term.

[372]
TOMORROW'S BUSINESS PROFESSIONALS SCHOLARSHIPS

Business Professionals of America
5454 Cleveland Avenue
Columbus, OH 43231-4021
(614) 895-7277   Fax: (614) 895-1165
Toll-free: (800) 334-2007
Web: www.bpa.org

Purpose   To provide financial assistance for college to members of the Business Professionals of America (BPA).

Eligibility   This program is open to BPA members who are either high school seniors or current college students. Applicants must have a GPA of 2.5 or higher. Along with their application, they must submit an essay of 250 to 500 words either

on how their involvement in BPA will influence their future or what part of BPA means the most to them. Selection is based on the essay, BPA involvement, community service participation, and non-BPA related extracurricular activities.

Financial data   A stipend is awarded (amount not specified).

Duration   1 year.

Additional information   Information is also available from Tomorrow's Business Professionals Scholarships, 232 Tumbleweed, Borger, TX 79007.

Number awarded   2 each year: 1 to a high school senior and 1 to a current college student.

Deadline   March of each year.

[373]
TRANSIT HALL OF FAME SCHOLARSHIP AWARDS

American Public Transportation Association
Attn: American Public Transportation Foundation
1666 K Street, N.W., Suite 1100
Washington, DC 20006
(202) 496-4803   Fax: (202) 496-4321
E-mail: pboswell@apta.com
Web: www.apta.com

Purpose   To provide financial assistance to undergraduate and graduate students who are preparing for a career in transportation.

Eligibility   This program is open to college sophomores, juniors, seniors, and graduate students who are preparing for a career in the transit industry. Any member organization of the American Public Transportation Association (APTA) can nominate and sponsor candidates for this scholarship. Nominees must be enrolled in a fully-accredited institution, have and maintain at least a 3.0 GPA, and be either employed by or demonstrate a strong interest in entering the public transportation industry. They must submit a 1,000-word essay on "In what segment of the public transportation industry will you make a career and why?" Selection is based on demonstrated interest in the transit field as a career, need for financial assistance, academic achievement, essay content and quality, and involvement in extracurricular citizenship and leadership activities.

Financial data   The stipend is at least $2,500. The winner of the Donald C. Hyde Memorial Essay Award receives an additional $500.

Duration   1 year; may be renewed.

Additional information   This program was established in 1987. There is an internship component, which is designed to provide substantive training and professional development opportunities. Each year, there are 4 named scholarships offered: the Jack R. Gilstrap Scholarship for the applicant who receives the highest overall score; the Parsons Brickerhoff-Jim Lammie Scholarship for an applicant dedicated to a public transportation engineering career; the Louis T. Klauder Scholarship for an applicant dedicated to a career in the rail transit industry as an electrical or mechanical engineer; and the Dan M. Reichard, Jr. Scholarship for an applicant dedicated to a career in the business administration/management area of the transit industry. In addition, the Donald C. Hyde Memorial Essay Award is presented to the applicant who submits the best response to the required essay component of the program.

Number awarded At least 6 each year.

Deadline June of each year.

[374]
TRAVIS C. TOMLIN SCHOLARSHIP

National Association of Black Accountants
Attn: Director, Center for Advancement of Minority
   Accountants
7249-A Hanover Parkway
Greenbelt, MD 20770
(301) 474-NABA, ext. 114   Fax: (301) 474-3114
E-mail: cquinn@nabainc.org
Web: www.nabainc.org

Purpose To provide financial assistance to student members of the National Association of Black Accountants (NABA) who are working on an undergraduate or graduate degree in a field related to accounting.

Eligibility This program is open to NABA members who are members of ethnic minority groups enrolled full time as 1) an undergraduate freshman, sophomore, junior, or first-semester senior majoring in accounting, business, or finance; or 2) a graduate student working on a master's degree in accounting. Applicants must have a GPA of 3.5 or higher in their major and 3.3 or higher overall. Selection is based on grades, financial need, and a 500-word autobiography that discusses career objectives, leadership abilities, community activities, and involvement in NABA.

Financial data The stipend ranges from $1,000 to $1,500 per year.

Duration 1 year.

Number awarded 1 each year.

Deadline December of each year.

[375]
TRI STATE SURVEYING AND PHOTOGRAMMETRY KRIS M. KUNZE MEMORIAL SCHOLARSHIP

American Congress on Surveying and Mapping
Attn: Office Administrator
6 Montgomery Village Avenue, Suite 403
Gaithersburg, MD 20879
(240) 632-9716, ext. 105   Fax: (240) 632-1321
E-mail: tmilburn@acsm.net
Web: www.acsm.net/scholar.html

Purpose To provide financial assistance to members of the American Congress on Surveying and Mapping who are interested in additional study in business.

Eligibility This program is open to members of the sponsoring organization enrolled in a 2-year or 4-year college or university. First priority is given to licensed Professional Land Surveyors or Certified Protogrammetrists taking college-level courses in business administration or business management. Second priority is certified land survey interns taking college-level courses in business administration or business management. Third priority is full-time students enrolled in a degree program in surveying and mapping but taking a program of study that includes business administration or business management. Selection is based on previous academic record

(30%), statement of study objectives (30%), letters of recommendation (20%), and professional activities (20%); if 2 or more applicants are judged equal based on those criteria, financial need may be considered.

Financial data The stipend is $1,000.

Duration 1 year.

Number awarded 1 each year.

Deadline November of each year.

[376]
TRIBAL BUSINESS MANAGEMENT PROGRAM

Catching the Dream
8200 Mountain Road, N.E., Suite 203
Albuquerque, NM 87110-7835
(505) 262-2351   Fax: (505) 262-0534
E-mail: NScholarsh@aol.com

Purpose To provide financial assistance for college to American Indian students interested in studying a field related to economic development for tribes.

Eligibility Native American students (with at least a quarter Indian blood and members of a U.S. tribe that is federally-recognized, state-recognized, or terminated) are eligible to apply for this program if they are majoring or planning to major in the 1 of the following fields: business administration, finance, management, economics, banking, hotel management, and related fields. Applicants must attend an accredited college or university and have above average GPA and ACT/SAT scores. Along with their application, they must submit a Certificate of Degree of Indian Blood, an essay, 3 letters of recommendation, official transcripts, standardized test scores, copies of applications to other scholarship sources, and a copy of their letter of admission. Selection is based on merit and student goals deemed most likely to improve the lives of Indian people. Financial need is not considered.

Financial data The amount awarded varies but is intended to cover expenses not paid for by other scholarships or assistance.

Duration 1 year.

Additional information The sponsor was formerly known as the Native American Scholarship Fund. This program was established in 2003.

Number awarded Varies; generally, 30 to 35 each year.

Deadline April of each year for fall term; September of each year for spring and winter terms; March of each year for summer school.

[377]
TRUCKLOAD CARRIERS ASSOCIATION SCHOLARSHIPS

Truckload Carriers Association
Attn: Scholarships
2200 Mill Road
Alexandria, VA 22314
(703) 838-1950   Fax: (703) 836-6610
E-mail: tca@truckload.org
Web: www.truckload.org/scholarships

Purpose To provide financial assistance for college to students associated with independent contractors who belong to the Truckload Carriers Association.

Eligibility This program is open to full-time college juniors or seniors in good standing who are the employee or the child, grandchild, or spouse of an employee of an independent contractor affiliated with a trucking company. Independent contractors affiliated with trucking companies may also apply. Applicants must be able to demonstrate financial need, character, integrity, and a GPA of 3.33 or higher. Along with their application, they must submit a 300-word essay on the impact their connection with the trucking industry has had on their life and academic career. Special consideration is given to students working on transportation and business degrees.

Financial data Stipends range from $1,500 to $3,000 per year.

Duration 1 semester; may be renewed automatically for 1 additional semester.

Number awarded Varies each year; recently, 15 of these scholarships were awarded.

Deadline May of each year.

[378]
TSCPA UNDERGRADUATE SCHOLARSHIPS

Texas Society of Certified Public Accountants
Attn: Accounting Education Foundation
14860 Montfort Drive, Suite 150
Dallas, TX 75240-6705
(972) 687-8500   Toll-free: (800) 428-0272, ext. 233
Fax: (972) 687-8682   E-mail: Sking@tscpa.net
Web: www.tscpa.org

Purpose To provide financial assistance to undergraduate accounting students in Texas who plan to become Certified Public Accountants.

Eligibility This program is open to college juniors in Texas who are majoring in accounting and planning to become Certified Public Accountants. They must be attending a college or university that participates in Accounting Education Foundation programs; be nominated by the chair of the accounting department of that university; be a U.S. citizen; have completed at least 54 semester credit hours; be enrolled full time; have a GPA of 3.5 or higher; and have completed 2 introductory accounting courses with a grade of "B" or better.

Financial data The stipend is $1,000 per year. Funds are sent to the recipient's school.

Duration 1 year; may be renewed 1 additional year as a college senior.

Additional information This program includes the following named scholarships: the Frank Hukill Memorial Scholarship and the M. Todd Welty Scholarship. Recipients are expected to take at least 2 accounting courses each semester.

Number awarded Varies each year; recently, 65 new and 38 renewal scholarships were awarded.

Deadline June of each year.

[379]
TTA FOUNDATION SCHOLARSHIP

Texas Telephone Association Foundation
Attn: Scholarship Committee
502 East 11th Street, Suite 400
Austin, TX 78701
(512) 472-1183   Toll-free: (512) 472-1293
E-mail: xinao@aams-texas.com
Web: www.tta.org

Purpose To provide financial assistance to high school seniors in Texas who are interested in majoring in fields of study related to telecommunications.

Eligibility Open to high school seniors in Texas who are U.S. citizens, have at least a 3.0 GPA, and will be attending a community college or university in the state. Special consideration is given to students who are planning to major in a field of particular interest to the telecommunications industry: mathematics, business, engineering, or computer sciences. Semifinalists are selected on the basis of career interests, extracurricular activities, demonstrated leadership, and financial need. They are asked to submit an essay; finalists are selected from that group.

Financial data The stipend is $1,000.

Duration 1 year.

Number awarded 10 each year.

Deadline March of each year.

[380]
TWIN CITIES CHAPTER MBA SCHOLARSHIPS

National Black MBA Association-Twin Cities Chapter
P.O. Box 2709
Minneapolis, MN 55402
(651) 223-7373   E-mail: scholar@nbmbaatc.org
Web: www.nbmbaatc.org/scholarships.html

Purpose To provide financial assistance to African American students from Minnesota who are interested in working on a bachelor's or master's degree in business administration.

Eligibility This program is open to African American students enrolled in a graduate business or management program; this includes undergraduate seniors who are about to enter graduate school. In addition, a scholarship is available to an undergraduate student working on a bachelor's degree in the field of business. Applicants must be residents of or attending school in Minnesota. Along with their application, they must submit an essay of 400 to 500 words. Undergraduate students must write on the aspects of their formal education that are likely to be of the most value to their future employer and why. Graduate students must write on the steps they are taking to prepare themselves to pursue the limited number of opportunities in the recessionary economic conditions prevailing in the country today. Selection is based on career aspirations, GPA, activities, work experience, and the essay.

Financial data Stipends range from $500 to $3,500.

Duration 1 year.

Number awarded Varies each year; recently, this sponsor awarded $17,500 in scholarships.

Deadline March of each year.

[381]
UNCF/HOUSEHOLD CORPORATE SCHOLARS PROGRAM

United Negro College Fund
Attn: Corporate Scholars Program
P.O. Box 1435
Alexandria, VA 22313-9998
Toll-free: (866) 671-7237   E-mail: internship@uncf.org
Web: www.uncf.org/internships/index.asp

Purpose To provide financial assistance and work experience to minority and other students majoring in fields related to business.

Eligibility This program is open to rising juniors majoring in accounting, business, computer science, finance, human resources, or marketing with a GPA of 3.0 or higher. Applicants must be interested in an internship with Household International, the program's sponsor, at 1 of the following sites: Bridgewater, New Jersey; Charlotte, North Carolina; Chesapeake, Virginia; Chicago, Illinois; Dallas, Texas; Indianapolis, Indiana; Jacksonville, Florida; Monterey, California; New Castle, Delaware; San Diego, California; or Tampa, Florida. Preference is given to applicants who reside in those areas, but students who live in other areas are also considered. African Americans, Hispanic Americans, American Indians, and Asian Americans are encouraged to apply. Along with their application, students must submit an essay on their personal and career goals and objectives, a letter of recommendation, and an official transcript.

Financial data This program provides a stipend of up to $10,000 per year and a paid internship.

Duration 8 to 10 weeks for the internships; 1 year for the scholarships, which may be renewed.

Number awarded Varies each year.

Deadline February of each year.

[382]
UNCF/SPRINT SCHOLARS PROGRAM

United Negro College Fund
Attn: Corporate Scholars Program
P.O. Box 1435
Alexandria, VA 22313-9998
Toll-free: (866) 671-7237   E-mail: internship@uncf.org
Web: www.uncf.org/internships/index.asp

Purpose To provide financial assistance and work experience to minority students who are majoring in selected business and science fields.

Eligibility This program is open to members of minority groups who are enrolled full time as juniors or seniors at a 4-year college or university in the United States. Applicants must have a GPA of 3.0 or higher and be majoring in accounting, business, computer engineering, computer information systems, computer science, economics, electrical engineering, finance, industrial engineering, journalism, marketing, management information systems, public relations, or statistics. They must be interested in a summer internship at Sprint. Along with their application, they must submit a 1-page personal statement describing their career interests and goals, a current resume, a letter of recommendation, official transcripts, and a financial need statement.

Financial data This program provides a paid internship and (upon successful completion of the internship) a need-based stipend of up to $7,500.

Duration 10 to 12 weeks for the internships; 1 year for the scholarships.

Additional information This program is sponsored by Sprint. Recipients may attend any of the 39 member institutions of the United Negro College Fund (UNCF), any other Historically Black College or University (HBCUs), or an accredited majority 4-year college or university.

Number awarded Varies each year.

Deadline October of each year.

[383]
UNDERGRADUATE SCHOLARSHIP PROGRAM OF THE ALABAMA SPACE GRANT CONSORTIUM

Alabama Space Grant Consortium
c/o University of Alabama in Huntsville
Materials Science Building, Room 205
Huntsville, AL 35899
(256) 890-6800   Fax: (256) 890-6061
E-mail: jfreasoner@matsci.uah.edu
Web: www.uah.edu/ASGC

Purpose To provide financial assistance to undergraduates who are studying the space sciences at universities participating in the Alabama Space Grant Consortium.

Eligibility This program is open to full-time students entering their junior or senior year at universities participating in the Alabama Space Grant Consortium. Applicants must be studying in a field related to space, including the physical, natural, and biological sciences; engineering, education; economics; business; sociology; behavioral sciences; computer science; communications; law; international affairs; and public administration. They must be U.S. citizens and have a GPA of 3.0 or higher. Individuals from underrepresented groups (African Americans, Hispanic Americans, American Indians, Pacific Islanders, Asian Americans, and women of all races) are encouraged to apply. Interested students should submit a completed application with a career goal statement, personal references, a brief resume, and transcripts. Selection is based on 1) academic qualifications, 2) quality of the career goal statement, and 3) an assessment of the applicant's motivation for a career in aerospace.

Financial data The stipend is $1,000 per year.

Duration 1 year; may be renewed 1 additional year.

Additional information The member universities are University of Alabama in Huntsville, Alabama A&M University, University of Alabama, University of Alabama at Birmingham, University of South Alabama, Tuskegee University, and Auburn University. Funding for this program is provided by NASA.

Number awarded Varies each year; recently, 37 of these scholarships were awarded.

Deadline February of each year.

[384]
UPS CORPORATE SCHOLARS PROGRAM
United Negro College Fund
Attn: Corporate Scholars Program
P.O. Box 1435
Alexandria, VA 22313-9998
Toll-free: (866) 671-7237   E-mail: internship@uncf.org
Web: www.uncf.org/internships/index.asp

Purpose To provide financial assistance and work experience to students majoring in designated fields at colleges and universities that are members of the United Negro College Fund (UNCF).

Eligibility This program is open to sophomores and juniors majoring in computer science, information technology, marketing, or mechanical engineering at UNCF-member institutions. Applicants must be interested in a summer internship with United Parcel Service (UPS), the program's sponsor. They must have a GPA of 3.0 or higher and be able to demonstrate financial need.

Financial data The students selected for this program receive paid internships and need-based scholarships that range up to $10,000 per year.

Duration 8 to 10 weeks for the internships; 1 year for the scholarships, which may be renewed.

Number awarded Varies each year.

Deadline March of each year.

[385]
URBAN FINANCIAL SERVICES COALITION OF DELAWARE SCHOLARSHIPS
Urban Financial Services Coalition of Delaware
P.O. Box 580
Wilmington, DE 19899-0580
(302) 286-2566
Web: www.ufscdel.org/scholarship.htm

Purpose To provide financial assistance to high school seniors in Delaware who plan to major in business in college.

Eligibility This program is open to seniors graduating from high schools in Delaware with a GPA of "C" or higher. Applicants must be planning to major in a business-related field at an accredited college or university. They must be able to demonstrate financial need.

Financial data The stipend is at least $1,000.

Duration 1 year; nonrenewable.

Additional information This program was established in 1993. The sponsor was formerly known as Urban Bankers of Delaware.

Number awarded 1 or more each year.

Deadline March of each year.

[386]
USDA/1890 NATIONAL SCHOLARS PROGRAM
Department of Agriculture
Recruitment and Employment Division
Attn: 1890 National Scholars Program Manager
Jamie L. Whitten Federal Building, Room 301-W
14th and Independence Avenue, S.W.
Washington, DC 20250-9600
(202) 720-6905
Web: 1890scholars.program.usda.gov

Purpose To provide financial assistance to high school seniors and graduates interested in majoring in a field related to agriculture or agribusiness at 1 of the 17 Historically Black 1890 Land Grant Institutions.

Eligibility This program is open to U.S. citizens who hold a high school diploma or GED certificate with a high school GPA of 3.0 or better and a combined verbal/math score of 1000 or more on the SAT or a composite score of 21 or more on the ACT. They must be planning to attend 1 of the 17 Historically Black 1890 Land Grant Institutions and study such fields as agriculture, agricultural business/management, agricultural economics, agricultural engineering/mechanics, agricultural production and technology, agronomy or crop science, animal sciences, botany, farm and range management, fish and game management, food sciences/technology, forestry and related services, home economics, horticulture, natural resources management, nutrition, soil conservation/soil science, wildlife management, or other related disciplines. Currently-enrolled bachelor's-level students attending an 1890 institution are not eligible.

Financial data Each award provides annual tuition, employment, employee benefits, use of a personal computer and software while receiving the scholarship, fees, books, and room and board.

Duration 4 years.

Additional information The Historically Black Land Grant institutions are: Alabama A&M University, Alcorn State University, University of Arkansas at Pine Bluff, Delaware State University, Florida A&M University, Fort Valley State University, Kentucky State University, Lincoln University of Missouri, Langston University, University of Maryland-Eastern Shore, North Carolina A&T State University, Prairie View A&M University, South Carolina State University, Southern University and A&M College, Tennessee State University, Tuskegee University, and Virginia State University. Applications must be submitted to the Liaison Officer of the U.S. Department of Agriculture at a participating 1890 institution.

Number awarded 34 or more each year: 2 at each of the participating universities.

Deadline January of each year.

[387]
UTAH AFFILIATE SCHOLARSHIP

American Woman's Society of Certified Public
    Accountants-Utah Affiliate
c/o Jodi Nichols
1008 North Omni Circle
Salt Lake City, UT 85750
(801) 378-5036   E-mail: jodinichols@attbi.com
Web: www.awscpa.org/affiliate_scholarships/utah.html

Purpose To provide financial assistance to women who are majoring in accounting at a college or university in Utah.

Eligibility This program is open to women who are majoring in accounting at a college or university in Utah.

Financial data A stipend is awarded (amount not specified).

Duration 1 year.

Number awarded 1 or more each year.

[388]
VERMONT DAR GOOD CITIZENSHIP SCHOLARSHIP

Vermont Student Assistance Corporation
Champlain Mill
Attn: Scholarship Programs
P.O. Box 2000
Winooski, VT 05404-2601
(802) 654-3798   Toll-free: (800) 642-3177
Fax: (802) 654-3765   TDD: (802) 654-3766
TDD: (800) 281-3341 (within VT) E-mail: info@vsac.org
Web: www.vsac.org

Purpose To provide financial assistance to high school seniors in Vermont who are interested in working on a college degree in the social sciences, including economics.

Eligibility This scholarship is available to graduating high school seniors in Vermont. Applicants must be planning to enroll in a postsecondary degree program in the social sciences, including (but not limited to) anthropology, archaeology, criminology, economics, geography, history, international relations, political science, sociology, and urban studies. Selection is based on financial need, academic achievement, a letter of recommendation, and required essays.

Financial data The stipend is $500.

Duration 1 year; nonrenewable.

Number awarded 1 each year.

Deadline March of each year.

[389]
VERMONT/NEW HAMPSHIRE DIRECT MARKETING GROUP SCHOLARSHIP

Vermont Student Assistance Corporation
Champlain Mill
Attn: Scholarship Programs
P.O. Box 2000
Winooski, VT 05404-2601
(802) 654-3798   Toll-free: (800) 642-3177
Fax: (802) 654-3765   TDD: (802) 654-3766
TDD: (800) 281-3341 (within VT) E-mail: info@vsac.org
Web: www.vsac.org

Purpose To provide financial assistance to residents of Vermont and New Hampshire who are interested in working on a degree in direct marketing.

Eligibility This scholarship is available to high school seniors, high school graduates, and currently-enrolled college students in New Hampshire and Vermont. Applicants must be enrolled or planning to enroll in an education or training program in a field related to direct marketing. Selection is based on academic achievement, financial need, a letter of recommendation, and required essays.

Financial data The maximum stipend is $1,000.

Duration 1 year; recipients may reapply.

[390]
VINCENT K. DERSCHEID SCHOLARSHIP

Wisconsin Institute of Certified Public Accountants
Attn: WICPA Educational Foundation
235 North Executive Drive, Suite 200
P.O. Box 1010
Brookfield, WI 53008-1010
(414) 785-0445
Toll-free: (800) 772-6939 (within WI and MN)
Fax: (414) 785-0838   E-mail: Tammy@wicpa.org
Web: www.wicpa.org

Purpose To provide financial assistance to college students in Wisconsin who are majoring in accounting.

Eligibility Applicants must be residents of Wisconsin, be attending a Wisconsin college or university, be a declared accounting major, and be in their junior year. Selection is based primarily on academic achievement. Secondary criteria include extracurricular activities, recommendations from educators, and community involvement. A student already receiving funding from the association is not eligible for this scholarship.

Financial data The amount of the scholarship is determined each year and depends upon the projected income from a restricted endowment fund. Recently, the stipend was $2,500.

Duration 2 years (junior and senior years).

Additional information A change of major, transfer to a nonaccredited business college, or transfer to a school outside of Wisconsin results in forfeiture of the scholarship.

Number awarded 1 each year.

Deadline October of each year.

[391]
VIRGINIA SOCIETY FOR HEALTHCARE HUMAN RESOURCES ADMINISTRATION SCHOLARSHIP

Virginia Society for Healthcare Human Resources
  Administration
c/o Janice Gibbs
Obici Hospital Human Resources Department
2800 Godwin Boulevard
Suffolk, VA 23434
(757) 934-4602   E-mail: jgibbs.obici.com

Purpose To provide financial assistance to undergraduate and graduate students in Virginia working on a degree in human relations and interested in a career in a health care setting.

Eligibility This program is open to residents of Virginia currently enrolled in an accredited college or university in the state and working on an undergraduate or graduate degree in human resources administration or a related field. Applicants must be at least a second-semester sophomore when the application is submitted and have a demonstrated interest in working in a health care setting. Selection is based on a 1-page statement outlining the applicant's life and work experiences that support an interest in human relations, specifically in a health care setting; official transcripts; and 2 letters of recommendation from faculty members.

Financial data The stipend is $1,000.

Duration 1 year.

Number awarded 1 each year.

Deadline August of each year.

[392]
VIRGINIA SOCIETY OF CERTIFIED PUBLIC ACCOUNTANTS MINORITY UNDERGRADUATE SCHOLARSHIP

Virginia Society of Certified Public Accountants
  Education Foundation
Attn: Educational Foundation
4309 Cox Road
P.O. Box 4620
Glen Allen, VA 23058-4620
(804) 270-5344   Toll-free: (800) 733-8272
Fax: (804) 273-1741   E-mail: vscpa@vscpa.com
Web: www.vscpa.com

Purpose To provide financial assistance to minority students enrolled in an undergraduate accounting program in Virginia.

Eligibility Applicants must be minority students (African Americans, Hispanic Americans, Native American Indians, or Asian Pacific Americans) currently enrolled in a Virginia college or university undergraduate accounting program. They must be U.S. citizens, be majoring in accounting, have completed at least 6 hours of accounting, be currently registered for 3 more credit hours of accounting, and have a GPA of 3.0 or higher. Along with their applications, they must submit a 1-page essay on how they are financing their education, how they plan to use their accounting education, and why they should be awarded this scholarship. Selection is based on the essay (50%), an official undergraduate transcript (15%), a current resume, (25%), and a faculty letter of recommendation (10%).

Financial data A stipend is awarded (amount not specified). A total of $10,000 is available for this program each year.

Duration 1 year.

Number awarded Varies each year; recently, 3 of these scholarships were awarded.

Deadline April of each year.

[393]
VIRGINIA SOCIETY OF CERTIFIED PUBLIC ACCOUNTANTS UNDERGRADUATE SCHOLARSHIP

Virginia Society of Certified Public Accountants
  Education Foundation
Attn: Educational Foundation
4309 Cox Road
P.O. Box 4620
Glen Allen, VA 23058-4620
(804) 270-5344   Toll-free: (800) 733-8272
Fax: (804) 273-1741   E-mail: vscpa@vscpa.com
Web: www.vscpa.com

Purpose To provide financial assistance to students enrolled in a Virginia college or university undergraduate accounting program.

Eligibility Applicants must be currently enrolled in a Virginia college or university undergraduate accounting program. They must be U.S. citizens, be majoring in accounting, have completed at least 6 hours of accounting, be currently registered for 3 more credit hours of accounting, and have a GPA of 3.0 or higher. Along with their applications, they must submit a 1-page essay on how they are financing their education, how they plan to use their accounting education, and why they should be awarded this scholarship. Selection is based on the essay (50%), an official undergraduate transcript (15%), a current resume, (25%), and a faculty letter of recommendation (10%).

Financial data A stipend is awarded (amount not specified). A total of $10,000 is available for this program each year.

Duration 1 year.

Number awarded Varies each year; recently, 9 of these scholarships were awarded.

Deadline April of each year.

[394]
WAL-MART STORES SCHOLARSHIPS

National FFA Organization
Attn: Scholarship Office
6060 FFA Drive
P.O. Box 68960
Indianapolis, IN 46268-0960
(317) 802-4321   Fax: (317) 802-5321
E-mail: scholarships@ffa.org
Web: www.ffa.org

Purpose To provide financial assistance to FFA members who are interested in majoring in a field related to agriculture or business in college.

Eligibility This program is open to members who are either graduating high school seniors planning to enroll full time in college or students already enrolled in college on a full-time basis. Applicants must be working on or planning to work on a 4-year degree in food science, food technology, food management, agricultural technology, computer systems technology, business management, retail management, supply chain management, transportation and logistics, product development, or product packaging. Students who can demonstrate strong financial need receive first priority. Second priority is given to students at the following universities: Iowa State University, Purdue University, Ohio State University, Cornell University, Western Michigan University, Mississippi State University, Colorado State University, Kansas State University, University of California at Davis, University of Nevada at Reno, New Mexico State University, Texas A&M University, or Clemson University. Selection is based on academic achievement (10 points for GPA, 10 points for SAT or ACT score, 10 points for class rank), leadership in FFA activities (30 points), leadership in community activities (10 points), and participation in the Supervised Agricultural Experience (SAE) program (30 points). U.S. citizenship is required.

Financial data The stipend is $2,500 per year. Funds are paid directly to the recipient.

Duration 2 years, as long as the recipient maintains a GPA of 3.0 or higher.

Additional information Funding for these scholarships is provided by Wal-Mart Stores, Inc.

Number awarded 12 each year.

Deadline February of each year.

[395]
WALGREENS DECA SCHOLARSHIPS

DECA
1908 Association Drive
Reston, VA 20191-1594
(703) 860-5000　　　　　　　Fax: (703) 860-4013
E-mail: decainc@aol.com
Web: www.deca.org/scholarships/index.html

Purpose To provide financial assistance to DECA members interested in studying business in college.

Eligibility This program is open to DECA members who are interested in working full time on a 2-year or 4-year degree in marketing, business, or marketing education. Applicants must be able to demonstrate evidence of DECA activities, academic achievement, leadership ability, and community service involvement. Selection is based on merit, not financial need.

Financial data The stipend is $1,000.

Duration 1 year.

Additional information This program, established in 2004, is sponsored by Walgreens.

Number awarded Up to 5 each year.

Deadline February of each year.

[396]
WALT DISNEY COMPANY FOUNDATION SCHOLARSHIP

Junior Achievement
Attn: Scholarships/Education Team
One Education Way
Colorado Springs, CO 80906-4477
(719) 540-6255　　　　　　　Fax: (719) 540-6175
E-mail: jascholarships@hotmail.com
Web: www.ja.org/programs/programs_schol_dis.shtml

Purpose To provide financial assistance to high school seniors who participated in the Junior Achievement (JA) program and are interested in majoring in business or the fine arts in college.

Eligibility This program is open to graduating high school seniors who have participated in the JA Company Program or JA Economics. Applicants must have an exceptional record of academic achievement and extracurricular activities. They must be interested in majoring in business administration or the fine arts in college. Letters of recommendation are required.

Financial data This scholarship provides full payment of tuition at the college or university of the recipient's choice plus a stipend of $200 cash per year for incidental fees.

Duration 4 years, provided the recipient maintains grades satisfactory to the college or university.

Additional information Funding for this program is provided by the Walt Disney Company Foundation. Recipients must attend a 4-year college or university.

Number awarded 1 each year.

Deadline January of each year.

[397]
WALTER FRESE MEMORIAL SCHOLARSHIP

Association of Government Accountants-Boston Chapter
c/o William A. Muench
10 Jordan Road
Hopkinton, MA 01748-2650
(508) 490-4019　　　　　　　E-mail: wmuench@dcaa.mil
Web: www.aga-boston-chapter.orgscholarship%20information

Purpose To provide financial assistance to high school seniors, undergraduates, or graduate students from New England or attending school in New England who are working on a degree in accounting or finance.

Eligibility Applicants must be a New England resident or enrolled in a New England area college or university; they must be beginning or currently working on an undergraduate or graduate degree in accounting or finance. Students in M.B.A. and M.P.A. programs are also eligible, if they are currently working in a government accounting, auditing, or finance position. Selection is based on scholastic achievement, leadership qualities, extracurricular activities, recommendations, writing ability, and an expressed interest in the field of government accounting, auditing, or financial management.

Financial data The stipend is $1,000.

Duration 1 year.

Number awarded 2 each year.

Deadline April of each year.

[398]
WASHINGTON D.C. CHAPTER SCHOLARSHIP PROGRAM

Armed Forces Communications and Electronics
Association-Washington D.C. Chapter
P.O. Box 1152
Arlington, VA 22211
Web: www.dcafcea.com/scholarships.htm

Purpose   To provide financial assistance to residents of the metropolitan Washington, D.C. area who are interested in majoring in engineering, science, or management information in college.

Eligibility   This program is open to residents of the metropolitan Washington, D.C. area who are U.S. citizens. Applicants may be either high school seniors or second-year students at a community college, but they must have been accepted to an accredited 4-year college or university in the United States. They must be planning to major in engineering (including computer technologies and management information systems), the "hard" sciences, or mathematics. Selection is based on academic achievement, school activities, community and civic activities, part-time work, letters of recommendation, and financial need.

Financial data   Stipends are either $3,500 for community college students or a total of $7,000 for high school seniors.

Duration   1 year for community college students or 3 years for high school seniors.

Additional information   Information is also available from E.F. "Ted" Bronson, The Bronson Group, 2121 Columbia Pike, Apartment 503, Arlington, VA 22204, (703) 892-2891, Fax: (703) 892- 1110, E-mail: efbronson@aol.com.

Number awarded   14 each year: 2 to community college students and 12 to high school seniors.

Deadline   April of each year.

[399]
WASHINGTON FASHION GROUP INTERNATIONAL SCHOLARSHIP

Fashion Group International of Washington
Attn: Linda Lizzio
P.O. Box 4998
Washington, DC 20008
(202) 997-1664

Purpose   To provide financial assistance for college or graduate school to residents of the Washington, D. C. area interested in preparing for a career in fashion or a fashion-related field.

Eligibility   This program is open to residents of the metropolitan area of Washington, defined to include the District of Columbia; the Maryland counties of Anne Arundel, Baltimore, Frederick, Howard, Montgomery, and Prince George's; the city of Baltimore; the Virginia counties of Arlington, Fairfax, Loudoun, and Prince William; and the Virginia cities of Alexandria, Fairfax, and Falls Church. Applicants must have graduated from high school by June, have been accepted by an accredited 2-year or 4-year institution, have demonstrated a genuine interest in fashion or fashion-related fields through education, work, or avocation, and be enrolled in a fashion or fashion-related (commercial arts, textiles and clothing design, interior design, journalism, merchandising, or photography)

degree granting program at the undergraduate or graduate level.

Financial data   The maximum stipend is $5,000.

Duration   1 year.

Number awarded   1 each year.

Deadline   February of each year.

[400]
WASHINGTON SOCIETY OF CPAS SCHOLARSHIPS FOR ACCOUNTING MAJORS

Washington Society of Certified Public Accountants
Attn: Scholarship Committee
902 140th Avenue N.E.
Bellevue, WA 98005-3480
(425) 644-4800   Toll-free: (800) 272-8273 (within WA)
Fax: (425) 562-8853
E-mail: memberservices@wscpa.org
Web: www.wscpa.org

Purpose   To provide financial assistance to undergraduate students in Washington who are majoring in accounting.

Eligibility   This program is open to accounting majors in Washington who have completed their sophomore year at an accredited 4-year institution or 2 terms at a 2-year institution. Preference is given to residents of Washington. Applicants must be U.S. citizens or have applied for citizenship and have a GPA of 3.0 or higher. Along with their application, they must submit essays on 1) what sparked their interest in working on a degree in accounting and what excites them about the profession; 2) their career goals; 3) their involvement in an extracurricular activity, organization, or community service experience and how it affected their life; and 4) why they should be awarded a scholarship. Selection is based on the essays, academic achievement, campus and/or community activities, work history, 2 letters of recommendation, and probability of success in obtaining a CPA license. Financial need is not considered.

Financial data   The stipend is $1,000 per year. Funds may be used to pay for tuition only.

Duration   1 year; nonrenewable.

Number awarded   8 each year.

Deadline   April of each year.

[401]
WAUSAU BENEFITS COLLEGE-TO-WORK SCHOLARSHIP

Wisconsin Foundation for Independent Colleges, Inc.
735 North Water Street, Suite 800
Milwaukee, WI 53202-4100
(414) 273-5980   Fax: (414) 273-5995
E-mail: info@wficweb.org
Web: www.wficweb.org/documents/coll_work.htm

Purpose   To provide financial assistance and work experience to students who are majoring in selected social service and business-related fields at private colleges in Wisconsin.

Eligibility   This program is open to full-time juniors and seniors at the 20 independent colleges or universities in Wisconsin who are preparing for a career in accounting, business, information systems, finance, marketing, nursing, or social work. They must have earned a GPA of 3.0 or higher and be interested in an internship at Wausau Benefits in Wausau,

Wisconsin. Along with their application, they must submit a 1-page autobiography, transcripts, a list of campus involvement and academic honors, a resume, 3 references, and 2 letters of recommendation.

Financial data The stipends are $3,500 for the scholarship and $1,500 for the internship.

Duration 1 year for the scholarship; 10 weeks for the internship.

Additional information The participating schools are Alverno College, Beloit College, Cardinal Stritch University, Carroll College, Carthage College, Concordia University of Wisconsin, Edgewood College, Lakeland College, Lawrence University, Marian College, Marquette University, Milwaukee Institute of Art & Design, Milwaukee School of Engineering, Mount Mary College, Northland College, Ripon College, St. Norbert College, Silver Lake College, Viterbo University, and Wisconsin Lutheran College. This program is sponsored by Wausau Benefits.

Number awarded 1 each year.

Deadline January of each year.

[402]
W.E. HAMMOND SCHOLARSHIP

New Mexico Society of Certified Public Accountants
Attn: Scholarships in Accounting
1650 University N.E., Suite 450
Albuquerque, NM 87102-1733
(505) 246-1699   Toll-free: (800) 926-2522
Fax: (505) 246-1686   E-mail: nmcpa@nmcpa.org
Web: www.nmcpa.org

Purpose To provide financial assistance to accounting students at New Mexico universities and colleges.

Eligibility This program is open to full-time students at New Mexico colleges and universities who have completed 12 semester hours in accounting, are currently enrolled in 6 or more accounting hours, have completed 75 hours overall, and have a cumulative GPA of 3.0 or higher. Selection is based on academic achievement, extracurricular activities, career objectives and goals in accounting, and financial need.

Financial data The stipend is $1,500.

Duration 1 year; may be renewed 1 additional year.

Number awarded 1 each year.

Deadline September of each year.

[403]
WELLS FARGO BANK SCHOLARSHIP

National FFA Organization
Attn: Scholarship Office
6060 FFA Drive
P.O. Box 68960
Indianapolis, IN 46268-0960
(317) 802-4321   Fax: (317) 802-5321
E-mail: scholarships@ffa.org
Web: www.ffa.org

Purpose To provide financial assistance to FFA members who are studying agriculture or agribusiness at designated universities in California.

Eligibility This program is open to members currently enrolled full time in college and working on a 4-year degree in agricultural and forestry production or management and

finance. Applicants must be sophomores or juniors at Santa Clara University, California State University at Fresno, California Polytechnic State University at San Luis Obispo, or the University of California at Davis. They must have a GPA of 3.0 or higher and be able to demonstrate financial need. Selection is based on academic achievement (10 points for GPA, 10 points for SAT or ACT score, 10 points for class rank), leadership in FFA activities (30 points), leadership in community activities (10 points), and participation in the Supervised Agricultural Experience (SAE) program (30 points). U.S. citizenship is required.

Financial data The stipend is $1,000. Funds are paid directly to the recipient.

Duration 1 year; nonrenewable.

Additional information Funding for this scholarship is provided by Wells Fargo Bank.

Number awarded 2 each year.

Deadline February of each year.

[404]
WILBUR-ELLIS COMPANY SCHOLARSHIPS

National FFA Organization
Attn: Scholarship Office
6060 FFA Drive
P.O. Box 68960
Indianapolis, IN 46268-0960
(317) 802-4321   Fax: (317) 802-5321
E-mail: scholarships@ffa.org
Web: www.ffa.org

Purpose To provide financial assistance to FFA members from designated states who are interested in studying a field related to agriculture in college.

Eligibility This program is open to members who are graduating high school seniors planning to enroll full time in college. Applicants must be residents of the following states: Arizona, California, Idaho, Indiana, Michigan, Minnesota, Montana, New Mexico, North Dakota, Ohio, Oregon, South Dakota, Texas, Utah, Washington, Wisconsin, or Wyoming. They must be planning to work on a 4-year degree in agricultural production, forestry, communication, education, management, finance, marketing, merchandising, sales, science, engineering, or social service. Selection is based on academic achievement (10 points for GPA, 10 points for SAT or ACT score, 10 points for class rank), leadership in FFA activities (30 points), leadership in community activities (10 points), and participation in the Supervised Agricultural Experience (SAE) program (30 points). Financial need is also considered in the selection process. U.S. citizenship is required.

Financial data The stipend is $1,000 per year. Funds are paid directly to the recipient.

Duration 1 year; nonrenewable.

Additional information Funding for this scholarship is provided by the Wilbur-Ellis Company.

Number awarded 5 each year.

Deadline February of each year.

[405]
WILLARD H. ERWIN, JR. SCHOLARSHIP

Greater Kanawha Valley Foundation
Attn: Scholarship Coordinator
1600 Huntington Square
900 Lee Street, East
P.O. Box 3041
Charleston, WV 25331-3041
(304) 346-3620   Fax: (304) 346-3640
E-mail: tgkvf@tgkvf.com
Web: www.tgkvf.com/scholar.html

Purpose To provide financial assistance to students in West Virginia who are working on an undergraduate or graduate degree in a field related to health care finance.

Eligibility This program is open to residents of West Virginia who are entering their junior, senior, or graduate year of study at a public college or university in the state. Applicants must have at least a 2.5 GPA and demonstrate good moral character. Preference is given to students working on a degree in business or some phase of health care finance. Selection is based on financial need, academic performance, leadership abilities, and contributions to school and community.

Financial data The stipend is $1,000 per year.

Duration Normally, 2 years.

Additional information Funding for this program is provided by the West Virginia Chapter of the Healthcare Financial Management Association.

Number awarded 1 each year.

Deadline February of each year.

[406]
WISCONSIN DECA SCHOLARSHIP AWARDS

Wisconsin DECA
c/o Wisconsin Department of Public Instruction
125 South Webster
P.O. Box 7841
Madison, WI 53707-7841
(608) 267-9253   Fax: (608) 267-9275
E-mail: marie.burbach@dpi.state.wi.us
Web: www.wideca.org

Purpose To provide financial assistance to DECA members from Wisconsin who are interested in working on a college degree in marketing, merchandising, management, or marketing education.

Eligibility This program is open to DECA members from Wisconsin who intend to work full time on a 2- or 4-year degree in marketing, merchandising, management, or marketing education. Applicants must submit essays on their involvement in DECA activities, involvement in other community activities, career objectives and ambitions, and how marketing education and DECA have helped them progress toward achieving those objectives. Selection is based on scholastic record (35 points), DECA activities (45 points), and general leadership ability (20 points). Financial need is not considered.

Financial data A stipend is awarded (amount not specified).

Duration 1 year.

Number awarded 1 or more each year.

[407]
WISCONSIN INSTITUTE OF CERTIFIED PUBLIC ACCOUNTANTS MINORITY SCHOLARSHIPS

Wisconsin Institute of Certified Public Accountants
Attn: WICPA Educational Foundation
235 North Executive Drive, Suite 200
P.O. Box 1010
Brookfield, WI 53008-1010
(414) 785-0445
Toll-free: (800) 772-6939 (within WI and MN)
Fax: (414) 785-0838   E-mail: Tammy@wicpa.org
Web: www.wicpa.org

Purpose To provide financial assistance to minority high school seniors in Wisconsin who are interested in majoring in accounting.

Eligibility This program is open to high school seniors who are residents of Wisconsin and African American, Hispanic, Native American, Indian, or Asian. Applicants must have earned a GPA of 3.0 or higher, be planning to attend a Wisconsin college or university, and be planning to begin academic work leading to an accounting major and a bachelor's degree.

Financial data The stipend is $375 per academic semester for the first 2 years, $500 per semester during the third year, and $750 per semester during the fourth year. The total award is $4,000 over 4 years. Funds may be used only for tuition and books.

Duration 4 years.

Number awarded Varies each year; recently, 2 of these scholarships were awarded.

Deadline February of each year.

[408]
WISCONSIN SPACE GRANT CONSORTIUM UNDERGRADUATE SCHOLARSHIPS

Wisconsin Space Grant Consortium
c/o University of Wisconsin at Green Bay
Natural and Applied Sciences
2420 Nicolet Drive
Green Bay, WI 54311-7001
(920) 465-2941   Fax: (920) 465-2376
E-mail: brandts@uwgb.edu
Web: www.uwgb.edu/wsgc

Purpose To provide financial support to undergraduate students at universities participating in the Wisconsin Space Grant Consortium (WSGC).

Eligibility This program is open to undergraduate students enrolled at 1 of the universities participating in the WSGC. Applicants must be U.S. citizens; be working full time on a bachelor's degree in space science, aerospace, or interdisciplinary space studies (including, but not limited to, engineering, the sciences, architecture, law, business, and medicine); and have a GPA of 3.0 or higher. The consortium especially encourages applications from underrepresented minorities, women, and students with disabilities. Selection is based on academic performance and potential for success.

Financial data Stipends up to $1,500 per year are available.

Duration 1 academic year.

Additional information Funding for this program is provided by the U.S. National Aeronautics and Space Administration. The schools participating in the consortium include the University of Wisconsin campuses at Green Bay, La Crosse, Madison, Milwaukee, Oshkosh, Parkside, and Whitewater; College of the Menominee Nation; Marquette University; Carroll College; Lawrence University; Milwaukee School of Engineering; Ripon College; and Medical College of Wisconsin.

Number awarded Varies each year; recently, 21 of these scholarships were awarded.

Deadline February of each year.

[409]
WOMEN IN NEED SCHOLARSHIPS

Educational Foundation for Women in Accounting
Attn: Foundation Administrator
P.O. Box 1925
Southeastern, PA 19399-1925
(610) 407-9229   Fax: (610) 644-3713
E-mail: info@efwa.org
Web: www.efwa.org/scholarships.htm

Purpose To provide financial support to women accounting students who are the sole source of support for themselves and their families.

Eligibility This program is open to women who, either through divorce or death of a spouse, have become the sole source of support for themselves and their family. They must wish to work on a degree in accounting as a means to gainful employment. Women who are single parents as a result of other circumstances are also considered. Applicants should be in their third, fourth, or fifth year of study. Selection is based on aptitude for accounting, commitment to the goal of working on a degree in accounting (including evidence of continued commitment after receiving this award), clear evidence that the candidate has established goals and a plan for achieving those goals, and financial need.

Financial data The stipend is $2,000 per year.

Duration 1 year; may be renewed 1 additional year if the recipient completes at least 12 hours each semester.

Number awarded 1 each year.

Deadline April of each year.

[410]
WOMEN'S TRANSPORTATION SEMINAR CHAPTER OF COLORADO ANNUAL SCHOLARSHIPS

Women's Transportation Seminar-Colorado Chapter
c/o Chris Proud, Scholarship Chair
CH2M Hill
9193 South Jamaica Street, South Building
Englewood, CO 80112
(720) 286-5702   Fax: (720) 286-9732
E-mail: cproud@ch2m.com
Web: www.wtsnational.org

Purpose To provide financial assistance to undergraduate and graduate students in Colorado preparing for a career in transportation.

Eligibility This program is open to students at colleges and universities in Colorado who are working on a bachelor's or graduate degree in a field related to transportation. Those fields may include engineering (civil, electrical, or mechanical), urban planning, finance, aviation, transit, or railways. Appli-

cants must submit an essay on their career goals after graduation and why they should receive this scholarship.

Financial data Undergraduate stipends are $1,000 or $250. Graduate stipends are $1,200.

Duration 1 year.

Additional information Winners are also nominated for scholarships offered by the national organization of the Women's Transportation Seminar.

Number awarded 3 each year: 2 to undergraduates and 1 to a graduate student.

Deadline November of each year.

[411]
WTS MINNESOTA CHAPTER SCHOLARSHIPS

Women's Transportation Seminar-Minnesota Chapter
c/o Jessica Overmohle, Director
URS Corporation
700 Third Street South
Minneapolis, MN 55415-1199
(612) 373-6404   Fax: (612) 370-1378
E-mail: Jessica_Overmohle@URSCorp.com
Web: www.wtsnational.org

Purpose To provide financial assistance to women working on an undergraduate or graduate degree in a transportation-related field at colleges and universities in Minnesota.

Eligibility This program is open to women currently enrolled in a undergraduate or graduate degree program at a college or university in Minnesota. Applicants must be preparing for a career in transportation or a transportation-related field and be majoring in a field such as transportation engineering, planning, finance, or logistics. They must have a GPA of 3.0 or higher. Along with their application, they must submit a 750-word statement on their career goals after graduation and why they think they should receive this award. Selection is based on transportation goals, academic record, and transportation-related activities or job skills.

Financial data The stipend is $1,000.

Duration 1 year.

Additional information Winners are also nominated for scholarships offered by the national organization of the Women's Transportation Seminar.

Number awarded 2 each year: 1 undergraduate and 1 graduate student.

Deadline November of each year.

[412]
WTS PUGET SOUND CHAPTER SCHOLARSHIP

Women's Transportation Seminar-Puget Sound Chapter
c/o Lorelei Mesic, Scholarship Co-Chair
W&H Pacific
3350 Monte Villa Parkway
Bothell, WA 98021-8972
(425) 951-4872   Fax: (425) 951-4808
E-mail: lmesic@whpacific.com
Web: www.wtspugetsound.org/nscholarships.html

Purpose To provide financial assistance to women undergraduate and graduate students from Washington who are working on a degree related to transportation and have financial need.

Eligibility This program is open to women who are residents of Washington, studying at a college in the state, or working as an intern in the state. Applicants must be currently enrolled in an undergraduate or graduate degree program in a transportation-related field, such as engineering, planning, finance, or logistics. They must have a GPA of 3.0 or higher and plans to prepare for a career in a transportation-related field. Minority candidates are encouraged to apply. Along with their application, they must submit a 500-word statement about their career goals after graduation, their financial need, and why they think they should receive this scholarship award. Selection is based on transportation goals, academic record, transportation-related activities or job skills, and financial need.

Financial data The stipend is $1,500.

Duration 1 year.

Additional information The winner is also nominated for scholarships offered by the national organization of the Women's Transportation Seminar.

Number awarded 1 each year.

Deadline October of each year.

[413]
WTS/ITS WASHINGTON INTELLIGENT TRANSPORTATION SYSTEMS SCHOLARSHIP

Women's Transportation Seminar-Puget Sound Chapter
c/o Lorelei Mesic, Scholarship Co-Chair
W&H Pacific
3350 Monte Villa Parkway
Bothell, WA 98021-8972
(425) 951-4872   Fax: (425) 951-4808
E-mail: lmesic@whpacific.com
Web: www.wtspugetsound.org/nscholarships.html

Purpose To provide financial assistance to undergraduate and graduate students from Washington working on a degree related to intelligent transportation systems (ITS).

Eligibility This program is open to students who are residents of Washington, studying at a college in the state, or working as an intern in the state. Applicants must be currently enrolled in an undergraduate or graduate degree program related to the design, implementation, operation, and maintenance of ITS technologies. They must be majoring in transportation or a related field, including transportation engineering, systems engineering, electrical engineering, planning, finance, or logistics, and be taking courses in such ITS-related fields of study as computer science, electronics, and digital communications. In addition, they must have a GPA of 3.0 or higher and plans to prepare for a career in a transportation-related field. Minority candidates are encouraged to apply. Along with their application, they must submit a 500-word statement about their career goals after graduation, how those relate to ITS, and why they think they should receive this scholarship award. Selection is based on that statement, academic record, and transportation-related activities or job skills. Financial need is not considered.

Financial data The stipend is $1,500.

Duration 1 year.

Additional information This program is co-sponsored by ITS Washington.

Number awarded 1 each year.

Deadline October of each year.

[414]
YOUNG FARMERS OF TEXAS SCHOLARSHIP

Texas FFA Association
614 East 12th Street
Austin, TX 78701
(512) 480-8045   Fax: (512) 472-0555
E-mail: txffa@texasffa.org
Web: www.texasffa.org/ffa/tfa-scho.html

Purpose To provide financial assistance for college to high school seniors in Texas who demonstrate outstanding personal qualities and involvement in FFA.

Eligibility This program is open to high school seniors in Texas who are FFA members and have been members at least 2 of the 3 previous years. Applicants must be planning to major in a field related to the agricultural or life sciences at a college or university in Texas. They must have completed at least 5 semesters of instruction in agriculture and/or agribusiness during high school and scored at least 950 on the SAT or 20 on the ACT. U.S. citizenship and ranking in the top half of their graduating class are also required. Selection is based on class rank (16 points), SAT or ACT scores (14 points), academic achievement in agricultural science and career related instruction (10 points), FFA achievements (30 points), financial need (10 points), and an interview (25 points).

Financial data The stipend is $2,000.

Duration 1 year.

Additional information The list of approved majors includes plant and soil sciences (agronomy, botany, clothing and textiles, floriculture, horticulture, plant science, soil science); natural and environmental sciences (aquaculture, atmospheric science, bioenvironmental science, entomology, forestry, fisheries, mariculture, marine biology, meteorology, range science, soil and water conservation, and wildlife science); human and animal sciences (animal science, dairy science, food and nutrition, food science, food technology, poultry science, preveterinary medicine, scientific nutrition, and zoology); support curriculums (agricultural development, agricultural business, agricultural economics, agricultural education, agricultural engineering, agricultural journalism, agricultural science, agricultural services, agricultural systems, biomedical engineering, chemical engineering, food engineering, land use and planning, landscape architecture, and recreation and parks); and basic sciences (biochemistry, biology, biomedical science, biotechnology, chemistry, genetics, microbiology, and pharmacology). Students may not apply for both 4-H and FFA scholarships.

Number awarded 1 each year.

[415]
4-H SAN ANTONIO LIVESTOCK EXPOSITION SCHOLARSHIP

Texas 4-H Foundation
Attn: Executive Director
Texas A&M University
7606 Eastmark Drive, Suite 101
Box 4-H
College Station, TX 77843-2473
(979) 845-1213   Fax: (979) 845-6495
E-mail: p-pearce@tamu.edu
Web: texas4-h.tamu.edu/foundation/schol.html

Purpose To provide financial assistance to 4-H members in Texas who are interested in studying a field related to agriculture (including economics, entrepreneurship, and finance) in college.

Eligibility This program is open to graduating seniors at high schools in Texas who have been actively participating in 4-H and plan to attend a college or university in the state to major in a field approved by the sponsor. Applicants must have passed all sections of the TAAS/TASP/TAKS test and have minimum scores of 910 on the SAT or 19 on the ACT. They must have exhibited, judged, or participated in the San Antonio Livestock Exposition. Selection is is based on GPA (25%), test scores (15%), 4-H experience (35%), financial need (20%), and a personal interview (5%).

Financial data Stipends range from $500 to $15,000.

Duration 1 year.

Additional information This program is funded by the San Antonio Livestock Exposition. Its list of approved fields includes (but is not limited to) accounting, advertising, agribusiness, agricultural communications, agricultural economics, agricultural education, agricultural engineering, agronomy, animal science, atmospheric science, banking and finance, basic medical science, biochemistry, biology, biomedical engineering, biomedical sciences, botany, business administration, cell and molecular biology, chemical engineering, chemistry, child development and family relationships, computer engineering, computer science, dairy science, dietetics, earth sciences, economics, engineering technology, entomology, entrepreneurship and strategic management, environmental conservation of natural resources, environmental and property law, equine science, family and consumer sciences, fashion design, fishery sciences, food and nutrition, food engineering, food science and technology, forestry, genetics, geology, horticulture, information science, journalism, landscape architecture, management, marine biology, marine engineering, marine sciences, marketing, mechanical engineering, medical technology, merchandising, meteorology, microbiology, neuroscience, nursing, pharmacy, physical therapy, poultry science, pre-dentistry, pre-law, pre-medicine, pre-optometry, pre-podiatry, radiological science, real estate, recreation and leisure studies, renewable natural resources, restaurant and hotel management, soil science, telecommunications, textiles and apparel, veterinary science, wildlife sciences, and zoology. Students who apply to the Texas FFA Association or the Texas chapter of Family, Career and Community Leaders of America (FCCLA) for a scholarship will have their 4-H application voided.

Number awarded Varies each year; recently, Texas 4-H awarded 156 scholarships with a total value of more than $1,000,000.

Deadline Students submit their applications to their county extension office, which must forward them to the district extension office by February of each year.

Fellowships

Described here are 177 funding opportunities designed to support students working on a graduate degree in business or related fields, including accounting, actuarial science, agricultural economics, banking, business administration, economics, finance, management, marketing and sales, personnel administration, and real estate. Usually no return of service or repayment is required. Note: other funding opportunities for graduate students working on a degree in business or a related field are also described in the Grants and Awards subsections.

[416]
ABBOTT LABORATORIES GRADUATE HEALTH ADMINISTRATION FELLOWSHIPS

Association of University Programs in Health
    Administration
Attn: Prizes, Fellowships and Scholarships
730 11th Street, N.W., Fourth Floor
Washington, DC 20001-4510
(201) 638-1448, ext. 131   Fax: (201) 638-3429
E-mail: aupha@aupha.org
Web: www.aupha.org

Purpose To provide financial assistance to students enrolled in graduate schools affiliated with the Association of University Programs in Health Administration (AUPHA).

Eligibility Eligible to be nominated for this program are students in health services administration at selected AUPHA graduate member programs in the United States and Canada. They should be enrolled in the second year of their studies. The 11 programs that can select nominees are identified in November. Recipients are selected on the basis of need and demonstrated leadership in management practice.

Financial data The stipend is $5,000.

Duration The fellowship is presented annually.

Additional information These fellowships are funded by Abbott Laboratories. Winning students are given the opportunity to visit Abbott Laboratories, a long-time leader in the health care field.

Number awarded 11 each year: 10 in the United States and 1 in Canada.

Deadline The participating schools are selected in November; nominations must be submitted by February.

[417]
ACCOUNTEMPS/AICPA STUDENT SCHOLARSHIP

American Institute of Certified Public Accountants
Attn: Academic and Career Development Division
1211 Avenue of the Americas
New York, NY 10036-8775
(212) 596-6223   Fax: (212) 596-6292
E-mail: educat@aicpa.org
Web: www.aicpa.org

Purpose To provide financial assistance to student affiliate members of the American Institute of Certified Public Accountants (AICPA) who are working on an undergraduate or graduate degree in accounting, finance, or information systems.

Eligibility This program is open to full-time undergraduate and graduate students who are AICPA student affiliate members with a declared major in accounting, finance, or information systems. Applicants must have completed at least 30 semester hours, including at least 6 semesters in accounting, with a GPA of 3.0 or higher and be a U.S. citizen. Students who will be transferring to a 4-year school must include an acceptance letter from that school. Selection is based on outstanding academic achievement, leadership, and future career interests.

Financial data The stipend is $2,500.

Duration 1 year.

Number awarded 2 each year.

Deadline March of each year.

[418]
AICPA FELLOWSHIPS FOR MINORITY DOCTORAL STUDENTS

American Institute of Certified Public Accountants
Attn: Academic and Career Development Division
1211 Avenue of the Americas
New York, NY 10036-8775
(212) 596-6270   Fax: (212) 596-6292
E-mail: educat@aicpa.org
Web: www.aicpa.org

Purpose To provide financial assistance to minority doctoral students who wish to prepare for a career teaching accounting at the college level.

Eligibility This program is open to minority students who have applied to and/or been accepted into a doctoral program with a concentration in accounting; have earned a master's degree or completed a minimum of 3 years of full-time work in accounting, are attending or planning to attend school full time; and agree not to work full time in a paid position, teach more than 1 course as a teaching assistant, or work more than 25% as a research assistant. U.S. citizenship is required. Preference is given to applicants who have attained a CPA designation. For purposes of this program, the American Institute of Certified Public Accountants (AICPA) considers minority students as those of Black, Native American, or Pacific Island races, or of Hispanic ethnic origin.

Financial data The stipend is $12,000 per year.

Duration 1 year; may be renewed up to 4 additional years.

Number awarded Varies each year; recently, 22 of these fellowships were awarded.

Deadline March of each year.

[419]
ALABAMA SPACE GRANT CONSORTIUM GRADUATE FELLOWSHIP PROGRAM

Alabama Space Grant Consortium
c/o University of Alabama in Huntsville
Materials Science Building, Room 205
Huntsville, AL 35899
(256) 890-6800   Fax: (256) 890-6061
E-mail: jfreasoner@matsci.uah.edu
Web: www.uah.edu/ASGC

Purpose To provide financial assistance for graduate study or research related to the space sciences at universities participating in the Alabama Space Grant Consortium.

Eligibility This program is open to full-time graduate students enrolled at the universities participating in the consortium. Applicants must be studying in a field related to space, including the physical, natural, and biological sciences; engineering; education; economics; business; sociology; behavioral sciences; computer science; communications; law; international affairs; and public administration. They must 1) present a proposed research plan related to space that includes an extramural experience at a field center of the National Aeronautics and Space Administration (NASA); 2) propose a multidisciplinary plan and course of study; 3) plan to be involved in consortium outreach activities; and 4) intend to prepare for a career in line with NASA's aerospace, science, and technology programs. U.S. citizenship is required. Individuals from underrepresented groups (African Americans, Hispanics, American Indians, Pacific Islanders, and women of all races) are encouraged to apply. Interested students should submit a completed application form, a description of the proposed research or study program, a schedule, a budget, a list of references, a vitae, and undergraduate and graduate transcripts. Selection is based on 1) academic qualifications, 2) quality of the proposed research program or plan of study and its relevance to the aerospace science and technology program of NASA, 3) quality of the proposed interdisciplinary approach, 4) merit of the proposed utilization of a NASA center to carry out the objectives of the program, 5) prospects for completing the project within the allotted time, and 6) applicant's motivation for a career in aerospace.

Financial data The award for 12 months includes $16,000 for a student stipend and up to $6,000 for a tuition/student research allowance.

Duration Up to 36 months.

Additional information The member universities are University of Alabama in Huntsville, Alabama A&M University, University of Alabama, University of Alabama at Birmingham, University of South Alabama, Tuskegee University, and Auburn University. Funding for this program is provided by NASA.

Number awarded Varies each year; recently, 11 of these fellowships were awarded.

Deadline February of each year.

[420]
ALAN B., '32, AND FLORENCE B., '35, CRAMMATTE FELLOWSHIP

Gallaudet University Alumni Association
Attn: Graduate Fellowship Fund Committee
Peikoff Alumni House
Gallaudet University
800 Florida Avenue, N.E.
Washington, DC 20002-3695
(202) 651-5060   Fax: (202) 651-5062
TTY: (202) 651-5060
E-mail: alumni.relations@gallaudet.edu
Web: www.gallaudet.edu

Purpose To provide financial assistance to deaf students who wish to work on a graduate degree in a field related to business at universities for people who hear normally.

Eligibility This program is open to deaf and hard of hearing graduates of Gallaudet University or other accredited academic institutions who have been accepted for graduate study in a business-related field at colleges or universities for people who hear normally. Applicants must be working on a doctorate or other terminal degree. Financial need is considered in the selection process.

Financial data The amount awarded varies, depending upon the needs of the recipient and the availability of funds.

Duration 1 year; may be renewed.

Additional information This fund is 1 of 11 designated funds included in the Graduate Fellowship Fund of the Gallaudet University Alumni Association. Recipients must carry a full-time semester load.

Number awarded Up to 1 each year.

Deadline April of each year.

[421]
ALBERT W. DENT STUDENT SCHOLARSHIP

American College of Healthcare Executives
One North Franklin Street, Suite 1700
Chicago, IL 60606-3529
(312) 424-2800   Fax: (312) 424-0023
E-mail: ache@ache.org
Web: www.ache.org

Purpose To provide financial assistance to minority graduate student members of the American College of Healthcare Executives.

Eligibility This program is open to student associates of the organization in good standing. Applicants must be minority students enrolled full time in a health care management graduate program, able to demonstrate financial need, and a U.S. or Canadian citizen.

Financial data The stipend is $3,500.

Duration 1 year.

Additional information The program was established and named in honor of Dr. Albert W. Dent, the foundation's first Black fellow and president emeritus of Dillard University.

Number awarded Varies each year.

Deadline March of each year.

[422]
AMERICAN SOCIETY OF WOMEN ACCOUNTANTS SCHOLARSHIPS

American Society of Women Accountants
Attn: Administrative Director
8405 Greensboro Drive, Suite 800
McLean, VA 22102
(703) 506-3265   Toll-free: (800) 326-2163
Fax: (703) 506-3266   E-mail: aswa@aswa.org
Web: www.aswa.org/scholarship.html

Purpose To provide financial assistance to undergraduate and graduate women interested in preparing for a career in accounting.

Eligibility This program is open to women who are enrolled in a college, university, or professional school as either part-time or full-time students working on a bachelor's or master's degree in accounting. Applicants must have completed at least 60 semester hours with a declared accounting major. Selection is based on career goals, communication skills, GPA, personal circumstances, and financial need. Membership in the American Society of Women Accountants (ASWA) is not required. Applications must be submitted to a local ASWA chapter.

Financial data The stipends range from $1,500 to $4,500 each.

Duration 1 year; recipients may reapply.

Additional information Founded in 1938 to assist women C.P.A.s, the organization has nearly 5,000 members in 30 chapters. Some chapters offer scholarships on the local/regional level. Funding for this program is provided by the Educational Foundation for Women in Accounting.

Number awarded Varies each year: recently, 8 of these scholarships were available, with a total value of $14,000.

Deadline Local chapters must submit their candidates to the national office by February of each year.

[423]
AMERICORPS PROMISE FELLOWS PROGRAM

Corporation for National and Community Service
1201 New York Avenue, N.W.
Washington, DC 20525
(202) 606-5000   Toll-free: (800) 942-2677
Fax: (202) 565-2784   TTY: (202) 565-2799
TTY: (800) 833-3722   E-mail: promise@cns.gov
Web: www.americorps.org/promise/about.html

Purpose To enable college graduates and other professionals to earn money for higher education purposes while serving as volunteers for public or nonprofit organizations that work to support children and youth.

Eligibility Participants in this program are selected by local and national nonprofit organizations that are engaged in coordinating activities intended to support children and youth. Each participating agency sets its own standards, but generally they require a bachelor's degree and/or professional experience in a particular field. Individuals with the following backgrounds are especially encouraged to apply: 1) advanced degree candidates concentrating in such areas as education, public policy, nonprofit management, social work, public health, and business; 2) professionals in nonprofits, corporations, other private sector organizations, and education who are ready for a new challenge; 3) alumni of AmeriCorps, Peace Corps, the military, and other service organizations; and 4) recent college graduates or part-time students looking for a chance to engage in service and gain leadership experience.

Financial data Full-time participants receive extensive professional development training, a living allowance of $13,000, and other benefits. After completing their service, they receive an education award of $4,725 that can be used to finance higher education or to pay off student loans.

Duration The length of the terms are established by each participating agency but are generally 1 year.

Additional information Applications are obtained from and submitted to the particular agency where the applicant wishes to serve; for a directory of participating agencies, contact the sponsor.

Number awarded Approximately 500 each year.

Deadline Each participating organization sets its own deadline.

[424]
ANNA C. KLUNE MEMORIAL SCHOLARSHIP

American Marketing Association-Connecticut Chapter
c/o Kristiana Sullivan, Scholarship Vice President
805 Brook Street
Building 4
Rocky Hill, CT 06067-3405
(860) 571-6213   Fax: (860) 571-7150
E-mail: ksullivan@cerc.com
Web: amact.marketingpower.com

Purpose To provide financial assistance to graduate students from Connecticut who are working on a degree in marketing.

Eligibility This program is open to Connecticut residents who are working on a master's degree in marketing or a related discipline (e.g., research, advertising). Applicants must have completed at least 50% of their program of study.

Financial data The stipend is $1,500.

Duration 1 year.
Number awarded 1 each year.
Deadline January of each year.

[425]
ANNA M. WINSTON FOUNDERS' SCHOLARSHIPS

National Association of Black Accountants
Attn: Director, Center for Advancement of Minority
    Accountants
7249-A Hanover Parkway
Greenbelt, MD 20770
(301) 474-NABA, ext. 114   Fax: (301) 474-3114
E-mail: cquinn@nabainc.org
Web: www.nabainc.org

Purpose To provide financial assistance to student members of the National Association of Black Accountants (NABA) who are working on an undergraduate or graduate degree in a field related to accounting.

Eligibility This program is open to NABA members who are members of ethnic minority groups enrolled full time as 1) an undergraduate freshman, sophomore, junior, or first-semester senior majoring in accounting, business, or finance; or 2) a graduate student working on a master's degree in accounting. Applicants must have a GPA of 3.5 or higher in their major and 3.3 or higher overall. Selection is based on grades, financial need, and a 500-word autobiography that discusses career objectives, leadership abilities, community activities, and involvement in NABA.

Financial data The stipend is $500 per year.

Duration 1 year.

Number awarded Varies each year.

Deadline December of each year.

[426]
APPRAISAL INSTITUTE EDUCATION TRUST SCHOLARSHIP

Appraisal Institute
Attn: Appraisal Institute Education Trust
550 West Van Buren Street, Suite 1000
Chicago, IL 60607
(312) 335-4100   Fax: (312) 335-4400
E-mail: ocarreon@appraisalinstitute.org
Web: www.appraisalinstitute.org

Purpose To provide financial assistance to graduate and undergraduate students majoring in real estate or allied fields.

Eligibility This program is open to U.S. citizens who are graduate or undergraduate students majoring in real estate appraisal, land economics, real estate, or related fields. Applicants must submit a statement regarding their general activities and intellectual interests in college; college training; activities and employment outside of college; contemplated line of study for a degree; and career they expect to follow after graduation. Selection is based on academic excellence.

Financial data The stipend is $3,000 for graduate students or $2,000 for undergraduate students.

Duration 1 year.

Number awarded At least 1 each year.

Deadline March of each year.

[427]
APPRAISAL INSTITUTE MASTER'S DEGREE PROGRAM SCHOLARSHIPS

Appraisal Institute
Attn: Appraisal Institute Education Trust
550 West Van Buren Street, Suite 1000
Chicago, IL 60607
(312) 335-4100   Fax: (312) 335-4400
E-mail: ocarreon@appraisalinstitute.org
Web: www.appraisalinstitute.org/education/masters.asp

Purpose To provide financial assistance to graduate students majoring in real estate or allied fields at designated universities.

Eligibility This program is open to U.S. citizens who are master's degree students in real estate appraisal. Applicants must be attending 1 of the following universities: Johns Hopkins University, New York University, Texas A&M University, University of Denver, Virginia Commonwealth University, or University of Southern California.

Financial data At least partial tuition is paid.

Duration 1 year.

Number awarded At least 1 each year.

Deadline March of each year.

[428]
ASMC MEMBERS' CONTINUING EDUCATION PROGRAM AWARD

American Society of Military Comptrollers
Attn: National Awards Committee
2034 Eisenhower Avenue, Suite 145
Alexandria, VA 22314-4650
(703) 549-0360   Toll-free: (800) 462-5637
E-mail: asmchq@aol.com
Web: www.asmconline.org

Purpose To provide financial assistance for continuing education to members of the American Society of Military Comptrollers (ASMC).

Eligibility Applicants for this assistance must have been members of the society for at least 2 full years and must have been active in the local chapter at some level (board member, committee chair or member, volunteer for chapter events, etc.). They must be enrolled in or planning to enroll in an academic institution in a field of study directly related to financial resource management, including business administration, economics, public administration, computer science, or operations research related to financial management, accounting, and finance. As part of the selection process, they must submit an essay of up to 500 words on their academic and career goals and financial need.

Financial data Stipends are $1,000 per year.

Duration 1 year.

Additional information The ASMC is open to all financial management professionals employed by the U.S. Department of Defense and Coast Guard, both civilian and military. The applicant whose service to the society is judged the most exceptional is designated the Dick Vincent Scholarship Winner.

Number awarded Up to 15 each year.

Deadline February of each year.

[429]
ASSOCIATION FOR THE ADVANCEMENT OF COST ENGINEERING INTERNATIONAL COMPETITIVE SCHOLARSHIPS

Association for the Advancement of Cost Engineering
209 Prairie Avenue, Suite 100
Morgantown, WV 26505
(304) 296-8444   Toll-free: (800) 858-COST
Fax: (304) 291-5728   E-mail: info@aacei.org
Web: www.aacei.org/education/scholarship.shtml

Purpose To provide financial assistance to undergraduate and graduate students in the United States or Canada working on a degree related to total cost management (the effective application of professional and technical expertise to plan and control resources, costs, profitability, and risk).

Eligibility Applicants may be undergraduate students (second year standing or higher) or graduate students. They must be enrolled full time in a degree program in the United States or Canada that is related to the field of cost management/cost engineering, including engineering, construction, manufacturing, technology, business, and computer science. Selection is based on academic record (35%), extracurricular activities (35%), and an essay (30%) on why the study of cost engineering or total cost management is important to their academic objectives and career goals.

Financial data Stipends range from $750 to $3,000 per year.

Duration 1 year.

Number awarded Varies each year; recently, 28 of these scholarships were awarded.

Deadline October of each year.

[430]
ASSOCIATION OF GOVERNMENT ACCOUNTANTS ACADEMIC MERIT SCHOLARSHIPS

Association of Government Accountants
Attn: National Awards Committee
2208 Mount Vernon Avenue
Alexandria, VA 22301-1314
(703) 684-6931   Toll-free: (800) AGA-7211, ext. 131
Fax: (703) 548-9367   E-mail: rortiz@agacgfm.org
Web: www.agacgfm.org/membership/awards

Purpose To provide financial assistance to members of the Association of Government Accountants (AGA) and their families who wish to work on a degree in financial management.

Eligibility This program is open to members of the association and their spouses, children, and grandchildren. Applicants may be pursuing or intending to pursue an undergraduate or graduate degree in a financial management discipline, including accounting, auditing, budgeting, economics, finance, information technology, or public administration. As part of the selection process, they must submit a 2-page essay on "Why I want a career in public financial management," high school or college transcripts, and a letter of recommendation from an AGA member. Financial need is not considered.

Financial data The annual stipends are $1,000 for full-time study or $500 for part-time study.

Duration 1 year; renewable.

Number awarded 16 each year: 8 to high school seniors and graduates (6 for full-time study and 2 for part-time study) and 8 to undergraduate and graduate students (6 for full-time study and 2 for part-time study).

Deadline March of each year.

[431]
ASSOCIATION OF LATINO PROFESSIONALS IN FINANCE AND ACCOUNTING SCHOLARSHIPS

Association of Latino Professionals in Finance and
    Accounting
Attn: Scholarships
510 West Sixth Street, Suite 400
Los Angeles, CA 90017
(213) 243-0004   Fax: (213) 243-0006
E-mail: scholarships@national.alpfa.org
Web: www.alpfa.org

Purpose To provide financial assistance to undergraduate and graduate students of Hispanic descent who are preparing for a career in a field related to finance or accounting.

Eligibility This program is open to full-time undergraduate and graduate students who have completed at least 15 undergraduate units at a college or university in the United States or Puerto Rico with a GPA of 3.0 or higher. Applicants must be of Hispanic heritage, defined as having 1 parent fully Hispanic or both parents half Hispanic. They must be working on a degree in accounting, finance, information technology, or a related field. Along with their application, they must submit a 2-page personal statement that addresses their Hispanic heritage and family background, personal and academic achievements, academic plans and career goals, efforts and plans for making a difference in their community, and financial need. U.S. citizenship or permanent resident status is required.

Financial data Stipends range from $1,000 to $5,000.

Duration 1 year.

Additional information The sponsoring organization was formerly named the American Association of Hispanic Certified Public Accountants. This program is administered by the Hispanic College Fund, 1717 Pennsylvania Avenue, Suite 460, Washington, DC 20006, (202) 296-5400, (800) 644-4223, Fax: (202) 296-3774, E-mail: hcf-info@hispanicfund.org.

Number awarded Varies each year; recently, 78 of these scholarships, worth $195,000, were awarded.

Deadline April of each year.

[432]
A.W. PERIGARD FUND SCHOLARSHIP

Society of Satellite Professionals International
Attn: Scholarship Program
New York Information Technology Center
55 Broad Street, 14th Floor
New York, NY 10004
(212) 809-5199   Fax: (212) 825-0075
E-mail: sspi@sspi.org
Web: www.sspi.org/html/scholarship.html

Purpose To provide financial assistance to students interested in majoring in satellite-related disciplines (including business) in college or graduate school.

Eligibility This program is open to high school seniors, undergraduates, and graduate students majoring or planning to major in fields related to satellite technologies, policies, or applications. Fields of study in the past have included broadcasting, business, distance learning, energy, government, imaging, meteorology, navigation, remote sensing, space law, and telecommunications. Applicants may be from any country. Selection is based on academic and leadership achievement, commitment to pursue educational and career opportunities in the satellite communications industry, potential for significant contribution to that industry, a personal statement of 500 to 750 words on interest in satellite communications and why they deserve the award, and a creative work (such as a research report, essay, article, videotape, artwork, computer program, or scale model of an antenna or spacecraft design) that reflects the applicant's interests and talents. Financial need is also considered.

Financial data The stipend is $2,000.

Duration 1 year.

Number awarded 1 each year.

Deadline May of each year.

[433]
AYLESWORTH FOUNDATION FOR THE ADVANCEMENT OF MARINE SCIENCE SCHOLARSHIPS

Florida Sea Grant College Program
Attn: Director
University of Florida
P.O. Box 110400
Gainesville, FL 32611-0400
(352) 392-5870   Fax: (352) 392-5113
Web: www.flseagrant.org

Purpose To provide financial assistance to undergraduate or graduate students working on a degree in a marine science-related field at any Florida university that participates in the Florida Sea Grant College Program.

Eligibility Eligible to be nominated by their department chair are undergraduate or graduate students who are working on a degree in an academic discipline that has direct application in marine science (ranging from biology and engineering to economics and food science) at a university or college in Florida that participates in the Florida Sea Grant College Program. These include: Florida A&M University, Florida Gulf Coast University, Florida Atlantic University, Florida Institute of Technology, Florida International University, Florida State University, Harbor Branch Oceanographic Institution, University of Miami, University of North Florida, University of South Florida, University of West Florida, Nova Southeastern University, University of Central Florida, and University of Florida. Financial need is the principal factor used in the selection process, although academic record, leadership, and personal character are also considered. Florida residents are given preference.

Financial data The maximum stipend awarded is 65% of the annual official university or college cost of attendance or $4,500, whichever is less.

Duration 1 year; renewable until the recipient completes the degree.

Additional information Since 1986, when the program was established, more than 60 students in 9 Florida universities have received funding.

Number awarded Generally, 4 or more each year.

Deadline November of each year.

[434]
BICK BICKSON SCHOLARSHIP FUND

Hawai'i Community Foundation
Attn: Scholarship Department
1164 Bishop Street, Suite 800
Honolulu, HI 96813
(808) 537-6333   Toll-free: (888) 731-3863
Fax: (808) 521-6286
E-mail: scholarships@hcf-hawaii.org
Web: www.hawaiicommunityfoundation.org

Purpose To provide financial assistance to Hawaii residents who are interested in studying marketing, law, or travel industry management in college or graduate school.

Eligibility This program is open to Hawaii residents who are interested in majoring in marketing, law, or travel industry management on the undergraduate or graduate school level. They must be able to demonstrate academic achievement (GPA of 2.7 or higher), good moral character, and financial need. In addition to filling out the standard application form, applicants must write a short statement indicating their reasons for attending college, their planned course of study, and their career goals.

Financial data The amounts of the awards depend on the availability of funds and the need of the recipient; recently, stipends averaged $1,250.

Duration 1 year.

Additional information Recipients may attend college in Hawaii or on the mainland. Recipients must be full-time students.

Number awarded Varies each year; recently, 2 of these scholarships were awarded.

Deadline February of each year.

[435]
BOSTON AFFILIATE SCHOLARSHIP

American Woman's Society of Certified Public
   Accountants-Boston Affiliate
c/o Julie Mead
Ziner, Kennedy & Lehan
2300 Crown Colony Drive
Quincy, MA 02169
E-mail: julie.m.mead@aexp.com
Web: www.awscpa.org

Purpose To provide financial assistance to women who are working on an undergraduate or graduate degree in accounting at a college or university in New England.

Eligibility This program is open to women who are attending a college in New England and majoring in accounting. Applicants must have completed at least 12 semester hours of accounting or tax courses and have a cumulative GPA of 3.0 or higher. They must be planning to graduate between May of next year and May of the following year or, for the 15-month graduate program, before September of the current year.

Financial data A stipend is awarded (amount not specified).

Duration 1 year.

Number awarded 1 or more each year.

Deadline April of each year.

[436]
BROADCAST CABLE FINANCIAL MANAGEMENT ASSOCIATION SCHOLARSHIP

Broadcast Cable Financial Management Association
932 Lee Street, Suite 204
Des Plaines, Il 60016
(847) 296-0200   Fax: (847) 296-7510
Web: www.bcfm.com

Purpose To provide financial assistance to members of the Broadcast Cable Financial Management Association who are interested in working on an undergraduate or graduate degree.

Eligibility All fully-paid members in good standing are eligible to apply for the scholarship. They must be interested in working on an undergraduate or graduate degree at an accredited college or university that has some relevance to their current job and/or to the broadcast or cable industries. To apply, individuals must submit an application, attach a current resume, include 2 letters of reference, and submit a 1-page essay that addresses the following: their current job responsibilities, the courses they intend to take, and a description of their career goals.

Financial data The stipend is generally $1,000.

Duration 1 year; recipients may reapply.

Number awarded Varies each year; a total of $5,000 is distributed annually.

Deadline March of each year.

[437]
BRYON BIRD GRADUATE SCHOLARSHIP

Kansas Society of Certified Public Accountants
Attn: Educational Foundation
1080 S.W. Wanamaker Road, Suite 200
P.O. Box 4291
Topeka, KS 66604-0291
(785) 272-4366   Toll-free: (800) 222-0452 (within KS)
Fax: (785) 262-4468   E-mail: kscpa@kscpa.org
Web: www.kscpa.org/scholarship.cfm

Purpose To provide financial assistance to graduate students in Kansas who are majoring in accounting.

Eligibility This program is open to graduate accounting students at each of the 6 regent institutions in Kansas and at Washburn University. Each institution may nominate 1 candidate.

Financial data The stipend is $1,750.

Duration 1 year.

Number awarded 1 each year.

Deadline February of each year.

[438]
BUILDING ACADEMIC GERIATRIC NURSING CAPACITY NURSE/MBA SCHOLARS PROGRAM

American Academy of Nursing
Attn: Building Academic Geriatric Nursing Capacity
  Program
600 Maryland Avenue, S.W., Suite 100 West
Washington, DC 20024-2571
(202) 651-7242   Fax: (202) 554-2641
E-mail: pfranklin@ana.org
Web: www.geriatricnursing.org

Purpose To provide funding to nurses interested in working on an M.B.A. degree to prepare for a career in the management of institutions serving the elderly.

Eligibility This program is open to registered nurses who hold a degree in nursing and have been accepted at a business institution to work on an M.B.A. degree. Applicants must be able to demonstrate a previous commitment to gerontology and specific examples of their ability to understand organizational and management challenges. They must demonstrate an established relationship with a gerontological nursing faculty member who will serve as a mentor during the fellowship period. Along with their application, they must submit a 3-page plan for professional development, including a description of goals, the competencies that are required to enhance their effectiveness in leadership, anticipated outcomes, and support from gerontology nursing faculty. U.S citizenship or permanent resident status is required.

Financial data The stipend is $50,000.

Duration 1 year.

Additional information This program, which began in 2001, is funded by a grant from the John A. Hartford Foundation.

Number awarded Varies each year; recently, 2 of these fellowships were awarded.

Deadline March of each year.

[439]
BUSH LEADERSHIP FELLOWS PROGRAM

Bush Foundation
East 900 First National Bank Building
332 Minnesota Street
St. Paul, MN 55101-1387
(651) 227-0891   Toll-free: (800) 605-7315
Fax: (651) 297-6485   E-mail: info@bushfoundation.org
Web: www.bushfoundation.org

Purpose To provide funding to mid-career professionals interested in obtaining further education to prepare themselves for higher-level responsibilities.

Eligibility This program is open to U.S. citizens or permanent residents who are at least 28 years of age. Applicants must have lived or worked for at least 1 continuous year immediately before the application deadline in Minnesota, North Dakota, South Dakota, or northwestern Wisconsin (Ashland, Barron, Bayfield, Buffalo, Burnett, Chippewa, Douglas, Dunn, Eau Claire, Florence, Forest, Iron, La Crosse, Lincoln, Oneida, Pepin, Pierce, Polk, Price, Rusk, St. Croix, Sawyer, Taylor, Trempealeau, Vilas, and Washburn counties). They should be employed full time with at least 5 years of work experience. Some experience in a policy-making or administrative capacity is desirable. Work experience may include

part-time and volunteer work. Most successful applicants have baccalaureate degrees or their equivalent. Fields of work have included public service, education, government, health, business, community development, engineering, architecture, science, farming, forestry, law, trade unions, law enforcement, journalism, and social work. They must be interested in pursuing full-time involvement in a learning experience that may include academic course work, internships, self-designed study programs, or various combinations of those and other kinds of learning experiences. Fellowships are not granted for applicants currently enrolled as full-time students, part-time study combined with full- or part-time employment, academic research, publications, or design and implementation of service programs or projects. Fellowships are unlikely to be awarded for full-time study plans built on academic programs designed primarily for part-time students, programs intended to meet the continuing education requirements for professional certification, completion of basic educational requirements for entry level jobs, segments of degree programs that cannot be completed within or near the end of the fellowship period, or projects that might more properly be the subjects of grant proposals from organizations. Selection is based on the applicants' personal qualities of integrity, adaptability, intelligence, and energy; work experience and community service record; fellowship plans; and goals.

Financial data Fellows receive monthly stipends for living expenses, an allowance for instructional expenses (50% of the first $8,000 plus 80% of expenses after $8,000), and reimbursements for travel expenses. The stipends paid to fellows participating in paid internships depend on the salary, if any, paid by the intern employer.

Duration From 2 to 18 months.

Additional information Awards are for full-time study and internships anywhere in the United States. This program began in 1965.

Number awarded Approximately 25 each year.

Deadline October of each year.

[440]
CALIFORNIA ASSOCIATION OF REALTORS SCHOLARSHIPS

California Association of Realtors
Attn: Scholarship Foundation
525 South Virgil Avenue
Los Angeles, CA 90020
(213) 739-8200   Fax: (213) 739-7202
E-mail: scholarship@car.org
Web: www.car.org

Purpose To provide financial assistance to students in California who are interested in a career in real estate.

Eligibility This program is open to undergraduate and graduate students enrolled at California colleges and universities who are interested in studying real estate brokerage, real estate finance, real estate management, real estate development, real estate appraisal, real estate planning, real estate law, or other related areas of study. Applicants must have completed at least 12 units prior to applying, be currently enrolled for at least 6 units per semester or term, have a cumulative GPA of 2.6 or higher, and have been legal residents of California for at least 1 year. Real estate licensees who wish to pursue advanced real estate designations, degrees, or credentials are also eligible.

Financial data The stipend is $2,000 for students at 4-year colleges or universities or $1,000 for students at 2-year colleges.

Duration 1 year; may be renewed 1 additional year.

Number awarded Varies each year.

Deadline May of each year.

[441]
CAREER ADVANCEMENT SCHOLARSHIPS

Business and Professional Women's Foundation
Attn: Scholarships
1900 M Street, N.W., Suite 310
Washington, DC 20036
(202) 293-1100, ext. 173　　　　Fax: (202) 861-0298
E-mail: dfrye@bpwusa.org
Web: www.bpwusa.org

Purpose To provide financial assistance for college or graduate school to mature women who are employed or seeking employment in selected fields.

Eligibility Applicants must be women who are at least 25 years of age, citizens of the United States, within 2 years of completing their course of study, officially accepted into an accredited program or course of study at an American institution (including those in Puerto Rico and the Virgin Islands), in financial need, and planning to use the desired training to improve their chances for advancement, train for a new career field, or enter/reenter the job market. They must be in a transitional period in their lives and be interested in studying 1 of the following fields: biological sciences, business studies, computer science, engineering, humanities, mathematics, paralegal studies, physical sciences, social science, teacher education certification, or for a professional degree (J.D., D.D.S., M.D.). Study at the Ph.D. level and for non-degree programs is not covered.

Financial data The stipend is $1,000 per year.

Duration 1 year; recipients may reapply.

Additional information The scholarship may be used to support part-time study as well as academic or vocational/paraprofessional/office skills training. The program was established in 1969. Scholarships cannot be used to pay for classes already in progress. The program does not cover study at the doctoral level, correspondence courses, postdoctoral studies, or studies in foreign countries. Training must be completed within 24 months.

Number awarded Varies each year; recently, 120 of these scholarships were awarded.

Deadline April of each year.

[442]
CARL H. MARRS SCHOLARSHIP FUND

Cook Inlet Region, Inc.
Attn: CIRI Foundation
2600 Cordova Street, Suite 206
Anchorage, AK 99503
(907) 263-5582　　　　Toll-free: (800) 764-3382
Fax: (907) 263-5588　　　　E-mail: tcf@ciri.com
Web: www.ciri.com/tcf/designated.html

Purpose To provide financial assistance for undergraduate or graduate studies in business-related fields to Alaska Natives who are original enrollees to Cook Inlet Region, Inc. (CIRI) and their lineal descendants.

Eligibility This program is open to Alaska Native enrollees under the Alaska Native Claims Settlement Act (ANCSA) of 1971 and their lineal descendants of Cook Inlet Region, Inc. There are no Alaska residency requirements or age limitations. Applicants must be accepted or enrolled full time in a 4-year undergraduate or a graduate degree program in business administration, economics, finance, organizational management, accounting, or a similar field. They must have a GPA of 3.7 or higher. Selection is based on academic achievement, rigor of course work or degree program, quality of a statement of purpose, student financial contribution, financial need, grade level, previous work performance, education and community activities, letters of recommendation, seriousness of purpose, and practicality of educational and professional goals.

Financial data The stipend is $18,000 per year.

Duration 1 year; may be renewed.

Additional information This program was established in 2001. Recipients must enroll in school on a full-time basis.

Number awarded 1 or more each year.

Deadline May of each year.

[443]
CAROLYN HUEY HARRIS SCHOLARSHIP

Alpha Omicron Pi Foundation
Attn: Scholarship Committee
5390 Virginia Way
P.O. Box 395
Brentwood, TN 37024-0395
(615) 370-0920　　　　Fax: (615) 370-4424
E-mail: foundation@alphaomicronpi.org
Web: www.aoiifoundation.org

Purpose To provide financial assistance for college or graduate school to collegiate and alumnae members of Alpha Omicron Pi, especially those from Georgia majoring in fields related to the communications industry.

Eligibility This program is open to collegiate members of Alpha Omicron Pi who wish to continue their undergraduate education and alumnae members who wish to work on a graduate degree. First preference is given to Lambda Sigma chapter members who are juniors or above and majoring in communications (including journalism, public relations, marketing, speech, and media) with a GPA of 3.0 or higher; second preference is given to members from other Georgia colleges; third preference is given to members from other states. Applicants must submit 50-word essays on the following topics: 1) the circumstances that have created their need for this scholarship, and 2) their immediate and long-term life objectives. Selection is based on academic excellence, dedication to serving the community and Alpha Omicron Pi, and financial need.

Financial data A stipend is awarded (amount not specified).

Duration 1 year.

Additional information Undergraduate recipients must enroll full time, but graduate recipients may enroll part time.

Number awarded 1 each year.

Deadline February of each year.

[444]
CATHY L. BROCK MEMORIAL SCHOLARSHIP
Institute for Diversity in Health Management
Attn: Education Program Coordinator
One North Franklin Street, 30th Floor
Chicago, IL 60606
Toll-free: (800) 233-0996   Fax: (312) 422-4566
E-mail: clopez@aha.org
Web: www.diversityconnection.com

Purpose To provide financial assistance to minority upper-division and graduate students in health care management or business management.

Eligibility This program is open to members of ethnic minority groups who are college juniors, seniors, or graduate students. Applicants must be accepted or enrolled in an accredited program in health care management or business management and have a GPA of 3.0 or higher. They must demonstrate commitment to a career in health services administration, financial need, solid extracurricular and community service activities, and a strong interest and experience in finance. U.S. citizenship or permanent resident status is required.

Financial data The stipend is $1,000.

Duration 1 year.

Number awarded 1 or more each year, depending on the availability of funds.

Deadline June of each year.

[445]
CEDARCREST FARMS SCHOLARSHIP
American Jersey Cattle Association
Attn: Dr. Cherie L. Bayer
6486 East Main Street
Reynoldsburg, OH 43068-2362
(614) 861-3636   Fax: (614) 861-8040
E-mail: cbayer@usjersey.com
Web: www.usjersey.com

Purpose To provide financial assistance to undergraduate and graduate students working on a degree related to the dairy industry.

Eligibility This program is open to undergraduate and graduate students who are working on a degree in large animal veterinary practice, dairy production, dairy manufacturing, or dairy product marketing. Applicants must have significant and extensive experience in breeding, managing, and showing Jersey cattle. They must demonstrate significant progress toward their intended degree and an intention to prepare for a career in agriculture. A GPA of 2.5 or higher is required. Financial need is not considered in the selection process.

Financial data The stipend is approximately $1,000.

Duration 1 year.

Number awarded 1 each year.

Deadline June of each year.

[446]
CHARLES V. CLEGHORN ACCOUNTING GRADUATE SCHOOL SCHOLARSHIP
Pennsylvania Institute of Certified Public Accountants
Attn: Careers in Accounting Team
1650 Arch Street, 17th Floor
Philadelphia, PA 19103-2099
(215) 496-9272   Toll-free: (888) CPA-2001 (within PA)
Fax: (215) 496-9212   E-mail: schools@picpa.org
Web: www.cpazone.org/scholar/graduate.asp

Purpose To provide financial assistance to students attending graduate business schools in Pennsylvania.

Eligibility This program is open to full-time graduate students enrolled in business schools in Pennsylvania. Their undergraduate degree must have been in accounting or a related field. Preference is given to candidates with an undergraduate degree from a Pennsylvania college or university. Applicants must be working on a graduate degree in accounting, business, computer science, taxation, or a related field. They must be nominated by a faculty member at their school (up to 2 students per school may be nominated). Selection is based on intellectual capacity, leadership potential, and financial need.

Financial data The stipend is $5,000 and is paid over a 2-year period. Recipients working on a business school degree that does not require 2 full years of study are awarded $2,500.

Duration 2 years.

Additional information Recipients must attend school on a full-time basis.

Number awarded 1 each year.

Deadline March of each year.

[447]
CHURCHARMENIA.COM FINANCE AND BUSINESS SCHOLARSHIP
Charles and Agnes Kazarian Eternal
   Foundation/ChurchArmenia.com
Attn: Educational Scholarships
30 Kennedy Plaza, Second Floor
Providence, RI 02903
E-mail: info@churcharmenia.com
Web: www.churcharmenia.com/scholarship1.html

Purpose To provide financial assistance to outstanding undergraduate or graduate students of Armenian descent who are working on a degree in business or finance.

Eligibility Applicants must be of Armenian descent and accepted to or qualified for a highly competitive undergraduate or graduate degree (including M.B.A.) program in economics, finance, or other similar field. They must submit a completed application form, official academic transcripts, 3-page personal statement, and up to 3 letters of recommendation. Applicants should provide examples of commitment to the community in terms of business experience or community service.

Financial data The stipend is $5,000.

Duration 1 year.

Number awarded 1 or more each year.

[448]
CIRI FOUNDATION SPECIAL EXCELLENCE SCHOLARSHIPS

Cook Inlet Region, Inc.
Attn: CIRI Foundation
2600 Cordova Street, Suite 206
Anchorage, AK 99503
(907) 263-5582   Toll-free: (800) 764-3382
Fax: (907) 263-5588   E-mail: tcf@ciri.com
Web: www.ciri.com/tcf/scholarship.html

Purpose To provide financial assistance for undergraduate or graduate studies to Alaska Natives who are original enrollees to Cook Inlet Region, Inc. (CIRI) and their lineal descendants.

Eligibility This program is open to Alaska Native enrollees under the Alaska Native Claims Settlement Act (ANCSA) of 1971 and their lineal descendants of Cook Inlet Region, Inc. There are no Alaska residency requirements or age limitations. Applicants must be accepted or enrolled full time in a 4-year undergraduate or a graduate degree program. They must have a GPA of 3.7 or higher. Preference is given to students working on a degree in business, education, mathematics, sciences, health services, or engineering. Selection is based on academic achievement, rigor of course work or degree program, quality of a statement of purpose, student financial contribution, financial need, grade level, previous work performance, education and community activities, letters of recommendation, seriousness of purpose, and practicality of educational and professional goals.

Financial data The stipend is $18,000 per year.

Duration 1 year; may be renewed.

Additional information This program was established in 1997. Recipients must enroll in school on a full-time basis.

Number awarded 1 or more each year.

Deadline May of each year.

[449]
COLORADO BROADCASTERS ASSOCIATION CONTINUING EDUCATION SCHOLARSHIPS

Colorado Broadcasters Association
Attn: Education Committee
2042 Boreas Pass Road
P.O. Box 2369
Breckenridge, CO 80424
(970) 547-1388   Fax: (970) 547-1384
E-mail: cobroadcasters@earthlink.net
Web: www.e-cba.org/scholarships.htm

Purpose To provide financial assistance for additional study in related fields to employees of broadcast stations that are members of the Colorado Broadcasters Association (CBA).

Eligibility This program is open to full-time employees who have worked for at least 1 year at a broadcast station that is a member of the CBA. Applicants must be interested in improving their education while continuing to work; examples of acceptable projects include 1) undergraduate and graduate courses in broadcasting, media programs at the college level, or academic work in other related fields, such as business or engineering; and 2) workshops and seminars offered by recognized national trade and professional organizations. Preference is given to projects leading to degrees or certificates. Applicants must submit a resume; a description of the course,

workshop, or program for which funding is sought; the cost of the course or program; a statement of their continuing educational and professional goals and their qualifications for the scholarship, a letter of recommendation from a supervisor or senior manager, and an explanation of any other special circumstances that might bear on their application.

Financial data The maximum award is $500.

Duration 1 year.

Number awarded Varies each year; a total of $3,000 is available for this program annually.

Deadline Applications may be submitted at any time and are considered on a first-come, first-served basis throughout the fiscal year (which begins in July).

[450]
COLORADO SOCIETY OF CPAS ETHNIC DIVERSITY SCHOLARSHIPS FOR COLLEGE STUDENTS

Colorado Society of Certified Public Accountants
Attn: CSCPA Educational Foundation
7979 East Tufts Avenue, Suite 500
Denver, CO 80237-2845
(303) 741-8613   Toll-free: (800) 523-9082 (within CO)
Fax: (303) 773-6344   E-mail: gmantz@cocpa.org
Web: www.cocpa.org/student_faculty/scholarships.asp

Purpose To provide financial assistance to minority undergraduate or graduate students in Colorado who are studying accounting.

Eligibility This program is open to African Americans, Hispanics, Asian Americans, Native Americans, and Pacific Islanders studying at a college or university in Colorado at the associate, baccalaureate, or graduate level. Applicants must have completed at least 1 intermediate accounting class, be declared accounting majors, have completed at least 8 semester hours of accounting classes, and have a GPA of at least 3.0. Selection is based first on scholastic achievement and second on financial need.

Financial data The stipend is $1,000. Funds are paid directly to the recipient's school to be used for books, tuition, room, board, fees, and expenses.

Duration 1 year; recipients may reapply.

Number awarded 2 each year.

Deadline June of each year.

[451]
COMMUNITY SERVICE SCHOLARSHIPS

Association of Government Accountants
Attn: National Awards Committee
2208 Mount Vernon Avenue
Alexandria, VA 22301-1314
(703) 684-6931   Toll-free: (800) AGA-7211, ext. 131
Fax: (703) 548-9367   E-mail: rortiz@agacgfm.org
Web: www.agacgfm.org/membership/awards

Purpose To provide financial assistance to undergraduate and graduate students majoring in financial management who are involved in community service.

Eligibility This program is open to graduating high school seniors, high school graduates, college and university undergraduates, and graduate students. Applicants must be working on or planning to work on a degree in a financial management discipline, including accounting, auditing, budgeting, economics, finance, information technology, or public administration. They must have a GPA of 2.5 or higher and be actively involved in community service projects. As part of the selection process, they must submit a 2-page essay on "My community service accomplishments," high school or college transcripts, and a reference letter from a community service organization. Selection is based on community service involvement and accomplishments; financial need is not considered.

Financial data The annual stipend is $1,000.

Duration 1 year; renewable.

Number awarded 2 each year: 1 to a high school senior or graduate and 1 to an undergraduate or graduate student.

Deadline March of each year.

[452]
CONSORTIUM FOR GRADUATE STUDY IN MANAGEMENT FELLOWSHIPS

Consortium for Graduate Study in Management
5585 Pershing Avenue, Suite 240
St. Louis, MO 63112
(314) 877-5500   Toll-free: (888) 658-6814
Fax: (314) 877-5505   E-mail: frontdesk@cgsm.org
Web: www.cgsm.org

Purpose To provide financial assistance and work experience to underrepresented racial minorities interested in preparing for a management career in business.

Eligibility Eligible to apply are African Americans, Hispanic Americans (Chicanos, Cubans, Dominicans, and Puerto Ricans), and Native Americans who have graduated from college and are interested in a career in business. An undergraduate degree in business or economics is not required. Applicants must be U.S. citizens and planning to work on an M.B.A. degree at 1 of the consortium's 13 schools. Preference is given to applicants under 31 years of age.

Financial data The fellowship pays full tuition and required fees. Summer internships with the consortium's cooperative sponsors, providing paid practical experience, are also offered.

Duration Up to 4 semesters. The participating schools are Carnegie Mellon University, Dartmouth College, Emory University, Indiana University, University of Michigan, New York University, University of North Carolina at Chapel Hill, University of Rochester, University of Southern California, University of Texas at Austin, University of Virginia, Washington University, and University of Wisconsin at Madison.

Additional information Fellowships are tenable at member schools only.

Number awarded Varies; up to 400 each year.

Deadline The early deadline is the end of November of each year. The final deadline is in January of each year.

[453]
CSCPA CANDIDATE'S AWARD

Connecticut Society of Certified Public Accountants
Attn: Educational Trust Fund
845 Brook Street, Building 2
Rocky Hill, CT 06067-3405
(860) 258-4800   Toll-free: (800) 232-2232 (within CT)
Fax: (860) 258-4859   E-mail: cscpa@cs-cpa.org
Web: www.cs-cpa.org

Purpose To provide financial assistance to college students in Connecticut who are majoring in accounting and going on to a fifth year of school.

Eligibility This program is open to college seniors going on to a fifth year in school in compliance with the 150-hour requirement of the Connecticut State Board of Accountancy to sit for the Uniform Certified Public Accountant Examination. Applicants must hold a baccalaureate degree from an accredited college or university, have earned at least a 3.5 overall GPA, and be enrolled in a formal program at a Connecticut college or university intended to satisfy the 150-hour requirement. Applicants must submit a completed application form and an official copy of their college or university academic transcript.

Financial data The stipend is $2,500.

Duration 1 year.

Number awarded 1 each year.

Deadline August of each year.

[454]
D. ANITA SMALL SCIENCE AND BUSINESS SCHOLARSHIP

Maryland Federation of Business and Professional
    Women's Clubs, Inc.
c/o Pat Schroeder, Chair
354 Driftwood Lane
Solomons, MD 20688
(410) 326-0167   Toll-free: (877) INFO-BPW
E-mail: patsc@csmd.edu
Web: www.bpwmaryland.org/HTML/scholarships.html

Purpose To provide financial assistance to women in Maryland who are interested in working on an undergraduate or graduate degree in a science or business-related field.

Eligibility This program is open to women in Maryland who are at least 21 years of age and have been accepted to a bachelor's or advanced degree program at an accredited Maryland academic institution. Applicants must be preparing for a career in 1 of the following or a related field: accounting, aeronautics, business administration, computer sciences, engineering, finance, information technology, mathematics, medical sciences (including nursing, laboratory technology, therapy, etc.), oceanography, or physical sciences. They must have a GPA of 3.0 or higher and be able to demonstrate financial need.

Financial data The stipend is $1,000 per year.

Duration 1 year.

Number awarded 1 or more each year.

Deadline May of each year.

[455]
DALLAS CHAPTER GRADUATE SCHOLARSHIP

National Black MBA Association-Dallas Chapter
Attn: Student Affairs Committee
P.O. Box 797174
Dallas, TX 75379-7174
(214) 853-4497   E-mail: stud_affairs@dallasmbas.org
Web: www.dallasmbas.org

Purpose To provide financial assistance to African American graduate students who are working on a master's degree in business administration in Texas.

Eligibility This program is open to African American students who are Texas residents and/or enrolled in a graduate business program at a college or university in Texas. Applicants must submit an official transcript, 2 letters of recommendation, an e-mail address, a resume of extracurricular/volunteer activities, a statement describing their projected college expense schedule, and a 2-page essay on a topic that changes annually but relates to African Americans in business.

Financial data Stipends are $2,000 for full-time students or $1,000 for part-time students.

Duration 1 year.

Number awarded Varies each year.

Deadline March of each year.

[456]
DANIEL B. GOLDBERG SCHOLARSHIP

Government Finance Officers Association
Attn: Scholarship Committee
203 North LaSalle Street, Suite 2700
Chicago, IL 60601-1210
(312) 977-9700   Fax: (312) 977-4806
Web: www.gfoa.org/services/scholarships.shtml

Purpose To provide financial assistance to master's degree students who are preparing for a career in state and local government finance.

Eligibility This program is open to graduate students who are enrolled in a full-time master's degree program and preparing for a career in public finance. Applicants must be college graduates, citizens or permanent residents of the United States or Canada, and able to provide a letter of recommendation from the dean of their graduate program. Selection is based on career plans, academic record, plan of study, letters of recommendation, and GPA. Financial need is not considered.

Financial data The stipend is $5,000.

Duration 1 year.

Number awarded 1 each year.

Deadline February of each year.

[457]
DAVID J. ARONSON SCHOLARSHIP

Massachusetts Society of Certified Public Accountants
Attn: MSCPA Educational Foundation
105 Chauncy Street, Tenth Floor
Boston, MA 02111
(617) 556-4000   Toll-free: (800) 392-6145
Fax: (617) 556-4126
E-mail: biannoni@MSCPAonline.org
Web: www.cpatrack.com/financial_aid/scholarship.php

Purpose To provide financial assistance to nontraditional students in Massachusetts who are preparing for a career in public accounting.

Eligibility This program is open to students in Massachusetts who have a nontraditional educational or personal background. Applicants must be enrolled full time in a graduate program leading to an M.B.A. or master's degree in taxation, accounting, or finance and be interested in preparing for a career in public accounting. Students who have spent at least 2 years in a full-time position prior to graduate school in order to facilitate a career change are favorably considered. Exceptional undergraduate students are encouraged to apply if they have spent at least 1 year away from full-time status, either working full time or pursuing other interests.

Financial data The stipend is $1,000.

Duration 1 year.

Number awarded 1 each year.

[458]
DAVID L. BOREN GRADUATE FELLOWSHIPS

Academy for Educational Development
Attn: National Security Education Program
1825 Connecticut Avenue, N.W.
Washington, DC 20009-5721
(202) 884-8285   Toll-free: (800) 498-9360
Fax: (202) 884-8407   E-mail: nsep@aed.org
Web: nsep.aed.org

Purpose To provide financial assistance to students who are working on a graduate degree and are interested in developing expertise in languages, cultures, and area studies of countries less commonly studied by Americans.

Eligibility This program is open to graduate students in professional and other disciplines who are interested in introducing an international component to their degree studies by focusing on an area of the world that is critical to national security and economic competitiveness. Fields of study include agriculture, anthropology, biology, business, economics, engineering and applied sciences, environmental sciences, history, law, public health, and sociology. Applicants in international affairs, policy studies, and political science often specialize in such subfields as democracy and governance and nonproliferation studies. Support is also provided for the study of the following languages: Albanian, Amharic, Arabic (and dialects), Armenian, Azeri, Belarusian, Bulgarian, Burmese, Cantonese, Czech, Farsi, Georgian, Hebrew, Hindi, Hungarian, Indonesian, Japanese, Kazakh, Khmer, Korean, Kurdish, Kyrgyz, Lingala, Macedonian, Malay, Mandarin, Mongolian, Polish, Portuguese, Romanian, Russian, Serbo-Croatian, Sinhala, Slovak, Slovene, Swahili, Tagalog, Tajik, Tamil, Thai, Turkish, Turkmen, Uighar, Ukrainian, Urdu, Uzbek, or Vietnamese. The study of French or Spanish is not supported unless the language instruction is at the advanced level or is combined with the study of business, the applied sciences, or engineering. Applicants must be U.S. citizens, enrolled in or applying to an accredited graduate school in the United States, and interested in internationalizing their educational experience or in enhancing an existing internationally-focused program. Part-time students are eligible to be considered for the fellowship, but they must be enrolled in a degree program. Selection is based on demonstrated academic excellence; a comprehensive, clear, and feasible proposal for study; a plan to develop, maintain, or advance language competence; evidence of ability to adapt to a different cultural environment; and the integration of the proposed program into the applicant's academic field and career goals.

Financial data The normal domestic stipend is $2,000 per semester; the stipend for overseas study is up to $10,000 per semester. The maximum level of support for a combined overseas and domestic program is $28,000.

Duration From 1 to 6 academic semesters.

Additional information Study outside the United States is strongly encouraged. This program is part of the National Security Education Program (NSEP), funded by the National Security Education Act, and administered by the Academy for Educational Development. All fellowships must include study of a language other than English and the corresponding culture that is appropriate for the degree program in which the student is enrolled. The program supports study abroad in areas of the world critical to national security; study will not be supported in most cases in western Europe, Canada, Australia, or New Zealand. Fellowship recipients incur a service obligation and must agree to work for the federal government or in the field of higher education subsequent to the fellowship period.

Number awarded Varies; generally, at least 300 per year.

Deadline January of each year.

[459]
DCBMBAA CHAPTER GRADUATE MBA SCHOLARSHIP PROGRAM

National Black MBA Association-Washington, DC
    Chapter
P.O. Box 14042
Washington, DC 20044
(202) 628-0138   E-mail: info@dcbmbaa.org
Web: www.dcbmbaa.org

Purpose To provide financial assistance to African American and other minority students from the Washington, D.C. area who are working on a graduate degree in business or management.

Eligibility This program is open to African American and other minority students who are enrolled in a full-time graduate business or management program in the United States, working on an M.B.A. degree; this includes current undergraduate seniors who have applied for admission to graduate school. Applicants must submit a completed application form, a photograph, a current resume, and an essay (up to 2 pages) on a topic that changes annually but focuses on minorities in business.

Financial data The stipend is at least $1,000.

Duration 1 year.

Number awarded 1 or more each year.

Deadline March of each year.

[460]
DELAWARE SHRM SCHOLARSHIPS

Delaware Society for Human Resource Management
c/o Noelle C. Robertson, Student Chapter Liaison
630 Martin Luther King Jr. Boulevard
P.O. Box 231
Wilmington, DE 19899-0231
(302) 429-3486   Fax: (302) 429-3816
E-mail: Noelle.Robertson@Connectiv.com
Web: www.shrmde.org

Purpose To provide financial assistance to students working on a bachelor's or master's degree in human resources at colleges and universities in Delaware.

Eligibility This program is open to 1) undergraduate students enrolled in a human resources program or related programs at a Delaware college, and 2) graduate students currently enrolled in a master's degree program at a Delaware college and clearly pursuing an emphasis area in human resources or related programs. Applicants must have a GPA of 3.0 or higher. Along with their application, they must submit a 2-page essay on their future objectives in the human resources field and why they chose this profession. Selection is based on total achievements and need.

Financial data The stipend is $2,500.

Duration 1 year.

Additional information The sponsor is the Delaware affiliate of the Society for Human Resource Management (SHRM).

Number awarded 4 each year.

Deadline September of each year.

[461]
DELL/UNCF CORPORATE SCHOLARS PROGRAM

United Negro College Fund
Attn: Corporate Scholars Program
P.O. Box 1435
Alexandria, VA 22313-9998
Toll-free: (866) 671-7237   E-mail: internship@uncf.org
Web: www.uncf.org/internships/index.asp

Purpose To provide financial assistance and work experience to undergraduate and graduate students, especially minorities, majoring in designated fields and interested in an internship at Dell Computer Corporation's corporate headquarters near Austin, Texas.

Eligibility This program is open to rising juniors and graduate students who are enrolled full time at institutions that are members of the United Negro College Fund (UNCF) or at any other 4-year college and university. Applicants must be majoring in business administration, computer science, engineering (computer, electrical, or mechanical), finance, human resources, management information systems, marketing, or supply chain management with a GPA of 3.0 or higher. Along with their application, they must submit a 1-page essay about themselves and their career goals, including information about their personal background and any particular challenges they have faced. Finalists are interviewed by a team of representatives from Dell, the program's sponsor.

Financial data The program provides a paid summer internship, housing accommodations in Austin, round-trip transportation to and from Austin, and (based on financial need and successful internship performance) a $10,000 scholarship.

Duration 10 to 12 weeks for the internship; 1 year for the scholarship.

Number awarded Varies each year.

Deadline January of each year.

[462]
DELOITTE DOCTORAL FELLOWSHIPS

Deloitte Foundation
Attn: Manager, Academic Development and University
   Relations
10 Westport Road
Wilton, CT 06897-0820
(203) 761-3179   Fax: (203) 563-2324
Web: www.deloitte.com

Purpose To provide financial assistance for study or research to doctoral candidates in accounting.

Eligibility This program is open to graduate students working on a doctoral degree in accounting at an accredited university who have completed 2 or more semesters of the program. Applicants should be preparing for careers in teaching.

Financial data The total grant is $25,000, disbursed in 4 payments: $2,500 when the director of the recipient's doctoral program considers that the fellow is 12 months from completing all required course work and examinations, $2,500 6 months later, $10,000 at the time the fellow's dissertation topic is approved and work on the dissertation begins, and $10,000 6 months later.

Duration 2 years: the final year of course work and the year immediately following, in which fellows are expected to complete their dissertations.

Number awarded Up to 10 each year.

Deadline October of each year.

[463]
DELTA MU DELTA SCHOLARSHIP AWARDS

Delta Mu Delta
Attn: Scholarship Chair
2 Salt Creek Lane LL6
Hinsdale, IL 60521
(630) 321-9522   Fax: (630) 214-6080
E-mail: dmd@dmd-ntl.org
Web: www.deltamudelta.org/scholarships.html

Purpose To provide financial assistance to undergraduate or graduate students majoring in business administration.

Eligibility This program is open to undergraduate and graduate students who are in at least the final term of their sophomore year and working on a degree in business administration. Although membership in Delta Mu Delta (a national honor society in business administration) is not required, applicants must be attending a school with a chapter of the society. Selection is based on scholarship, leadership, character, motivation, potential, and need.

Financial data Stipends are $2,000, $1,500, $1,000, $750, or $500.

Duration 1 year.

Number awarded Varies each year; recently, 39 of these scholarship were awarded: 1 at $2,000 (the Mildred R. Marion Award), 2 at $1,500 (the Albert J. Escher Award and the A.J. Foranoce Award), 4 at $1,000, 11 at $750 (including the Helen D. Snow Award, the Balwant Singh Award, and the Abderrahman Robana Award), and 21 at $500 (including the Eta Chapter Award).

Deadline February of each year.

[464]
DEREK HUGHES/NAPSLO EDUCATIONAL FOUNDATION INSURANCE SCHOLARSHIP

NAPSLO Educational Foundation
Attn: Insurance Scholarship Committee
6405 North Cosby Avenue, Suite 201
Kansas City, MO 64151
(816) 741-3910   Fax: (816) 741-5409
E-mail: foundation@napslo.org
Web: www.napslo.org

Purpose To provide financial assistance to undergraduate and graduate students working on a adegree in a field of importance to the insurance industry.

Eligibility This program is open to students who are enrolled or accepted for enrollment in an undergraduate or graduate program, working on a degree in actuarial science, business, economics, insurance, finance, management, risk management, statistics, or any field that relates to a career in insurance. They must have a GPA of 3.0 or higher (entering freshmen must also rank in the top 25% of their high school class). Students must submit a completed application, a college transcript, an essay, and 2 letters of recommendation. Financial need is considered in the selection process.

Financial data The stipend is $2,000.

Duration 1 year; recipients may reapply.

Additional information This program includes several named scholarships: Rolland L. Wiegers, Herbert Kaufman, Kevin A. McLaughlin, and Scott W. Polley Memorial Scholarship (for students majoring in insurance who qualify based on a combination of merit and financial need). Also offered as part of the program is the September 11 Scholarship, for children of insurance professionals killed in the 2001 terrorist attacks. This program is sponsored by the National Association of Professional Surplus Lines Offices (NAPSLO) Educational Foundation.

Number awarded 10 to 12 each year.

Deadline May of each year.

[465]
EARL G. GRAVES NAACP SCHOLARSHIP

National Association for the Advancement of Colored
   People
Attn: Education Department
4805 Mt. Hope Drive
Baltimore, MD 21215-3297
(410) 580-5760   Toll-free: (877) NAACP-98
E-mail: youth@naacpnet.org
Web: www.naacp.org

Purpose To provide financial assistance to upper-division and graduate students majoring in business.

Eligibility This program is open to full-time juniors, seniors, and graduate students majoring in business. Applicants must be currently in good academic standing, making satisfactory progress toward an undergraduate or graduate degree, and in the top 20% of their class. Along with their application, they must submit a 1-page essay on their interest in their major and a career, their life's ambition, what they hope to accomplish in their lifetime, and what they consider their most significant contribution to their community. Financial need is not considered in the selection process.

Financial data The stipend is $5,000 per year.

Duration 1 year.

Additional information Information is also available from the United Negro College Fund, Scholarships and Grants Administration, 8260 Willow Oaks Corporate Drive, Fairfax, VA 22031, (703) 205-3400.

Number awarded Varies each year; recently, 20 of these scholarships were awarded.

Deadline April of each year.

[466]
EDNA A. LAUTERBACH SCHOLARSHIP

Community Foundation for the Capital Region
Attn: Scholarship Coordinator
Executive Park Drive
Albany, NY 12203
(518) 446-9638   Fax: (518) 446-9708
E-mail: info@cfcr.org
Web: www.cfcr.org/scholarships/scholarships.htm

Purpose To provide financial assistance to nurses in New York who are interested in taking business-related courses in college or graduate school.

Eligibility This program is open to nurses in New York (registered and licensed practical nurses) who 1) plan to or are engaged in running a business related to health care and 2) want to take business-related courses in college or pursue other appropriate training. Applicants must demonstrate that the proposed classes/training will improve their ability to run a business. Financial need is considered in the selection process.

Financial data The amount awarded varies each year.

Additional information This program was established in the memory of a former president of Competent Care, Inc. and American Care, Inc.

Duration 1 year.

Number awarded Varies each year.

Deadline July of each year.

[467]
EDUCATIONAL FOUNDATION
COLLEGE/UNIVERSITY SCHOLARSHIPS

Colorado Society of Certified Public Accountants
Attn: CSCPA Educational Foundation
7979 East Tufts Avenue, Suite 500
Denver, CO 80237-2845
(303) 741-8613   Toll-free: (800) 523-9082 (within CO)
Fax: (303) 773-6344   E-mail: gmantz@cocpa.org
Web: www.cocpa.org/student_faculty/scholarships.asp

Purpose To provide financial assistance to undergraduate

and graduate students in Colorado who are studying accounting.

Eligibility This program is open to undergraduate and graduate students at colleges and universities in Colorado who have completed at least 8 semester hours of accounting courses (including at least 1 intermediate accounting class) and have a GPA, both overall and in accounting, of at least 3.0. Selection is based first on scholastic achievement and second on financial need.

Financial data The stipend is $1,000. Funds are paid directly to the recipient's school to be used for books, tuition, room, board, fees, and expenses.

Duration 1 year; recipients may reapply.

Number awarded 20 each year.

Deadline June of each year for fall semester or quarter; November of each year for winter quarter or spring semester.

[468]
ELIZABETH C. AND JOHN L. RICKETTS
GRADUATE SCHOOL SCHOLARSHIP

Pennsylvania Institute of Certified Public Accountants
Attn: Careers in Accounting Team
1650 Arch Street, 17th Floor
Philadelphia, PA 19103-2099
(215) 496-9272   Toll-free: (888) CPA-2001 (within PA)
Fax: (215) 496-9212   E-mail: schools@picpa.org
Web: www.cpazone.org/scholar/graduate.asp

Purpose To provide financial assistance to students attending graduate business schools in Pennsylvania.

Eligibility This program is open to full-time graduate students enrolled in business schools in Pennsylvania. Their undergraduate degree must have been in accounting or a related field. Preference is given to candidates with an undergraduate degree from a Pennsylvania college or university. Applicants must be working on a graduate degree in accounting, business, computer science, taxation, or a related field. They must be nominated by a faculty member at their school (up to 2 students per school may be nominated). Selection is based on intellectual capacity, leadership potential, and financial need.

Financial data The stipend is $5,000 and is paid over a 2-year period. Recipients working on a business school degree that does not require 2 full years of study are awarded $2,500.

Duration 2 years.

Additional information Recipients must attend school on a full-time basis.

Number awarded 1 each year.

Deadline March of each year.

[469]
ELLEN H. RICHARDS FELLOWSHIP

American Association of Family and Consumer Sciences
Attn: Manager of Awards and Grants
1555 King Street
Alexandria, VA 22314-2752
(703) 706-4600   Toll-free: (800) 424-8080, ext. 119
Fax: (703) 706-4663   E-mail: staff@aafcs.org
Web: www.aafcs.org/fellowships/brochure.html

Purpose To provide financial assistance to graduate students in the field of family and consumer sciences.

Eligibility Graduate students working on a degree in family and consumer sciences with an emphasis on administration are eligible to apply for this award. Applicants should have worked in an administrative area (such as supervision, college or university administration, cooperative extension, or business) and must be U.S. citizens or permanent residents with clearly defined plans for full-time graduate study. Selection is based on scholarship and special aptitudes for advanced study and research, educational and/or professional experiences, professional contributions to family and consumer sciences, and significance of the proposed research problem to the public well-being and the advancement of family and consumer sciences. Applicants are encouraged to have at least 1 year of professional family and consumer sciences work experience, serving in such positions as a graduate/undergraduate assistant, trainee, or intern.

Financial data The stipend is $3,500.

Duration 1 year.

Additional information This fellowship was first awarded for the academic year 1917-18. The application fee is $40. The association reserves the right to reconsider an award in the event the student receives a similar award for the same academic year.

Number awarded 1 each year.

Deadline January of each year.

[470]
ELLIOTT C. ROBERTS, SR. SCHOLARSHIP

Institute for Diversity in Health Management
Attn: Education Program Coordinator
One North Franklin Street, 30th Floor
Chicago, IL 60606
Toll-free: (800) 233-0996   Fax: (312) 422-4566
E-mail: clopez@aha.org
Web: www.diversityconnection.com

Purpose To provide financial assistance to minority graduate students in health care management or business management.

Eligibility This program is open to members of ethnic minority groups who are second-year graduate students. Applicants must be accepted or enrolled in an accredited program in health care management or business management and have a GPA of 3.0 or higher. They must demonstrate commitment to a career in health services administration, financial need, solid extracurricular activities, and a commitment to community service. U.S. citizenship or permanent resident status is required.

Financial data The stipend is $1,000.

Duration 1 year.

Number awarded 1 or more each year, depending on the availability of funds.

Deadline June of each year.

[471]
EMAF FELLOWSHIP PROGRAM

Society for Human Resource Management
Attn: Employment Management Association Foundation
1800 Duke Street
Alexandria, VA 22314-3499
(703) 548-3440   Toll-free: (800) 283-SHRM
Fax: (703) 535-6490   TDD: (703) 548-6999
E-mail: wflowers@shrm.org
Web: www.shrm.org/emaf/fellow.asp

Purpose To provide financial assistance to students enrolled or planning to enroll in a graduate program in the human resources field.

Eligibility Students are eligible to apply if they are 1) full-time college seniors who intend to prepare for a career in human resources in a generalist or employment/staffing capacity and have been accepted into an accredited graduate program; 2) full-time graduate students currently working on a degree that will lead them to a career in human resources in a generalist or employment/staffing capacity who have a GPA of 3.0 or higher; or 3) experienced degree holders who are returning to school for the purpose of re-careering or career advancement and have been accepted in an accredited graduate program related to the human resources generalist or employment/staffing field. U.S. citizenship is required. Selection is based on demonstrated scholastic achievement, leadership ability, work experience, and commitment to a career in a human resources field. At least 1 of the awards is designated for a qualified applicant from an ethnic or racial group underrepresented in the profession.

Financial data The stipend is $5,000, payable in 2 equal installments. Funds are made payable jointly to the recipient and the recipient's school.

Duration 1 year; recipients may reapply but may receive only 1 additional award.

Additional information This program includes 1 fellowship designated as the Richard Gast Fellowship. Funding for this program is provided by the Employment Management Association Foundation; the program is administered by Scholarship America, One Scholarship Way, P.O. Box 297, St. Peter, MN 56082, (507) 931-1682, (800) 537-4180, Fax: (507) 931-9168, E-mail: smsinfo@csfa.org.

Number awarded Up to 5 each year.

Deadline January of each year.

[472]
ETHNIC MINORITY POSTGRADUATE SCHOLARSHIP PROGRAM

National Collegiate Athletic Association
Attn: Leadership Advisory Board
700 West Washington Avenue
P.O. Box 6222
Indianapolis, IN 46206-6222
(317) 917-6477   Fax: (317) 917-6888
Web: www.ncaa.org

Purpose To provide funding to ethnic minority graduate students who are interested in preparing for a career in intercollegiate athletics.

Eligibility This program is open to members of minority groups who have been accepted into a program at a National Collegiate Athletic Association (NCAA) member institution that will prepare them for a career in intercollegiate athletics (athletics administrator, coach, athletic trainer, or other career that provides a direct service to intercollegiate athletics). Applicants must be U.S. citizens, have performed with distinction as a student body member at their respective undergraduate institution, and be entering the first semester or term of their postgraduate studies. Selection is based on the applicant's involvement in extracurricular activities, course work, commitment to preparing for a career in intercollegiate athletics, and promise for success in that career. Financial need is not considered.

Financial data The stipend is $6,000; funds are paid to the college or university of the recipient's choice.

Duration 1 year; nonrenewable.

Number awarded 16 each year; 3 of the scholarships are reserved for applicants who completed undergraduate study at an NCAA Division III institution.

Deadline February of each year.

[473]
FINANCIAL WOMEN INTERNATIONAL OF HAWAII SCHOLARSHIP

Hawai'i Community Foundation
Attn: Scholarship Department
1164 Bishop Street, Suite 800
Honolulu, HI 96813
(808) 537-6333   Toll-free: (888) 731-3863
Fax: (808) 521-6286
E-mail: scholarships@hcf-hawaii.org
Web: www.hawaiicommunityfoundation.org

Purpose To provide financial assistance to women in Hawaii who are studying business on the upper-division or graduate school level.

Eligibility This program is open to Hawaii residents who are majoring in business or a business-related field as a junior, senior, or graduate student. They must be able to demonstrate academic achievement (GPA of 3.5 or higher), good moral character, and financial need. Applications must be accompanied by a short statement indicating reasons for attending college, planned course of study, and career goals.

Financial data The amounts of the awards depend on the availability of funds and the need of the recipient; recently, stipends averaged $800.

Duration 1 year.

Additional information This program was established in 1998.

Number awarded Varies each year; recently, 2 of these scholarships were awarded.

Deadline February of each year.

[474]
FLORIDA BANKERS EDUCATIONAL FOUNDATION GRANTS

Florida Bankers Association
Attn: Florida Bankers Educational Foundation
1001 Thomasville Road, Suite 201
P.O. Box 1360
Tallahassee, FL 32302-1360
(850) 224-2265, ext. 139   Fax: (850) 224-2423
E-mail: lnewton@flbankers.net
Web: www.floridabankers.com

Purpose To provide financial assistance to undergraduate and graduate students who are interested in preparing for a career in Florida banking.

Eligibility This program is open to undergraduate and graduate students who have at least 5 years of full-time experience working in Florida banking. Applicants must be Florida residents, registered at 1 of 27 participating colleges or universities in the state, and taking banking-related classes. They must have a GPA of 2.5 or higher. Along with their application, they must submit 2 letters of recommendation from their place of employment: 1 from the bank president or other high-level employee and 1 from an immediate supervisor. Selection is based on interest in Florida banking, scholastic achievement, aptitude, ability, leadership, personality, and character.

Financial data The amount of assistance is based on the number of semester hours the student has remaining until graduation. The maximum award is $1,500 per year for the freshman and sophomore years, $2,000 per year for the junior and senior years, and $5,000 as a graduate student.

Duration Up to 4 years as an undergraduate and another 2 years as a graduate student.

Additional information Recipients must maintain a 2.5 GPA and take at least 12 credit hours per calendar year.

Number awarded Several each year.

Deadline February, May, August, or November of each year.

[475]
FOSTER G. MCGAW STUDENT SCHOLARSHIP

American College of Healthcare Executives
One North Franklin Street, Suite 1700
Chicago, IL 60606-3529
(312) 424-2800   Fax: (312) 424-0023
E-mail: ache@ache.org
Web: www.ache.org

Purpose To provide financial assistance to graduate student members of the American College of Healthcare Executives.

Eligibility This program is open to student members in good standing who are enrolled full time in an accredited graduate program in health care management. Applicants must be U.S. or Canadian citizens and be recommended by the director of their program.

Financial data The stipend is $3,500.
Duration 1 year; nonrenewable.
Number awarded Varies each year.
Deadline March of each year.

[476]
GEORGE A. NIELSEN PUBLIC INVESTOR SCHOLARSHIP

Government Finance Officers Association
Attn: Scholarship Committee
203 North LaSalle Street, Suite 2700
Chicago, IL 60601-1210
(312) 977-9700   Fax: (312) 977-4806
Web: www.gfoa.org/services/scholarships.shtml

Purpose To provide financial assistance to public employees who are undergraduate and graduate students and have research or career interests in the investment of public funds.
Eligibility This program is open to employees (for at least 1 year) of a local government or other public entity who are enrolled or planning to enroll in an undergraduate or graduate program in public administration, finance, business administration, or a related field. Applicants must be citizens or permanent residents of the United States or Canada and able to provide a letter of recommendation from their employer. They must have a research or career interest in the efficient and productive investment of public funds. Financial need is not considered in the selection process.
Financial data The stipend is $5,000 or $2,500.
Duration 1 year.
Additional information Funds for this program are provided by George A. Nielsen LLP.
Number awarded Each year, either 1 scholarship at $5,000 or 2 at $2,500 are awarded.
Deadline February of each year.

[477]
GEORGIA GOVERNMENT FINANCE OFFICERS ASSOCIATION SCHOLARSHIP

Georgia Government Finance Officers Association
Attn: Scholarship Selection Committee
P.O. Box 6473
Athens, GA 30604-6473
(706) 542-8162   Fax: (706) 542-9856
E-mail: ggfoa@cviog.uga.edu
Web: www.ggfoa.org/Scholarships/scholarships.htm

Purpose To provide financial assistance to undergraduate or graduate students in Georgia who are preparing for a career in public finance.
Eligibility This program is open to undergraduate or graduate students who are preparing for a career in public finance and are currently enrolled or accepted (for graduate school) as full-time students at a college or university in Georgia. Applicants must have a GPA of 3.0 or higher. Along with their application, they must submit a letter of recommendation from the head of the applicable program (e.g., public administration, accounting, finance, business) and a 2-page statement describing their proposed career plans and plan of study. Preference is given to members of the Georgia Government Finance Officers Association (GGFOA) and employees

of GGFOA governmental entities who are eligible for in-state tuition.
Financial data The stipend is $3,000.
Duration 1 year.
Number awarded 2 each year.
Deadline June of each year.

[478]
GEORGIA SOCIETY OF CPAS SCHOLARSHIP PROGRAM

Georgia Society of CPAs
Attn: Educational Foundation
3353 Peachtree Road, N.E., Suite 400
Atlanta, GA 30326-1414
(404) 231-8676   Toll-free: (800) 330-8889, ext. 2943
Fax: (404) 237-1291   E-mail: gscpaweb@gscpa.org
Web: www.gscpa.org

Purpose To provide financial assistance to upper-division and graduate students who are majoring in accounting in Georgia.
Eligibility This program is open to residents of Georgia who have demonstrated a commitment to a career in accounting. Applicants must be 1) rising junior or senior undergraduate accounting majors, or 2) graduate students enrolled in a master's degree in accounting or a business administration program. They must be enrolled in an accredited public or private college or university in Georgia with a GPA of 3.0 or higher either overall or in their accounting courses. Along with their application, they must submit documentation of financial need, transcripts, a resume, and a 250-word essay on their personal career goals and how this scholarship will help them attain those goals.
Financial data A stipend is awarded (amount not specified).
Duration 1 year.
Additional information This program includes the following named scholarships: the Time + Plus Scholarship, the Robert H. Lange Memorial Scholarship, the Julius M. Johnson Memorial Scholarship, and the Paychex Entrepreneur Scholarship.
Number awarded Varies each year; recently, 36 of these scholarships were awarded.
Deadline April of each year.

[479]
GORDON SCHEER SCHOLARSHIP

Colorado Society of Certified Public Accountants
Attn: CSCPA Educational Foundation
7979 East Tufts Avenue, Suite 500
Denver, CO 80237-2845
(303) 741-8613   Toll-free: (800) 523-9082 (within CO)
Fax: (303) 773-6344   E-mail: gmantz@cocpa.org
Web: www.cocpa.org/student_faculty/scholarships.asp

Purpose To provide financial assistance to undergraduate and graduate students in Colorado who are studying accounting.
Eligibility This program is open to undergraduate and graduate students at colleges and universities in Colorado who have completed at least 1 intermediate accounting class and

have a GPA, both overall and in accounting, of at least 3.5. Selection is based on scholastic achievement.

Financial data The stipend is $1,250. Funds are paid directly to the recipient's school to be used for books, tuition, room, board, fees, and expenses.

Duration 1 year; recipients may reapply.

Number awarded 1 each year.

Deadline June of each year.

[480]
HARRY S. TRUMAN SCHOLARSHIP PROGRAM

Harry S. Truman Scholarship Foundation
Attn: Executive Secretary
712 Jackson Place, N.W.
Washington, DC 20006
(202) 395-4831   Fax: (202) 395-6995
E-mail: office@truman.gov
Web: www.truman.gov

Purpose To provide financial assistance to undergraduate students who have outstanding leadership potential, plan to prepare for a career in government or other public service, and wish to attend graduate school in the United States or abroad to prepare themselves for a public service career.

Eligibility Students must be nominated to be considered for this program. Nominees must be full-time students with junior standing at a 4-year institution, committed to a career in government or public service, in the upper quarter of their class, and U.S. citizens or nationals. Each participating institution may nominate up to 4 candidates (and up to 3 additional students who completed their first 2 years at a community college); community colleges and other 2-year institutions may nominate former students who are enrolled as full-time students with junior-level academic standing at accredited 4-year institutions. Selection is based on extent and quality of community service and government involvement, academic performance, leadership record, suitability of the nominee's proposed program of study for a career in public service, and writing and analytical skills. Priority is given to candidates who plan to enroll in a graduate program that specifically trains them for a career in public service, including government at any level, uniformed services, public interest organizations, nongovernmental research and/or educational organizations, public and private schools, and public service oriented non-profit organizations. The fields of study may include agriculture, biology, engineering, environmental management, physical and social sciences, and technology policy, as well as such traditional fields as economics, education, government, history, international relations, law, nonprofit management, political science, public administration, public health, and public policy. Interviews are required.

Financial data The scholarship provides up to $26,000: up to $2,000 for the senior year of undergraduate education and as much as $24,000 for graduate studies. All scholars are eligible to receive up to $12,000 for the first year of graduate study. They are eligible to receive up to $12,000 for their final year of graduate study if they provide assurance that they will enter public service immediately upon graduation or completion of a judicial clerkship after graduation.

Duration 1 year of undergraduate study and up to 3 years of graduate study, as long as the recipient maintains satisfactory academic performance.

Additional information Recipients may attend graduate school in the United States or in foreign countries.

Number awarded 75 to 80 each year: a) 1 "state" scholarship is available to a qualified resident nominee in each of the 50 states, the District of Columbia, Puerto Rico, and (considered as a single entity) Guam, the Virgin Islands, American Samoa, and the Commonwealth of the Northern Mariana Islands; and b) up to 30 at-large scholars.

Deadline February of each year.

[481]
HARVEY FELLOWS PROGRAM

Mustard Seed Foundation
Attn: Harvey Fellows Program
3330 Washington Boulevard, Suite 100
Arlington, VA 22201
(703) 524-5620   Fax: (703) 524-5643
Web: www.msfdn.org

Purpose To provide financial aid to Christian students to attend prestigious graduate schools in the United States or abroad and to "pursue leadership positions in strategic fields where Christians appear to be underrepresented."

Eligibility This program is open to American and foreign students. The most competitive applicants are those whose intended vocational fields are demonstrated to have a significant impact on society and to be of high priority for Christian involvement. These fields include but are not limited to: government, corporate, and university research; international economics and finance in public and private sectors; journalism and media; film production and visual and performing arts; public policy and federal, state, and major city government; research, teaching, and administration at premier colleges and universities. Vocations that are not considered a priority for this scholarship include: work within a church or religious organization; civil service; elementary and secondary education; general business; homemaking; farming; nonprofit relief and economic development; military service; private practice law or medicine; clinical psychology or counseling; social work; professional sports; and other fields that traditionally have attracted a higher percentage of Christians. Selection is based on the applicant's description of his or her Christian faith; demonstrated commitment and accountability to the local church; vocational plans; argument for the lack of a distinctive Christian voice in that field; demonstrated leadership within the discipline; potential to impact people and systemic structures within the field; ability to affect the chosen field (often demonstrated by current publishing and research success, professional experiences and exposure, and recommendations). Financial need is not a factor. Preference is given to candidates with at least 2 years of study remaining and to those whose research or project interests are not explicitly Christian in nature.

Financial data Each fellow is awarded an annual $14,000 stipend. Funds must be used at a "premier" graduate degree program, subject to approval by the selection committee. Fellows may use their stipends for tuition, living expenses, research tools or travel, studio space, professional conferences, and interview travel.

Duration Up to 2 years for most master's degree programs and up to 3 years for law and doctoral programs. Due to the nature of the program, 1-year fellowships are rarely awarded.

Additional information   This fellowship was first awarded in 1994. A significant component of the program is a 1-week summer institute where fellows meet in Washington, D.C. to explore the integration of faith, learning, and vocation. The sponsor pays program costs; fellows are responsible for transportation to and from the institute. Recipients must attend 1 of the top 5 institutions (anywhere in the world) in their field of study. Christian colleges and small liberal arts schools are excluded, because, according to the sponsors, they "have not yet found" any that are "nationally acknowledged in professional publications or national rankings as top five institutions."

Number awarded   Varies each year; recently, 17 were awarded.

Deadline   November of each year.

[482]
H.B. EARHART FELLOWSHIPS

Earhart Foundation
2200 Green Road, Suite H
Ann Arbor, MI 48105

Purpose   To provide financial assistance to outstanding graduate students in the social sciences (including economics) and humanities.

Eligibility   Faculty sponsors are invited to nominate talented graduate students in the social sciences or humanities (especially economics, philosophy, international affairs, and government/politics) who are interested in preparing for a career in college or university teaching. Only invited nominations are accepted; direct applications from candidates or from non-invited sponsors are not accepted.

Financial data   Stipends range from $2,500 to $12,500. Some fellows also receive tuition.

Duration   1 year.

Number awarded   Varies each year; recently, 51 fellowships were awarded at 29 institutions; of those, 34 included payment of tuition.

[483]
HELENE M. OVERLY MEMORIAL GRADUATE SCHOLARSHIP

Women's Transportation Seminar
Attn: National Headquarters
1666 K Street, N.W., Suite 1100
Washington, DC 20006
(202) 496-4340   Fax: (202) 496-4349
E-mail: wts@wtsnational.org
Web: www.wtsnational.org

Purpose   To provide financial assistance to women graduate students interested in preparing for a career in transportation.

Eligibility   This program is open to women who are enrolled in a graduate degree program in a transportation-related field (e.g., transportation engineering, planning, finance, or logistics). Applicants must have at least a 3.0 GPA and be interested in a career in transportation. They must submit a 750-word statement about their career goals after graduation and why they think they should receive the scholarship award. Applications must be submitted first to a local chapter; the chapters forward selected applications for consideration on

the national level. Minority women are particularly encouraged to apply. Selection is based on transportation involvement and goals, job skills, and academic record.

Financial data   The stipend is $6,000.

Duration   1 year.

Additional information   This program was established in 1981.

Number awarded   1 each year.

Deadline   Applications must be submitted by November to a local WTS chapter.

[484]
HIMSS FOUNDATION SCHOLARSHIPS

Healthcare Information and Management Systems
   Society
Attn: HIMSS Foundation Scholarship Program
   Coordinator
230 East Ohio Street, Suite 500
Chicago, IL 60611-3269
(312) 664-4467   Fax: (312) 664-6143
Web: www.himss.org/asp/scholarships.asp

Purpose   To provide financial assistance to upper-division or graduate student members of the Healthcare Information and Management Systems Society (HIMSS) who are interested in the field of health care information and management systems.

Eligibility   This program is open to student members of the society, although an application for membership, including dues, may accompany the scholarship application. Applicants must be upper-division or graduate students enrolled in an accredited program designed to prepare them for a career in health care information or management systems, which may include industrial engineering, health care informatics, operations research, computer science and information systems, mathematics, and quantitative programs in business administration and hospital administration. Selection is based on academic achievement and demonstration of leadership potential, including communication skills and participation in society activity.

Financial data   The stipend is $5,000. The award includes an all-expense paid trip to the annual HIMSS conference and exhibition.

Duration   1 year.

Additional information   This program was established in 1986 for undergraduate and master's degree students. The first Ph.D. scholarship was awarded in 2002.

Number awarded   3 each year: 1 to an undergraduate student, 1 to a master's degree student, and 1 to a Ph.D. candidate.

Deadline   October of each year.

[485]
HRA-NCA ACADEMIC SCHOLARSHIPS

Human Resource Association of the National Capital
   Area
Attn: Chair, College Relations
P.O. Box 7503
Arlington, VA 22207
(703) 241-0229   Fax: (703) 532-9473
E-mail: info@hra-nca.org
Web: hra-nca.org/studentservices.asp

Purpose To provide financial assistance to students working on an undergraduate or graduate degree in human
resources at colleges and universities in the Washington, D.C.
metropolitan area.

Eligibility This program is open to undergraduate and graduate students working on a degree in human resources or a
related field at a college or university in the Washington, D.C.
metropolitan area. Applicants must have completed at least
half of their degree program and have at least a full semester
remaining. Selection is based on academic performance and
commitment to human resources as demonstrated by participation in a student chapter of the Society for Human
Resource Management (SHRM), an internship, or relevant
work experience or community service.

Financial data The stipend is $1,500.

Duration 1 year.

Additional information The Human Resource Association
of the National Capital Area (HRA-NCA) is the local affiliate of
SHRM.

Number awarded 2 each year.

Deadline Applications are generally due in spring of each
year.

[486]
HUMANE STUDIES FELLOWSHIPS

Institute for Humane Studies at George Mason University
3301 North Fairfax Drive, Suite 440
Arlington, VA 22201-4432
(703) 993-4880   Toll-free: (800) 697-8799
Fax: (703) 993-4890   E-mail: ihs@gmu.edu
Web: www.TheIHS.org

Purpose To provide financial assistance to undergraduate
and graduate students in the United States or abroad who
intend to pursue "intellectual careers" and have demonstrated
an interest in classical liberal principles.

Eligibility This program is open to students who will be full-
time college juniors, seniors, or graduate students planning
academic or other intellectual careers, including law, public
policy, and journalism. Applicants must have a clearly demonstrated interest in the classical liberal/libertarian tradition of
individual rights and market economics. Applications from
students outside the United States or studying abroad receive
equal consideration. Selection is based on academic or professional performance, relevance of work to the advancement
of a free society, and potential for success.

Financial data The maximum stipend is $12,000.

Duration 1 year; may be renewed upon reapplication.

Additional information As defined by the sponsor, the
core principles of the classical liberal/libertarian tradition
include the recognition of individual rights and the dignity and
worth of each individual; protection of these rights through the

institutions of private property, contract, the rule of law, and
freely evolved intermediary institutions; voluntarism in all
human relations, including the unhampered market mechanism in economic affairs; and the goals of free trade, free
migration, and peace. This program began in 1983 as Claude
R. Lambe Fellowships. The application fee is $25.

Number awarded Approximately 100 each year.

Deadline December of each year.

[487]
HYPERTHERM–INTERNATIONAL HYTECH LEADERSHIP SCHOLARSHIP

American Welding Society
Attn: AWS Foundation, Inc.
550 N.W. LeJeune Road
Miami, FL 33126
(305) 445-6628   Toll-free: (800) 443-9353, ext. 461
Fax: (305) 443-7559   E-mail: found@aws.org
Web: www.aws.org

Purpose To provide financial assistance to graduate students working on a degree in engineering management within
the welding and cutting industry.

Eligibility This program is open to graduate students working on an advanced degree in engineering management within
the welding and cutting industry. Applicants must have graduated with an overall GPA of 2.8 or higher. They may be citizens of any country attending an academic institution in any
country. Along with their application, they must submit a personal statement on their proposed advanced academic and
post-academic plans. Financial need is not required, but priority is given to applicants who can demonstrate a financial
need.

Financial data A stipend is awarded (amount not specified).

Duration 1 year.

Number awarded 1 each year.

Deadline January of each year.

[488]
IBM PHD FELLOWSHIP PROGRAM

IBM Corporation
Attn: University Relations
1133 Westchester Avenue
White Plains, NY 10604
Toll-free: (800) IBM-4YOU   TTY: (800) IBM-3383
E-mail: phdfellow@us.ibm.com
Web: www-306.ibm.com

Purpose To provide financial assistance and work experience to students working on a Ph.D. in a research area of
broad interest to IBM (including business).

Eligibility Students nominated for this fellowship should be
enrolled full time in an accredited U.S. or Canadian college
or university and should have completed at least 1 year of
graduate study in the following fields: business, chemistry,
computer science, electrical engineering, materials sciences,
mathematics, mechanical engineering, physics, or related disciplines. They should be planning a career in research. Nominations must be made by a faculty member and endorsed by
the department head. IBM values diversity and encourages
nominations of women, minorities, and others who contribute

to that diversity. Selection is based on the applicants' potential for research excellence, the degree to which their technical interests align with those of IBM, and academic progress to date.

Financial data Fellows receive tuition, fees, and a stipend of $17,500 per year.

Duration 1 year; may be renewed up to 3 additional years, provided the recipient is renominated, interacts with IBM's technical community, and demonstrates continued progress and achievement.

Additional information Recipients are offered an internship at 1 of the IBM Research Division laboratories and are given an IBM ThinkPad.

Number awarded Varies each year.

Deadline December of each year.

[489]
IDDBA SCHOLARSHIP

International Dairy-Deli-Bakery Association
Attn: Scholarship Committee
313 Price Place, Suite 202
P.O. Box 5528
Madison, WI 53705-0528
(608) 238-7908   Fax: (608) 238-6330
E-mail: iddba@iddba.org
Web: www.iddba.org

Purpose To provide financial assistance for undergraduate or graduate study to students interested in a career in the food industry who are employed in a supermarket dairy, deli, or bakery department (or related companies).

Eligibility This program is open to high school seniors, college students, vocational/technical students, and graduate students. Applicants must be currently employed in a supermarket dairy, deli, or bakery department or be employed by a company that services those departments (e.g., food manufacturers, brokers, or wholesalers). They must be majoring in a food-related field, e.g., culinary arts, baking/pastry arts, food science, business, or marketing. Employees of restaurants, retail bakeries, bakery-cafes, or other food service establishments not associated with a supermarket are not eligible. While a GPA of 2.5 or higher is required, this may be waived for first-time applicants. Selection is based on academic achievement, work experience, and a statement of career goals and/or how their degree will be beneficial to their job. Financial need is not considered.

Financial data Stipends range from $250 to $1,000. Funds are paid jointly to the recipient and the recipient's school. If the award exceeds tuition fees, the excess may be used for other educational expenses.

Duration 1 year; recipients may reapply.

Number awarded Varies each year; a total of $75,000 is available for this program annually.

Deadline Applications must be submitted prior to the end of March, June, September, or December of each year.

[490]
IMA MEMORIAL EDUCATION FUND SCHOLARSHIPS

Institute of Management Accountants
Attn: Committee on Students
10 Paragon Drive
Montvale, NJ 07645-1760
(201) 573-9000   Toll-free: (800) 638-4427, ext. 1543
Fax: (201) 573-8438   E-mail: students@imanet.org
Web: www.imanet.org

Purpose To provide financial assistance to student members of the Institute of Management Accountants (IMA) who are interested in preparing for a career in a field related to management accounting.

Eligibility This program is open to undergraduate and graduate student IMA members who have a GPA of 2.8 or higher. Applicants must be preparing for a career in management accounting, financial management, or information technology. They must submit a 2-page statement on their reasons for applying for the scholarship, reasons that they deserve the award, specific contributions to the IMA, ideas on how they will promote awareness and increase membership and certification within IMA, and their career goals and objectives. Selection is based on that statement, academic merit, IMA participation, the quality of the presentation, a resume, and letters of recommendation.

Financial data Stipends range from $1,000 to $2,500 per year.

Duration 1 year.

Additional information Up to 30 finalists in each category (including the scholarship winners) receive a scholarship to take 5 parts of the Certified Management Accountant (CMA) and/or Certified in Financial Management (CFM) examination within a year of graduation.

Number awarded Varies each year.

Deadline February of each year.

[491]
INEZ ELEANOR RADELL FELLOWSHIP

American Association of Family and Consumer Sciences
Attn: Manager of Awards and Grants
1555 King Street
Alexandria, VA 22314-2752
(703) 706-4600   Toll-free: (800) 424-8080, ext. 119
Fax: (703) 706-4663   E-mail: staff@aafcs.org
Web: www.aafcs.org/fellowships/brochure.html

Purpose To provide financial assistance to graduate students in the field of family and consumer sciences.

Eligibility This program is open to graduate students working on a degree in the design, construction, and/or marketing of clothing for the aged and/or disabled adults. Applicants must have earned a baccalaureate degree in family and consumer sciences with an undergraduate major in clothing, art, merchandising, business, or a related field. They must be U.S. citizens or permanent residents with clearly defined plans for full-time graduate study. Selection is based on scholarship and special aptitudes for advanced study and research, educational and/or professional experiences, professional contributions to family and consumer sciences, and significance of the proposed research problem to the public well-being and the advancement of family and consumer sciences. Applicants are encouraged to have at least 1 year of professional family and consumer sciences work experience, serving in such positions as a graduate/undergraduate assistant, trainee, or intern.

Financial data The stipend is $3,500.

Duration 1 year.

Additional information This program was initiated in 1979. The application fee is $40. The association reserves the right to reconsider an award in the event the student receives a similar award for the same academic year.

Number awarded 1 each year.

Deadline January of each year.

[492]
INTERNATIONAL PUBLIC MANAGEMENT ASSOCIATION FOR HUMAN RESOURCES GRADUATE STUDY FELLOWSHIP

International Public Management Association for Human Resources
Attn: Fellowship Committee
1617 Duke Street
Alexandria, VA 22314
(703) 549-7100   Fax: (703) 684-0948
Web: www.ipma-hr.org

Purpose To provide funding to members of the International Public Management Association for Human Resources (IPMA-HR) who are interested in working on a law degree or a master's degree in public administration, business administration, or a related field.

Eligibility This program is open to students working on a graduate degree in public administration, business administration, the law, or a related field. Ph.D. candidates are not eligible. Applicants must have been professional members of the association (student members are not eligible) for at least 1 year and have at least 5 years of full-time professional experience. Selection is based on academic record, demonstrated leadership abilities, and commitment to public service. Financial need is not considered in the selection process.

Financial data The maximum stipend is $2,000 per year.

Duration 1 year; may be renewed for 1 additional year.

Additional information This program was started in 1982.

Number awarded 2 each year.

Deadline May of each year.

[493]
INVESTING IN THE FUTURE SCHOLARSHIP

Charles and Agnes Kazarian Eternal
    Foundation/ChurchArmenia.com
Attn: Educational Scholarships
30 Kennedy Plaza, Second Floor
Providence, RI 02903
E-mail: info@churcharmenia.com
Web: www.churcharmenia.com/scholarship1.html

Purpose To provide financial assistance to outstanding undergraduate or graduate students of Armenian descent who are preparing for a career in finance, business, medicine, or research.

Eligibility Applicants must be of Armenian descent and accepted to or qualified for highly competitive undergraduate

or graduate degree programs focusing on finance, medicine, business, or research. They must submit a completed application form, official academic transcripts, 3-page personal statement, and up to 3 letters of recommendation. Selection is based on academic record, financial need, and future ability to make an investment or return to the Armenian community.

Financial data The stipend is $10,000.

Duration 1 year.

Number awarded 1 or more each year.

[494]
JAMES C. & ELIZABETH R. CONNER FOUNDATION SCHOLARSHIPS

James C. & Elizabeth R. Conner Foundation
204 South Wellington
P.O. Box 1315
Marshall, TX 75671
(903) 938-0331   Fax: (903) 938-0334

Purpose To provide financial assistance to graduate students in engineering, physical science, medical science, or business.

Eligibility This program is open to U.S. citizens who have received a bachelor's degree and are interested in working on a master's degree or a doctorate in the following fields: engineering, physical science, medical science, or business. Applicants may not be married. They must be in the upper 10% of their college graduating class and be attending a college or university in the southwestern states. Selection is based on academic performance, character, ambition, and career plans.

Financial data The amount awarded varies but is generally around $6,000 per year.

Duration 1 year; may be renewed.

Number awarded Varies; generally, 2 each year.

[495]
JCC ASSOCIATION SCHOLARSHIP PROGRAM

Jewish Community Centers Association
Attn: Scholarship Coordinator
15 East 26th Street, Tenth Floor
New York, NY 10010-1579
(212) 532-4949   Fax: (212) 481-4174
E-mail: recruiter@jcca.org
Web: www.jccworks.com/scholarships.html

Purpose To provide financial assistance to graduate students who are interested in preparing for a professional career at a Jewish Community Center (JCC).

Eligibility Applicants must have a bachelor's degree from an accredited college or university; have an undergraduate GPA of 3.0 or higher; and be knowledgeable about the JCC movement, its values and mission statement, and relevant issues in the Jewish community and in Israel. They must be working on a graduate degree in social work, Jewish communal service, nonprofit management, business administration, public policy, sports management, health and physical education, Jewish studies, education, or other relevant field. Along with their application, they must submit a personal essay on their interest in JCC work and their understanding of the JCC movement, references, and transcripts. Preference is given to applicants committed to a career in the JCC movement. Finalists are interviewed.

Financial data The stipend is $10,000 per year.

Duration 2 years.

Additional information Recipients attending schools that require field work must request a placement in a JCC, preferably during the second year. All recipients must make a 2-year commitment to work in a JCC or YM-YWHA following graduation.

Number awarded Several each year.

Deadline January of each year.

[496]
JCC ASSOCIATION TUITION ASSISTANCE

Jewish Community Centers Association
Attn: Scholarship Coordinator
15 East 26th Street, Tenth Floor
New York, NY 10010-1579
(212) 532-4949   Fax: (212) 481-4174
E-mail: recruiter@jcca.org
Web: www.jccworks.com/scholarships.html

Purpose To provide financial assistance to graduate students who are currently working full time at a Jewish Community Center (JCC).

Eligibility This program is open to graduate students who are currently working full time in the JCC movement. Applicants must be committed to a career in the JCC movement; be able to demonstrate leadership potential; have an undergraduate GPA of 3.0 or higher; and be knowledgeable about the JCC movement, its values and mission statement, and relevant issues in the Jewish community and in Israel. They must be working on a graduate degree in social work, Jewish communal service, nonprofit management, business administration, public policy, sports management, health and physical education, Jewish studies, education, or other relevant field. Along with their application, they must submit a personal essay on their interest in JCC work and their understanding of the JCC movement, references, and transcripts. Finalists are interviewed.

Financial data The stipend is $3,000 per year.

Duration 2 years.

Additional information Recipients must continue to work full time in the JCC movement.

Number awarded Several each year.

Deadline January of each year.

[497]
J.J. BARR SCHOLARSHIP

National Association of Water Companies
Attn: Scholarship Committee
1725 K Street, N.W., Suite 1212
Washington, DC 20006-1401
(202) 833-8383   Fax: (202) 331-7442
E-mail: darcy@nawc.com
Web: www.nawc.com/scholarship.html

Purpose To provide financial assistance for graduate school to students planning careers in the investor-owned community water supply business.

Eligibility This program is open to U.S. citizens who are 1) graduating college seniors entering a graduate degree pro-

gram; 2) current graduate students; and 3) current water utility industry employees entering a graduate degree program. Applicants must be working on or planning to work on a graduate degree in engineering, biology, chemistry, business administration, or any other field that may lead to a career or continuation of a career in the investor-owned public water supply business. Their undergraduate or graduate institution must be located in a state that is included within the geographical boundaries of chapters of the National Association of Water Companies (NAWC). Financial need is considered in the selection process.

Financial data The stipend is $5,000; the award check is payable to the awardee and college, to be used toward payment of educational expenses. The recipient's college receives an additional $500.

Duration 1 year.

Additional information The NAWC is the trade association of 320 companies in 42 states that provide water to communities. Chapters are currently located in California, the Carolinas, Delaware, Florida, Illinois, Indiana, Missouri, the New England states, New Jersey, New York, Ohio, Pennsylvania, and Washington.

Number awarded 1 each year.

Deadline March of each year.

[498]
JOHN L. CAREY SCHOLARSHIPS

American Institute of Certified Public Accountants
Attn: Academic and Career Development Division
1211 Avenue of the Americas
New York, NY 10036-8775
(212) 596-6221   Fax: (212) 596-6292
E-mail: educat@aicpa.org
Web: www.aicpa.org/members/div/career/mini/jlcs.htm

Purpose To provide financial assistance to liberal arts degree recipients who are interested in working on a graduate degree in accounting.

Eligibility Applicants for these scholarships must hold a liberal arts degree from an accredited institution in the United States. They must be accepted into, or be in the process of applying to, a graduate degree program in accounting that will enable them to sit for the C.P.A. examination at a college or university whose business administration program is accredited by the AACSB. Selection is based on demonstrated academic achievement, leadership, future career interests, and an essay on academic and professional goals.

Financial data The stipend is $5,000 per year.

Duration 1 year; may be renewed for 1 additional year, if recipients are making satisfactory progress toward graduation.

Number awarded Up to 7 each year.

Deadline March of each year.

[499]

JOHN MCLENDON MEMORIAL MINORITY POSTGRADUATE SCHOLARSHIP AWARD

National Association of Collegiate Directors of Athletics
Attn: NACDA Foundation
24651 Detroit Road
P.O. Box 16428
Cleveland, OH 44116
(440) 892-4000   Fax: (440) 892-4007
E-mail: bhorning@nacda.com
Web: nacda.collegesports.com

Purpose To provide financial assistance to minority college seniors who are interested in working on a graduate degree in athletics administration.

Eligibility This program is open to minority college students who are seniors, are attending school on a full-time basis, have a GPA of 3.0 or higher, intend to attend graduate school to earn a degree in athletics administration, and are involved on the college or community level. Candidates are not required to be student athletes. Current graduate students are not eligible.

Financial data The stipend is $10,000. In addition, 1 recipient each year is offered the opportunity to serve a 9-month internship in the office of the National Association of Collegiate Directors of Athletics (NACDA).

Duration 1 year.

Additional information Recipients must maintain full-time status during the senior year to retain their eligibility. They must attend NACDA-member institutions.

Number awarded 5 each year.

Deadline January of each year.

[500]

KIRBY MCDONALD EDUCATION ENDOWMENT SCHOLARSHIP FUND

Cook Inlet Region, Inc.
Attn: CIRI Foundation
2600 Cordova Street, Suite 206
Anchorage, AK 99503
(907) 263-5582   Toll-free: (800) 764-3382
Fax: (907) 263-5588   E-mail: tcf@ciri.com
Web: www.ciri.com/tcf/designated.html

Purpose To provide financial assistance for undergraduate or graduate studies to Alaska Natives who are original enrollees to Cook Inlet Region, Inc. (CIRI) and their lineal descendants.

Eligibility This program is open to Alaska Native enrollees under the Alaska Native Claims Settlement Act (ANCSA) of 1971 and the lineal descendants of Cook Inlet Region, Inc. There are no Alaska residency requirements or age limitations. Applicants must be accepted or enrolled full time in a 4-year undergraduate or a graduate degree program. Preference is given to students in the culinary arts, business administration, or engineering. They must have a GPA of 2.5 or higher. Selection is based on academic achievement, rigor of course work or degree program, quality of a statement of purpose, student financial contribution, financial need, grade level, previous work performance, education and community activities, letters of recommendation, seriousness of purpose, and practicality of educational and professional goals.

Financial data The stipend is $9,000 per year, $7,000 per year, or $2,000 per semester, depending on GPA.

Duration 1 year (2 semesters).

Additional information This program was established in 1991. Recipients must attend school on a full-time basis.

Deadline May of each year.

[501]

KPMG MINORITY ACCOUNTING DOCTORAL SCHOLARSHIPS

KPMG Foundation
Attn: Scholarship Administrator
Three Chestnut Ridge Road
Montvale, NJ 07645-0435
(201) 307-7932   Fax: (201) 307-7093
E-mail: fionarose@kpmg.com
Web: kpmgfoundation.org/graduate.html

Purpose To provide funding to underrepresented minority students working on a doctoral degree in accounting.

Eligibility Applicants must be African Americans, Hispanic Americans, or Native Americans. They must be U.S. citizens or permanent residents and accepted or enrolled in a full-time accounting doctoral program. Along with their application, they must submit a brief letter explaining their reason for working on a Ph.D. in accounting.

Financial data The stipend is $10,000 per year.

Duration 1 year; may be renewed up to 4 additional years.

Additional information These funds are not intended to replace funds normally made available by the recipient's institution. The foundation recommends that the recipient's institution also award, to the recipient, a $5,000 annual stipend, a teaching or research assistantship, and a waiver of tuition and fees.

Number awarded Varies each year; recently, 14 new scholarships were awarded and another 65 were renewed.

Deadline April of each year.

[502]

KSCPA GRADUATE SCHOLARSHIPS

Kansas Society of Certified Public Accountants
Attn: Educational Foundation
1080 S.W. Wanamaker Road, Suite 200
P.O. Box 4291
Topeka, KS 66604-0291
(785) 272-4366   Toll-free: (800) 222-0452 (within KS)
Fax: (785) 262-4468   E-mail: kscpa@kscpa.org
Web: www.kscpa.org/scholarship.cfm

Purpose To provide financial assistance to graduate students in Kansas who are majoring in accounting.

Eligibility This program is open to graduate accounting students at each of the 6 regent institutions in Kansas and at Washburn University. Applicants must be studying accounting.

Financial data The stipend is $1,500.

Duration 1 year.

Number awarded 7 each year: 1 at each of the participating institutions.

Deadline June of each year.

[503]
LAURELS FUND SCHOLARSHIPS

Educational Foundation for Women in Accounting
Attn: Foundation Administrator
P.O. Box 1925
Southeastern, PA 19399-1925
(610) 407-9229   Fax: (610) 644-3713
E-mail: info@efwa.org
Web: www.efwa.org/laurels.htm

Purpose To provide financial support to women doctoral students in accounting.

Eligibility This program is open to women who are working on a Ph.D. degree in accounting and have completed their comprehensive examinations. Selection is based on academic achievement in course work and research activities, volunteer work in which the applicant has made significant or long-term commitments, and financial need.

Financial data Stipends range from $1,000 to $5,000 per year.

Duration 1 year; may be renewed up to 3 additional years.

Additional information This program was established in 1978.

Number awarded Varies each year. A total of $20,000 is available for this program each year.

Deadline March of each year.

[504]
LEADERSHIP FOUNDATION GRADUATE SCHOLARSHIPS

Delta Sigma Pi
Attn: Leadership Foundation
330 South Campus Avenue
P.O. Box 230
Oxford, OH 45056-0230
(513) 523-1907, ext. 230   Fax: (513) 523-7292
E-mail: foundation@dspnet.org
Web: www.dspnet.org

Purpose To provide financial assistance to graduate students who have been elected to membership in Delta Sigma Pi, a business education honor society.

Eligibility Eligible to apply are currently-enrolled graduate students who are majoring in business and have been members in good standing of the honor society. Selection is based on 2 letters of recommendation, standardized test (GMAT, LSAT, or GRE) scores, a personal essay on reasons for having pursued an undergraduate curriculum in business administration and objective in working on a graduate degree, a personal essay on fraternal and community involvement since initiation, a personal statement of financial need, and undergraduate or graduate transcripts.

Financial data The stipend is $1,500.

Duration 1 year; recipients may reapply.

Additional information This program consists of the following named scholarships the Howard B. Johnson (Kappa–Georgia State) Scholarship, the Thomas M. Mocella (Beta–Northwestern) Scholarship, the Lester A. White (Alpha–New York) Scholarship, and the Ben H. Wolfenberger (Beta Psi–Louisiana Tech) Scholarship.

Number awarded 4 each year.

Deadline June of each year.

[505]
LEGACY SCHOLARSHIPS

Legacy, Inc.
P.O. Box 3813
Montgomery, AL 36109
(334) 270-5921   Toll-free: (800) 240-5115 (within AL)
Fax: (334) 270-5527
Web: www.legacyenved.org/fund/fund_college.htm

Purpose To provide financial assistance to upper-division and graduate students in Alabama who are interested in preparing for an environmentally-related career.

Eligibility Open to upper-division (juniors and seniors) and graduate students who reside in Alabama, are enrolled in a college or university in the state, and are planning to prepare for an environmentally-related career. Given the interdisciplinary nature of environmental education, it is not a requirement that all applicants have an environmental title attached to their major; some examples of career fields that have been funded in the past include: business, education, government, law, medicine, public relations, and geography. Finalists are interviewed.

Financial data Undergraduates receive up to $1,500; graduate students receive up to $2,000.

Duration 1 year,

Additional information Legacy's scholarship funds are made available, in part, from proceeds derived from the sale of Alabama's "Protect Our Environment" license tag.

Number awarded 20 each year: 10 to undergraduates, 4 to master's degree students, and 6 to doctoral students.

Deadline May of each year.

[506]
LITTLE FAMILY FOUNDATION MBA FELLOWSHIP AWARDS

Junior Achievement
Attn: Scholarships/Education Team
One Education Way
Colorado Springs, CO 80906-4477
(719) 540-6255   Fax: (719) 540-6175
E-mail: jascholarships@hotmail.com
Web: www.ja.org/programs/programs_schol_littl.shtml

Purpose To provide financial assistance to students working on M.B.A. degrees at selected universities who have participated in the Junior Achievement (JA) program.

Eligibility This program is open to students planning to work full time on an M.B.A. degree at any of 17 selected universities. Applicants must have participated in any of JA's high school programs or taught as a volunteer in at least 2 classes of JA's K-8 programs. They must have graduated from college and worked in business for at least 2 years after college.

Financial data The stipend is $2,500 per year. The participating university provides a matching grant of another $2,500 per year.

Duration 1 year; may be renewed for 1 additional year.

Additional information This program is sponsored by the Little Family Foundation. The participating universities are Carnegie Mellon University, Cornell University, Dartmouth College (Amos Tuck School of Business Management), Duke University, Harvard University, Indiana University, MIT (Alfred P. Sloan School of Management), Northwestern University

(Kellogg School of Management), University of Cincinnati, University of Michigan, University of Notre Dame, University of Pennsylvania (Wharton School), University of Pittsburgh, University of Rhode Island, University of Rochester (William E. Simon School), University of Washington, and Yale School of Management.

Number awarded Varies each year.

[507]
MARGARET H. TERRELL FELLOWSHIPS
American Association of Family and Consumer Sciences
Attn: Manager of Awards and Grants
1555 King Street
Alexandria, VA 22314-2752
(703) 706-4600   Toll-free: (800) 424-8080, ext. 119
Fax: (703) 706-4663   E-mail: staff@aafcs.org
Web: www.aafcs.org/fellowships/brochure.html

Purpose To provide financial assistance to graduate students interested in institutional management or food service systems administration.

Eligibility Graduate students working on a degree in family and consumer sciences with an emphasis on institutional management or food service systems administration are eligible to apply for this award if they are U.S. citizens or permanent residents and present clearly defined plans for full-time graduate study. Selection is based on academic record and special aptitudes for advanced study and research, educational and/or professional experiences, professional contributions to family and consumer sciences, and significance of the proposed research problem to the public well-being and the advancement of family and consumer sciences. Applicants are encouraged to have at least 1 year of professional family and consumer sciences work experience, serving in such positions as a graduate/undergraduate assistant, trainee, or intern.

Financial data The stipend is $3,500.

Duration 1 year.

Additional information The application fee is $40. The association reserves the right to reconsider an award in the event the student receives a similar award for the same academic year.

Number awarded 2 each year.

Deadline January of each year.

[508]
MARINE CORPS SPECIAL EDUCATION PROGRAM
U.S. Marine Corps
Manpower and Reserve Affairs (MMOA-5)
Attn: Undergraduate and Graduate Education Programs
3280 Russell Road
Quantico, VA 22134-5103
(703) 784-9284   Fax: (703) 784-9844
E-mail: esparzaja@manpower.usmc.mil
Web: www.usmc.mil

Purpose To provide financial assistance to commissioned Marine Corps officers who are interested in earning an advanced degree in selected fields.

Eligibility This program is open to selected commissioned Marine Corps officers at the rank of first lieutenant through

lieutenant colonel. Applicants must be interested in earning a postgraduate degree in specified disciplines (recently: aeronautical engineering, acquisition and contract management, combat systems science and technology, computer science, defense systems analysis, electrical engineering, environmental management, financial management, information systems technology, information warfare systems, leadership development, manpower systems analysis, material logistics support, modeling virtual environmental simulation, operations analysis, public affairs, space systems operations, and system acquisition management). They must be planning to attend the Naval Postgraduate School, the United States Naval Academy, the Air Force Institute of Technology, or (for designated programs) approved civilian institutions.

Financial data Commissioned officers selected to participate in this program receive their regular Marine Corps pay while attending a college or university on a full-time basis, as well as full payment for the cost of tuition (to a maximum of $10,000 per year at a civilian institution). Other allowances include reimbursement of up to $150 per academic year for required textbooks and up to $200 for typing a required thesis.

Duration Up to the equivalent of 2 academic years.

Additional information Officers must agree not to tender their resignation or request retirement while enrolled in the program. They must also agree to remain on active duty, after completion of degree requirements or upon separation from the program for any other reason, for 3 years or, if the enrollment in school is longer than 1 calendar year, for 4 years.

Number awarded Varies each year. Recently, 26 officers were selected to participate in this program.

Deadline August of each year.

[509]
MARION MACCARRELL SCOTT SCHOLARSHIP
Hawai'i Community Foundation
Attn: Scholarship Department
1164 Bishop Street, Suite 800
Honolulu, HI 96813
(808) 537-6333   Toll-free: (888) 731-3863
Fax: (808) 521-6286
E-mail: scholarships@hcf-hawaii.org
Web: www.hawaiicommunityfoundation.org

Purpose To provide financial assistance to residents of Hawaii for undergraduate or graduate studies in fields related to achieving world cooperation and international understanding.

Eligibility This program is open to graduates of public high schools in Hawaii. They must plan to attend school as full-time students (on the undergraduate or graduate level) on the mainland, majoring in history, government, political science, anthropology, economics, geography, international relations, law, psychology, philosophy, or sociology. They must be residents of the state of Hawaii, able to demonstrate financial need, interested in attending an accredited 2- or 4- year college or university, and able to demonstrate academic achievement (GPA of 2.8 or higher). Along with their application, they must submit an essay on their commitment to world peace that includes their learning experiences (courses, clubs, community activities, or travel) related to achieving world peace and international understanding and explaining how their experiences have enhanced their ability to achieve those goals.

Financial data The amounts of the awards depend on the availability of funds and the need of the recipient; recently, stipends averaged $2,097.

Duration 1 year.

Number awarded Varies each year; recently, 233 of these scholarships were awarded.

Deadline February of each year.

[510]
MARK MILLER AWARD

National Association of Black Accountants
Attn: Director, Center for Advancement of Minority
  Accountants
7249-A Hanover Parkway
Greenbelt, MD 20770
(301) 474-NABA, ext. 114   Fax: (301) 474-3114
E-mail: cquinn@nabainc.org
Web: www.nabainc.org

Purpose To provide financial assistance to student members of the National Association of Black Accountants (NABA) who are working on an undergraduate or graduate degree in a field related to accounting.

Eligibility This program is open to NABA members who are members of ethnic minority groups enrolled full time as 1) an undergraduate freshman, sophomore, junior, or first-semester senior majoring in accounting, business, or finance; or 2) a graduate student working on a master's degree in accounting. Applicants must have a GPA of 2.0 or higher in their major and 2.5 or higher overall. Selection is based on grades, financial need, and a 500-word autobiography that discusses career objectives, leadership abilities, community activities, and involvement in NABA.

Financial data The stipend is $1,000 per year.

Duration 1 year.

Number awarded 1 each year.

Deadline December of each year.

[511]
MARY CRAIG SCHOLARSHIP FUND

American Society of Women Accountants-Billings Big
  Sky Chapter
820 Division Street
Billings, MT 59101
Web: www.imt.net/~aswa

Purpose To provide financial assistance to students working on a bachelor's or master's degree in accounting at a college or university in Montana.

Eligibility This program is open to students working on a bachelor's or master's degree in accounting at an accredited Montana college or university. Applicants must have completed at least 60 semester hours. Selection is based on career goals, communication skills, GPA, personal circumstances, and financial need. Membership in the American Society of Women Accountants is not required.

Financial data The stipend is $1,500.

Duration 1 year.

Additional information Information is also available from Jane Crowder, (406) 248-2990, E-mail: jane_bowl@yahoo.com.

Number awarded 1 each year.

Deadline March of each year.

[512]
MARY M. FRAIJO SCHOLARSHIPS

American Society of Women Accountants-Inland
  Northwest Chapter
Attn: Leslie Miller
P.O. Box 3202
Spokane, WA 99220-3202
(509) 444-6832   E-mail: editor@aswa4.org
Web: www.aswa4.org/appform.htm

Purpose To provide financial assistance to women from the Inland Northwest area (Washington and Idaho) who are interested in working on an undergraduate or graduate degree in accounting.

Eligibility This program is open to women whose primary residence is Washington or Idaho. Applicants must be either 1) part-time or full-time students working on a bachelor's or master's degree in accounting who have completed a minimum of 60 semester hours with a declared accounting major; or 2) students enrolled in a formal 2-year accounting program at a community college, junior college, or accredited trade school who have completed the first year of the accounting program. Membership in the American Society of Women Accountants is not required. Selection is based on a statement of career goals, communication skills, financial needs and circumstances, GPA, and personal circumstances.

Financial data The amount of the award depends on the availability of funds.

Duration 1 year; may reapply.

Number awarded 3 or 4 each year.

Deadline March of each year.

[513]
MARYLAND ASSOCIATION OF CERTIFIED PUBLIC ACCOUNTANTS SCHOLARSHIP PROGRAM

Maryland Association of Certified Public Accountants
Attn: MACPA Educational Foundation
901 Dulaney Valley Road, Suite 710
Towson, MD 21204-2683
(410) 296-6250   Toll-free: (800) 782-2036
Fax: (410) 296-8713   E-mail: info@macpa.org
Web: www.macpa.org

Purpose To provide financial assistance to residents of Maryland working on an undergraduate or graduate degree in accounting.

Eligibility This program is open to Maryland residents attending a college or university in the state and taking enough undergraduate or graduate courses to qualify as a full-time student at their school. Applicants must have completed at least 60 total credit hours at the time of the award, including at least 6 hours in accounting courses. They must have a GPA of 3.0 or higher and be able to demonstrate financial need. U.S. citizenship is required.

Financial data Stipends are at least $1,000. The exact amount of the award depends upon the recipient's financial need.

Duration 1 year; may be renewed until completion of the 150-hour requirement and eligibility for sitting for the C.P.A. examination in Maryland. Renewal requires continued full-time enrollment and a GPA of 3.0 or higher.

Number awarded Several each year.

Deadline April of each year.

[514]
MASSACHUSETTS SOCIETY OF CERTIFIED PUBLIC ACCOUNTANTS MASTERS GRANT PROGRAM

Massachusetts Society of Certified Public Accountants
Attn: MSCPA Educational Foundation
105 Chauncy Street, Tenth Floor
Boston, MA 02111
(617) 556-4000   Toll-free: (800) 392-6145
Fax: (617) 556-4126
E-mail: biannoni@MSCPAonline.org
Web: www.cpatrack.com/financial_aid/scholarship.php

Purpose To provide financial assistance to students working on a master's degree in accounting in Massachusetts.

Eligibility This program is open to residents of Massachusetts who hold an undergraduate degree in accounting and are planning to enroll in a master's degree program in the state with a concentration in accounting or its equivalent. Applicants must intend to seek a position or continue working or teaching in accounting-related areas in Massachusetts following completion of their master's degree. They must be able to demonstrate financial need.

Financial data The stipend is $2,500 per year.

Duration 1 year; recipients may be granted 1 additional year of support.

Number awarded 1 each year.

[515]
MCKNIGHT DOCTORAL FELLOWSHIP PROGRAM

Florida Education Fund
201 East Kennedy Boulevard, Suite 1525
Tampa, FL 33602
(813) 272-2772   Fax: (813) 272-2784
E-mail: mdf@fl-educ-fd.org
Web: www.fl-educ-fd.org/mdf.html

Purpose To provide financial assistance to African American graduate students in Florida who are interested in teaching at colleges and universities in the state.

Eligibility This program is open to African Americans who are working on a Ph.D. degree at 1 of 10 universities in Florida. Fellowships may be in any discipline in the arts and sciences, mathematics, business, or engineering; preference is given to the following fields of study: agriculture, biology, business administration, chemistry, computer science, engineering, marine biology, mathematics, physics, and psychology. Academic programs that lead to professional degrees (such as the M.D., D.B.A., D.D.S., J.D., or D.V.M.) are not covered by the fellowship. Graduate study in education, whether leading to an Ed.D. or a Ph.D., is generally not included. U.S.

citizenship is required. Because this program is intended to increase African American graduate enrollment at the 10 participating universities, currently-enrolled doctoral students at these universities are not eligible to apply.

Financial data Each award covers annual tuition up to $5,000 and provides an annual stipend of $12,000. Recipients are also eligible for the Fellows Travel Fund, which supports recipients who wish to attend and present papers at professional conferences.

Duration 3 years; an additional 2 years of support may be provided by the university if the recipient maintains satisfactory performance and normal progress toward the Ph.D. degree.

Additional information The universities participating in this program are: Barry University, Florida Agricultural and Mechanical University, Florida Atlantic University, Florida Institute of Technology, Florida International University, Florida State University, University of Central Florida, University of Florida, University of Miami, and University of South Florida.

Number awarded Up to 25 each year.

Deadline January of each year.

[516]
M.E. FRANKS SCHOLARSHIP

International Association of Food Industry Suppliers
Attn: IAFIS Foundation
1451 Dolley Madison Boulevard
McLean, VA 22101-3850
(703) 761-2600   Fax: (703) 761-4334
E-mail: info@iafis.org
Web: www.iafis.org

Purpose To provide financial assistance to outstanding undergraduate and graduate students who are interested in working on a degree in a field related to food science, dairy foods, or agribusiness.

Eligibility This program is open to students working on a degree in dairy foods, food science, food technology, food marketing, agricultural economics, or agricultural business management on the undergraduate or graduate school level. Undergraduate students must be entering their junior or senior year. Graduate students must be working on a master's or Ph.D. degree. U.S. or Canadian citizenship is required. Applicants in food science departments must provide evidence that they will enroll in at least 1 specialized course in the processing, chemistry, or microbiology of milk or dairy products and 1 additional course with an emphasis in dairy processing, dairy product sensory evaluation, chemistry, or microbiology. Students in dairy science departments must provide evidence of enrollment in a dairy foods option or specialization. Completed applications should be submitted to the applicant's department head/chairperson, who then forwards them on to the foundation office. Selection is based on academic performance; commitment to a career in the food industry; and evidence of leadership ability, character, initiative and integrity. Graduate students are also evaluated on their statement of purpose for their master's or Ph.D. thesis proposal. Age, sex, race, and financial need are not considered in the selection process.

Financial data The stipend is $3,000 per year. Funds are paid directly to the recipient.

Duration 1 year; nonrenewable.

Additional information This program is administered by the International Association of Food Industry Suppliers on behalf of the Dairy Recognition and Education Foundation, which provides the funding. Recipients must enroll in school full time.

Number awarded Up to 8 each year: 4 to undergraduates and up to 4 to graduate students.

Deadline November of each year.

[517]
MEDICAL SERVICE CORPS INSERVICE PROCUREMENT PROGRAM (MSC-IPP)

U.S. Navy
Attn: Naval Medical Education and Training Command
Code OG3
8901 Wisconsin Avenue, 16th Floor, Tower 1
Bethesda, MD 20889-5611
(301) 319-4520 E-mail: mscipp@nmetc.med.navy.mil
Web: nshs.med.navy.mil/mscipp/mscipp.htm

Purpose To provide funding to Navy and Marine enlisted personnel who wish to earn an undergraduate or graduate degree in selected health care specialties while continuing to receive their regular pay and allowances.

Eligibility This program is open to enlisted personnel who are serving on active duty in pay grades E-5 through E-9 of the U.S. Navy, U.S. Marine Corps, Naval Reserve (including the Training and Administration of the Reserve Program), and the Marine Corps Reserve (including the Active Reserve Program). Applicants must be interested in working on a degree to become commissioned in the following medical specialties: 1) health care administration (HCA), for personnel who have a bachelor's degree in business/health care administration or a management-related discipline with a GPA of 2.5 or higher and wish to work on a master's degree in health care administration, public health administration, or business administration with a health care emphasis; 2) radiation health officer (RHO), for enlisted radiation health technicians, nuclear medicine technologists, submarine independent duty corpsmen, and biomedical technologists who have completed 60 hours of college credit with a GPA of 3.0 or higher and wish to complete a bachelor's degree in medical physics, radiation health physics, radiological science, or nuclear engineering; 3) environmental health officer (EHO) or industrial hygiene officer (IHO), for enlisted preventive medicine technicians and independent duty corpsmen who have completed 60 hours of college credit with a GPA of 3.0 or higher and wish to completed a bachelor's degree in natural science (biology, chemistry, or physics) for EHO or industrial hygiene for IHO; 4) entomology officer, for enlisted preventive medicine technicians and independent duty corpsmen who wish to work on a full-time graduate degree in entomology and have a GPA of 3.0 or higher; or 5) pharmacy officer, for enlisted pharmacy technicians who have been accepted into an accredited Pharm.D. program, have a GPA of 3.0 or higher, and can complete their degree within 48 months. Applicants for graduate programs must submit GRE or GMAT scores less than 5 years old. All applicants must be U.S. citizens who can be commissioned before they reach their 40th birthday.

Financial data Participants receive payment of tuition, mandatory fees, a book allowance, and full pay and allow-

ances for their enlisted pay grade. They are eligible for advancement while in college.

Duration 24 to 48 months of full-time, year-round study, until completion of a relevant degree.

Additional information Following graduation, participants are commissioned in the Medical Service Corps and attend Officer Indoctrination School.

Number awarded Varies each year.

Deadline August of each year.

[518]
MELVILLE H. COHEE STUDENT LEADER CONSERVATION SCHOLARSHIPS

Soil and Water Conservation Society
945 S.W. Ankeny Road
Ankeny, IA 50021-9764
(515) 289-2331 Toll-free: (800) THE SOIL
Fax: (515) 289-1227 E-mail: swcs@swcs.org
Web: www.swcs.org/t_membership_scholar.htm

Purpose To provide financial assistance to student officers of the Soil and Water Conservation Society (SWCS) who are interested in working on undergraduate or graduate studies with a focus on natural resource conservation.

Eligibility Applicants must have been members of the society for more than 1 year, have served for 1 academic year or longer as a student chapter officer for a chapter with at least 15 members, have earned a GPA of 3.0 or higher, be in school at least half time, not be an employee or immediate family member of the scholarship selection committee, and be in the junior or senior year of undergraduate study or the first or second year of graduate study in conservation or resource-related fields (such as agricultural economics, soils, planned land use management, forestry, wildlife biology, agricultural engineering, hydrology, rural sociology, agronomy, or water management) or related environmental protection or resource management fields at an accredited college or university. Financial need is not considered in the selection process.

Financial data The stipend is $1,000.

Duration 1 year.

Additional information This scholarship may not be combined with other SWCS scholarships or internships.

Number awarded 2 each year.

Deadline February of each year.

[519]
METRO NEW YORK CHAPTER MBA SCHOLARSHIP AWARD

National Black MBA Association-New York Chapter
P.O. Box 8138
New York, NY 10116
(212) 439-5100
Web: www.nyblackmba.org/html/studentrel.asp

Purpose To provide financial assistance to minority students from New York working on an M.B.A. or equivalent degree.

Eligibility This program is open to minority students who are either 1) enrolled full time in an accredited New York graduate business or management program working toward an M.B.A. or equivalent degree, or 2) residents of New York enrolled in a graduate business or management program working toward an M.B.A. or equivalent degree. Applicants must submit a 3-page essay on a topic that changes annually but recently was "What significant changes have corporations made to implement Customer Relationship Management?" Financial need is not considered in the selection process.

Financial data A stipend is awarded (amount not specified).

Duration 1 year.

Number awarded 1 or more each year.

Deadline September of each year.

[520]
METRO NEW YORK CHAPTER PHD SCHOLARSHIP AWARD

National Black MBA Association-New York Chapter
P.O. Box 8138
New York, NY 10116
(212) 439-5100
Web: www.nyblackmba.org/html/studentrel.asp

Purpose To provide financial assistance to minority students from New York working on a Ph.D. degree in business or management.

Eligibility This program is open to minority students who are either 1) enrolled full time in an accredited New York graduate business or management program working toward a Ph.D. degree, or 2) residents of New York enrolled in a graduate business or management program working toward a Ph.D. degree. Applicants must submit a 4-page essay on a topic that changes annually but recently was "Select a corporation and describe how it has implemented Decision Support Systems (DSS) into its strategic planning." Financial need is not considered in the selection process.

Financial data A stipend is awarded (amount not specified).

Duration 1 year.

Number awarded 1 or more each year.

Deadline September of each year.

[521]
MICHIGAN ACCOUNTANCY FOUNDATION FIFTH/GRADUATE YEAR STUDENT SCHOLARSHIPS

Michigan Association of Certified Public Accountants
Attn: Michigan Accountancy Foundation
5480 Corporate Drive, Suite 200
P.O. Box 5068
Troy, MI 48007-5068
(248) 267-3700   Toll-free: (888) 877-4CPE
Fax: (248) 267-3737   E-mail: maf@michcpa.org
Web: www.michcpa.org/maf/scholarships.asp

Purpose To provide financial assistance to students at Michigan colleges and universities who are working on a degree in accounting.

Eligibility This program is open to U.S. citizens enrolled full time at accredited Michigan colleges and universities with a declared concentration in accounting. Applicants must have completed at least 50% of their school's requirements toward completion of their junior year. They must intend to or have successfully passed the Michigan C.P.A. examination and intend to practice public accounting in the state. Along with

their application, they must submit a statement about their educational and career aspirations, including on- and off-campus activities, professional goals, current professional accomplishments, and a summary of personal and professional activities (including community involvement). Documentation of financial need may also be included.

Financial data The stipend is $4,000 per year.

Duration 1 year; may be renewed for the fifth or graduate year of study, provided that all requirements continue to be met and that funding is available.

Number awarded Varies each year; recently, 15 of these scholarships were awarded.

Deadline January of each year.

[522]
MID-ATLANTIC CHAPTER SCHOLARSHIPS

Society of Satellite Professionals International
Attn: Scholarship Program
New York Information Technology Center
55 Broad Street, 14th Floor
New York, NY 10004
(212) 809-5199   Fax: (212) 825-0075
E-mail: sspi@sspi.org
Web: www.sspi.org/html/scholarship.html

Purpose To provide financial assistance to students in designated mid-Atlantic states who are interested in working on an undergraduate or graduate degree in satellite-related disciplines (including business).

Eligibility This program is open to high school seniors, college undergraduates, and graduate students majoring or planning to major in fields related to satellite technologies, policies, or applications. Fields of study in the past have included broadcasting, business, distance learning, energy, government, imaging, meteorology, navigation, remote sensing, space law, and telecommunications. Applicants must be attending or planning to attend school in Delaware, the District of Columbia, Maryland, Virginia, or West Virginia. Selection is based on academic and leadership achievement, commitment to pursue educational and career opportunities in the satellite communications industry, potential for significant contribution to that industry, a personal statement of 500 to 750 words on their interest in satellite communications and why they deserve the award, and a creative work (such as a research report, essay, article, videotape, artwork, computer program, or scale model of an antenna or spacecraft design) that reflects the applicant's interests and talents. Financial need is not considered.

Financial data The stipend is $4,000.

Duration 1 year.

Number awarded 1 to 3 each year.

Deadline May of each year.

[523]
MINNESOTA SPACE GRANT CONSORTIUM SCHOLARSHIPS AND FELLOWSHIPS

Minnesota Space Grant Consortium
c/o University of Minnesota
Department of Aerospace Engineering and Mechanics
107 Akerman Hall
110 Union Street S.E.
Minneapolis, MN 55455
(612) 626-9295   Fax: (612) 626-1558
E-mail: mnsgc@aem.umn.edu
Web: www.aem.umn.edu

Purpose To provide financial assistance for space-related studies (including economics) to undergraduate and graduate students in Minnesota.

Eligibility This program is open to graduate and undergraduate full-time students at institutions that are affiliates of the Minnesota Space Grant Consortium. U.S. citizenship and a GPA of 3.2 or higher are required. Eligible fields of study include the physical sciences (astronomy, astrophysics, chemistry, computer science, mathematics, physics, planetary geoscience, and planetary science), life sciences (biology, biochemistry, botany, health science/nutrition, medicine, molecular/cellular biology, and zoology), social sciences (anthropology, architecture, art, economics, education, history, philosophy, political science/public policy, and psychology), earth sciences (atmospheric science, climatology/meteorology, environmental science, geography, geology, geophysics, and oceanography), and engineering (agricultural, aeronautical, aerospace, architectural, bioengineering, chemical, civil, computer, electrical, electronic, environmental, industrial, materials science, mechanical, mining, nuclear, petroleum, engineering science, and engineering mechanics). The Minnesota Space Grant Consortium is a component of the U.S. National Aeronautics and Space Administration (NASA) Space Grant program, which encourages participation by women, underrepresented minorities, and persons with disabilities.

Financial data This program awards approximately $125,000 in undergraduate scholarships and $25,000 in graduate fellowships each year. The amounts of the awards are set by each of the participating institutions, which augment funding from this program with institutional resources.

Duration 1 year; renewable.

Additional information This program is funded by NASA. The member institutions are: Augsburg College, Bethel College, Bemidji State University, College of St. Catherine, Carleton College, Concordia College, Fond du Lac Community College, Itasca Community College, Leech Lake Tribal College, Macalaster College, Normandale Community College, Southwest State University, University of Minnesota at Duluth, University of Minnesota at Twin Cities, and University of St. Thomas.

Number awarded 8 to 12 undergraduate scholarships and 2 to 3 graduate fellowships are awarded each year.

Deadline March of each year.

[524]
MINORITIES IN GOVERNMENT FINANCE SCHOLARSHIP

Government Finance Officers Association
Attn: Scholarship Committee
203 North LaSalle Street, Suite 2700
Chicago, IL 60601-1210
(312) 977-9700   Fax: (312) 977-4806
Web: www.gfoa.org/services/scholarships.shtml

Purpose To provide financial assistance to minority undergraduate and graduate students who are preparing for a career in state and local government finance.

Eligibility This program is open to upper-division undergraduate and graduate students who are enrolled in a full-time program and preparing for a career in public finance. Applicants must be members of a minority group, citizens or permanent residents of the United States or Canada, and able to provide a letter of recommendation from the dean of their school. Selection is based on career plans, academic record, plan of study, letters of recommendation, and GPA. Financial need is not considered.

Financial data The stipend is $5,000.

Duration 1 year.

Additional information Funding for this program is provided by Fidelity Investments Tax-Exempt Services Company.

Number awarded 1 or more each year.

Deadline February of each year.

[525]
MISSISSIPPI SOCIETY OF CERTIFIED PUBLIC ACCOUNTANTS GRADUATE SCHOLARSHIPS

Mississippi Society of Certified Public Accountants
Attn: MSCPA Awards, Education and Scholarships
   Committee
Highland Village, Suite 246
P.O. Box 16630
Jackson, MS 39236
(601) 366-3473   Toll-free: (800) 772-1099 (within MS)
Fax: (601) 981-6-79   E-mail: mail@ms-cpa.org
Web: www.ms-cpa.org

Purpose To provide financial assistance to graduate students majoring in accounting at 4-year institutions in Mississippi.

Eligibility This program is open to residents of Mississippi who are enrolled or planning to enroll in a graduate accounting program in Mississippi. Students must be nominated by their academic institution. Nominees must submit a completed application form, transcripts (GPA of 3.0 or higher both overall and in accounting classes), a copy of their GMAT score, and a 1-page essay explaining why they plan a career in accounting. Selection is based on the essay, academic excellence, recommendations, financial need, and campus involvement.

Financial data The stipend is $1,000. Checks are made payable to the recipient's school.

Duration 1 year.

Additional information This program includes the Ross/Nickey Scholarship and the Gary E. Thornton Memorial Scholarship.

Number awarded 2 each year.

Deadline June of each year.

[526]
MR. & MRS. SIDNEY A. SPARKS COLLEGIAN OF THE YEAR
Delta Sigma Pi
Attn: Leadership Foundation
330 South Campus Avenue
P.O. Box 230
Oxford, OH 45056-0230
(513) 523-1907, ext. 230   Fax: (513) 523-7292
E-mail: foundation@dspnet.org
Web: www.dspnet.org

Purpose To provide financial assistance for graduate school to outstanding members of Delta Sigma Pi, a business education honor society.

Eligibility This scholarship is awarded to an undergraduate member of the society who is planning to go to graduate school. Nominees must submit an essay on their plans as a collegian of the year; information on their Delta Sigma Pi activities, positions, and honors; other extracurricular activities, positions, and honors; employment history; and academic accomplishments.

Financial data The national award is a $3,000 graduate scholarship. In addition, each regional winner receives a $400 scholarship and each provincial winner receives a $500 scholarship.

Duration 1 year; the award must be used for graduate study within 10 years following completion of an undergraduate program.

Additional information The national winner serves as a voting member of the Delta Sigma Pi board of directors for 2 years.

Number awarded 1 national winner is selected each year.

Deadline Nominations must be submitted by October of each year. The nominee must then complete and submit an application by November.

[527]
NABA CORPORATE SCHOLARSHIPS
National Association of Black Accountants
Attn: Director, Center for Advancement of Minority
    Accountants
7249-A Hanover Parkway
Greenbelt, MD 20770
(301) 474-NABA, ext. 114   Fax: (301) 474-3114
E-mail: cquinn@nabainc.org
Web: www.nabainc.org

Purpose To provide financial assistance to student members of the National Association of Black Accountants (NABA) who are working on an undergraduate or graduate degree in a field related to accounting.

Eligibility This program is open to NABA members who are members of ethnic minority groups enrolled full time as 1) an undergraduate freshman, sophomore, junior, or first-semester senior majoring in accounting, business, or finance; or 2) a graduate student working on a master's degree in accounting. Applicants must have a GPA of 3.5 or higher in their major and 3.3 or higher overall. Selection is based on grades, financial need, and a 500-word autobiography that discusses

career objectives, leadership abilities, community activities, and involvement in NABA.

Financial data Stipends range from $1,000 to $5,000 per year.

Duration 1 year.

Number awarded Varies each year.

Deadline December of each year.

[528]
NAIW EDUCATION FOUNDATION COLLEGE SCHOLARSHIPS
National Association of Insurance Women
Attn: NAIW Education Foundation
5310 East 31st Street, Suite 302
Tulsa, OK 74135
(918) 622-1816   Toll-free: (866) 349-1816
Fax: (918) 622-1821
E-mail: foundation@naiwfoundation.org
Web: www.naiwfoundation.org/college.htm

Purpose To provide financial assistance to college and graduate students working on a degree in insurance and risk management.

Eligibility This program is open to candidates for a bachelor's degree or higher with a major or minor in insurance, risk management, or actuarial science. Applicants must 1) be completing or have completed their second year of college; 2) have an overall GPA of 3.0 or higher; 3) have successfully completed at least 2 insurance or risk management-related courses; and 4) not be receiving full reimbursement for the cost of tuition, books, or other educational expenses from their employer or any other outside source. Selection is based on academic record and honors, extracurricular and personal activities, work experience, 3 letters of recommendation, and a 500-word essay on career path and goals.

Financial data Stipends range from $1,000 to $4,000 per year; funds are paid jointly to the institution and to the student.

Duration 1 year.

Additional information The National Association of Insurance Women established the NAIW Educational Foundation in 1993. It provides financial assistance to both men and women interested in careers in the insurance industry.

Number awarded Varies each year; recently, 15 of these scholarships were awarded.

Deadline February each year.

[529]
NATIONAL ASSOCIATION OF BLACK ACCOUNTANTS NATIONAL SCHOLARSHIP
National Association of Black Accountants
Attn: Director, Center for Advancement of Minority
    Accountants
7249-A Hanover Parkway
Greenbelt, MD 20770
(301) 474-NABA, ext. 114   Fax: (301) 474-3114
E-mail: cquinn@nabainc.org
Web: www.nabainc.org

Purpose To provide financial assistance to student members of the National Association of Black Accountants (NABA) who are working on an undergraduate or graduate degree in a field related to accounting.

Eligibility This program is open to NABA members who are members of ethnic minority groups enrolled full time as 1) an undergraduate freshman, sophomore, junior, or first-semester senior majoring in accounting, business, or finance; or 2) a graduate student working on a master's degree in accounting. Applicants must have a GPA of 3.5 or higher in their major and 3.3 or higher overall. Selection is based on grades, financial need, and a 500-word autobiography that discusses career objectives, leadership abilities, community activities, and involvement in NABA.

Financial data The stipend ranges from $3,000 to $6,000 per year.

Duration 1 year.

Number awarded 1 each year.

Deadline December of each year.

[530]
NATIONAL BLACK MBA ASSOCIATION NATIONAL SCHOLARSHIP PROGRAM

National Black MBA Association
180 North Michigan Avenue, Suite 1400
Chicago, IL 60601
(312) 236-2622, ext. 8086   Fax: (312) 236-4131
E-mail: scholarship@nbmbaa.org
Web: www.nbmbaa.org

Purpose To provide financial assistance to minority students interested in working on an M.B.A. degree.

Eligibility This program is open to minority students enrolled full time in a graduate business or management program in the United States. Applicants must submit a 2-page essay on 1 of 3 topics that change annually. Selection is based on the essay, a resume, transcripts, and 3 letters of recommendation. Selected finalists are interviewed.

Financial data Stipends range from $2,500 to $6,000.

Duration 1 year.

Additional information Recipients must agree to attend the NBMBAA annual convention, participate in limited public relations activities at the convention, and attend the awards program.

Number awarded 25 each year.

Deadline April of each year.

[531]
NATIONAL BLACK MBA ASSOCIATION PHD FELLOWSHIP PROGRAM

National Black MBA Association
180 North Michigan Avenue, Suite 1400
Chicago, IL 60601
(312) 236-2622, ext. 8086   Fax: (312) 236-4131
E-mail: scholarship@nbmbaa.org
Web: www.nbmbaa.org

Purpose To provide financial assistance to minority students interested in working on a doctoral degree in a field related to business.

Eligibility This program is open to minority students who are enrolled full time in an accredited business, management, or related doctoral program. Applicants must submit a 5-page

essay on a topic that changes annually; recently, the topic was "What is one of the major questions in your field that needs to be addressed? What unique perspective can black scholars provide to this discussion?" Selection is based on the quality of the paper, including its importance, accuracy, completeness, clarity, and presentation.

Financial data Stipends are $11,000 or $6,000.

Duration 1 year.

Additional information Recipients must agree to attend the NBMBAA annual convention, participate in limited public relations activities at the convention, attend the awards program, and become lifetime members.

Number awarded 2 each year: 1 at $11,000 and 1 at $6,000.

Deadline April of each year.

[532]
NATIONAL HISPANIC FOUNDATION FOR THE ARTS SCHOLARSHIP PROGRAM

National Hispanic Foundation for the Arts
1010 Wisconsin Avenue, N.W., Suite 210
Washington, D.C. 20007
(202) 293-8330   Fax: (202) 965-5252
Web: www.hispanicarts.org/application.html

Purpose To provide financial assistance to Hispanic American graduate students at selected universities who are interested in preparing for a career in the media, arts, and communications industries.

Eligibility This program is open to full-time graduate students at designated universities who are enrolled in disciplines leading to careers in the entertainment arts and industry. Those disciplines include, but are not limited to, drama/theater, costume design, set design, lighting design, music, film (writing, directing, or producing), broadcast communications, entertainment law, and business administration (with an emphasis on entertainment management). Applicants must have a GPA of 3.0 or higher and be able to demonstrate financial need. They must be U.S. citizens of Hispanic descent (1 parent fully Hispanic or both parents half Hispanic). Preference is given to students who can demonstrate special talent in areas related to the entertainment arts and industry; they may submit portfolios and/or video/audio tapes of their work.

Financial data Stipends are based on the need of the recipient and the availability of funds.

Additional information The designated university programs are New York University Tisch School of the Arts, Columbia University School of the Arts, Harvard University Lampoon magazine comedy writers, Yale University Drama Department, University of Texas at Austin Communications School, the University of California at Los Angeles, Northwestern University Drama Department, and the University of Southern California. This program is administered by the Hispanic Scholarship Fund, 55 Second Street, Suite 1500, San Francisco, CA 94105, (877) HSF-INFO, E-mail: specialprograms@hsf.net.

Number awarded Varies each year.

[533]
NATIONAL OCEANIC AND ATMOSPHERIC ADMINISTRATION EDUCATIONAL PARTNERSHIP PROGRAM WITH MINORITY SERVING INSTITUTIONS GRADUATE SCIENCES PROGRAM

Oak Ridge Institute for Science and Education
Attn: Education and Training Division
P.O. Box 117
Oak Ridge, TN 37831-0117
(865) 576-9272   Fax: (865) 241-5220
E-mail: babcockc@orau.gov
Web: www.orau.gov/orise.htm

Purpose To provide financial assistance and summer research experience to graduate students at minority serving institutions who are majoring in scientific fields of interest to the National Oceanic and Atmospheric Administration (NOAA).

Eligibility This program is open to graduate students working on master's or doctoral degrees at minority serving institutions, including Hispanic Serving Institutions (HSIs), Historically Black Colleges and Universities (HBCUs), and Tribal Colleges and Universities (TCUs). Applicants must be majoring in biology, chemistry, computer science, economics, engineering, geography, geology, mathematics, physical science, physics, social science, or other fields specific to NOAA, such as cartography, environmental planning, fishery biology, hydrology, meteorology, or oceanography. They must also be interested in participating in a training program during the summer at a NOAA research facility.

Financial data During the school year, the program provides payment of tuition and fees, books, housing, meals, and travel expenses. During the summer, students receive a salary and benefits.

Duration 2 years of study plus 16 weeks of research training during the summer.

Additional information This program is funded by NOAA and administered by the Education and Training Division (ETD) of Oak Ridge Institute for Science and Education (ORISE).

Number awarded 5 each year.

Deadline January of each year.

[534]
NEHRA FUTURE STARS IN HR SCHOLARSHIPS

Northeast Human Resources Association
Attn: Scholarship Awards
One Washington Street, Suite 101
Wellesley, MA 02481
(781) 235-2900   Fax: (781) 237-8745
E-mail: info@nehra.com
Web: www.nehra.com/scholarships.php

Purpose To provide financial assistance to undergraduate and graduate students at colleges and universities in New England who are preparing for a career in human resources.

Eligibility This program is open to full-time undergraduate and graduate students at accredited colleges and universities in New England. Applicants must have completed at least 1 course related to human resources and have a GPA of 3.0 or higher. Along with their application, they must submit 2 essays. 1) why they are interested in becoming a human

resources professional; and 2) what qualities they believe are critical to the success of a human resources professional, which of those they currently possess, and how they intend to acquire the others. Selection is based on interest in becoming a human resources professional, academic success, leadership skills, and participation in non-academic activities. The applicant who is judged most outstanding receives the John D. Erdlen Scholarship Award.

Financial data Stipends are $3,000 or $2,500 per year.

Duration 1 year; may be renewed.

Additional information The sponsor is an affiliate of the Society for Human Resource Management (SHRM).

Number awarded 4 each year: 1 at $3,000 (the John D. Erdlen Scholarship Award) and 3 at $2,500.

Deadline March of each year

[535]
NEW HAMPSHIRE SOCIETY OF CERTIFIED PUBLIC ACCOUNTANTS SCHOLARSHIP PROGRAM

New Hampshire Society of Certified Public Accountants
Attn: Financial Careers Committee
1750 Elm Street, Suite 403
Manchester, NH 03104
(603) 622-1999   Fax: (603) 626-0204
E-mail: info@nhscpa.org
Web: nhscpa.org/student.htm

Purpose To provide financial assistance to undergraduate and graduate students in New Hampshire who are preparing for a career as a certified public accountant.

Eligibility This program is open to residents of New Hampshire who are 1) entering their junior or senior year in an accounting or business program at an accredited 4-year college or university or 2) full-time graduate students in an accredited master's degree program in accounting or business. A recommendation or appraisal from the person in charge of the applicant's accounting program must be included in the application package. Selection is based on academic record, not financial need, although if academic measures between 2 or more students are the same, financial need may be considered secondarily.

Financial data A stipend is awarded (amount not specified).

Duration 1 year.

Number awarded 2 or more each year.

Deadline October of each year.

[536]
NEW HAMPSHIRE/VERMONT CHAPTER HFMA CONTINUING EDUCATION SCHOLARSHIP

Healthcare Financial Management Association-New
  Hampshire/Vermont Chapter
c/o Jeffrey D. Walla, Scholarship Committee
Berry, Dunn, McNeil & Parker
46 Centerra Parkway, Suite 210
Lebanon, NH 03766
(603) 653-0015   Fax: (603) 640-6195
Web: www.nhvthfma.org

Purpose To provide financial assistance to members of the New Hampshire/Vermont chapter of the Healthcare Financial

Management Association (HFMA) who are working on a degree in health care financial management.

Eligibility This program is open to chapter members who are enrolled in a bachelor's or master's program at an accredited college or university in the field of health care finance or administration. Applicants must have accumulated at least 40 founders award points. They may only apply for 1 course per college term. Along with their application, they must submit a description of their financial need, the benefit they will receive by attending the course, their desire to further their education, and anything else they feel is important. The program in which they wish to enroll may be located in any state.

Financial data The maximum stipend is $1,000. Funds are paid directly to the school.

Duration Funding is provided for 1 course; recipients may apply for support for 1 additional course if they earn a GPA of 3.0 or higher for the first course.

Number awarded 2 each year.

Deadline October or May of each year.

[537]
NEW JERSEY HFMA MEMBER SCHOLARSHIP

Healthcare Financial Management Association-New
  Jersey Chapter
c/o Gabrielle Parseghian, Scholarship Committee Chair
P.O. Box 6422
Bridgewater, NJ 08807
(732) 583-7428   Fax: (732) 583-7428
E-mail: gabbyparseghian@yahoo.com
Web: www.hfmanj.org

Purpose To provide financial assistance to members of the New Jersey Chapter of the Healthcare Financial Management Association (HFMA) and their families who are interested in working on a degree related to health care administration.

Eligibility Applicants must have been a member of the chapter for at least 2 years or the spouse or dependent of a 2-year member. They must be enrolled in an accredited college, university, nursing school, or other allied health professional school. Preference is given to applicants working on a degree in finance, accounting, health care administration, or a field of study related to health care. Along with their application, they must submit an essay describing their educational and professional goals and the role of this scholarship in helping achieve those. Selection is based on the essay, merit, academic achievement, civic and professional activities, course of study, and content of the application. Financial need is not considered.

Financial data A total of $3,000 is available for this program each year.

Duration 1 year.

Number awarded Varies each year; recently, the sponsor offered 2 scholarships at $1,500 each.

Deadline March of each year.

[538]
NEW JERSEY SOCIETY OF CERTIFIED PUBLIC ACCOUNTANTS COLLEGE SCHOLARSHIP PROGRAM

New Jersey Society of Certified Public Accountants
Attn: Student Programs Coordinator
425 Eagle Rock Avenue, Suite 100
Roseland, NJ 07068-1723
(973) 226-4494, ext. 209   Fax: (973) 226-7425
E-mail: njscpa@njscpa.org
Web: www.njscpa.org

Purpose To provide financial assistance to upper-division and graduate students in New Jersey who are preparing for a career as a certified public accountant.

Eligibility This program is open to residents of New Jersey who are attending a college or university in the state. Applicants must be 1) juniors who are majoring or concentrating in accounting; or 2) graduate students entering an accounting-related program. Students may apply directly or be nominated by the accounting department chair at their college. Selection is based on academic achievement (GPA of 3.0 or higher).

Financial data Stipends range from $500 to $4,000.

Duration 1 year. Each student may receive only 1 undergraduate and 1 graduate scholarship during their academic career.

Number awarded Varies each year. Recently, 46 of these scholarships were awarded: 1 at $4,000, 35 at $3,000, 3 at $2,000, 2 at $1,000, 3 at $750, and 2 at $500.

Deadline January of each year.

[539]
NEW MEXICO GRADUATE SCHOLARSHIP PROGRAM

New Mexico Commission on Higher Education
Attn: Financial Aid and Student Services
1068 Cerrillos Road
P.O. Box 15910
Santa Fe, NM 87506-5910
(505) 827-1217   Toll-free: (800) 279-9777
Fax: (505) 827-7392 E-mail: highered@che.state.nm.us
Web: www.nmche.org/collegefinance/gradshol.asp

Purpose To provide financial assistance for graduate education in selected fields to underrepresented groups in New Mexico.

Eligibility Applicants for this program must be New Mexico residents who are members of underrepresented groups, particularly minorities and women. Preference is given to 1) students enrolled in business, engineering, computer science, mathematics, or agriculture and 2) American Indian students enrolled in any graduate program. All applicants must be U.S. citizens or permanent residents enrolled in graduate programs at public institutions of higher education in New Mexico.

Financial data The maximum stipend is $7,500 per year.

Duration 1 year; may be renewed.

Additional information Information is available from the dean of graduate studies at the participating New Mexico public institution. Recipients must serve 10 hours per week in an unpaid internship or assistantship.

Number awarded Varies each year, depending on the availability of funds.

Deadline Deadlines are established by the participating institutions.

[540]
NIB GRANT M. MACK MEMORIAL SCHOLARSHIP

American Council of the Blind
Attn: Coordinator, Scholarship Program
1155 15th Street, N.W., Suite 1004
Washington, DC 20005
(202) 467-5081   Toll-free: (800) 424-8666
Fax: (202) 467-5085   E-mail: info@acb.org
Web: www.acb.org

Purpose To provide financial assistance to students who are blind and working on an undergraduate or graduate degree in business or management.

Eligibility All legally blind persons who are majoring in business or management (undergraduate or graduate) and are U.S. citizens or resident aliens are eligible to apply. In addition to letters of recommendation and copies of academic transcripts, applications must include an autobiographical sketch. A cumulative GPA of 3.3 or higher is generally required. Selection is based on demonstrated academic record, involvement in extracurricular and civic activities, and academic objectives. The severity of the applicant's visual impairment and his/her study methods are also taken into account.

Financial data The stipend is $2,000. In addition, the winner receives a $1,000 cash scholarship from the Kurzweil Foundation and, if appropriate, a Kurzweil-1000 Reading System.

Duration 1 year.

Additional information This scholarship is sponsored by National Industries for the Blind (NIB) in honor of a dedicated leader of the American Council of the Blind. Scholarship winners are expected to be present at the council's annual conference; the council will cover all reasonable expenses connected with convention attendance.

Number awarded 1 each year.

Deadline February of each year.

[541]
NYWICI FOUNDATION SCHOLARSHIPS

New York Women in Communications, Inc.
Attn: NYWICI Foundation
355 Lexington Avenue, 17th Floor
New York, NY 10017-6603
(212) 297-2133   Fax: (212) 370-9047
E-mail: nywicipr@nywici.org
Web: www.nywici.org/foundation.scholarships.html

Purpose To provide financial assistance for college or graduate school to residents of designated eastern states who are interested in preparing for a career in the communications profession.

Eligibility This program is open to 1) seniors graduating from high schools in the state of New York; 2) undergraduate students who are permanent residents of New York, New Jersey, Connecticut, or Pennsylvania; 3) graduate students who are permanent residents of New York, New Jersey, Connecticut, or Pennsylvania; and 4) current members of New York Women in Communications, Inc. (NYWICI) who are returning

to school. Applicants must be majoring in a communications-related major (advertising, broadcasting, communications, journalism, marketing, new media, or public relations) and have a GPA of 3.5 or higher in their major and 3.0 overall. Along with their application, they must submit a resume that includes school and extracurricular activities, significant achievements, academic honors and awards, and community service work; a statement of their future goals in the communications profession; a 300- to 500-word personal essay describing how events in their lives have inspired them to achieve success and overcome difficulty in the face of any financial and/or other obstacles; 2 letters of recommendation; and an official transcript.

Financial data The maximum stipend is $10,000.

Duration 1 year.

Number awarded 1 or more each year.

Deadline January of each year.

[542]
O.J. BOOKER SCHOLARSHIP AWARD

Healthcare Financial Management Association-Georgia
   Chapter
c/o Judy King Williams, Awards Chair
McKesson Information Solutions
5995 Windward Parkway
Alpharetta, GA 30005
(404) 338-3749   Fax: (404) 338-6101
E-mail: JudyKing.Williams@mcKesson, com
Web: www.georgiahfma.org/scholarships.asp

Purpose To provide financial assistance to members of the Georgia chapter of the Healthcare Financial Management Association (HFMA) who are planning to enter the health care financial management industry.

Eligibility This program is open to student members of the HFMA Georgia chapter who are nominated by a chapter member. Letters of nomination should include the place of employment, degree of program being pursued, and reason for nomination. Nominees must be enrolled full time in a program to prepare for a career in the health care financial management industry.

Financial data The stipend is $1,500.

Duration 1 year.

Additional information This program was established in 1987.

Number awarded 1 each year.

[543]
OMAHA CHAPTER SCHOLARSHIPS

American Society of Women Accountants-Omaha
   Chapter
c/o Beth Byrne, Scholarship Committee
823 Auburn Lane
Papillion, NE 68046
Web: www.geocities.com/aswaomaha/scholarships.htm

Purpose To provide financial assistance to accounting students in Nebraska.

Eligibility This program is open to part- and full-time students working on a bachelor's or master's degree in accounting at a college or university in Nebraska. Applicants must have completed at least 00 semester hours. They are not required to be a member of the American Society of Women Accountants. Selection is based on academic achievement, extracurricular activities and honors, a statement of career goals and objectives, letters of recommendation, and financial need.

Financial data A total of $2,000 is available for this program each year.

Duration 1 year.

Additional information The highest ranked recipient is entered into the national competition for scholarships that range from $1,500 to $4,500.

Number awarded Varies each year; recently, 3 of these scholarships were awarded.

Deadline January of each year.

[544]
OREGON STATE FISCAL ASSOCIATION SCHOLARSHIP

Oregon Student Assistance Commission
Attn: Grants and Scholarships Division
1500 Valley River Drive, Suite 100
Eugene, OR 97401-2146
(541) 687-7395   Toll-free: (800) 452-8807, ext. 7395
Fax: (541) 687-7419
E-mail: awardinfo@mercury.osac.state.or.us
Web: www.osac.state.or.us

Purpose To provide financial assistance for college or graduate school to members of the Oregon State Fiscal Association and their children.

Eligibility This program is open to members of the association and their children who are enrolled or planning to enroll at a college or university in Oregon as an undergraduate or graduate student. Members must study public administration, finance, economics, or related fields, but they may enroll part time. Children may enroll in any program of study, but they must be full-time students.

Financial data Scholarship amounts vary, depending upon the needs of the recipient.

Duration 1 year.

Number awarded Varies each year.

Deadline February of each year.

[545]
OSCAR AND ROSETTA FISH FUND

Hawai'i Community Foundation
Attn: Scholarship Department
1164 Bishop Street, Suite 800
Honolulu, HI 96813
(808) 537-6333   Toll-free: (888) 731-3863
Fax: (808) 521-6286
E-mail: scholarships@hcf-hawaii.org
Web: www.hawaiicommunityfoundation.org

Purpose To provide financial assistance to Hawaii residents who are interested in studying business at 1 of the campuses of the University of Hawaii.

Eligibility This program is open to Hawaii residents who are interested in studying business on the undergraduate or graduate school level at any campus of the University of Hawaii except Manoa. Applicants must be able to demonstrate academic achievement (GPA of 2.7 or higher), good moral char-

acter, and financial need. In addition to filling out the standard application form, applicants must write a short statement indicating their reasons for attending college, their planned course of study, and their career goals.

Financial data The amounts of the awards depend on the availability of funds and the need of the recipient; recently, stipends averaged $2,000.

Duration 1 year.

Additional information This program was established in 1999. Recipients must be full-time students.

Number awarded Varies each year; recently, 27 of these scholarships were awarded.

Deadline February of each year.

[546]
OSCPA EDUCATIONAL FOUNDATION COLLEGE SCHOLARSHIPS

Oregon Society of Certified Public Accountants
Attn: OSCPA Educational Foundation
10206 S.W. Laurel Street
Beaverton, OR 97005-3209
(503) 641-7200   Toll-free: (800) 255-1470, ext. 29
Fax: (503) 626-2942   E-mail: oscpa@orcpa.org
Web: www.orcpa.org

Purpose To provide financial assistance to undergraduate and graduate students in Oregon who are working on a degree in accounting.

Eligibility This program is open to Oregon college and university students who are working full time on an undergraduate or master's degree in accounting. Applicants must have a GPA of 3.2 or higher in accounting/business classes and overall. Along with their application, they must submit 3 letters of recommendation and a recent transcript. Selection is based on scholastic ability and interest in the accounting profession.

Financial data For graduate students and undergraduates enrolled in or transferring to 4-year colleges and universities, stipends range from $1,000 to $3,000. For students enrolled in community colleges, the stipend is $500.

Duration 1 year.

Number awarded Varies each year.

Deadline February of each year.

[547]
PAUL HAGELBARGER MEMORIAL SCHOLARSHIP

Alaska Society of Certified Public Accountants
341 West Tudor Road, Suite 105
Anchorage, AK 99503
(907) 562-4334   Toll-free: (800) 478-4334
Fax: (907) 562-4025
Web: www.akcpa.org/scholarships.htm

Purpose To provide financial assistance to upper-division and graduate students at colleges and universities in Alaska who are preparing for a career in public accounting.

Eligibility This program is open to juniors, seniors, and graduate students majoring in accounting at 4-year colleges and universities in Alaska. Applicants must submit brief essays on their educational goals, career goals, and financial need. Selection is based on academic achievement, intent to prepare for a career in public accounting in Alaska, and financial need.

Financial data The stipend is at least $2,000.

Duration 1 year.

Additional information This program was established in 1964.

Number awarded 1 or more each year.

Deadline November of each year.

[548]
PBI MEDIA SCHOLARSHIP

Society of Satellite Professionals International
Attn: Scholarship Program
New York Information Technology Center
55 Broad Street, 14th Floor
New York, NY 10004
(212) 809-5199   Fax: (212) 825-0075
E-mail: sspi@sspi.org
Web: www.sspi.org/html/scholarship.html

Purpose To provide financial assistance to students interested in majoring in satellite-related disciplines (including business) in college or graduate school.

Eligibility This program is open to high school seniors, college undergraduates, and graduate students majoring or planning to major in fields related to satellite technologies, policies, or applications. Fields of study in the past have included broadcasting, business, distance learning, energy, government, imaging, meteorology, navigation, remote sensing, space law, and telecommunications. Applicants may be from any country. Selection is based on academic and leadership achievement, commitment to pursue educational and career opportunities in the satellite communications industry, potential for significant contribution to that industry, a personal statement of 500 to 750 words on interest in satellite communications and why they deserve the award, and a creative work (such as a research report, essay, article, videotape, artwork, computer program, or scale model of an antenna or spacecraft design) that reflects the applicant's interests and talents. This award recognizes innovative work in the satellite field that emphasizes the commercial and/or humanitarian aspects of new technologies and services. It is conferred on the applicant who best analyzes the entrepreneurial possibilities of new satellite services, technologies, or applications from a profit-driven or public service-oriented perspective. Financial need is not considered.

Financial data The stipend is $2,000.

Duration 1 year.

Number awarded 1 each year.

Deadline May of each year.

[549]
PFIZER/UNCF CORPORATE SCHOLARS PROGRAM

United Negro College Fund
Attn: Corporate Scholars Program
P.O. Box 1435
Alexandria, VA 22313-9998
Toll-free: (866) 671-7237   E-mail: internship@uncf.org
Web: www.uncf.org/internships/index.asp

Purpose To provide financial assistance and work experience to minority undergraduate and graduate students majoring in designated fields and interested in an internship at a Pfizer facility.

Eligibility This program is open to sophomores, juniors, graduate students, and first-year law students who are African American, Hispanic American, Asian/Pacific Islander American, or American Indian/Alaskan Native. Applicants must have a GPA of 3.0 or higher and be enrolled at an institution that is a member of the United Negro College Fund (UNCF) or at another targeted college or university. They must be working on 1) a bachelor's degree in animal science, business, chemistry (organic or analytical), human resources, logistics, microbiology, organizational development, operations management, pre-veterinary medicine, or supply chain management; 2) a master's degree in chemistry (organic or analytical), finance, human resources, or organizational development; or 3) a law degree. Eligibility is limited to U.S. citizens, permanent residents, asylees, refugees, and lawful temporary residents. Along with their application, they must submit a 1-page essay about themselves and their career goals, including information about their interest in Pfizer (the program's sponsor), their personal background, and any particular challenges they have faced.

Financial data The program provides an internship stipend of up to $5,000, housing accommodations near Pfizer Corporate facilities, and (based on successful internship performance) a $15,000 scholarship.

Duration 8 to 10 weeks for the internship; 1 year for the scholarship.

Additional information Opportunities for first-year law students include the summer internship only.

Number awarded Varies each year.

Deadline January of each year.

[550]
PI GAMMA MU SCHOLARSHIPS

Pi Gamma Mu
Attn: Executive Director
1001 Millington, Suite B
Winfield, KS 67156
(316) 221-3128
Web: www.pigammamu.org/scholarship.html

Purpose To provide financial assistance to members of Pi Gamma Mu (international honor society in the social sciences) who are interested in working on a graduate degree in selected disciplines.

Eligibility This program is open to members in good standing who are interested in working on a graduate degree in 1 of the following areas: sociology, anthropology, political science, history, economics, international relations, public administration, criminal justice, law, cultural geography, social psychology, or social work. Applications are not accepted from students working on a degree in business administration. Preference is given to applicants ready to enter or just beginning their first year of graduate school. Financial need is considered. Applications must be accompanied by a transcript, a statement describing why the applicant is interested in working on a graduate degree in the social sciences, and at least 3 letters of recommendation from professors in the field.

Financial data Awards are either $2,000 or $1,000.

Duration 1 year.

Number awarded 10 each year: 3 at $2,000 and 7 at $1,000.

Deadline January of each year.

[551]
PIKES PEAK CHAPTER SCHOLARSHIP PROGRAM

Institute of Management Accountants-Pikes Peak
    Chapter
Attn: Scholarship Selection Committee
P.O. Box 752
Colorado Springs, CO 80901-0752
(719) 637-8539
E-mail: scholarships@pikespeakima.org
Web: www.pikespeakima.org

Purpose To provide financial assistance to undergraduate and graduate students interested in preparing for a career in management accounting or financial management.

Eligibility This program is open to students who are 1) attending a 2-year college in business administration or accounting and planning to continue their education in a 4- or 5-year management accounting or financial management program; 2) attending a 4-year undergraduate institution in business administration, accounting, or finance; or 3) working on a graduate degree with a declared major in management accounting or financial management or have majored in management accounting or financial management as an undergraduate. Applicants must be members of the Institute of Management Accountants (IMA) studying in the United States or Puerto Rico at a regionally-accredited institution. Selection is based on academic merit, quality of the application presentation, demonstrated community leadership, and potential for success in expressed career goals in a financial management position.

Financial data The stipend is $500.

Duration 1 academic year; nonrenewable.

Number awarded 1 each year.

Deadline January of each year.

[552]
PRINT AND GRAPHICS SCHOLARSHIP FOUNDATION FELLOWSHIPS

Print and Graphics Scholarship Foundation
Attn: Scholarship Competition
200 Deer Run Road
Sewickley PA 15143-2600
(412) 741-6860, ext. 161   Toll-free: (800) 910-GATF
Fax: (412) 741-2311   E-mail: pgsf@gatf.org
Web: www.gain.net/employment/scholarships.html

Purpose To provide financial assistance to graduate students interested in preparing for careers in the graphic communications industries.

Eligibility To be eligible to apply for an award, students must 1) plan to seek employment at the managerial or educational level in the graphic communications industry; 2) have demonstrated ability and special aptitude for advanced education in such fields as mathematics, chemistry, physics, industrial education, engineering, and business technology, provided the area of study has potential application in the printing, publishing, and packaging industries; and 3) be either a college senior who expects to complete a baccalaureate degree during the academic year and has been admitted as a full-time graduate student or a currently-enrolled graduate student who has at least 1 year of study remaining. Selection is based on college academic records, rank in class, recommendations, biographical records which indicate academic honors, extracurricular interests, and work experience.

Financial data Stipends range from $1,500 to $4,000 per year. Funds are paid directly to the institution selected by the award winner and credited to the account of the fellow, who may not withdraw more than 60% of the deposit during the first half of the academic year.

Duration 1 year.

Number awarded Varies each year.

Deadline January of each year.

[553]
PUBLIC EMPLOYEE RETIREMENT RESEARCH AND ADMINISTRATION SCHOLARSHIP

Government Finance Officers Association
Attn: Scholarship Committee
203 North LaSalle Street, Suite 2700
Chicago, IL 60601-1210
(312) 977-9700   Fax: (312) 977-4806
Web: www.gfoa.org/services/scholarships.shtml

Purpose To provide financial assistance to graduate students preparing for careers in the field of public sector retirement benefits.

Eligibility This program is open to full- or part-time students enrolled in a graduate program in public administration, finance, business administration, or social sciences. Applicants must be college graduates, citizens or permanent residents of the United States or Canada, and able to provide a letter of recommendation from the dean of their graduate program. Selection is based on career plans, academic record, plan of study, letters of recommendation, and GPA. Financial need is not considered.

Financial data The stipend is $4,000.

Duration 1 year.

Additional information Funds for this program are provided by the ICMA Retirement Corporation.
Number awarded 1 each year.
Deadline February of each year.

[554]
PUBLIC SERVICE SCHOLARSHIPS

Hispanic Scholarship Fund Institute
1001 Connecticut Avenue, N.W., Suite 632
Washington, DC 20036
(202) 296-0009   Fax: (202) 296-3633
E-mail: info@hsfi.org
Web: www.hsfi.org/sch_pss.html

Purpose To provide financial assistance to undergraduate and graduate students interested in preparing for a career in a field of interest to the U.S. Department of Agriculture (USDA), including business administration.

Eligibility This program is open to 1) full-time undergraduates and 2) master's degree students (who may be enrolled part time) at accredited institutions in the United States. Applicants must be U.S. citizens or permanent residents majoring in a field of interest to the USDA: accounting, agribusiness, agriculture, business administration, civil engineering, computer science, economics, finance, food sciences, information technology, management, mathematics, nutrition, soil science, or statistics. They must have a GPA of 2.75 or higher and a strong interest in a career in public service with the USDA. Along with their application, they must submit a 2-page essay on why a career in public service interests them, how their academic major connects with their stated USDA career goal, why the USDA should invest in them through this program, and how they believe the USDA will benefit from this investment. Selection is based mainly on academic achievement, commitment to public service, and interest in federal employment with the USDA, but financial need is also considered.

Financial data The program provides recipients with full payment of tuition and fees, employment with USDA (including employee benefits), a fully-equipped personal computer, and networking opportunities.

Duration 1 year; may be renewed.

Additional information After graduation, recipients must be prepared to work for USDA for 1 year for each year of educational assistance they receive. For a list of the USDA agencies, the academic majors in which they are interested, and the locations where they offer employment, contact the sponsor or see the web site.

Number awarded Approximately 30 each year.
Deadline April of each year.

[555]
PUGET SOUND CHAPTER HELENE M. OVERLY MEMORIAL SCHOLARSHIP

Women's Transportation Seminar-Puget Sound Chapter
c/o Lorelei Mesic, Scholarship Co-Chair
W&H Pacific
3350 Monte Villa Parkway
Bothell, WA 98021-8972
(425) 951-4872   Fax: (425) 951-4808
E-mail: lmesic@whpacific.com
Web: www.wtspugetsound.org/nscholarships.html

Purpose To provide financial assistance to women graduate students from Washington working on a degree related to transportation.

Eligibility This program is open to women who are residents of Washington, studying at a college in the state, or working as an intern in the state. Applicants must be currently enrolled in a graduate degree program in a transportation-related field, such as engineering, planning, finance, or logistics. They must have a GPA of 3.0 or higher and plans to prepare for a career in a transportation-related field. Minority candidates are encouraged to apply. Along with their application, they must submit a 750-word statement about their career goals after graduation and why they think they should receive this scholarship award. Selection is based on that statement, academic record, and transportation-related activities or job skills. Financial need is not considered.

Financial data The stipend is $1,700.
Duration 1 year.
Additional information The winner is also nominated for scholarships offered by the national organization of the Women's Transportation Seminar.
Number awarded 1 each year.
Deadline October of each year.

[556]
RALPH AND VALERIE THOMAS SCHOLARSHIP

National Association of Black Accountants
Attn: Director, Center for Advancement of Minority Accountants
7249-A Hanover Parkway
Greenbelt, MD 20770
(301) 474-NABA, ext. 114   Fax: (301) 474-3114
E-mail: cquinn@nabainc.org
Web: www.nabainc.org

Purpose To provide financial assistance to student members of the National Association of Black Accountants (NABA) who are working on an undergraduate or graduate degree in a field related to accounting.

Eligibility This program is open to NABA members who are members of ethnic minority groups enrolled full time as 1) an undergraduate freshman, sophomore, junior, or first-semester senior majoring in accounting, business, or finance; or 2) a graduate student working on a master's degree in accounting. Applicants must have a GPA of 3.5 or higher in their major and 3.3 or higher overall. Selection is based on grades, financial need, and a 500-word autobiography that discusses career objectives, leadership abilities, community activities, and involvement in NABA.

Financial data The stipend is $1,000 per year.
Duration 1 year.

Number awarded 1 each year.
Deadline December of each year.

[557]
RAY FOLEY MEMORIAL SCHOLARSHIP PROGRAM

American Wholesale Marketers Association
Attn: Distributors Education Foundation
2750 Prosperity Avenue, Suite 530
Fairfax, VA 22031
(703) 208-3358   Toll-free: (800) 482-2962
Fax: (703) 573-5738   E-mail: info@awmanet.org
Web: www.awmanet.org/edu/edu-schol.html

Purpose To provide financial assistance to undergraduate or graduate students who are employed by or related to an employee of a member of the American Wholesale Marketers Association (AWMA) and working on a degree in business.

Eligibility This program is open to full-time undergraduate and graduate students working on a degree in a business course of study (accounting or business administration) at an accredited college or university. Applicants must be employed by an AWMA wholesaler distributor member or be an immediate family member (spouse, child, stepchild) of an employee of an AWMA wholesaler distributor member. They must be able to demonstrate interest in a career in distribution of candy, tobacco, and convenience products. Selection is based on academic merit and career interest in the candy/tobacco/convenience-products wholesale industry.

Financial data The scholarships are $5,000 per year. Funds are paid directly to the college or university to cover tuition, on-campus room and board, and other direct costs; any remaining funds are paid to the student for reimbursement of school-related expenses, when appropriate receipts are available.

Duration 1 year; nonrenewable.

Additional information The American Wholesale Marketers Association (AWMA) resulted from the 1991 merger of the National Association of Tobacco Distributors (NATD) and the National Candy Wholesalers Association (NCWA). This scholarship was established in memory of Ray Foley, the late executive vice president of the NCWA.

Number awarded 2 each year.
Deadline May of each year.

[558]
RICHARD P. COVERT, PH.D., FHIMSS SCHOLARSHIP

Healthcare Information and Management Systems
  Society
Attn: HIMSS Foundation Scholarship Program
  Coordinator
230 East Ohio Street, Suite 500
Chicago, IL 60611-3269
(312) 664-4467   Fax: (312) 664-6143
Web: www.himss.org/asp/scholarships.asp

Purpose To provide financial assistance to student members of the Healthcare Information and Management Systems Society (HIMSS) who are working on a degree in management engineering.

Eligibility This program is open to student members of the society, although an application for membership, including dues, may accompany the scholarship application. Applicants must be upper-division or graduate students working on a degree in management engineering. Selection is based on academic achievement and demonstration of leadership potential, including communication skills and participation in society activity.

Financial data The stipend is $5,000. The award includes an all-expense paid trip to the annual HIMSS conference and exhibition.

Duration 1 year.

Additional information This program was established in 2004.

Number awarded 1 each year.
Deadline October of each year.

[559]
RITCHIE-JENNINGS MEMORIAL SCHOLARSHIPS PROGRAM

Association of Certified Fraud Examiners
Attn: Scholarship Program
The Gregor Building
716 West Avenue
Austin, TX 78701-2727
(512) 478-9070   Toll-free: (800) 245-3321
Fax: (512) 478-9297   E-mail: scholarships@cfenet.com
Web: www.cfenet.com/services/scholarships.asp

Purpose To provide financial assistance to undergraduate and graduate students working on an accounting or criminal justice degree.

Eligibility This program is open to students working full time on an undergraduate or graduate degree in accounting or criminal justice. Applicants must submit a short essay on why they deserve the award and how fraud awareness will affect their professional career development. Selection is based on the essay, academic achievement, and several letters of recommendation (including at least 1 from a certified fraud examiner).

Financial data The stipend is $1,000.

Duration 1 year.

Additional information This program was established in 1995 and given its current name in 1998.

Number awarded 15 each year.
Deadline May of each year.

[560]
ROBERT H. RUMLER MBA SCHOLARSHIP PROGRAM

Holstein Association USA.
Attn: Executive Secretary
One Holstein Place
P.O. Box 808
Brattleboro, VT 05302-0808
(802) 254-4551   Toll-free: (800) 952-5200, ext. 4231
Fax: (802) 254-8251
Web: www.holsteinusa.com

Purpose To provide financial assistance to college graduates who majored in dairy science and now want to work on a master's degree in business administration.

Eligibility Eligible to apply are college graduates who graduated from an accredited agricultural college or university with a bachelor's degree in dairy production or its equivalent. They should have ranked in the upper third of their graduating class. Work experience is a plus. They must be interested in working on an M.B.A. degree. Applicants may be either entering the program or returning as a second-year full-time student. Selection is based on academic record, work experience, extracurricular activities, leadership abilities, and interest in applying business techniques to agriculture. Financial need is not considered.

Financial data The stipend is $3,000.

Duration 1 year; recipients may reapply for 1 additional year.

Additional information This program was established in 1984.

Number awarded 1 each year.

Deadline April of each year.

[561]
ROBERT H. THOMAS SCHOLARSHIP FUND

Healthcare Financial Management Association-Virginia
  Chapter
c/o Herbert D. Harvey, Scholarship Committee Chair
Obici Health System
2800 Godwin Boulevard
Suffolk, VA 23435
(757) 934-4642   E-mail: hharvey@obici.com
Web: www.vahfma.org

Purpose To provide financial assistance to members of the Virginia chapter of the Healthcare Financial Management Association (HFMA) who are interested in a program of continuing education.

Eligibility This program is open to HFMA members in Virginia who are interested in working on an advanced degree, completing a certification program, taking undergraduate courses, or engaging in other educational activities to enhance their career. Selection is based primarily on a 2-page essay that describes their academic goals, how the scholarship will help them achieve those goals, and how they expect their career to be improved.

Financial data The stipend is $1,000.

Duration 1 year.

Number awarded 1 each year.

Deadline April of each year.

[562]
SARA TATEM SCHOLARSHIP

Virginia Organization of Nurse Executives
c/o Linda Cecil, Scholarship Committee Chair
Carilion Medical Center
P.O. Box 184
Elliston, VA 24087
(540) 981-7353   Fax: (540) 344-2431
E-mail: lcecil@carilion.com
Web: www.hospitalconnect.com

Purpose To provide financial assistance to nurses working on a graduate degree in business or administration in Virginia.

Eligibility This program is open to students enrolled full or part time in an NLN-approved program in nursing at the mas-

ter's, D.N.S., or Ph.D. level in Virginia. Applicants must be majoring or conducting research in 1) nursing administration, 2) a health-related program combined with an M.B.A. or M.H.A., or 3) an M.B.A. or M.H.A. program. They must hold a Virginia nursing license.

Financial data The stipend is $1,000.

Duration 1 year.

Number awarded 2 each year.

Deadline September of each year.

[563]
SCHOLARSHIPS FOR MINORITY ACCOUNTING STUDENTS

American Institute of Certified Public Accountants
Attn: Academic and Career Development Division
1211 Avenue of the Americas
New York, NY 10036-8775
(212) 596-6223   Fax: (212) 596-6292
E-mail: educat@aicpa.org
Web: www.aicpa.org

Purpose To provide financial assistance to underrepresented minorities interested in studying accounting at the undergraduate or graduate school level.

Eligibility Undergraduate applicants must be minority students who are enrolled full time, have completed at least 30 semester hours of college work (including at least 6 semester hours in accounting), be majoring in accounting with an overall GPA of 3.3 or higher, and be U.S. citizens or permanent residents. Minority students who are interested in a graduate degree must be 1) in the final year of a 5-year accounting program; 2) an undergraduate accounting major currently accepted or enrolled in a master's-level accounting, business administration, finance, or taxation program; or 3) any undergraduate major currently accepted in a master's-level accounting program. Selection is based primarily on merit (academic and personal achievement); financial need is evaluated as a secondary criteria. For purposes of this program, the American Institute of Certified Public Accountants (AICPA) considers minority students to be those of Black, Native American/Alaskan Native, Pacific Island, or Hispanic ethnic origin.

Financial data The maximum stipend is $5,000 per year.

Duration 1 year; may be renewed, if recipients are making satisfactory progress toward graduation.

Additional information These scholarships are granted by the institute's Minority Educational Initiatives Committee.

Number awarded Varies each year; recently, 187 students received funding through this program.

Deadline June of each year.

[564]
SEALASKA HERITAGE INSTITUTE 7(I) SCHOLARSHIPS

Sealaska Corporation
Attn: Sealaska Heritage Institute
One Sealaska Plaza, Suite 201
Juneau, AK 99801-1249
(907) 586-9177   Toll-free: (888) 311-4992
Fax: (907) 586-9293
E-mail: scholarship@sealaska.com
Web: www.sealaskaheritage.org

Purpose To provide financial assistance for undergraduate or graduate study to Native Alaskans who have a connection to Sealaska Corporation and are majoring in designated fields.

Eligibility This program is open to 1) Alaska Natives who are enrolled to Sealaska Corporation, and 2) Native lineal descendants of Alaska Natives enrolled to Sealaska Corporation, whether or not the applicant owns Sealaska Corporation stock. Applicants must be enrolled or accepted for enrollment as full-time undergraduate or graduate students. Along with their application, they must submit 2 essays: 1) their personal history and educational goals, and 2) their past history of and expected contributions to the Alaska Native community. Financial need is also considered in the selection process. The following areas of study qualify for these awards: natural resources (environmental sciences, engineering, conservation biology, fisheries, geology, marine science/biology, forestry, wildlife management, and mining technology); business administration (accounting, finance, marketing, international business, international commerce and trade, management of information systems, human resources management, economics, computer information systems, and industrial management); and other special fields (cadastral surveys, chemistry, equipment/machinery operators, industrial safety specialists, occupational health specialists, plastics engineers, trade specialists, physics, mathematics, and marine trades and occupations).

Financial data The amount of the award depends on the availability of funds, the number of qualified applicants, class standing, and cumulative GPA.

Duration 1 year; may be renewed up to 5 years for a bachelor's degree, up to 3 years for a master's degree, up to 2 years for a doctorate, or up to 3 years for vocational study. The maximum total support is limited to 9 years. Renewal depends on recipients' maintaining full-time enrollment and a GPA of 2.5 or higher.

Additional information Funding for this program is provided from Alaska Native Claims Settlement Act (ANSCA) Section 7(i) revenue sharing provisions.

Number awarded Varies each year.

Deadline February of each year.

[565]
SEATTLE CHAPTER SCHOLARSHIPS

American Society of Women Accountants-Seattle
  Chapter
c/o Anne Macnab
800 Fifth Avenue, Suite 101
Seattle, WA 98104-3191
E-mail: scholarship@aswaseattle.com
Web: www.aswaseattle.com/scholarships.htm

Purpose To provide financial assistance to students working on a bachelor's or master's degree in accounting at a college or university in Washington.

Eligibility This program is open to part-time and full-time students working on an associate, bachelor's, or master's degree in accounting at a college or university in Washington. Applicants must have completed at least 30 semester hours and have maintained a GPA of at least 2.5 overall and 3.0 in accounting. Membership in the American Society of Women Accountants is not required. Selection is based on career goals, communication skills, GPA, personal circumstances, and financial need.

Financial data The amounts of the awards vary. Recently, a total of $12,000 was available for this program. Funds are paid directly to the recipient's school.

Duration 1 year.

Number awarded April of each year.

Deadline Varies each year.

[566]
SEATTLE PROFESSIONAL CHAPTER SCHOLARSHIPS

Association for Women in Communications-Seattle
  Professional Chapter
Attn: Scholarship Chair
1319 Dexter Avenue North, Number 370
Seattle, WA 98109
(206) 654-2929   Fax: (206) 285-5220
E-mail: awcseattle@qwest.net
Web: www.seattleawc.org/scholarships.html

Purpose To provide financial assistance to upper-division and graduate students in Washington who are preparing for a career in the communications industry.

Eligibility This program is open to Washington state residents who are enrolled at a 4-year college or university in the state as a junior, senior, or graduate student (sophomores at 2-year colleges applying to a 4-year institution are also eligible). Applicants must be majoring, or planning to major, in a communications program, including print and broadcast journalism, television and radio production, film, advertising, public relations, marketing, graphic design, multimedia design, photography or technical communication. Selection is based on demonstrated excellence in communications; contributions made to communications on campus and in the community; scholastic achievement; financial need; and writing samples from journalism, advertising, public relations, or broadcasting.

Financial data The stipend is $1,500. Funds are paid directly to the recipient's school and must be used for tuition and fees.

Duration 1 year.

Number awarded 2 each year.

Deadline February of each year.

[567]
SHRM FOUNDATION GRADUATE SCHOLARSHIPS

Society for Human Resource Management
Attn: Foundation Administrator
1800 Duke Street
Alexandria, VA 22314-3499
(703) 535-6020   Toll-free: (800) 283-SHRM
Fax: (703) 535-6490   TDD: (703) 548-6999
E-mail: speyton@shrm.org
Web: www.shrm.org/students/ags_published

Purpose To provide financial assistance to graduate student members of the Society for Human Resource Management (SHRM).

Eligibility This program is open to graduate student members of the society. Applicants must be enrolled in a master's degree program, pursuing an emphasis area in human relations and/or industrial relations, and have completed at least 12 hours of graduate course work with a GPA of 3.5 or higher.

Financial data The stipend is $5,000.

Duration 1 year.

Number awarded 1 each year.

Deadline October of each year.

[568]
SHRM FOUNDATION REGIONAL ACADEMIC SCHOLARSHIPS

Society for Human Resource Management
Attn: Member Chapter Relations Department
1800 Duke Street
Alexandria, VA 22314-3499
(703) 548-3440   Toll-free: (800) 283-SHRM
Fax: (703) 535-6490   TDD: (703) 548-6999
E-mail: shrm@shrm.org
Web: www.shrm.org/students/ags_published

Purpose To provide financial assistance to regular (nonstudent) members of the Society for Human Resource Management (SHRM) who are interested in pursuing an an undergraduate or graduate degree in human resource management while working full time.

Eligibility This program is open to national professional, general, and association members of the society who are employed full time in human resources and working on either an undergraduate or graduate degree in the field at an accredited institution of higher learning, either through correspondence, online, and/or classroom learning. Applicants must submit a 1-page essay in which they discuss their contribution to the human resource profession to date, their future goals as a human resources professional, how this scholarship will help to achieve those goals, and their financial need. Selection is based on human resource work experience and involvement (50%), volunteer activity (20%), financial need (20%), and letters of reference (10%).

Financial data The stipend is $3,000.

Duration 1 year.

Number awarded 5 each year: 1 in each of the society's 5 regions.

Deadline April of each year.

[569]
SMITH BARNEY WOMEN IN BUSINESS SCHOLARSHIPS

Nevada Women's Fund
770 Smithridge Drive, Suite 300
Reno, NV 89502
(702) 786-2335   Fax: (702) 786-8152
E-mail: info@nevadawomensfund.com
Web: www.nevadawomensfund.com/scholarships

Purpose To provide funding to women in Nevada who are interested in working on an undergraduate or graduate education.

Eligibility This program is open to women who are working on or planning to work on an academic degree or vocational training on the undergraduate or graduate level. Preference is given to northern Nevada residents and those attending northern Nevada institutions. Selection is based on academic achievement, financial need, work experience, community involvement, other life experiences, family responsibilities, and the applicant's plan after completing study. Women of all ages are eligible. An interview may be required.

Financial data Stipends are $1,000 or $500. A total of $6,000 is available for these scholarships each year.

Duration 1 year; may be renewed.

Number awarded Varies each year. Recently, 7 of these scholarships were awarded: 5 at $1,000 and 2 at $500.

Deadline February of each year.

[570]
SOUTH CAROLINA ASSOCIATION OF CPA'S SCHOLARSHIP PROGRAM

South Carolina Association of Certified Public
   Accountants
Attn: Educational Fund, Inc.
570 Chris Drive
West Columbia, SC 29169
(803) 791-4181   Toll-free: (888) 557-4814
Fax: (803) 791-4196
Web: www.scacpa.org

Purpose To provide financial assistance to upper-division and graduate students majoring in accounting in South Carolina.

Eligibility This program is open to South Carolina residents who are majoring in accounting at a college or university in the state. Applicants must be juniors, seniors, or graduate students with a GPA of 3.25 or higher overall and 3.5 or higher in accounting. They must submit their college transcripts, a listing of awards and other scholarships, 2 letters of reference, a resume, a 250-word essay on their personal career goals, and certification of their accounting major. Financial need is not considered in the selection process.

Financial data Stipends range from $500 to $1,500. Funds are paid to the recipient's school.

Duration 1 year.

Number awarded Varies each year.

Deadline June of each year.

[571]
SPACE SYSTEMS/LORAL SCHOLARSHIP

Society of Satellite Professionals International
Attn: Scholarship Program
New York Information Technology Center
55 Broad Street, 14th Floor
New York, NY 10004
(212) 809-5199   Fax: (212) 825-0075
E-mail: sspi@sspi.org
Web: www.sspi.org/html/scholarship.html

Purpose To provide financial assistance to women interested in majoring in satellite-related disciplines (including business) in college or graduate school.

Eligibility This program is open to high school seniors, college undergraduates, and graduate students majoring or planning to major in fields related to satellite technologies, policies, or applications. Fields of study in the past have included broadcasting, business, distance learning, energy, government, imaging, meteorology, navigation, remote sensing, space law, and telecommunications. Applicants must be women born and living in the United States. Selection is based on academic and leadership achievement, commitment to pursue educational and career opportunities in the satellite communications industry, potential for significant contribution to that industry, a personal statement of 500 to 750 words on interest in satellite communications and why they deserve the award, and a creative work (such as a research report, essay, article, videotape, artwork, computer program, or scale model of an antenna or spacecraft design) that reflects the applicant's interests and talents. Financial need is not considered.

Financial data The stipend ranges from $2,000 to $5,000.

Duration 1 year.

Number awarded 1 each year.

Deadline May of each year.

[572]
STANLEY H. STEARMAN SCHOLARSHIP AWARD

National Society of Accountants
Attn: NSA Scholarship Foundation
1010 North Fairfax Street
Alexandria, VA 22314-1574
(703) 549-6400, ext. 1312
Toll-free: (800) 966-6679, ext. 1312
Fax: (703) 549-2512   E-mail: snoell@nsacct.org
Web: www.nsacct.org

Purpose To provide funding for the undergraduate and graduate study of accounting to relatives of active or deceased members of the National Society of Accountants.

Eligibility Both undergraduate and graduate students may apply for this award. They must be working on a degree in accounting, have a GPA of 3.0 or higher, be enrolled full time at an accredited college or university, and be the relative (spouse, son, daughter, grandchild, niece, nephew, or son- or daughter-in-law) of an active National Society of Accountants' member or deceased member. Applicants must submit a letter of intent outlining their reasons for seeking the award, their intended career objective, and how this scholarship award would be used to accomplish that objective. Selection is based on academic attainment, demonstrated leadership ability, and financial need.

Financial data The stipend is $2,000 per year.

Duration Up to 3 years.

Number awarded 1 each year.

Deadline March of each year.

[573]
STUART CAMERON AND MARGARET MCLEOD MEMORIAL SCHOLARSHIP

Institute of Management Accountants
Attn: Committee on Students
10 Paragon Drive
Montvale, NJ 07645-1760
(201) 573-9000   Toll-free: (800) 638-4427, ext. 1543
Fax: (201) 573-8438   E-mail: students@imanet.org
Web: www.imanet.org

Purpose To provide financial assistance to undergraduate or graduate student members of the Institute of Management Accountants (IMA) who are interested in preparing for a career in management accounting or financial management.

Eligibility This program is open to undergraduate and graduate student IMA members who have a GPA of 2.8 or higher. Applicants must be preparing for a career in management accounting, financial management, or information technology. They must submit a 2-page statement on their reasons for applying for the scholarship, reasons that they deserve the award, specific contributions to the IMA, ideas on how they will promote awareness and increase membership and certification within IMA, and their career goals and objectives. Selection is based on that statement, academic merit, IMA participation, quality of the presentation, a resume, and letters of recommendation.

Financial data The stipend is $5,000.

Duration 1 year.

Additional information The recipient is required to participate in the parent chapter, at the council level, or at the national level.

Number awarded 1 each year.

Deadline February of each year.

[574]
TDC SCHOLARSHIP

National Association of Black Accountants
Attn: Director, Center for Advancement of Minority
    Accountants
7249-A Hanover Parkway
Greenbelt, MD 20770
(301) 474-NABA, ext. 114   Fax: (301) 474-3114
E-mail: cquinn@nabainc.org
Web: www.nabainc.org

Purpose To provide financial assistance to student members of the National Association of Black Accountants (NABA) who are working on an undergraduate or graduate degree in a field related to accounting.

Eligibility This program is open to NABA members who are members of ethnic minority groups enrolled full time as 1) an undergraduate freshman, sophomore, junior, or first-semester senior majoring in accounting, business, or finance; or 2) a graduate student working on a master's degree in accounting. Applicants must have a GPA of 2.0 or higher in their major and 2.5 or higher overall. Selection is based on grades, financial need, and a 500-word autobiography that discusses career objectives, leadership abilities, community activities, and involvement in NABA.

Financial data The stipend is $1,000 per year.

Duration 1 year.

Number awarded 1 each year.

Deadline December of each year.

[575]
TEXAS BUSINESS HALL OF FAME SCHOLARSHIPS

Texas Business Hall of Fame
c/o International Meeting Managers, Inc.
4550 Post Oak Place, Suite 342
Houston, TX 77027
(713) 993-9433   Fax: (713) 960-0488
E-mail: info@texasbusiness.org
Web: www.texasbusiness.org

Purpose To provide financial assistance to students in Texas who are working on their master's in business administration degree.

Eligibility Eligible to apply are students working full time on an M.B.A. degree at a university in Texas. Applicants must be U.S. citizens. Interviews may be required. Applications will not be accepted without the nomination of the student's Dean. Selection is based on leadership traits, academic achievement (at least a 3.5 GPA), a propensity for entrepreneurial achievement, and outstanding moral character.

Financial data Each stipend is $5,000. To date, the sponsor has awarded more than $1.8 million in scholarships to students preparing for a business career at Texas' leading institutions of higher learning.

Duration 1 year.

Number awarded Varies each year; recently, 14 were awarded.

[576]
THOMPSON SCHOLARSHIP FOR WOMEN IN SAFETY

American Society of Safety Engineers
Attn: ASSE Foundation
1800 East Oakton Street
Des Plaines, IL 60018
(847) 768-3441   Fax: (847) 296-9220
E-mail: mrosario@asse.org
Web: www.asse.org

Purpose To provide financial assistance to women working on a graduate degree in safety-related fields.

Eligibility This program is open to women who are working on a graduate degree in safety engineering, safety management, occupational health nursing, occupational medicine, risk management, ergonomics, industrial hygiene, fire safety, environmental safety, environmental health, or another safety-related field. Applicants must be full-time students who have completed at least 9 semester hours with a GPA of 3.5 or higher. Their undergraduate GPA must have been 3.0 or higher. As part of the selection process, they must submit 2 essays of 300 words or less: 1) why they are seeking a degree in safety, a brief description of their current activities, and how those relate to their career goals and objectives; and 2) why

they should be awarded this scholarship (including career goals and financial need).

Financial data The stipend is $1,000 per year.

Duration 1 year; nonrenewable.

Number awarded 1 each year.

Deadline November of each year.

[577]
TRANSIT HALL OF FAME SCHOLARSHIP AWARDS

American Public Transportation Association
Attn: American Public Transportation Foundation
1666 K Street, N.W., Suite 1100
Washington, DC 20006
(202) 496-4803   Fax: (202) 496-4321
E-mail: pboswell@apta.com
Web: www.apta.com

Purpose To provide financial assistance to undergraduate and graduate students who are preparing for a career in transportation.

Eligibility This program is open to college sophomores, juniors, seniors, and graduate students who are preparing for a career in the transit industry. Any member organization of the American Public Transportation Association (APTA) can nominate and sponsor candidates for this scholarship. Nominees must be enrolled in a fully-accredited institution, have and maintain at least a 3.0 GPA, and be either employed by or demonstrate a strong interest in entering the public transportation industry. They must submit a 1,000-word essay on "In what segment of the public transportation industry will you make a career and why?" Selection is based on demonstrated interest in the transit field as a career, need for financial assistance, academic achievement, essay content and quality, and involvement in extracurricular citizenship and leadership activities.

Financial data The stipend is at least $2,500. The winner of the Donald C. Hyde Memorial Essay Award receives an additional $500.

Duration 1 year; may be renewed.

Additional information This program was established in 1987. There is an internship component, which is designed to provide substantive training and professional development opportunities. Each year, there are 4 named scholarships offered: the Jack R. Gilstrap Scholarship for the applicant who receives the highest overall score; the Parsons Brickerhoff-Jim Lammie Scholarship for an applicant dedicated to a public transportation engineering career; the Louis T. Klauder Scholarship for an applicant dedicated to a career in the rail transit industry as an electrical or mechanical engineer; and the Dan M. Reichard, Jr. Scholarship for an applicant dedicated to a career in the business administration/management area of the transit industry. In addition, the Donald C. Hyde Memorial Essay Award is presented to the applicant who submits the best response to the required essay component of the program.

Number awarded At least 6 each year.

Deadline June of each year.

[578]
TRAVIS C. TOMLIN SCHOLARSHIP

National Association of Black Accountants
Attn: Director, Center for Advancement of Minority
   Accountants
7249-A Hanover Parkway
Greenbelt, MD 20770
(301) 474-NABA, ext. 114   Fax: (301) 474-3114
E-mail: cquinn@nabainc.org
Web: www.nabainc.org

Purpose To provide financial assistance to student members of the National Association of Black Accountants (NABA) who are working on an undergraduate or graduate degree in a field related to accounting.

Eligibility This program is open to NABA members who are members of ethnic minority groups enrolled full time as 1) an undergraduate freshman, sophomore, junior, or first-semester senior majoring in accounting, business, or finance; or 2) a graduate student working on a master's degree in accounting. Applicants must have a GPA of 3.5 or higher in their major and 3.3 or higher overall. Selection is based on grades, financial need, and a 500-word autobiography that discusses career objectives, leadership abilities, community activities, and involvement in NABA.

Financial data The stipend ranges from $1,000 to $1,500 per year.

Duration 1 year.

Number awarded 1 each year.

Deadline December of each year.

[579]
TWIN CITIES CHAPTER MBA SCHOLARSHIPS

National Black MBA Association-Twin Cities Chapter
P.O. Box 2709
Minneapolis, MN 55402
(651) 223-7373   E-mail: scholar@nbmbaatc.org
Web: www.nbmbaatc.org/scholarships.html

Purpose To provide financial assistance to African American students from Minnesota who are interested in working on a bachelor's or master's degree in business administration.

Eligibility This program is open to African American students enrolled in a graduate business or management program; this includes undergraduate seniors who are about to enter graduate school. In addition, a scholarship is available to an undergraduate student working on a bachelor's degree in the field of business. Applicants must be residents of or attending school in Minnesota. Along with their application, they must submit an essay of 400 to 500 words. Undergraduate students must write on the aspects of their formal education that are likely to be of the most value to their future employer and why. Graduate students must write on the steps they are taking to prepare themselves to pursue the limited number of opportunities in the recessionary economic conditions prevailing in the country today. Selection is based on career aspirations, GPA, activities, work experience, and the essay.

Financial data Stipends range from $500 to $3,500.

Duration 1 year.

Number awarded Varies each year; recently, this sponsor awarded $17,500 in scholarships.

Deadline March of each year.

[580]
UNITED CHURCH OF CHRIST FELLOWSHIP PROGRAM IN HEALTH AND HUMAN SERVICE MANAGEMENT

United Church of Christ
Attn: Council for Health and Human Service Ministries
700 Prospect Avenue East
Cleveland, OH 44115-1100
(216) 736-2250   Fax: (216) 736-2251
E-mail: nehringa@ucc.org
Web: www.ucc.org

Purpose To provide financial assistance to United Church of Christ clergy and lay members who wish to work on a graduate degree in health and human service management.

Eligibility This program is open to clergy with ecclesiastical standing and active lay members of a community of faith who have earned at least a baccalaureate degree. Candidates must be able to articulate their faith motivation for entering a ministry of health and human service management. They must qualify for admission and successfully complete any accredited academic program in theology and/or management as full-time students; successfully complete any state or federal examinations and obtain licensure as required by their administrative discipline; complete all residency, mentoring, and special project assignments at sponsoring institutions; and accept full-time employment, if offered, in an organization of the United Church of Christ (UCC) for a period of 5 years following completion of the fellowship. Fields of study include: long-term care and retirement housing; hospital and community health services; services to children, youth, and families; and services to persons with developmental disabilities. Applications from women and persons of color are especially encouraged.

Financial data The amount of the award is negotiable, based on the costs of the program.

Duration Varies, depending on the background of the fellow and the training required.

Number awarded 1 each year.

[581]
VIRGINIA SOCIETY FOR HEALTHCARE HUMAN RESOURCES ADMINISTRATION SCHOLARSHIP

Virginia Society for Healthcare Human Resources
   Administration
c/o Janice Gibbs
Obici Hospital Human Resources Department
2800 Godwin Boulevard
Suffolk, VA 23434
(757) 934-4602   E-mail: jgibbs.obici.com

Purpose To provide financial assistance to undergraduate and graduate students in Virginia working on a degree in human relations and interested in a career in a health care setting.

Eligibility This program is open to residents of Virginia currently enrolled in an accredited college or university in the state and working on an undergraduate or graduate degree in human resources administration or a related field. Applicants must be at least a second-semester sophomore when the application is submitted and have a demonstrated interest in working in a health care setting. Selection is based on a 1-page statement outlining the applicant's life and work experiences that support an interest in human relations, specifically in a health care setting; official transcripts; and 2 letters of recommendation from faculty members.

Financial data The stipend is $1,000.

Duration 1 year.

Number awarded 1 each year.

Deadline August of each year.

[582]
VIRGINIA SOCIETY OF CERTIFIED PUBLIC ACCOUNTANTS GRADUATE SCHOLARSHIPS

Virginia Society of Certified Public Accountants
  Education Foundation
Attn: Educational Foundation
4309 Cox Road
P.O. Box 4620
Glen Allen, VA 23058-4620
(804) 270-5344   Toll-free: (800) 733-8272
Fax: (804) 273-1741   E-mail: vscpa@vscpa.com
Web: www.vscpa.com

Purpose To provide financial assistance to students working on a graduate degree in accounting in Virginia.

Eligibility This program is open to U.S. citizens who are currently enrolled or have been accepted in a graduate accounting program at a college or university in Virginia. They must have a GPA of 3.0 or higher. Along with their applications, they must submit a 1-page essay on how they are financing their education, how they plan to use their accounting education, and why they should be awarded this scholarship. Selection is based on the essay (50%), an official undergraduate transcript (15%), a current resume, (25%), and a faculty letter of recommendation (10%).

Financial data A stipend is awarded (amount not specified). A total of $10,000 is available for this program each year.

Duration 1 year.

Number awarded Varies each year; recently, 3 of these scholarships were awarded.

Deadline April of each year.

[583]
WALTER FRESE MEMORIAL SCHOLARSHIP

Association of Government Accountants-Boston Chapter
c/o William A. Muench
10 Jordan Road
Hopkinton, MA 01748-2650
(508) 490-4019   E-mail: wmuench@dcaa.mil
Web: www.aga-boston-
chapter.orgscholarship%20information

Purpose To provide financial assistance to high school seniors, undergraduates, or graduate students from New England or attending school in New England who are working on a degree in accounting or finance.

Eligibility Applicants must be a New England resident or enrolled in a New England area college or university; they must be beginning or currently working on an undergraduate or graduate degree in accounting or finance. Students in M.B.A. and M.P.A. programs are also eligible, if they are currently working in a government accounting, auditing, or finance position. Selection is based on scholastic achievement, leadership qualities, extracurricular activities, recom-

mendations, writing ability, and an expressed interest in the field of government accounting, auditing, or financial management.

Financial data The stipend is $1,000.

Duration 1 year.

Number awarded 2 each year.

Deadline April of each year.

[584]
WASHINGTON FASHION GROUP INTERNATIONAL SCHOLARSHIP

Fashion Group International of Washington
Attn: Linda Lizzio
P.O. Box 4998
Washington, DC 20008
(202) 997-1664

Purpose To provide financial assistance for college or graduate school to residents of the Washington, D. C. area interested in preparing for a career in fashion or a fashion-related field.

Eligibility This program is open to residents of the metropolitan area of Washington, defined to include the District of Columbia; the Maryland counties of Anne Arundel, Baltimore, Frederick, Howard, Montgomery, and Prince George's; the city of Baltimore; the Virginia counties of Arlington, Fairfax, Loudoun, and Prince William; and the Virginia cities of Alexandria, Fairfax, and Falls Church. Applicants must have graduated from high school by June, have been accepted by an accredited 2-year or 4-year institution, have demonstrated a genuine interest in fashion or fashion-related fields through education, work, or avocation, and be enrolled in a fashion or fashion-related (commercial arts, textiles and clothing design, interior design, journalism, merchandising, or photography) degree granting program at the undergraduate or graduate level.

Financial data The maximum stipend is $5,000.

Duration 1 year.

Number awarded 1 each year.

Deadline February of each year.

[585]
WILLARD H. ERWIN, JR. SCHOLARSHIP

Greater Kanawha Valley Foundation
Attn: Scholarship Coordinator
1600 Huntington Square
900 Lee Street, East
P.O. Box 3041
Charleston, WV 25331-3041
(304) 346-3620   Fax: (304) 346-3640
E-mail: tgkvf@tgkvf.com
Web: www.tgkvf.com/scholar.html

Purpose To provide financial assistance to students in West Virginia who are working on an undergraduate or graduate degree in a field related to health care finance.

Eligibility This program is open to residents of West Virginia who are entering their junior, senior, or graduate year of study at a public college or university in the state. Applicants must have at least a 2.5 GPA and demonstrate good moral character. Preference is given to students working on a degree in business or some phase of health care finance.

Selection is based on financial need, academic performance, leadership abilities, and contributions to school and community.

Financial data The stipend is $1,000 per year.

Duration Normally, 2 years.

Additional information Funding for this program is provided by the West Virginia Chapter of the Healthcare Financial Management Association.

Number awarded 1 each year.

Deadline February of each year.

[586]
WILMA ALLISON MOORE SCHOLARSHIP

Saint Paul Foundation
Attn: Program Associate
600 Fifth Street Center
55 Fifth Street East
St. Paul, MN 55101-1797
(651) 325-4230   Toll-free: (800) 875-6167
Fax: (651) 224-8123
E-mail: lab@saintpaulfoundation.org
Web: www.saintpaulfoundation.org/scholarships

Purpose To provide financial assistance to students working on a master's degree in elementary education at the University of Minnesota or a master's degree in industrial relations at another university.

Eligibility This program is open to students entering or enrolled in 1) a master's degree program in elementary education at the Minneapolis campus of the University of Minnesota, or 2) a master's degree program in industrial relations at an accredited college or university. Preference is given to members of Alpha Kappa Alpha sorority, African American women working on a degree in elementary education at the University of Minnesota, natives of St. Paul, natives of Minneapolis, and current residents of the Twin Cities. Along with their application, they must submit a 2-page personal statement on their educational plan and career goals, including motivating factors or important experiences that have influenced their decision to prepare for their chosen career; industrial relations students should address whether or not they are concentrating in labor relations with an emphasis on organized labor, particularly within the field of education. Selection is based on academic performance, leadership and participation in school and community activities, clear educational and career goals, work experience, and financial need.

Financial data A stipend is awarded (amount not specified).

Duration 1 year; nonrenewable.

Number awarded 1 each year.

Deadline May of each year.

[587]
WISCONSIN INSTITUTE OF CERTIFIED PUBLIC ACCOUNTANTS 150-HOUR SCHOLARSHIPS

Wisconsin Institute of Certified Public Accountants
Attn: WICPA Educational Foundation
235 North Executive Drive, Suite 200
P.O. Box 1010
Brookfield, WI 53008-1010
(414) 785-0445
Toll-free: (800) 772-6939 (within WI and MN)
Fax: (414) 785-0838   E-mail: Tammy@wicpa.org
Web: www.wicpa.org

Purpose To provide financial assistance to students in Wisconsin working to meet the 150-hour accounting education requirement.

Eligibility This program is open to students at universities in Wisconsin who are enrolled in the fifth year of academic work leading to a master's degree in accounting. Applicants must be working to complete the 150-hour accounting education requirement.

Financial data The stipend is $5,000 per year.

Duration 1 year.

Additional information This program was established in 2001.

Number awarded Varies each year; recently, 7 of these scholarships were awarded.

Deadline February of each year.

[588]
WOMEN'S ENHANCEMENT POSTGRADUATE SCHOLARSHIP PROGRAM

National Collegiate Athletic Association
Attn: Leadership Advisory Board
700 West Washington Avenue
P.O. Box 6222
Indianapolis, IN 46206-6222
(317) 917-6477   Fax: (317) 917-6888
Web: www.ncaa.org

Purpose To provide funding for women who are interested in working on a graduate degree in intercollegiate athletics.

Eligibility This program is open to women who have been accepted into a program at a National Collegiate Athletic Association (NCAA) member institution that will prepare them for a career in intercollegiate athletics (athletics administrator, coach, athletic trainer, or other career that provides a direct service to intercollegiate athletics). Applicants must be U.S. citizens, have performed with distinction as a student body member at their respective undergraduate institution, and be entering the first semester or term of their postgraduate studies. Selection is based on the applicant's involvement in extracurricular activities, course work, commitment to preparing for a career in intercollegiate athletics, and promise for success in that career. Financial need is not considered.

Financial data The stipend is $6,000; funds are paid to the college or university of the recipient's choice.

Duration 1 year; nonrenewable.

Number awarded 16 each year; 3 of the scholarships are reserved for applicants who completed undergraduate study at an NCAA Division III institution.

Deadline February of each year.

[589]
WOMEN'S TRANSPORTATION SEMINAR CHAPTER OF COLORADO ANNUAL SCHOLARSHIPS

Women's Transportation Seminar-Colorado Chapter
c/o Chris Proud, Scholarship Chair
CH2M Hill
9193 South Jamaica Street, South Building
Englewood, CO 80112
(720) 286-5702   Fax: (720) 286-9732
E-mail: cproud@ch2m.com
Web: www.wtsnational.org

Purpose To provide financial assistance to undergraduate and graduate students in Colorado preparing for a career in transportation.

Eligibility This program is open to students at colleges and universities in Colorado who are working on a bachelor's or graduate degree in a field related to transportation. Those fields may include engineering (civil, electrical, or mechanical), urban planning, finance, aviation, transit, or railways. Applicants must submit an essay on their career goals after graduation and why they should receive this scholarship.

Financial data Undergraduate stipends are $1,000 or $250. Graduate stipends are $1,200.

Duration 1 year.

Additional information Winners are also nominated for scholarships offered by the national organization of the Women's Transportation Seminar.

Number awarded 3 each year: 2 to undergraduates and 1 to a graduate student.

Deadline November of each year.

[590]
WSEHA GRADUATE SCHOLARSHIP

Washington State Environmental Health Association
Attn: Executive Secretary
103 Sea Pine Lane
Bellingham, WA 98226-9363
(360) 756-2040   Fax: (360) 756-2080
E-mail: kerri@wseha.org
Web: www.wseha.org

Purpose To provide financial assistance to student members of the Washington State Environmental Health Association (WSEHA) who are interested in working on a graduate degree.

Eligibility This program is open to members of the association who are interested in pursuing an advanced degree that will materially promote the practice of environmental health in Washington state. Applicants must have been accepted as a graduate student at an accredited institution of higher education in a program leading to a master's or doctoral degree in an area related to the practice of environmental health, including managerial or policy arenas. Examples of eligible degree programs include a master of public health (M.P.H.), master of science (M.S.) in a related technical discipline (e.g., food protection, air pollution, water and wastewater, solid waste, vector control and housing, toxics and hazardous substances, hazardous waste, toxicology, GIS, groundwater hydrology), master of business administration (M.B.A.), master of public administration (M.P.A.), doctor of public health (Dr.P.H.), or doctor of philosophy (Ph.D.) in a related technical discipline.

Applicants must demonstrate their intent to employ their acquired knowledge to improve the practice of environmental health in Washington following graduation.

Financial data A stipend is awarded (amount not specified).

Duration 1 year.

Additional information Information is also available from the Student Scholarship Committee Chair, Chuck Treser, 3045 N.W. 57th Street, Seattle, WA 98107, (206) 616-2097, Fax: (206) 543-8123, E-mail: ctreser@u.washington.edu. Recipients must attend the association's annual educational conference to accept the scholarship award.

Number awarded 1 each year.

Deadline March of each year.

[591]
WTS MINNESOTA CHAPTER SCHOLARSHIPS

Women's Transportation Seminar-Minnesota Chapter
c/o Jessica Overmohle, Director
URS Corporation
700 Third Street South
Minneapolis, MN 55415-1199
(612) 373-6404   Fax: (612) 370-1378
E-mail: Jessica_Overmohle@URSCorp.com
Web: www.wtsnational.org

Purpose To provide financial assistance to women working on an undergraduate or graduate degree in a transportation-related field at colleges and universities in Minnesota.

Eligibility This program is open to women currently enrolled in a undergraduate or graduate degree program at a college or university in Minnesota. Applicants must be preparing for a career in transportation or a transportation-related field and be majoring in a field such as transportation engineering, planning, finance, or logistics. They must have a GPA of 3.0 or higher. Along with their application, they must submit a 750-word statement on their career goals after graduation and why they think they should receive this award. Selection is based on transportation goals, academic record, and transportation-related activities or job skills.

Financial data The stipend is $1,000.

Duration 1 year.

Additional information Winners are also nominated for scholarships offered by the national organization of the Women's Transportation Seminar.

Number awarded 2 each year: 1 undergraduate and 1 graduate student.

Deadline November of each year.

[592]
WTS PUGET SOUND CHAPTER SCHOLARSHIP

Women's Transportation Seminar-Puget Sound Chapter
c/o Lorelei Mesic, Scholarship Co-Chair
W&H Pacific
3350 Monte Villa Parkway
Bothell, WA 98021-8972
(425) 951-4872   Fax: (425) 951-4808
E-mail: lmesic@whpacific.com
Web: www.wtspugetsound.org/nscholarships.html

Purpose To provide financial assistance to women undergraduate and graduate students from Washington who are working on a degree related to transportation and have financial need.

Eligibility This program is open to women who are residents of Washington, studying at a college in the state, or working as an intern in the state. Applicants must be currently enrolled in an undergraduate or graduate degree program in a transportation-related field, such as engineering, planning, finance, or logistics. They must have a GPA of 3.0 or higher and plans to prepare for a career in a transportation-related field. Minority candidates are encouraged to apply. Along with their application, they must submit a 500-word statement about their career goals after graduation, their financial need, and why they think they should receive this scholarship award. Selection is based on transportation goals, academic record, transportation-related activities or job skills, and financial need.

Financial data The stipend is $1,500.

Duration 1 year.

Additional information The winner is also nominated for scholarships offered by the national organization of the Women's Transportation Seminar.

Number awarded 1 each year.

Deadline October of each year.

[593]
WTS/ITS WASHINGTON INTELLIGENT TRANSPORTATION SYSTEMS SCHOLARSHIP

Women's Transportation Seminar-Puget Sound Chapter
c/o Lorelei Mesic, Scholarship Co-Chair
W&H Pacific
3350 Monte Villa Parkway
Bothell, WA 98021-8972
(425) 951-4872   Fax: (425) 951-4808
E-mail: lmesic@whpacific.com
Web: www.wtspugetsound.org/nscholarships.html

Purpose To provide financial assistance to undergraduate and graduate students from Washington working on a degree related to intelligent transportation systems (ITS).

Eligibility This program is open to students who are residents of Washington, studying at a college in the state, or working as an intern in the state. Applicants must be currently enrolled in an undergraduate or graduate degree program related to the design, implementation, operation, and maintenance of ITS technologies. They must be majoring in transportation or a related field, including transportation engineering, systems engineering, electrical engineering, planning, finance, or logistics, and be taking courses in such ITS-related fields of study as computer science, electronics, and digital communications. In addition, they must have a GPA of 3.0 or higher and plans to prepare for a career in a transportation-related field. Minority candidates are encouraged to apply. Along with their application, they must submit a 500-word statement about their career goals after graduation, how those relate to ITS, and why they think they should receive this scholarship award. Selection is based on that statement, academic record, and transportation-related activities or job skills. Financial need is not considered.

Financial data The stipend is $1,500.

Duration 1 year.

Additional information This program is co-sponsored by ITS Washington.

Number awarded 1 each year.

Deadline October of each year.

Grants

Described here are 33 programs that provide funds for innovative efforts, projects, creative activities, or research to either undergraduate or graduate students in a business-related field, including accounting, actuarial science, agricultural economics, banking, business administration, economics, finance, management, marketing and sales, personnel administration, and real estate. For information on funding available to support undergraduate studies, see the Scholarships subsection; for information on funding available to support graduate studies, see the Fellowships subsection.

[594]
AEFA PREDOCTORAL SCHOLARS PROGRAM

American Education Finance Association
Attn: Executive Director
8365 South Armadillo Trail
Evergreen, CO 80439
(303) 674-0857   Fax: (303) 670-8986
Web: www.aefa.cc/newscholars.php

Purpose To provide funding to doctoral students and recent master's degree recipients who are interested in conducting research utilizing the databases of the National Center for Education Statistics (NCES).

Eligibility This program is open to 1) students who are currently enrolled in a doctoral program, and 2) individuals who received a master's degree during the preceding 4 years. Applicants must be interested in conducting research in elementary, secondary, and higher education finance. They must describe the issue to be investigated, the research methodology, the data sources to be used, the importance and relevance of the issue to education finance, and plans for disseminating the findings.

Financial data The grant is $3,000. Awards also include a 1-year membership in the American Education Finance Association (AEFA).

Duration 1 year.

Additional information Information is also available from Dan D. Goldhaber, University of Washington, Evans School of Public Affairs, Center on Reinventing Public Education, Parrington 327, Box 353055, Seattle, WA 98195-3055, (206) 685-2214, E-mail: dgoldhab@u.washington.edu.

Number awarded 2 each year.

Deadline December of each year.

[595]
AES/PHEAA DISSERTATION FELLOWSHIP

Pennsylvania Higher Education Assistance Agency
Attn: State Grant and Special Programs Division
1200 North Seventh Street
Harrisburg, PA 17102-1444
(717) 720-2800   Toll-free: (800) 692-7392
TDD: (717) 720-2366   E-mail: info@pheaa.org
Web: www.pheaa.org/specialprograms/index.shtml

Purpose To provide funding for dissertation research to students in universities in Pennsylvania in fields related to the educational mission of American Education Services (AES) and the Pennsylvania Higher Education Assistance Agency (PHEAA).

Eligibility This program is open to doctoral candidates at Pennsylvania universities working in the fields of higher education, economics, psychology, public policy, sociology, and related fields. Applicants must be conducting policy-driven research that supports the AES/PHEAA mission: creating access to education. Examples of eligible topics include financial aid policies and college attendance costs; early outreach programs; and student recruitment, retention, and degree attainment. The thesis proposal must have been approved by the student's dissertation committee. Selection is based on the relationship of the proposed research to the AES/PHEAA mission, quality and significance of the proposed research, applicant's ability as evidenced by scholarly achievements and publications, feasibility of the work plan, letters of recom-

mendation, and commitment of the thesis advisor to the goals of the fellowship.

Financial data Fellows receive a stipend of $25,000 per year; additional funds for tuition for required thesis research credits, professional development (including conferences), and other research-related expenses; and a laptop computer and software.

Duration 18 months.

Additional information This program was established in 2003. Information is also available from American Education Services, 1200 North Seventh Street, Harrisburg, PA 17102, (717) 720-2794, Fax: (717) 720-3971, E-mail: research@aesSuccess.org.

Number awarded 1 or more each year.

Deadline November of each year.

[596]
ALABAMA SPACE GRANT CONSORTIUM GRADUATE FELLOWSHIP PROGRAM

Alabama Space Grant Consortium
c/o University of Alabama in Huntsville
Materials Science Building, Room 205
Huntsville, AL 35899
(256) 890-6800   Fax: (256) 890-6061
E-mail: jfreasoner@matsci.uah.edu
Web: www.uah.edu/ASGC

Purpose To provide financial assistance for graduate study or research related to the space sciences at universities participating in the Alabama Space Grant Consortium.

Eligibility This program is open to full-time graduate students enrolled at the universities participating in the consortium. Applicants must be studying in a field related to space, including the physical, natural, and biological sciences; engineering; education; economics; business; sociology; behavioral sciences; computer science; communications; law; international affairs; and public administration. They must 1) present a proposed research plan related to space that includes an extramural experience at a field center of the National Aeronautics and Space Administration (NASA); 2) propose a multidisciplinary plan and course of study; 3) plan to be involved in consortium outreach activities; and 4) intend to prepare for a career in line with NASA's aerospace, science, and technology programs. U.S. citizenship is required. Individuals from underrepresented groups (African Americans, Hispanics, American Indians, Pacific Islanders, and women of all races) are encouraged to apply. Interested students should submit a completed application form, a description of the proposed research or study program, a schedule, a budget, a list of references, a vitae, and undergraduate and graduate transcripts. Selection is based on 1) academic qualifications, 2) quality of the proposed research program or plan of study and its relevance to the aerospace science and technology program of NASA, 3) quality of the proposed interdisciplinary approach, 4) merit of the proposed utilization of a NASA center to carry out the objectives of the program, 5) prospects for completing the project within the allotted time, and 6) applicant's motivation for a career in aerospace.

Financial data The award for 12 months includes $16,000 for a student stipend and up to $6,000 for a tuition/student research allowance.

Duration Up to 36 months.

Additional information The member universities are University of Alabama in Huntsville, Alabama A&M University, University of Alabama, University of Alabama at Birmingham, University of South Alabama, Tuskegee University, and Auburn University. Funding for this program is provided by NASA.

Number awarded Varies each year; recently, 11 of these fellowships were awarded.

Deadline February of each year.

[597]
ALBERT M. GREENFIELD FOUNDATION DISSERTATION FELLOWSHIP

Library Company of Philadelphia
Attn: Librarian
1314 Locust Street
Philadelphia, PA 19107-5698
(215) 546-3181   Fax: (215) 546-5167
E-mail: jgreen@librarycompany.org
Web: www.librarycompany.org

Purpose To support dissertation research in fields and disciplines relating to the history of North America (particularly in the 18th and 19th centuries) at the Library Company of Philadelphia.

Eligibility This program is open to doctoral candidates interested in conducting dissertation research at the Library Company. The project proposal should demonstrate that the library has primary sources directly related to the intended research. The library's collection is particularly strong in Afro-Americana, German-Americana, American Judaica, history of women, domestic economy, banking and business, medicine, agriculture, natural history, philanthropy, education, art (including Philadelphia-area prints and photographs), architecture, technology, local and regional history, and the history of printing and publishing. The library also has a significant collection of British and Continental books and pamphlets from the 17th to 19th centuries.

Financial data The stipend is $1,800 per month.

Duration 1 academic year or 1 semester.

Number awarded Either 1 fellowship for a year or 2 for a semester are supported each year.

Deadline February of each year.

[598]
ALFRED D. CHANDLER, JR. TRAVELING FELLOWSHIPS IN BUSINESS HISTORY AND INSTITUTIONAL ECONOMIC HISTORY

Harvard Business School
Attn: Business History Review
South Hall 104
Soldiers Field
Boston, MA 02163
(617) 495-1003   Fax: (617) 495-0594
E-mail: wfriedman@hbs.edu
Web: www.hbs.edu/bhr/awards.html

Purpose To provide funding to students and scholars interested in conducting research in business history or institutional economic history.

Eligibility This program is open to 3 categories of applicants: 1) Harvard University graduate students in history, eco-

nomics, business administration, or a related discipline (such as sociology, government, or law) whose research requires travel to distant archives or repositories; 2) graduate students or nontenured faculty in those fields from other North American universities whose research requires travel to the Boston/Cambridge area; and 3) Harvard College undergraduates writing senior theses in those fields whose research requires similar travel. Applicants must be interested in conducting library and archival research in business history or institutional economic history, broadly defined.

Financial data Grants range from $1,000 to $3,000.

Duration These awards are granted annually.

Number awarded Varies; a total of $15,000 is available for this program each year.

Deadline November of each year.

[599]
AMERICAN HISTORY AND CULTURE SHORT-TERM FELLOWSHIPS

Library Company of Philadelphia
Attn: Librarian
1314 Locust Street
Philadelphia, PA 19107-5698
(215) 546-3181   Fax: (215) 546-5167
E-mail: jgreen@librarycompany.org
Web: www.librarycompany.org/Fellowships.htm

Purpose To support graduate and postdoctoral research in fields and disciplines relating to the history of North America (particularly in the 18th and 19th centuries).

Eligibility This program is open to candidates interested in conducting dissertation, postdoctoral, and advanced research. The project proposal should demonstrate that the Library Company has primary sources directly related to the intended research. The library's collection is particularly strong in Afro-Americana, German-Americana, American Judaica, history of women, domestic economy, banking and business, medicine, agriculture, natural history, philanthropy, education, art (including Philadelphia-area prints and photographs), architecture, technology, local and regional history, and the history of printing and publishing. The library also has a significant collection of British and Continental books and pamphlets from the 17th to 19th centuries.

Financial data The stipend is $1,800 per month.

Duration 1 month.

Additional information The Society for Historians of the Early American Republic (SHEAR) sponsors 2 fellowships that support research in American history in the early national period. The William Reese Company supports fellowships for research in American bibliography and the history of the book in the Americas. The William H. Helfand Fellowship supports research in the social history of medicine in American to 1900. The Library Company's Program in Early American Economy and Society (PEAES) offers 4 fellowships for research in that field. The Balch Institute for Ethnic Studies supports research in the HSP/Balch collections on the ethnic and immigrant experience in the United States and/or American cultural, social, political, or economic history since 1875. The American Society for Eighteenth-Century Studies (ASECS) sponsors a fellowship for research on projects related to the U.S. 18th century. Fellows are assisted in finding reasonably priced accommodations.

Number awarded Approximately 31 each year.
Deadline February of each year.

[600]
ASSOCIATION FOR WOMEN IN SCIENCE PREDOCTORAL AWARDS

Association for Women in Science
Attn: AWIS Educational Foundation
1200 New York Avenue, N.W., Suite 650
Washington, DC 20005
(202) 326-8940   Toll-free: (866) 657-AWIS
Fax: (202) 326-8960   E-mail: awisedfd@awis.org
Web: www.awis.org/resource/edfoundation.html

Purpose To provide research funding to predoctoral women students interested in preparing for careers in the natural and social sciences (including economics).

Eligibility This program is open to women enrolled in a Ph.D. program who have passed their department's qualifying exam and expect to complete their degree within 2 years. Applicants must be enrolled in a program in a natural or social science, including anthropology, archaeology, astronomy, biology, chemistry, computer and information science, demography, economics, engineering, geography, geoscience, history of science, linguistics, mathematics, philosophy of science, physics, political science, psychology, or sociology. Foreign students are eligible if they are enrolled in a U.S. institution of higher education. Selection is based on academic achievement, the importance of the research question addressed, the quality of the research, and the applicant's potential for future contributions to science or engineering.

Financial data The stipends are $1,000. Citations of merit are $300. Funds may be used for any aspect of education, including tuition, books, housing, research, travel and meeting registration, or publication costs.

Duration 1 year.

Additional information This program includes the Amy Lutz Rechel Award for a student in the field of plant biology, the Luise Meyer-Schutzmeister Award for a student in physics, the Diane H. Russell Award for a student in the fields of biochemistry or pharmacology, the Gail Naughton Graduate Award for an outstanding graduate student, and the Ruth Satter Memorial Awards for women who interrupted their education for 3 years or more to raise a family. Information is also available from Barbara Filner, President, AWIS Educational Foundation, 7008 Richard Drive, Bethesda, MD 20817-4838.

Number awarded 5 to 10 each year.
Deadline January of each year.

[601]
BEHAVIORAL SCIENCES STUDENT FELLOWSHIPS IN EPILEPSY

Epilepsy Foundation
Attn: Research Department
4351 Garden City Drive
Landover, MD 20785-7223
(301) 459-3700   Toll-free: (800) EFA-1000
Fax: (301) 577-2684   TDD: (800) 332-2070
E-mail: grants@efa.org
Web: www.epilepsyfoundation.org/research/grants.cfm

Purpose To provide funding to undergraduate and graduate students interested in working on a summer research training project in a field relevant to epilepsy (including economics).

Eligibility This program is open to undergraduate and graduate students in a behavioral science program relevant to epilepsy research or clinical care, including, but not limited to, sociology, social work, psychology, anthropology, nursing, economics, vocational rehabilitation, counseling, and political science. Applicants must be interested in pursuing an epilepsy research project under the supervision of a qualified mentor. Because the program is designed as a training opportunity, the quality of the training plans and environment are considered in the selection process. Other selection criteria include the quality of the proposed project, the relevance of the proposed work to epilepsy, the applicant's interest in the field of epilepsy, the applicant's qualifications, and the mentor's qualifications, including his or her commitment to the student and the project. U.S. citizenship is not required, but the project must be conducted in the United States. Applications from women, members of minority groups, and people with disabilities are especially encouraged.

Financial data The grant is $3,000.

Duration 3 months during the summer.

Additional information This program is supported by the American Epilepsy Society, Abbott Laboratories, Ortho-McNeil Pharmaceutical Corporation, and Pfizer Inc.

Number awarded Varies each year; recently, 4 of these fellowships were awarded.

Deadline February of each year.

[602]
BYRON HANKE FELLOWSHIP FOR GRADUATE RESEARCH ON COMMUNITY ASSOCIATIONS

Community Associations Institute Research Foundation
Attn: Manager, Research Foundation Programs
225 Reinekers Lane, Suite 300
Alexandria, VA 22314-2875
(703) 548-8600, ext. 340   Fax: (703) 684-1581
E-mail: sayres@caionline.org
Web: www.cairf.org/schol/hanke.html

Purpose To provide funding to graduate students interested in working on research related to community associations.

Eligibility Applicants must be enrolled in an accredited master's, doctoral, or law program. They may be working in any subject area, but their proposed research must relate to community associations (organizations that govern common-interest communities of any kind—condominiums, cooperatives, townhouse developments, planned unit developments, and other developments where homeowners support an asso ciation with mandatory financial assessments and are subject to use and aesthetic restrictions). Academic disciplines include law, economics, sociology, and urban planning. The foundation is especially interested in substantive papers from the social sciences which place community association housing within political or economic organizational models. Minority applicants are particularly encouraged to apply. Selection is based on academic achievement, faculty recommendations, demonstrated research and writing ability, and nature of the proposed topic and its benefit to the study and understanding of community associations.

Financial data Grants range from $2,000 to $4,000. Funds are paid in 2 equal installments and may be used for tuition, books, or other educational expenses.

Duration 1 year.

Additional information The foundation may publish the final project. Recipients must provide the foundation with a copy of their final project.

Deadline Applications may be submitted at any time.

[603]
CASUALTY ACTUARIAL SOCIETY/SOCIETY OF ACTUARIES PH.D. GRANTS

Society of Actuaries
Attn: Committee on Knowledge Extension Research
475 North Martingale Road, Suite 800
Schaumburg, IL 60173-2226
(847) 706-3565   Fax: (847) 706-3599
E-mail: sbaker@soa.org
Web: www.soa.org/academic

Purpose To encourage graduate students to complete research on topics related to actuarial science and to prepare for an academic career in North America.

Eligibility This program is open to individuals who have been admitted to Ph.D. candidacy by their institution and who have a thesis topic that deals with actuarial science or a related area. Grants are awarded on the basis of individual merit. The relevance of the thesis topic is the primary consideration in the evaluation process. Preference is given to candidates who are likely to prepare for an academic career in North America. Preference is also given to candidates who are members of, or are working toward becoming members of, the Casualty Actuarial Society or the Society of Actuaries.

Financial data The grant is $10,000 per academic year.

Duration 1 year; may be renewed for up to 2 additional years.

Additional information The Casualty Actuarial Society and the Society of Actuaries are international research, education, and membership organizations that promote the advancement of the state of actuarial science.

Number awarded Varies each year; recently, 3 new and 3 renewal grants were awarded.

Deadline February of each year.

[604]
CHARLES G. KOCH SUMMER FELLOW PROGRAM

Institute for Humane Studies at George Mason University
3301 North Fairfax Drive, Suite 440
Arlington, VA 22201-4432
(703) 993-4880   Toll-free: (800) 697-8799
Fax: (703) 993-4890   E-mail: ihs@gmu.edu
Web: www.TheIHS.org

Purpose To provide students and recent graduates with experience at a market-oriented research organization in Washington, D.C.

Eligibility This program is open to undergraduates, graduate students, and recent graduates. Applicants must be planning careers in public policy and be interested in a program that includes seminars on market-based public policy and policy analysis as well as an internship at a market-oriented research organization in Washington, D.C. Along with their application, they must submit 1) a list of the 5 intellectual figures or books that have most influenced their philosophical and political thinking; 2) a 1-page resume listing their academic and professional experience, honors and awards, extracurricular activities, and 2 references; 3) a 250-word statement on their career goals and how this fellowship would help them reach those; 4) a 500-word statement about which policy issues and potential host organizations interest them and why; and 5) a 500-word essay on a major issue of public policy.

Financial data The program provides a $1,500 stipend, round-trip airfare to the Washington area, books and study materials, and housing in the Virginia suburbs of Washington.

Duration 10 weeks during the summer: 2 weeks for seminars at the Institute for Humane Studies in Arlington, Virginia and 8 weeks for the internship.

Number awarded 40 each year.

Deadline February of each year.

[605]
DELOITTE DOCTORAL FELLOWSHIPS

Deloitte Foundation
Attn: Manager, Academic Development and University Relations
10 Westport Road
Wilton, CT 06897-0820
(203) 761-3179   Fax: (203) 563-2324
Web: www.deloitte.com

Purpose To provide financial assistance for study or research to doctoral candidates in accounting.

Eligibility This program is open to graduate students working on a doctoral degree in accounting at an accredited university who have completed 2 or more semesters of the program. Applicants should be preparing for careers in teaching.

Financial data The total grant is $25,000, disbursed in 4 payments: $2,500 when the director of the recipient's doctoral program considers that the fellow is 12 months from completing all required course work and examinations, $2,500 6 months later, $10,000 at the time the fellow's dissertation topic is approved and work on the dissertation begins, and $10,000 6 months later.

Duration 2 years: the final year of course work and the year immediately following, in which fellows are expected to complete their dissertations.

Number awarded Up to 10 each year.

Deadline October of each year.

[606]
DISSERTATION FELLOWSHIP IN BUSINESS AND AMERICAN CULTURE

Newcomen Society of the United States
Attn: Director of Publications
412 Newcomen Road
Exton, PA 19341-1999
(610) 363-6600   Fax: (610) 363-0612
Toll-free: (800) 466-7604   E-mail: info@newcomen.org
Web: www.newcomen.org/dissertation.html

Purpose To provide funding to doctoral candidates interested in working on a dissertation in American business history.

Eligibility This program is open to doctoral candidates interested in preparing for a career studying and teaching the history of American business. Applicants must be able to devote full-time effort to research, writing, and graduate study. Preference is given to candidates who are already writing their dissertations.

Financial data The stipend is $10,000.

Duration 9 months.

Number awarded 1 each year.

[607]
DWIGHT EISENHOWER/CLIFFORD ROBERTS GRADUATE FELLOWSHIPS

Eisenhower Institute
915 15th Street, N.W., Eighth Floor
Washington, DC 20005
(202) 628-4444   Fax: (202) 628-4445
E-mail: apark@eisenhowerinstitute.org
Web: www.eisenhowerinstitute.org

Purpose To provide financial assistance to doctoral candidates completing their dissertations on selected subjects at designated universities.

Eligibility This program is open to doctoral candidates completing their dissertations at a participating university. Applicants must be majoring in international relations, security studies, government, economics, business administration, or history.

Financial data The stipend is $10,000 per year.

Duration 1 year.

Additional information The participating universities are Chicago, Columbia, Cornell, Harvard, Kansas, Princeton, Stanford, Texas at Austin, Vanderbilt, Virginia, and Washington of St. Louis.

Number awarded 4 each year.

[608]
FELLOWSHIPS IN SCIENCE AND INTERNATIONAL AFFAIRS

Harvard University
John F. Kennedy School of Government
Belfer Center for Science and International Affairs
Attn: Fellowship Coordinator
79 John F. Kennedy Street
Cambridge, MA 02138
(617) 495-3745   Fax: (617) 495-8963
E-mail: kathleen_siddell@harvard.edu
Web: bcsia.ksg.harvard.edu

Purpose To provide funding for research (by professionals, postdoctorates, or graduate students) in areas of interest to the Belfer Center for Science and International Affairs at Harvard University in Cambridge, Massachusetts.

Eligibility The postdoctoral fellowship is open to recent recipients of the Ph.D. or equivalent degree, university faculty members, and employees of government, military, international, humanitarian, and private research institutions who have appropriate professional experience. Applicants for predoctoral fellowships must have passed general examinations. Lawyers, economists, physical scientists, and others of diverse disciplinary backgrounds are also welcome to apply. The program especially encourages applications from women, minorities, and citizens of all countries. All applicants must be interested in conducting research in 1 of the 5 major program areas of the center: the international security program; the environment and natural resources program; the science, technology, and public policy program; the World Peace Foundation program on intrastate conflict, conflict prevention, and conflict resolution; and the Caspian Studies program. Fellowships may also be available in other specialized programs, such as science, technology, and globalization; managing the atom; domestic preparedness for terrorism; science and technology for sustainability; and energy technology innovation.

Financial data The stipend is $34,000 for postdoctoral research fellows or $20,000 for predoctoral research fellows. Health insurance is also provided.

Duration 10 months.

Number awarded A limited number each year.

Deadline January of each year.

[609]
GRANTS FOR HEALTH SERVICES DISSERTATION RESEARCH

Agency for Healthcare Research and Quality
Attn: Division of Grants Management
2101 East Jefferson Street, Suite 601
Rockville, MD 20852-4908
(301) 594-1843   Fax: (301) 594-3210
E-mail: Adeal@ahrq.gov
Web: www.ahrq.gov

Purpose To provide financial assistance to doctoral candidates engaged in research for a dissertation that examines some aspect of the health care system.

Eligibility This program is open to student enrolled in an accredited research doctoral degree (e.g., Ph.D., Sc.D., Dr.P.H., Ed.D.) program. Applicants must have completed all requirements for the doctoral degree other than the dissertation. The dissertation topic must relate to health services research, including social, behavioral, biostatistical, epidemiological, economic, education, policy, management, medical, nursing, or health sciences. Priority is given to research on health issues related to designated populations, including racial and ethnic minorities, women, children, older adults, low income groups, and individuals with special health care needs (such as individuals with disabilities and individuals who need chronic care or end-of-life health care). U.S. citizenship is not required, but candidates who are neither U.S. citizens nor permanent residents must apply through their institution.

Financial data Total direct costs may not exceed $30,000. Funds may be used for the investigator's salary, direct project expenses (travel, data purchasing, data processing, and supplies), and matriculation fees. The institution will receive facilities and administrative costs of 8% of total allowable direct costs exclusive of tuition and related fees, health insurance, and expenditures for equipment.

Duration Normally for 12 months or less, but may be for up to 17 months.

Number awarded Up to 30 each year.

Deadline January, May, or September of each year.

[610]
HAMBURG FELLOWSHIP PROGRAM

Stanford University
Center for International Security and Cooperation
Attn: Fellowship Program Coordinator
Encina Hall, Room E210
616 Serra Street
Stanford, CA 94305-6165
(650) 723-9626   Fax: (650) 723-0089
E-mail: barbara.platt@stanford.edu
Web: www.cisac.stanford.edu

Purpose To provide funding to doctoral students who are interested in working on their dissertation at Stanford University's Center for International Security and Cooperation (which must focus on issues related to preventing deadly conflict).

Eligibility This program is open to advanced doctoral students who have completed all of the curricular and residency requirements at their own institutions and who are engaged in the research and write-up stage of their dissertations in a field related to the prevention of deadly conflict. Applicants must be interested in writing their dissertation at Stanford University's Center for International Security and Cooperation. Fields of study may include anthropology, economics, history, law, political science, sociology, medicine, or the natural and physical sciences. Specific topics might include issues of policing, judiciaries, and civil-military relations; the use of sanctions and other economic tools for the prevention of conflict; early warning mechanisms, mediation processes, and other forms of third-party intervention; environmental degradation and its effects on deadly conflict; the role of non-lethal weapons and other military technologies in preventing conflict; the role of leadership in prevention of conflict. Applications from women and minorities are encouraged.

Financial data The stipend is $20,000. Reimbursement for some travel and health insurance expenses may be available for fellows and their immediate dependents.

Duration 9 months.

Additional information This program began in 1997. It honors Dr. David Hamburg, the retiring president of the Carnegie Corporation of New York, whose gift to the center made the program possible. Fellows join faculty, research staff, and other fellows at the center, where they have an office to ensure their integration into the full spectrum of research activities.

Number awarded Varies each year.

Deadline January of each year.

[611]
HERB SOCIETY OF AMERICA RESEARCH GRANT PROGRAM

Herb Society of America
9019 Kirtland Chardon Road
Kirtland, OH 44094
(440) 256-0514   Fax: (440) 256-0541
E-mail: herbs@herbsociety.org
Web: www.herbsociety.org

Purpose To fund research involving the use of herbs.

Eligibility This program is open to persons who are proposing a scientific, academic, or artistic investigation of herbal plants. Fields of study may include horticulture, science, literature, history, art, and/or economics. Although both undergraduate and graduate students may apply, they may use the funds only for specific research on herbal projects, not as financial aid for education. Research should involve plants using the horticultural rather than the botanical definition of herbs. Proposals may not exceed 500 words. Finalists will be interviewed.

Financial data Up to $5,000 per year. Funds may not be used for travel.

Duration Up to 1 year.

Additional information Progress reports are required 3 times during the year.

Number awarded 1 or 2 grants are awarded each year.

Deadline January of each year.

[612]
INDEPENDENT INSTITUTE INTERNSHIPS

Independent Institute
Attn: Academic Affairs Director
100 Swan Way
Oakland, CA 94621-1428
(510) 632-1366, ext. 117   Fax: (510) 568-6040
E-mail: cclose@independent.org
Web: www.independent.org

Purpose To provide research experience at the Independent Institute in Oakland, California to college students interested in public policy issues.

Eligibility This program is open to undergraduate students, preferably those studying economics, law, public policy, political science, or related social sciences. Applicants must be interested in conducting policy research on such topics as high technology and antitrust, environmental policy, crime and security, money and finance, or health and welfare. They must submit a copy of their college transcript, 2 writing samples, a letter explaining their academic and career goals, and an indication of when they prefer to start and end their internship.

Financial data The stipend is $700 per month.

Duration 8 weeks, year-round.

Number awarded Varies each year.

Deadline Applications may be submitted at any time.

[613]
INSTITUTE FOR SUPPLY MANAGEMENT DOCTORAL DISSERTATION GRANT PROGRAM

Institute for Supply Management
Attn: Senior Vice President
2055 East Centennial Circle
P.O. Box 22160
Tempe, AZ 85285-2160
(480) 752-6276, ext. 3029
Toll-free: (800) 888-6276, ext. 3029
Fax: (480) 752-7890   E-mail: jcavinato@ism.ws
Web: www.ism.ws/OnlineGuides/doctoralgrant.cfm

Purpose To provide financial support to doctoral candidates who are conducting dissertation research in purchasing or related fields.

Eligibility Eligible to apply are doctoral candidates who are working on a Ph.D. or D.B.A. in purchasing, business, management, logistics, economics, industrial engineering, or a related field at an accredited university in the United States. Candidates must be citizens or permanent residents of the United States. Examples of research projects that could be funded include: purchasing and supply measurement, supply networks, costing/pricing models and applications, electronic supply development, supply's role in corporate success, or strategic development of supply. To apply, students must submit an application form; official transcripts from all academic institutions attended; 3 letters of recommendation; a proposal (up to 25 pages) that discusses hypotheses, significance of the study, research methodology, and value of the research to the field of purchasing; and a letter of endorsement from the applicant's major advisor, stating that the dissertation topic is acceptable.

Financial data The grant is $10,000.

Duration 1 year.

Additional information The sponsoring organization was previously known as the National Association of Purchasing Management.

Number awarded 4 each year.

Deadline January of each year.

[614]
INSTITUTE ON GLOBAL CONFLICT AND COOPERATION DISSERTATION FELLOWSHIPS

University of California at San Diego
Attn: Institute on Global Conflict and Cooperation
Robinson Building Complex
9500 Gilman Drive
La Jolla, CA 92093-0518
(858) 534-7224   Fax: (858) 534-7655
E-mail: cgilhoi@ucsd.edu
Web: www-igcc.ucsd.edu

Purpose To provide funding to doctoral students at the 9 University of California campuses who are interested in conducting dissertation research on the causes of international conflict (including economic aspects).

Eligibility This program is open to doctoral students (including J.D./Ph.D. and M.D./Ph.D. candidates) at the 9 University of California campuses: Berkeley, Davis, Irvine, Los Angeles, Riverside, San Diego, San Francisco, Santa Barbara, and Santa Cruz. Applicants must be currently enrolled and have advanced to candidacy for their Ph.D. Doctoral students from all disciplines are eligible, but they should be interested in conducting dissertation research on international conflict. Preference is given to proposals that relate to the causes of international conflict, ethnic conflict, and terrorism; international and regional cooperation on health, technology, culture, and social issues; international dispute resolution; international and regional cooperation on security, economic, and legal issues; international environmental policy; innovations in international cooperation; the economics, politics, and sociology of transnational flows of capital, goods, technology, and people; transnational social movements and nongovernmental organizations; and gender issues and international politics. Standard dissertation fellowships have been offered to candidates from such disciplines as anthropology, communications, economics, energy resources, environmental studies, geography, history, legal studies, philosophy, political science, religious studies, sociology, and urban development. U.S. citizenship is not required.

Financial data The stipend is $12,000. Travel and research support up to $4,000 may also be awarded for the first year only.

Duration 1 year; may be renewed for 1 additional year.

Additional information This program has also offered special scholarships in the past and may do so again. Those include a foreign policy studies dissertation fellowship (which requires residency in the Washington, D.C. office of the institute) and the Herbert York Fellowship (for students conducting research on international policy issues in natural science, engineering, or science policy, including at least 1 academic quarter at the Lawrence Livermore or Los Alamos National Laboratories).

Number awarded Varies each year; recently, 14 of these fellowships were available.

Deadline January of each year.

[615]
INTERNATIONAL SECURITY AND COOPERATION PREDOCTORAL FELLOWSHIPS

Stanford University
Center for International Security and Cooperation
Attn: Fellowship Program Coordinator
Encina Hall, Room E210
616 Serra Street
Stanford, CA 94305-6165
(650) 723-9626   Fax: (650) 723-0089
E-mail: barbara.platt@stanford.edu
Web: www.cisac.stanford.edu

Purpose To provide funding to doctoral students who are interested in writing a dissertation on the problems of arms control and international security at Stanford University's Center for International Security and Cooperation.

Eligibility Students currently enrolled in doctoral programs at academic institutions in the United States who would benefit from access to the facilities offered by the center are eligible to apply. Fields of study might include anthropology, economics, history, law, political science, sociology, medicine, or the natural and physical sciences. Topics suitable for support might include the causes and prevention of terrorism; security relationships around the world; U.S.-Russian strategic relations; peacekeeping; prevention of deadly conflicts; U.S. defense and arms control policies; proliferation of nuclear, chemical, and biological weapons; security in south and east Asia; the commercialization of national defense technologies; and ethnic and civil conflict. The center is especially interested in receiving applications from minorities and women.

Financial data The stipend is $20,000. Additional funds may be available for dependents and travel.

Duration 9 months.

Number awarded Varies; generally, 4 each year.

Deadline January of each year.

[616]
LAND ECONOMICS FOUNDATION GRADUATE SCHOLARSHIP

Lambda Alpha International
Attn: Land Economics Foundation
710 East Ogden Avenue, Suite 600
Naperville, IL 60563-8614
(630) 579-3284   Fax: (630) 369-2488
E-mail: lai@lai.org
Web: www.lai.org/lef/index.html

Purpose To provide funding to graduate students interested in working on a paper in a field related to land economics.

Eligibility This program is open to graduate students at universities in the United States and Canada who are working on a degree in land economics, architecture, law, geography, urban planning, landscape architecture, environmental planning, civil engineering, government, public administration, real estate, or urban studies. Applicants must be interested in working on a project that will result in completion of a paper. As part of the application, they must indicate the project objectives, the relationship to and impact on other work being done in the same field, the target audience, the proposed procedures they will use, the proposed time schedule, and any other financial resources needed and/or available. Selection is based on the significance of the contribution of the paper to the field of land economics, the qualifications of the applicant relative to the paper's goals and implementation requirement, the soundness of the proposal, and the overall quality of the application.

Financial data The grant is $3,000.

Duration 1 year; may be renewed for 1 additional year.

Additional information Lambda Alpha International is an international honorary society of land economics professionals; it was founded in 1930. The sponsoring organization has the right to publish the paper or ask the student to present it at a meeting.

Number awarded 1 each year.

Deadline February of each year.

[617]
LUNG HEALTH RESEARCH DISSERTATION GRANTS

American Lung Association
Attn: Grants and Awards
61 Broadway, Sixth Floor
New York, NY 10006
(212) 315-8793   Toll-free: (800) LUNG-USA
Fax: (212) 265-5642
Web: www.lungusa.org/research

Purpose To provide funding to doctoral candidates interested in conducting dissertation research on issues relevant to people with lung disease (including economic issues).

Eligibility This program is open to full-time doctoral students in the behavioral and social sciences who have an academic career focus; fields of study include psychology, sociology, nursing, epidemiology, health economics, biostatistics, health policy, health care administration, and public health. Nurses in any field who are interested in lung disease may also apply. Individuals with an M.D. degree who wish to acquire a Ph.D. are not eligible. Generally, individuals conducting laboratory research that does not involve patients or patient data are not eligible. Applicants must be U.S. citizens, permanent residents, or foreign residents authorized to work in the United States and enrolled in a U.S. institution. Selection is based on the applicant's education and experience; the scientific merit, innovation, and feasibility of the research plan and its relevance to the mission of the American Lung Association; and the research environment.

Financial data The grant is $21,000 per year (including up to $16,000 for stipend and $5,000 for research support).

Duration Up to 2 years.

Number awarded 1 or more each year.

Deadline September of each year.

[618]
MILLER CENTER FELLOWSHIPS IN CONTEMPORARY HISTORY, PUBLIC POLICY AND AMERICAN POLITICS

University of Virginia
Attn: Miller Center of Public Affairs
2201 Old Ivy Road
P.O. Box 400406
Carlottesville, VA 22904-4406
(443) 924-4694   Fax: (434) 982-2739
E-mail: mplynch@virginia.edu
Web: www.millercenter.virginia.edu

Purpose To provide funding to Ph.D. candidates and other scholars who are completing dissertations or books on 20th-century politics and governance in the United States.

Eligibility This program is open to 1) Ph.D. candidates who are completing their dissertations and 2) independent scholars who are writing books. Applicants may be working in a broad range of disciplines, including history, political science, policy studies, law, political economy, and sociology, but their project must relate to 20th-century U.S. politics and governance. Selection is based on the scholarly quality of the proposal and its potential to shed new light on important public policy questions.

Financial data The stipend is $18,000 per year.

Duration 1 year.

Additional information Recipients are encouraged, but not required, to be in residence at the Miller Center of Public Affairs at the University of Virginia. Fellows are expected to complete their dissertation or book during the fellowship year.

Number awarded Up to 10 each year.

Deadline January of each year.

[619]
NATIONAL OCEANIC AND ATMOSPHERIC ADMINISTRATION EDUCATIONAL PARTNERSHIP PROGRAM WITH MINORITY SERVING INSTITUTIONS GRADUATE SCIENCES PROGRAM

Oak Ridge Institute for Science and Education
Attn: Education and Training Division
P.O. Box 117
Oak Ridge, TN 37831-0117
(865) 576-9272   Fax: (865) 241-5220
E-mail: babcockc@orau.gov
Web: www.orau.gov/orise.htm

Purpose To provide financial assistance and summer research experience to graduate students at minority serving institutions who are majoring in scientific fields of interest to the National Oceanic and Atmospheric Administration (NOAA).

Eligibility This program is open to graduate students working on master's or doctoral degrees at minority serving institutions, including Hispanic Serving Institutions (HSIs), Historically Black Colleges and Universities (HBCUs), and Tribal Colleges and Universities (TCUs). Applicants must be majoring in biology, chemistry, computer science, economics, engineering, geography, geology, mathematics, physical science, physics, social science, or other fields specific to NOAA, such as cartography, environmental planning, fishery biology, hydrology, meteorology, or oceanography. They must also be interested in participating in a training program during the summer at a NOAA research facility.

Financial data During the school year, the program provides payment of tuition and fees, books, housing, meals, and travel expenses. During the summer, students receive a salary and benefits.

Duration 2 years of study plus 16 weeks of research training during the summer.

Additional information This program is funded by NOAA and administered by the Education and Training Division (ETD) of Oak Ridge Institute for Science and Education (ORISE).

Number awarded 5 each year.

Deadline January of each year.

[620]
NATIONAL OCEANIC AND ATMOSPHERIC ADMINISTRATION STUDENT RESEARCH PARTICIPATION PROGRAM

Oak Ridge Institute for Science and Education
Attn: Education and Training Division
P.O. Box 117
Oak Ridge, TN 37831-0117
(865) 576-8158   Fax: (865) 241-5220
E-mail: riderh@orau.gov
Web: www.orau.gov/orise.htm

Purpose To provide funding to students who wish to participate in research and development activities during the summer at the National Oceanic and Atmospheric Administration (NOAA) headquarters and field centers.

Eligibility This program is open to undergraduate and graduate students in business, computer sciences, engineering, physical sciences, or life sciences. Applicants must propose to participate in research and development activities at NOAA headquarters (Silver Spring, Maryland) or field centers. U.S. citizenship or permanent resident status is required.

Financial data The weekly stipend ranges from $420 to $515, depending on academic level; also provided is limited travel reimbursement for round-trip transportation between the facility and home or campus.

Duration 10 weeks during the summer.

Additional information This program is funded by NOAA through an interagency agreement with the U.S. Department of Energy and administered by the Education and Training Division (ETD) of Oak Ridge Institute for Science and Education (ORISE).

Number awarded Varies each year.

Deadline Applications may be submitted at any time.

[621]
PROGRAM IN EARLY AMERICAN ECONOMY AND SOCIETY LONG-TERM FELLOWSHIPS

Library Company of Philadelphia
Attn: Program in Early American Economy and Society
1314 Locust Street
Philadelphia, PA 19107-5698
(215) 546-3181   Fax: (215) 546-5167
E-mail: cmatson@librarycompany.org
Web: www.librarycompany.org

Purpose To support postdoctoral and dissertation research on early American economic history at the Library Company of Philadelphia.

Eligibility This program is open to 1) postdoctoral scholars, and 2) doctoral candidates working on their dissertations. Applicants must be interested in conducting research at the library on the origins and development of early American business to roughly the 1850s. They must need to use the printed and manuscript collections related to the history of commerce, finance, technology, manufacturing, agriculture, internal improvements, and political economy that are held by the library and by other institutions in its vicinity.

Financial data The stipends are $40,000 for postdoctoral scholars or $17,500 for doctoral candidates. Awards may be divided between 2 recipients, each of whom would receive $20,000 (if postdoctoral scholars) or $8,750 (if doctoral candidates).

Duration 9 months, starting in September. If the awards are divided, each recipient would be supported for approximately 1 academic semester.

Number awarded 2 (or 4) each year: 1 (or 2) to postdoctoral scholars and 1 (or 2) to doctoral candidates.

Deadline February of each year.

[622]
STATE FARM COMPANIES FOUNDATION DOCTORAL DISSERTATION AWARDS

State Farm Companies Foundation
Attn: Doctoral Dissertation Award
One State Farm Plaza
Bloomington, IL 61710-0001
(309) 766-2161   Fax: (309) 766-3700
Web: www.statefarm.com/foundati/doctoral.htm

Purpose To provide financial assistance to doctoral candidates whose dissertation topic relates to insurance and risk management or to business.

Eligibility This program is open to doctoral candidates who have completed a major portion of their course work for a degree in either business or insurance and risk management. Applicants must be U.S. citizens who have started writing, but not yet completed, a dissertation on a business topic that relates to general business principles and issues or an insurance and risk management topic that directly relates to or benefits the insurance industry. Selection is based on academic achievement, quality of the dissertation proposal, and recommendations from the dissertation advisor and faculty members.

Financial data The program awards $10,000 to the student recipient and $3,000 to the recipient's school.

Duration 1 year.

Number awarded Generally 6 each year: 3 in each category.

Deadline March of each year.

[623]
WILLY Z. SADEH GRADUATE STUDENT AWARD IN SPACE ENGINEERING AND SPACE SCIENCES

American Institute of Aeronautics and Astronautics
Attn: Student Programs Director
1801 Alexander Bell Drive, Suite 500
Reston, VA 20191-4344
(703) 264-7536   Toll-free: (800) 639-AIAA, ext. 536
Fax: (703) 264-7551   E-mail: stephenb@aiaa.org
Web: www.aiaa.org

Purpose To provide financial assistance for graduate research in space science and engineering.

Eligibility This program is open to graduate students who are specializing in space-based research at an accredited college or university anywhere in the world. Applicants must be enrolled in a graduate degree program that requires research in 1) space engineering pertaining to agricultural engineering, bioengineering, civil engineering and infrastructure, fluid dynamics, or geotechnical engineering; 2) space life sciences, encompassing agricultural sciences, biology, biosphere and life support sciences, food sciences and human nutrition, physiology, or plant sciences; or 3) space policy concerning

economics, history, law, public policy, or science and technology. Selection is based on student academic accomplishments, research record, letter of recommendation, and quality of the research proposal (content, methodology, originality, and practical application).

Financial data The grant is $5,000. The fellow also receives travel stipends to attend the AIAA Aerospace Sciences Meeting and the International Astronautical Federation Congress.

Duration 1 year; nonrenewable.

Additional information This program was instituted in 2000.

Number awarded 1 each year.

Deadline January of each year.

[624]
WISCONSIN SPACE GRANT CONSORTIUM GRADUATE FELLOWSHIPS

Wisconsin Space Grant Consortium
c/o University of Wisconsin at Green Bay
Natural and Applied Sciences
2420 Nicolet Drive
Green Bay, WI 54311-7001
(920) 465-2941   Fax: (920) 465-2376
E-mail: brandts@uwgb.edu
Web: www.uwgb.edu/wsgc

Purpose To provide financial assistance to graduate students at member institutions of the Wisconsin Space Grant Consortium (WSGC) who are interested in conducting aerospace, space science, or other interdisciplinary aerospace-related research.

Eligibility This program is open to graduate students enrolled at the universities participating in the WSGC. Applicants must be U.S. citizens; be enrolled full time in a master's or Ph.D. program related to space science, aerospace, or interdisciplinary aerospace studies (including, but not limited to, engineering, the sciences, architecture, law, business, and medicine); have a GPA of 3.0 or higher; and be interested in conducting space-related research. The consortium especially encourages applications from underrepresented minorities, women, persons with disabilities, and those pursuing interdisciplinary aerospace studies. Selection is based on academic performance and space-related promise.

Financial data Grants up to $5,000 per year are provided.

Duration 1 academic year.

Additional information Funding for this program is provided by the U.S. National Aeronautics and Space Administration. The schools participating in the consortium include the University of Wisconsin campuses at Green Bay, La Crosse, Madison, Milwaukee, Oshkosh, Parkside, and Whitewater; College of the Menominee Nation; Marquette University; Carroll College; Lawrence University; Milwaukee School of Engineering; Ripon College; and Medical College of Wisconsin.

Number awarded Varies each year; recently, 7 of these fellowships were awarded.

Deadline February of each year.

[625]
WISCONSIN SPACE GRANT CONSORTIUM UNDERGRADUATE RESEARCH AWARDS

Wisconsin Space Grant Consortium
c/o University of Wisconsin at Madison
Space Science and Engineering Center
1225 West Dayton Street, Room 251
Madison, WI 53706-1280
(608) 263-4206   Fax: (608) 263-5974
E-mail: toma@ssec.wisc.edu
Web: www.uwgb.edu/wsgc

Purpose To provide funding to undergraduate students at colleges and universities participating in the Wisconsin Space Grant Consortium (WSGC) who are interested in conducting space-related research.

Eligibility This program is open to undergraduate students enrolled at 1 of the institutions participating in the WSGC. Applicants must be U.S. citizens; be enrolled full time in an undergraduate program related to space science, aerospace, or interdisciplinary space studies; and have a GPA of 3.0 or higher. They must be proposing to create and implement a small research project of their own design as academic year, summer, or part-time employment that is directly related to their interests and career objectives in space science, aerospace, or space-related studies. Students must request a faculty or research staff member on their campus to act as an advisor; the consortium locates a scientist or engineer from 1 of the research-intensive universities to serve as a second mentor for successful applicants. The consortium especially encourages applications from students pursuing interdisciplinary space studies (e.g., engineering, the sciences, architecture, law, business, and medicine), underrepresented minorities, women, and persons with disabilities. Selection is based on academic performance and space-related promise.

Financial data Stipends up to $3,500 per year or summer session are available. An additional $500 may be awarded for exceptional expenses, such as high travel costs.

Duration 1 academic year or summer.

Additional information Funding for this program is provided by the U.S. National Aeronautics and Space Administration. The schools participating in the consortium include the University of Wisconsin campuses at Green Bay, La Crosse, Madison, Milwaukee, Oshkosh, Parkside, and Whitewater; College of the Menominee Nation; Marquette University; Carroll College; Lawrence University; Milwaukee School of Engineering; Ripon College; and Medical College of Wisconsin.

Number awarded Varies each year; recently, 9 of these grants were awarded.

Deadline February of each year.

[626]
YOUNG COMMUNICATORS FELLOWSHIPS

Institute for Humane Studies at George Mason University
3301 North Fairfax Drive, Suite 440
Arlington, VA 22201-4432
(703) 993-4880   Toll-free: (800) 697-8799
Fax: (703) 993-4890   E-mail: ihs@gmu.edu
Web: www.TheIHS.org/tab1/ycf.html

Purpose To provide funding for research and other training to upper-division and graduate students as well as recent graduates who are interested in a career in communications.

Eligibility This program is open to college juniors and seniors, graduate students, and recent graduates. Applicants must have a clearly demonstrated interest in the "classical liberal" tradition of individual rights and market economics; intend to prepare for a career in journalism, film, writing (fiction or nonfiction), publishing, or market-oriented public policy; and have arranged or applied for an internship, training program, or other short-term opportunity related to their intended career. Applications are not accepted for tuition or living expenses associated with a degree.

Financial data The program provides a stipend of up to $2,500 and housing and travel assistance up to $2,500 (if required).

Duration Up to 12 weeks.

Number awarded Varies each year.

Deadline March of each year for summer programs; up to 10 weeks in advance for programs at other times of the year.

Awards

Described here are 48 competitions, prizes, and honoraria granted to undergraduate or graduate students in recognition or support of their personal accomplishments, professional contributions, or service in business or a related field. Prizes received solely as the result of entering contests are excluded.

[627]
AAMI YOUNG INVESTIGATOR COMPETITION

Association for the Advancement of Medical
    Instrumentation
Attn: Education Department
1110 North Glebe Road, Suite 220
Arlington, VA 22201-4795
(703) 525-4890, ext. 212
Toll-free: (800) 332-2264, ext. 212
Fax: (703) 276-0793   E-mail: ahaynes@aami.org
Web: www.aami.org/awards/yic.html

Purpose To recognize and reward student authors of outstanding research papers on medical instrumentation and technology (along with management issues).

Eligibility This competition is open to undergraduate, graduate, and medical students; interns; residents; postdoctoral fellows; and recent (within 6 months) graduates from accredited programs in the fields of engineering, computer science, medicine, physical and medical sciences, management, administration, or public health. Applicants must submit an abstract of a research paper for presentation at the annual meeting of the Association for the Advancement of Medical Instrumentation (AAMI). The abstract must relate to 1 or more of the following categories: 1) innovative medical instrumentation of medical devices having direct applications to patient care; 2) new applications of existing technology to improve patient management; or 3) clinical outcomes of patient safety studies directly related to the application of current or future medical technology.

Financial data The first-prize winner receives $1,500 and a plaque.

Duration The competition is held annually.

Additional information This competition was first held in 1995.

Number awarded 1 each year.

Deadline October of each year.

[628]
AFP SCHOLAR'S AWARD

Association for Financial Professionals
Attn: Membership Department
7315 Wisconsin Avenue, Suite 600 West
Bethesda, MD 20814-3211
(301) 907-2862   Fax: (301) 907-2864
E-mail: student@AFPonline.org
Web: www.AFPonline.org/pub/rec/scholars_award.html

Purpose To recognize and reward outstanding papers on financial management written by undergraduate or graduate students who have participated in the Corporate Treasury Management (CTM) Program of the Association for Financial Professionals (AFP).

Eligibility Eligible to apply are business and finance students who are AFP student members or participants in the CTM Program. This is a merit competition. Selection is based on an original paper (10 to 12 pages in length) written by each candidate and submitted by their sponsor (faculty member). Papers must cover a subject related to treasury or financial management. They must be original and not previously submitted to any other award program.

Financial data The winner receives a $5,000 scholarship, complimentary registration to the annual conference of the AFP, and reimbursement of up to $1,000 in travel expenses.

Duration The competition is held annually.

Additional information Winning papers may be published as a feature in the association's journal, *AFP Exchange.*

Number awarded 1 each year.

Deadline June of each year.

[629]
AGRI-ENTREPRENEURSHIP AWARDS PROGRAM

National FFA Organization
Attn: Agri-Entrepreneurship Education Program
6060 FFA Drive
P.O. Box 68960
Indianapolis, IN 46268-0960
(317) 802-4255   Fax: (317) 802-5255
E-mail: ag_ent@ffa.org
Web: www.ffa.org

Purpose To recognize and reward high school student members of FFA who engage in entrepreneurial activities.

Eligibility This program is open to current members who have established an agricultural enterprise that takes advantage of an opportunity that others have overlooked. Their application should explain how they have mobilized resources to pursue the opportunity, developed a strategy that includes marketing and financial components, and made a convincing case that the business will be successful. Candidates first compete at the state level, and winners advance to the national competition.

Financial data Each state winner receives $100; states with more than 20 applicants award a $50 second prize. National winners receive $1,000.

Duration The competition is held annually.

Additional information This program is sponsored by the Ewing Marion Kauffman Foundation of Kansas City, Missouri as a special project of the National FFA Foundation.

Number awarded 10 each year.

Deadline July of each year.

[630]
AGRICULTURAL MECHANICS CAREER DEVELOPMENT EVENT

National FFA Organization
Attn: Career Development Events
6060 FFA Drive
P.O. Box 68960
Indianapolis, IN 46268-0960
(317) 802-4263   Fax: (317) 802-5263
E-mail: cde@ffa.org
Web: www.ffa.org

Purpose To recognize and reward members of FFA who score highest on a written examination on agricultural mechanics and management.

Eligibility Current members in teams of 3 or 4 high school seniors enter to solve a complex, multi-system agricultural problem. The problem scenario is presented to the team on the day of the event and members utilize the materials and equipment provided to undertake and prepare a written, computer mechanics generated solution. Each year, a different theme area is emphasized, rotating among integrated pest management (formerly chemical application) in 2005, animal production systems in 2006, materials handling systems (formerly forage systems) in 2007, and processing systems in 2008. Within each of those theme emphasis areas, the systems that are covered include machinery and equipment systems, industry and marketing systems, energy systems, structural systems, and environmental and natural resource systems. The winning teams in state competitions advance to the national finals. At those finals, individual participants complete a written examination. and demonstrate problem-solving and hands-on performance skills.

Financial data Each member of the winning team receives a $1,000 scholarship. In addition, the highest scoring individual receives $900, the second highest individual receives $750, the third highest individual receives $600, the fourth through tenth highest individuals receive $500 each, and the 11th highest individual receives $250. If the national winning team is composed of only 3 members, 4 additional scholarships of $250 are also awarded.

Duration The competition is held annually.

Additional information This competition is sponsored by the Bridgestone/Firestone Trust Fund and Firestone Agricultural Tire Company. Each entry in team or individual events is charged an entry processing fee of $25. Members of winning teams are not eligible to receive individual awards.

Number awarded 1 team and 11 individual winners are selected each year.

Deadline July of each year.

[631]
AGRICULTURAL SALES CAREER DEVELOPMENT EVENT

National FFA Organization
Attn: Career Development Events
6060 FFA Drive
P.O. Box 68960
Indianapolis, IN 46268-0960
(317) 802-4263   Fax: (317) 802-5263
E-mail: cde@ffa.org
Web: www.ffa.org

Purpose To recognize and reward members of FFA who score highest in a competition related to sales of agricultural products.

Eligibility Current members are eligible to enter as a team of 4 high school seniors. Teams are presented with information about a product, including the market situation, area demographics, company information, present and/or potential retail and/or wholesale outlets, community information, storage information, transportation and distribution information, and existing marketing problems. Based on that information, teams develop a presentation that identifies the demographic consumer group for which the product will be targeted, the key features and benefits of the product, potential customer objections, and strategies to address those objections. The winning teams in state competitions advance to the national finals. At those finals, participants also complete as individuals by taking an objective written test, making a sales presentation, and competing in 1 of 4 practicums on topics that rotate annually (2005: horticulture industry; 2006: animal industry; 2007: crop industry). The topics include customer

relations, promotion and advertising, telephone order taking, customer service, and prospecting for new customers.

Financial data Each member of the winning team receives a $1,000 scholarship. In addition, the highest scoring individual receives $900, the second highest individual receives $750, the third highest individual receives $600, the fourth through tenth highest individuals receive $500 each, and the 11th highest individual receives $250.

Duration The competition is held annually.

Additional information This competition is sponsored by Monsanto Company. Each entry in team or individual events is charged an entry processing fee of $25. Members of winning teams are not eligible to receive individual awards.

Number awarded 1 team and 11 individual winners are selected each year.

Deadline July of each year.

[632]
AMERICAN ENTERPRISE SPEECH CONTEST

National Management Association
Attn: American Enterprise Speech Contest
2210 Arbor Boulevard
Dayton, OH 45439-1580
(937) 294-0421   Fax: (937) 294-2374
E-mail: nma@nma1.org
Web: nma1.org/aespeech/index.htm

Purpose To recognize and reward outstanding high school speeches on the American competitive enterprise system.

Eligibility Eligible to compete are students in grades 9-12 in a high school within an area of a sponsoring chapter of the National Management Association (NMA). Contestants prepare speeches of 4 to 6 minutes on a topic related to the economic system of the United States. Non-economic issues (social, medical, environmental, political, etc.) may be utilized, but only if focused on business/entrepreneurial issues or approaches. No audio/visual aids are allowed with the presentations, and speeches may not be read verbatim, although notes are allowed. Winners of the chapter contests advance to council competition, from which winners proceed to compete in 1 of the 6 areas of the NMA. The 6 area winners then compete in the national contest. Speeches are judged on the basis of content (50%), delivery (30%), and language (20%).

Financial data Chapter awards are determined by each chapter, up to a maximum of $500 for the first-place winner; each council also determines its own awards, to a maximum of $750 for the first-place winner. In each of the area contests, first prize is $2,000, second $1,500, and third $1,000. In the national contest, first prize is $10,000, second $5,000, third $3,000, and fourth through sixth $500. All prizes are in the form of savings bonds.

Additional information All costs for prizes and transportation at chapter and council levels are paid by the individual chapters and councils. The national level of NMA supplies the area prizes, national prizes, and transportation reimbursements for area winners to compete in the national contest.

Number awarded 18 area and 6 national winners are selected each year; the number of chapter and council prizes awarded varies.

Deadline Chapter contests are held in January or early February of each year, council contests in February or March, area contests in April and May, and the national contest in September or October.

[633]
ATTORNEY-CPA FOUNDATION
GRADUATE/PROFESSIONAL ESSAY CONTEST

American Association of Attorney-Certified Public
  Accountants Foundation
Attn: Executive Director
24196 Alicia Parkway, Suite K
Mission Viejo, CA 92691
(949) 768-0336   Toll-free: (888) ATTY-CPA
Fax: (949) 768-7062
E-mail: aaacpa@attorney-cpa.com
Web: www.attorney-cpa.com/essay.html

Purpose To recognize and reward outstanding essays written by graduate or professional school students on a topic related to law and accounting.

Eligibility Graduate and professional students are invited to enter this essay contest. The topic of the essay changes annually but always deals with the law and accounting; recently, the topic related to the ethical rules of independence, conflicts of interest, and confidentiality that are based on core values of both the legal and accounting professions. The submitted essay should be approximately 30 pages, including footnotes and endnotes.

Financial data The grand prize is $2,500, the runner-up prize is $1,500, third prize is $500, fourth prize is $500, and regional prizes are $250.

Duration The competition is held annually.

Number awarded 8 each year: 1 grand prize, 1 runner-up, 1 third prize, 1 fourth prize, and 4 regional prizes.

Deadline May of each year.

[634]
ATTORNEY-CPA FOUNDATION
UNDERGRADUATE ESSAY CONTEST

American Association of Attorney-Certified Public
  Accountants Foundation
Attn: Executive Director
24196 Alicia Parkway, Suite K
Mission Viejo, CA 92691
(949) 768-0336   Toll-free: (888) ATTY-CPA
Fax: (949) 768-7062
E-mail: aaacpa@attorney-cpa.com
Web: www.attorney-cpa.com/essay.html

Purpose To recognize and reward outstanding undergraduate student essays on a topic related to accounting.

Eligibility Undergraduate accounting students are invited to enter this essay contest. The topic of the essay changes annually but always deals with the law and accounting; recently, the topic was "Corporate directors' fiduciary duties—From auditor selection to executive compensation, what standards apply?" The essay should be no more than 20 pages, including footnotes or endnotes.

Financial data The grand prize is $2,500, the runner-up prize is $1,500, third prize is $500, fourth prize is $500, and regional prizes are $250.

Duration The competition is held annually.

Number awarded 8 each year: 1 grand prize, 1 runner-up, 1 third prize, 1 fourth prize, and 4 regional prizes.

Deadline May of each year.

[635]
AWORLDCONNECTED.ORG ESSAY CONTEST

A World Connected
c/o Institute for Humane Studies
George Mason University
3301 North Fairfax Drive, Suite 440
Arlington, VA 22201
(703) 993-4880   Toll-free: (800) 697-8799
Fax: (703) 993-4890
E-mail: info@aworldconnected.org
Web: www.aworldconnected.org

Purpose To recognize and reward undergraduate and graduate students and other young people who submit outstanding essays related to globalization and the economy.

Eligibility This competition is open to 1) full-time undergraduate and graduate students of any age, and 2) other people 25 years of age and younger. Entrants may be from any country and any academic discipline. High school students are not eligible. Applicants must submit an essay, up to 2,500 words in length, on the following topic: "Why are some countries rich and others poor? How has globalization contributed to the wealth or poverty of nations?" Essays must be in English. Selection is based on the essays' clarity, rigor, and eloquence.

Financial data First prize is $5,000, second $2,500, third $1,500, and honorable mentions $250.

Duration The competition is held annually.

Additional information This competition was first held in 2003.

Number awarded 7 each year: 3 prize winners and 4 honorable mentions.

Deadline April of each year.

[636]
BANK OF AMERICA ACHIEVEMENT AWARDS

Bank of America Foundation
Attn: Achievement Awards Program
CA5-704-08-03
315 Montgomery Street, Eighth Floor
San Francisco, CA 94104-1866
(415) 953-0927   Toll-free: (888) 488-9802
Fax: (415) 622-3469
Web: www.bankofamerica.com/foundation

Purpose To recognize and reward high school seniors in California who show outstanding ability is selected areas.

Eligibility Eligible are high school seniors in California who are chosen by faculty committees in their schools. The committees select students to receive certificates in specific study areas (agriculture, art, business, communications, computer studies, drama, English, English as a Second Language, foreign language, history, home economics, mathematics, music, religious studies, science, social science, and trades and industrial studies). Small high schools (those with 199 or fewer students in grades 10-12) may award a total of 7 certificates and large high schools (those with 200 or more students) present a total of 14 certificates. In addition, the faculty committees select graduating seniors to receive plaques in 4 general study areas (applied arts, fine arts, liberal arts, and science and mathematics); certificate winners may not also receive plaques; the number of plaques awarded by each high school also depends on the size of the school (2 plaques with enrollment of 1 to 199 students in grades 10-12, 3 plaques with 200 to 599 students, and 4 plaques for schools with more than 600 students). Winners of plaques are then eligible to enter the Achievement Awards competition. Of all plaque winners statewide, 320 finalists (8 in each of 10 regions in each of the 4 general study areas) are selected to enter competitions involving 1) an essay judged on written expression, logical progression, ability to focus on topic, and creative interpretation, and 2) a group discussion judged on cooperation, sound and logical thinking, oral communication and command of English, and originality of thought.

Financial data The cash awards are $2,000 for first-place winners, $1,500 for second-place winners, $1,000 for third-place winners, and $500 for other participating finalists.

Duration Prizes are awarded annually.

Additional information This program was established in 1948.

Number awarded All 320 finalists receive cash awards; the top 40 finalists (1 in each general study area in each region) receive first-place awards and other finalists receive awards depending on their scores in the competition.

Deadline Schools must select their plaque recipients before the end of January of each year.

[637]
BIRCH TELECOM COMPETITION ROCKS! SCHOLARSHIP PROGRAM & ESSAY CONTEST

Birch Telecom
Attn: Scholarship Committee
2114 Central, Suite 300
Kansas City, MO 64108
(816) 300-5716   E-mail: eblackwell@birch.com
Web: www.birch.com/scholarship

Purpose To recognize and reward outstanding essays written by high school seniors in selected states on the value of competition.

Eligibility Open to high school seniors who are U.S. citizens or permanent residents and living in 1 of the following states: Alabama, Florida, Georgia, Kansas, Louisiana, Missouri, Mississippi, North Carolina, Oklahoma, South Carolina, Tennessee, or Texas. Interested students must submit an essay on the value of competition: lower prices, better service, more innovative products, etc. Entrants also need to have taken the ACT or SAT and be scheduled to enroll at a college or university in the fall following the competition.

Financial data Awards range from $500 to $2,500; in total, $25,000 is distributed annually.

Duration These are 1-time awards; nonrenewable.

Number awarded 24 each year: 4 at $2,500; 10 at $1,000; and 10 at $500.

Deadline March of each year.

[638]
CAREER DEVELOPMENT EVENTS SCHOLARSHIPS

National FFA Organization
Attn: Career Development Events
6060 FFA Drive
P.O. Box 68960
Indianapolis, IN 46268-0960
(317) 802-4263   Fax: (317) 802-5263
E-mail: cde@ffa.org
Web: www.ffa.org

Purpose To recognize and reward members of FFA who score highest in various competitions that are part of the Career Development Events.

Eligibility These competitions are open to members, but they are usually limited to high school seniors. Currently, the organization conducts 23 different competitions and 1 activity, most of which begin as state activities from which winners compete at national finals. Each competition has its own rules and procedures. Most involve competitions in which teams of 3 or 4 students demonstrate their knowledge of different agricultural specialties through written examinations or practicums. Team members also compete as individuals in related activities.

Financial data Each competition presents awards differently, but in many of them each member of the winning team receives a $1,000 scholarship and the highest scoring individual receives $900, the second highest individual receives $750, the third highest individual receives $600, the fourth through tenth highest individuals receive $500 each, and the 11th highest individual receives $250. Other competitions simply provide $1,000 scholarships to winners.

Duration The competitions are held annually.

Additional information The events currently offered are in agricultural communications, agricultural issues forum, agricultural mechanics, agricultural sales, agronomy, creed speaking, dairy cattle evaluation, dairy foods, dairy handling, environmental and natural resources, extemporaneous public speaking, farm business management, floriculture, food science and technology, forestry, horse evaluation, job interview, livestock evaluation, marketing plan, meats evaluation and technology, nursery and landscape, parliamentary procedure, poultry evaluation, and prepared public speaking. The competitions are supported by a number of corporate sponsors. Each entry in team or individual events is charged an entry processing fee of $25. Members of winning teams are not eligible to receive individual awards.

Number awarded 1 team and 11 individual winners are selected each year in most competitions.

Deadline The deadline to enter most competitions is in July of each year.

[639]
CBAI ANNUAL SCHOLARSHIP PROGRAM

Community Bankers Association of Illinois
Attn: CBAI Foundation for Community Banking
901 Community Drive
Springfield, IL 62703-5184
(217) 529-2265   Toll-free: (800) 736-2224 (within IL)
Fax: (217) 529-9484   E-mail: cbaicom@cbai.com
Web: www.cbai.com/scholarship.htm

Purpose To recognize and reward high school seniors in Illinois who enter an essay competition on a topic related to banking.

Eligibility This program is open to seniors graduating from high schools in Illinois. Applicants must submit a 2-page essay on a topic that changes annually but relates to the sponsor's mission of increasing public awareness of community banks and their contributions to society. Recently, the topic was "Does technology help or hinder the philosophy of community banking?" Applications are available at banks that are members of the Community Bankers Association of Illinois (CBAI). Selection is based on an understanding of community banking philosophy, accurate information, clear and concise sentences, logical organization, proper grammar, correct punctuation and spelling, and conclusion and summary.

Financial data Prizes range up to $4,000.

Duration The competition is held annually.

Number awarded 13 each year; a total of $16,500 in prizes is awarded.

Deadline February of each year.

[640]
CONNECTICUT CHAPTER HFMA GRADUATE SCHOLARSHIP

Healthcare Financial Management Association-
  Connecticut Chapter
c/o Andy Czerniewski, Scholarship Committee Chair
VNA of Central Connecticut
One Long Wharf Drive
New Haven, CT 06511-5991
(203) 777-5521, ext. 1700   Fax: (203) 495-7483
E-mail: aczerniewski@vnascc.org
Web: www.cthfma.org/Scholarship.asp

Purpose To recognize and reward graduate students in fields related to health care financial management at colleges and universities in Connecticut who submit outstanding essays on topics in the field.

Eligibility This competition is open to graduate students at colleges and universities in Connecticut, children of members of the Connecticut chapter of the Healthcare Financial Management Association (HFMA), and residents of Connecticut commuting to a college or university in a state that borders Connecticut. Applicants must be enrolled in a business, finance, accounting, or information systems program and have an interest in health care or be enrolled in a nursing or allied health program. They must submit an essay, up to 5 pages, on 1 of the following topics: 1) how modifications in state Medicaid program benefits and provider reimbursement rates and policies have impacted the beneficiaries and health care providers; 2) the impact of the Health Insurance Portability and Accountability Act on the delivery of patient care; or 3) the implications of the shortage of health care delivery per-

sonnel on the delivery of patient care. Finalists may be interviewed.

Financial data The winner receives a $2,000 fellowship, membership in the Connecticut chapter of HFMA and its scholarship committee, and waiver of chapter program fees for 1 year.

Duration The competition is held annually.

Number awarded 1 each year.

Deadline March of each year.

[641]
CONNECTICUT CHAPTER HFMA UNDERGRADUATE SCHOLARSHIP

Healthcare Financial Management Association-
  Connecticut Chapter
c/o Andy Czerniewski, Scholarship Committee Chair
VNA of Central Connecticut
One Long Wharf Drive
New Haven, CT 06511-5991
(203) 777-5521, ext. 1700   Fax: (203) 495-7483
E-mail: aczerniewski@vnascc.org
Web: www.cthfma.org/Scholarship.asp

Purpose To recognize and reward, with college scholarships, undergraduate students in fields related to health care financial management at colleges and universities in Connecticut who submit outstanding essays on topics in the field.

Eligibility This competition is open to undergraduate students at colleges and universities in Connecticut, children of members of the Connecticut chapter of Healthcare Financial Management Association (HFMA), and residents of Connecticut commuting to a college or university in a state that borders Connecticut. Applicants must be enrolled in a business, finance, accounting, or information systems program and have an interest in health care or be enrolled in a nursing or allied health program. They must submit an essay, up to 3 pages, on what they see as the most significant challenge facing the health care industry today and their proposal for a practical and feasible solution. Finalists may be interviewed.

Financial data The winner receives a $1,000 scholarship, membership in the Connecticut chapter of HFMA and its scholarship committee, and waiver of chapter program fees for 1 year.

Duration The competition is held annually.

Number awarded 1 each year.

Deadline March of each year.

[642]
DELOITTE NATIONAL STUDENT CASE STUDY SEMINAR

Deloitte Foundation
Attn: Manager, Academic Development and University
  Relations
10 Westport Road
Wilton, CT 06897-0820
(203) 761-3248   Fax: (203) 563-2324
Web: www.deloitte.com

Purpose To recognize and reward accounting students who participate in an accounting competition.

Eligibility This program is open to accounting students at universities in the United States. The sponsoring firm's

Accounting Research Department develops case studies of accounting problems. Teams of students from participating universities present their cases and solutions to a panel of active and retired partners of the firm who play the role of senior management or the audit committee of a client company. The panel members raise questions and issues for response and discussion, and then rank the teams based on their presentations and ability to identify and resolve the relevant accounting issues.

Financial data Each participant on the winning team receives a $1,000 scholarship and those on the second-place team receive $500. Other participating student finalists receive $250.

Duration The competition is held annually.

Additional information This competition, held at the Deloitte Development Center in Scottsdale, Arizona, was first conducted in 1996.

Number awarded Varies each year; recently, 6 teams participated in the competition finals.

[643]
DR. KEITH DAVIS GRADUATE SCHOLARSHIPS

Sigma Iota Epsilon
c/o Colorado State University
Management Department
324 Rockwell Hall
Fort Collins, CO 80523-1275
(970) 491-7200   Fax: (970) 491-3522
E-mail: brenda.ogden@colostate.edu
Web: www.sienational.com

Purpose To recognize and reward outstanding papers written on management topics by graduate student members of Sigma Iota Epsilon (SIE), the national honorary and professional management fraternity.

Eligibility Any active graduate student member may submit a scholarly paper on an appropriate management subject (e.g., organization and management theory, organizational behavior, personnel and human resources, management education and development, social issues in management, organizational development and change, organizational communications and information systems, organizational development and change, organization and the natural environment, managerial and organizational cognition, managerial consultation, business policy and strategy, health care administration, management history, public and nonprofit sector management, women in management, international management, conflict management, careers, entrepreneurship, or research methods). Papers should be between 15 and 20 pages. Students may submit a paper previously written for a class assignment, but it may not include grades or comments. Papers primarily focused on another discipline (e.g., marketing, finance, real estate, business law) are not eligible.

Financial data The author of the winning paper receives a $1,250 cash scholarship and a plaque. The runners-up receive $500 each.

Duration The competition is held annually.

Number awarded 3 each year: 1 winner and 2 runners-up (1 master's degree student and 1 doctoral degree student).

Deadline May of each year.

[644]
EXTEMPORANEOUS PUBLIC SPEAKING CAREER DEVELOPMENT EVENT

National FFA Organization
Attn: Career Development Events
6060 FFA Drive
P.O. Box 68960
Indianapolis, IN 46268-0960
(317) 802-4263   Fax: (317) 802-5263
E-mail: cde@ffa.org
Web: www.ffa.org

Purpose To recognize and reward FFA members who present outstanding extemporaneous speeches on agricultural topics (including agrimarketing).

Eligibility Eligible are current members who are regularly enrolled in agricultural education or who are still in high school but have completed all the agricultural education offered. On the local level, the event superintendent prepares 12 topics, 3 each from the following categories: agriscience and technology, agrimarketing and international agricultural relations, food and fiber systems, and urban agriculture. Participants have 30 minutes in which to prepare a speech, from 4 to 6 minutes in length, on 1 of the topics selected at random from the pool of 12; they may use up to 5 items of reference material in preparing their speeches. Each state FFA organization may send 1 speaker to compete at the annual National FFA convention. Selection is based on content related to topic, organization of material, voice, stage presence, power of expression, response to questions, and general effect.

Financial data The awards are $1,000.

Duration The contest is held annually.

Additional information This competition is sponsored by the American Farm Bureau Federation.

Number awarded 4 national winners receive awards each year.

Deadline July of each year.

[645]
FARM BUSINESS MANAGEMENT CAREER DEVELOPMENT EVENT

National FFA Organization
Attn: Career Development Events
6060 FFA Drive
P.O. Box 68960
Indianapolis, IN 46268-0960
(317) 802-4263   Fax: (317) 802-5263
E-mail: cde@ffa.org
Web: www.ffa.org

Purpose To recognize and reward members of FFA who score highest in a competition related to the management of a farming business.

Eligibility Current members are eligible to enter as a team of 3 or 4 high school seniors. Teams are allowed 1 hour to engage in an activity that involves the use of farm business management skills and resource and resource information. The winning teams in state competitions advance to the national finals. At those finals, individuals also participate by completing a written test that demonstrates their knowledge and abilities in applying economic principles to agriculture and agribusiness.

Financial data Each member of the winning team receives a $1,000 scholarship. In addition, the highest scoring individual receives $900, the second highest individual receives $750, the third highest individual receives $600, the fourth through tenth highest individuals receive $500 each, and the 11th highest individual receives $250. If the national winning team is composed of only 3 members, 4 additional scholarships of $250 are also awarded.

Duration The competition is held annually.

Additional information This competition is sponsored by John Deere & Company of Moline, Illinois. Each entry in team or individual events is charged an entry processing fee of $25. Members of winning teams are not eligible to receive individual awards.

Number awarded 1 team and 11 individual winners are selected each year.

Deadline July of each year.

[646]
FFA PROFICIENCY AWARDS

National FFA Organization
Attn: Proficiency Awards
6060 FFA Drive
P.O. Box 68960
Indianapolis, IN 46268-0960
(317) 802-4255   Fax: (317) 802-5255
E-mail: proficiency@ffa.org
Web: www.ffa.org

Purpose To recognize and reward FFA members who demonstrate outstanding performance in the Supervised Agricultural Experience (SAE) program.

Eligibility This program is open to members who either are current high school students or graduated from high school within the past year. High school graduates must have completed at least 3 full years of instruction in agricultural education. Applicants must have participated in an SAE program either in a placement type or an entrepreneurship type. Placement SAE programs involve work or experience-only (paid or unpaid) activities, including directed laboratory, improvement, and research/experimentation experiences; examples include working at a nursery, grooming at a horse stable, developing a research program, or volunteering at a local park. Entrepreneurship SAE programs involve ownership of an agricultural production or agribusiness enterprise. The award areas include agricultural communications, agricultural mechanics design and fabrication, agricultural mechanics energy systems, agricultural mechanics repair and maintenance, agricultural processing, agricultural sales, agricultural services, aquaculture, beef production, dairy production, diversified agricultural production, diversified crop production, diversified horticulture, diversified livestock production, emerging agricultural technology, environmental sciences and natural resources management, equine science, fiber and/or oil crop production, floriculture, food science and technology, forage production, forest management and products, fruit production, grain production, home and/or community development, landscape management, nursery operations, outdoor recreation, poultry production, sheep production, small animal production and care, specialty animal production, specialty crop production, swine production, turf grass management, vegetable production, and wildlife production and management. In some of these areas, students compete separately for place

ment types and entrepreneurship types; in other areas, placement SAE programs compete with entrepreneurship SAE programs. The total number of award areas varies each year, depending on the areas offered and whether there are separate or combined placement and entrepreneurship competitions. Recently, a total of 49 award areas were offered. Students are first judged at the state level on their SAE program. Selection is based on 1) skills and competencies learned that relate to an agricultural career field; 2) financial achievements, including growth in scope; 3) personal growth and development through FFA activities; 4) evidence of student accomplishments based on available resources and opportunities; and 5) communication skills, as demonstrated in the written portions of applications and clear concise answers during interviews. State winners then compete for national awards.

Financial data Each state winner receives a framed certificate and a $100 cash award. Each national finalist receives a plaque and a $250 cash award. Each national winner receives an additional plaque and an additional $250 cash award.

Duration The competition is held annually.

Additional information Funding for this program is provided by many corporate and organizational sponsors.

Number awarded Varies each year.

Deadline February of each year.

[647]
GENDER ISSUES IN ACCOUNTING
MANUSCRIPT AWARD

American Accounting Association
Attn: Gender Issues in Accounting Section
5717 Bessie Drive
Sarasota, FL 34233-2399
(941) 921-7747   Fax: (941) 923-4093
E-mail: office@aaahq.org
Web: accounting.rutgers.edu

Purpose To recognize and reward outstanding research manuscripts on gender issues in accounting.

Eligibility This competition is open to accounting faculty members and Ph.D. students who submit a manuscript that is unpublished and not accepted for publication by a journal at the time of the submission. The research must focus on an aspect of gender issues in accounting. At least 1 of the authors must be a member of the Gender Issues in Accounting section of the American Accounting Association.

Financial data The awards are $500.

Duration The awards are presented annually.

Number awarded 2 each year: 1 to a faculty member and 1 to a Ph.D. student.

Deadline March of each year.

[648]
GEORGIA SOCIETY OF CPAS ACADEMIC EXCELLENCE AWARD PROGRAM

Georgia Society of CPAs
Attn: Educational Foundation
3353 Peachtree Road, N.E., Suite 400
Atlanta, GA 30326-1414
(404) 231-8676   Toll-free: (800) 330-8889, ext. 2943
Fax: (404) 237-1291   E-mail: gscpaweb@gscpa.org
Web: www.gscpa.org

Purpose To recognize and reward graduates of colleges and institutions in Georgia who have demonstrated outstanding achievement in accounting.

Eligibility These awards are presented to students graduating from institutions in Georgia who are 1) the senior at a 4-year institution with the highest overall academic average and a major in accounting, or 2) the graduate of a 2-year institution with the highest combined GPA in the 2 courses in principles of accounting.

Financial data The award at 4-year institutions is $500; the award at 2-year institutions is $250.

Duration The awards are presented annually.

Number awarded 1 student at each institution receives an award.

Deadline Nominations must be submitted by April of each year.

[649]
GOLDEN KEY BUSINESS ACHIEVEMENT AWARDS

Golden Key International Honour Society
621 North Avenue N.E., Suite C-100
Atlanta, GA 30308
(404) 377-2400   Toll-free: (800) 377-2401
Fax: (678) 420-6757
E-mail: scholarships@goldenkey.org
Web: www.goldenkey.org

Purpose To recognize and reward members of the Golden Key International Honour Society who submit outstanding papers on topics related to the field of business.

Eligibility This program is open to undergraduate, graduate, and postgraduate members of the society who submit a paper or report, up to 10 pages in length, on a topic related to business. Applicants must also submit 1) an essay, up to 2 pages in length, describing the assignment for writing the paper, the greatest challenge in writing the paper, the lessons learned from completing the assignment, and what they would change if they could redo the paper; 2) a letter of recommendation; and 3) academic transcripts. Selection of the winners is based on academic achievement and the quality of the paper.

Financial data The winner receives a $1,000 scholarship, second place a $750 scholarship, and third place a $500 scholarship.

Duration These awards are presented annually.

Additional information This program began in 2001.

Number awarded 3 each year.

Deadline February of each year.

[650]
HENRY B. GONZALEZ AWARD

Financial Markets Center
P.O. Box 334
Philomont, VA 20131
(540) 338-7754   Fax: (540) 338-7757
Web: www.fmcenter.org

Purpose To recognize and reward outstanding essays, written by students and others, on central bank reform.

Eligibility This annual contest is open to all entrants, including students enrolled in graduate and undergraduate programs, who submit a paper (up to 15,000 words) on the subject of central bank reform. Entries may be sweeping in scope or focused on a specific aspect of the Federal Reserve's structure, governance, operations, staffing, culture, or statutory authority. Preference is given to clearly-written entries accessible to a broad audience.

Financial data The winning entry receives a cash award of $2,500 and is published by the sponsor.

Duration The competition is held annually.

Number awarded 1 each year.

[651]
HILL-ROM MANAGEMENT ESSAY COMPETITION IN HEALTHCARE ADMINISTRATION

American College of Healthcare Executives
Attn: Associate Director, Division of Research and
    Development
One North Franklin Street, Suite 1700
Chicago, IL 60606-3529
(312) 424-9444   Fax: (312) 424-0023
E-mail: ache@ache.org
Web: www.ache.org/Faculty_Students/hillrom.cfm

Purpose To recognize and reward undergraduate graduate student members of the American College of Healthcare Executives (ACHE) who submit outstanding essays on health care administration.

Eligibility This competition is open to ACHE student associates or affiliates who are enrolled in an undergraduate or graduate program in health care management at an accredited college or university in the United States or Canada. Applicants must submit an essay, up to 15 pages in length, on a topic with a focus on such health management topics as strategic planning and policy; accountability of and/or relationships among board, medical staff, and executive management; financial management; human resources management; systems management; plant and facility management; comprehensive systems of services; quality assessment and assurance; professional, public, community, or interorganization relations; government relations or regulation; marketing; education; research; or law and ethics. Selection is based on significance of the subject to health care management, innovativeness in approach to the topic, thoroughness and precision in developing the subject, practical usefulness for guiding management action, and clarity and conciseness of expression.

Financial data The first-place winners in each division (undergraduate and graduate) receive $3,000 and their programs receive $1,000. The second-place winner receives $2,000 and third $1,000.

Duration The competition is held annually.

Additional information This program was established in 1989.

Number awarded 6 each year: 3 undergraduate and 3 graduate students.

Deadline December of each year.

[652]
HOWARD N. MCINTOSH MEMORIAL AWARD

Junior Achievement of Delaware, Inc.
522 South Walnut Street
Wilmington, DE 19801-5230
(302) 654-4510   Toll-free: (866) JA-TODAY
Fax: (302) 654-0783
Web: delaware.ja.org/programs_evaluations.html

Purpose To recognize and reward outstanding high school seniors in Delaware's Junior Achievement (JA) program.

Eligibility This program is open to high school seniors who are student members of JA in Delaware. Applicants must submit brief essays describing what JA has meant to them, how it has affected their performance in school and other activities, and their chief ambitions for the future. They must have been actively involved in the JA program and able to demonstrate that, as a result of their participation, they have improved their communication skills, poise, self confidence, and competitiveness.

Financial data The award is $500.

Duration The award is presented annually.

Additional information Junior Achievement of Delaware serves the state of Delaware, Salem County in New Jersey, and Cecil County in Maryland.

Number awarded 1 each year.

Deadline April of each year.

[653]
INSTITUTE FOR BRAND LEADERSHIP ESSAY CONTEST

Institute for Brand Leadership
1000 Potomac Street, N.W., Suite 122
Washington, DC 20007
(202) 337-1106   Fax: (202) 333-2659
E-mail: contactus@instituteforbrandleadership.org
Web: www.instituteforbrandleadership.org

Purpose To recognize and reward the authors of outstanding essays on the importance of brands.

Eligibility This contest is open to students and others, anywhere in the world. Applicants must submit an essay, of 1,500 to 2,500 words, on this topic: "Why and under what conditions are people more likely to buy brand names than their generic counterparts?" They should apply a theory from a particular discipline or area of study to answer the question. Selection is based on the plausibility of the theory (20 points), the clarity with which the author ties the idea to a particular discipline or area of study (20 points), the plausibility of the argument in terms of brand practice (20 points), the feasibility of operationalizing the hypothesis (20 points), the clarity, understandability, and organization of the essay (10 points), and the effectiveness of communicating the link between theory and practice (10 points).

Financial data First prize is $3,000, second $1,500, and third $500.

Duration The contest is held annually.

Additional information The Institute for Brand Leadership, founded in 1997, established this contest in 2001.

Number awarded 3 each year.

Deadline October of each year.

[654]
INSTITUTE OF MANAGEMENT ACCOUNTANTS NATIONAL STUDENT VIDEO CASE COMPETITION

Institute of Management Accountants
Attn: Committee on Students
10 Paragon Drive
Montvale, NJ 07645-1760
(201) 573-9000   Toll-free: (800) 638-4427, ext. 294
Fax: (201) 573-8438   E-mail: students@imanet.org
Web: www.imanet.org

Purpose To recognize and reward students who respond to a published case in management accounting with a video presentation.

Eligibility Each year a case in management accounting is distributed to student chapters of the Institute of Management Accountants (IMA), Beta Alpha Psi chapters, IMA academic mentors, and IMA chapter presidents; it is also published in *Strategic Finance*. Each college and university in the country may select a team or teams of 3 to 5 students. No more than half of the team may be master's degree candidates; doctoral degree candidates are not eligible. The team prepares a video, up to 15 minutes in length, presenting a solution to the case. Each team member is required to be an equal part of the presentation. Selection is based on content, style of presentation, and response to the case requirements. Judges select 4 videos as finalists, and those team members are invited to the final competition at the IMA Annual Conference & Expo. The 4 finalist teams present their video solutions and respond to additional questions on which they are judged.

Financial data The winning team receives $5,000 and each runner-up team receives $3,000.

Duration The competition is held annually.

Number awarded 1 winner and 3 runners-up are selected each year.

Deadline January of each year.

[655]
LORD ACTON ESSAY COMPETITION

Acton Institute for the Study of Religion and Liberty
161 Ottawa N.W., Suite 301
Grand Rapids, MI 49503
(616) 454-3080   Fax: (616) 454-9454
E-mail: awards@acton.org
Web: www.acton.org/programs/students/essay

Purpose To recognize and reward scholars, practitioners, and graduate students who author outstanding essays on the themes of religion and liberty.

Eligibility This competition is open to seminarians, graduate students, priests, pastors, scholars, and professors, regardless of religious affiliation or denomination. Applicants must submit a scholarly paper, op-editorial, article (published or unpublished), or treatise. Entries should discuss the interrelationships among religious believers and institutions, the mediating structures of society, and economic and political systems. There are no page requirements or limits. Applications from those outside the United States and those studying abroad receive equal consideration. Selection is based on the integration of economic, theological, and political thought.

Financial data First place is $2,000, second $1,000, and third $500.

Duration The competition is held annually.

Additional information This competition was first held in 1992. The 3 prize winners and 2 honorable mentions are published on the sponsor's web site.

Number awarded 3 cash prizes are awarded each year.

Deadline November of each year.

[656]
MARKETING PLAN CAREER DEVELOPMENT EVENT

National FFA Organization
Attn: Career Development Events
6060 FFA Drive
P.O. Box 68960
Indianapolis, IN 46268-0960
(317) 802-4263   Fax: (317) 802-5263
E-mail: cde@ffa.org
Web: www.ffa.org

Purpose To recognize and reward members of FFA who score highest in a competition related to developing a marketing plan.

Eligibility Current members are eligible to enter as a team of 3 high school seniors. Teams research and present a marketing plan for an agricultural product, supply, or service. The winning teams in state competitions advance to the national finals. The written plan is judged on its market analysis (10 points), business proposal (5 points), strategies and action plan (10 points), evaluation (5 points), and budget (5 points). The live presentation is judged on demonstrated understanding of the 5 parts of the marketing plan (25 points), evidence of meaningful original market research (15 points), effectiveness of the presentation (10 points), and questions and answers (15 points).

Financial data Each member of the first-place team receives a $1,000 scholarship, second-place team $600, third-place team $500, and fourth-place team $250.

Duration The competition is held annually.

Additional information This competition is sponsored by Data Transmission Network of Omaha, DuPont Company, and the National FFA Foundation. Each entry is charged a processing fee of $25.

Number awarded 4 teams are selected each year.

Deadline September of each year.

[657]
MARYLAND BANKERS ASSOCIATION ESSAY CONTEST

Maryland Bankers Association
186 Duke of Gloucester Street
Annapolis, MD 21401
(410) 269-5977   Toll-free: (800) 327-5977
Fax: (410) 269-1874
Web: www.mdbankers.com

Purpose To recognize and reward, with college scholarships, high school seniors in Maryland who submit outstanding essays on a topic related to banking.

Eligibility This competition is open to seniors graduating from high schools in Maryland. Applicants must submit a 2-page essay on a topic that changes annually but relates to banking. Recently, students were asked how they would improve their community's money management skills if they were a bank president.

Financial data Prizes are a $1,000 scholarship for first place, a $500 scholarship for second, and a $250 scholarship for third.

Duration The competition is held annually.

Number awarded 3 each year.

Deadline January of each year.

[658]
MASSACHUSETTS SOCIETY OF CERTIFIED PUBLIC ACCOUNTANTS STUDENT MANUSCRIPT CONTEST

Massachusetts Society of Certified Public Accountants
Attn: MSCPA Educational Foundation
105 Chauncy Street, Tenth Floor
Boston, MA 02111
(617) 556-4000   Toll-free: (800) 392-6145
Fax: (617) 556-4126
E-mail: biannoni@MSCPAonline.org
Web: www.cpatrack.com/financial_aid/scholarship.php

Purpose To recognize and reward undergraduate students in Massachusetts who submit outstanding papers on accounting.

Eligibility This competition is open to undergraduate accounting students at colleges and universities in Massachusetts. Applicants must submit a 2,000-word paper covering financial reporting, accounting principles, socio-economic accounting, interface with computers, auditing, taxation accounting systems, managerial accounting, or management services. Papers may be innovative, descriptive, or evaluative.

Financial data Prizes are $1,500 for first place (the William Holmes Award), $1,000 for second, and $500 for third.

Duration The competition is held annually.

Additional information Outstanding manuscripts are considered for publication on CPA Review Online.

Number awarded 3 each year.

Deadline May of each year.

[659]
MISS AMERICA COMPETITION AWARDS

Miss America Pageant
Attn: Scholarship Department
Two Miss America Way, Suite 1000
Atlantic City, NJ 08401
(609) 345-7571, ext. 27   Toll-free: (800) 282-MISS
Fax: (609) 347-6079   E-mail: info@missamerica.org
Web: www.missamerica.org

Purpose To provide educational scholarships to participants in the Miss America Pageant on local, state, and national levels.

Eligibility To enter an official Miss America Preliminary Pageant, candidates must meet certain basic requirements and agree to abide by all the rules of the local, state, and national Miss America Pageants. Among the qualifications required are that the applicant be female, between the ages of 17 and 24, a resident of the town or state in which they first compete, in good health, of good moral character, and a citizen of the United States. A complete list of all eligibility requirements is available from each local and state pageant. A number of special awards are also presented to national contestants: the Active International Scholarship for Business and Marketing is presented to the highest scoring contestant who lists business, marketing, or a related business career as a stated ambition; the Bernie Wayne Performing Arts Award is presented to the contestant with the highest talent score among those women with performing arts as a stated ambition; the Eleanor (Big Mama) Andrews Scholarship is presented to the non-finalist contestant with the highest talent score among those women with performing arts as a stated ambition; the Charles and Theresa Brown Scholarships are presented to Miss America, the 4 runners-up, Miss Alaska, Miss Hawaii, Miss Illinois, and Miss Ohio; and the Quality of Life Awards are presented to the 3 contestants who demonstrate the most outstanding commitment to enhancing the quality of life for others through volunteerism and community service.

Financial data More than $45 million in cash and tuition assistance is awarded annually at the local, state, and national Miss America Pageants. At the national level, a total of $455,000 is awarded: Miss America receives $50,000 in scholarship money, the first runner-up $40,000, second runner-up $30,000, third runner-up $25,000, fourth runner-up $20,000, semifinalists $10,000 each, finalists $6,000 each, and national contestants $5,000 each. Among the preliminary winners, those for community achievement in interview receive $5,000, those for artistic expression in talent receive $4,000, those for on-stage knowledge and awareness receive $3,000, those for presence and poise in evening wear receive $2,000, and those for lifestyle and fitness in swimsuit receive $2,000. In addition, the overall knowledge and community achievement in interview winner receives $5,000, the overall artistic expression in talent winner receives $4,000, and the overall elegance and lifestyle winner (including both evening wear and swimsuit) receives $3,000. Of the special awards presented to national contestants, the Active International Scholarship for Business and Marketing is $3,000; the Bernie Wayne Performing Arts Award is $2,500; the Charles and Theresa Brown Scholarships are $2,500 each; and the Quality of Life Awards are $6,000 for first place, $400 for second, and $3,000 for third.

Duration The pageants are held every year.

Additional information The Miss America Pageant has been awarding scholarships since 1945. Scholarships are to be used for tuition, room, board, supplies, and other college expenses. Use of the scholarships must begin within 4 years from the date of the award (5 years if the recipient is Miss America) unless a reasonable extension is requested and granted. Training under the scholarship should be continuous and completed within 10 years from the date the scholarship is activated; otherwise, the balance of the scholarship may be canceled without further notice.

Deadline Varies, depending upon the date of local pageants leading to the state and national finals.

Number awarded At the national level, 52 contestants (1 from each state, the District of Columbia, and the Virgin Islands) share the awards.

[660]
NATIONAL AD 2 STUDENT CREATIVE COMPETITION

National Ad 2
c/o Tod Visdal, Howard & Frost
Attn: National Ad 2 Student Creative Competition
3131 Western Avenue, Suite 520
Seattle, WA 98121
(206) 378-1909, ext. 12   Fax: (206) 378-1910
E-mail: visdal@msn.com
Web: www.ad2.org

Purpose To recognize and reward outstanding advertising art created by college students.

Eligibility Eligible to compete are students currently enrolled, full or part time, in an accredited college, university, or commercial art school in the United States. Applicants must have at least a 2.0 GPA, be majoring in advertising or a closely-related field (e.g., art, communications, journalism, marketing, public relations), and submit a complete advertisement. Advertising elements (e.g., logos, illustrations, photography) will not be considered, nor will work developed for paying customers or group efforts. Entries must be submitted in 1 of the following formats: print, outdoor, radio, television, or web. Selection is based on followed instructions (10 points), use of media (20 points), creativity (50 points), professionalism (10 points), and meets the challenge (10 points).

Financial data The grand-prize winner receives $1,000 plus complimentary registration and travel vouchers for the sponsor's national conference.

Duration The competition is held annually.

Additional information Local Ad 2 chapters may host a local competition for prizes. There is at least a $5 entry fee.

Number awarded 1 each year.

Deadline March of each year.

[661]
NATIONAL AD 2 STUDENT CREATIVE COMPETITION
National Ad 2
c/o Tod Visdal, Williams-Helde Marketing
  Communications
711 Sixth Avenue North, Suite 200
Seattle, WA 98109
(206) 226-7367   E-mail: visdal@msn.com
Web: www.ad2.org/education/education.htm

Purpose To recognize and reward students who enter an advertising competition.

Eligibility This competition is open to students enrolled full or part time in an accredited U.S. college, university, or commercial art school. Applicants must have a "C" or better average overall and be majoring in advertising or a closely-related field (e.g., art, communication, journalism, marketing, or public relations). They must submit a complete advertisement in 1 of the following formats: print, outdoor, radio, television, or web. The work must be the student's own individual effort and developed specifically for this competition. Entries must be submitted through a local Ad 2 Club.

Financial data The prize is $1,000.

Duration The competition is held annually.

Additional information National Ad 2 is a division of the American Advertising Federation (AAF) for members under 32 years of age. The winner also receives a free trip to the AAF national conference. The entry fee is $5.

Number awarded 1 each year.

Deadline March of each year.

[662]
NEW JERSEY SOCIETY OF CERTIFIED PUBLIC ACCOUNTANTS ACCOUNTING MANUSCRIPT CONTEST
New Jersey Society of Certified Public Accountants
Attn: Student Programs Coordinator
425 Eagle Rock Avenue, Suite 100
Roseland, NJ 07068-1723
(973) 226-4494, ext. 209   Fax: (973) 226-7425
E-mail: njscpa@njscpa.org
Web: www.njscpa.org

Purpose To recognize and reward outstanding manuscripts on accounting written by college students in New Jersey.

Eligibility The contest is open to sophomores and juniors who are attending 2-year or 4-year colleges or universities in New Jersey and majoring in accounting. They are invited to submit a manuscript on accounting (up to 1,000 words). All submissions must be original work that has not been previously published. Students must select a faculty member to serve as a mentor in the development of the article. No co-authored manuscripts are accepted. Manuscripts are judged on the basis of content, creativity, clarity, ability to communicate effectively the relevance of accountancy to the topic, and ability to communicate information that is relevant to New Jersey businesses.

Financial data First place is a $3,000 scholarship; honorable mentions are $1,000.

Duration The competition is held annually.

Additional information The winning manuscript is published in *New Jersey Business* magazine, which is also the co-sponsor of this award. The topic changes annually; recently it was "What is the importance of corporate ethics in financial reporting?"

Number awarded Up to 4 each year: 1 first prize and up to 3 honorable mentions.

Deadline January of each year.

[663]
NEW JERSEY SOCIETY OF CERTIFIED PUBLIC ACCOUNTANTS HIGH SCHOOL SCHOLARSHIP PROGRAM
New Jersey Society of Certified Public Accountants
Attn: Student Programs Coordinator
425 Eagle Rock Avenue, Suite 100
Roseland, NJ 07068-1723
(973) 226-4494, ext. 209   Fax: (973) 226-7425
E-mail: njscpa@njscpa.org
Web: www.njscpa.org

Purpose To provide recognize and reward seniors in New Jersey high schools who are interested in preparing for a career as a certified public accountant and take a statewide accounting exam.

Eligibility This program is open to all New Jersey high school seniors who are planning to major in accounting in college. Applications for a 1-hour accounting aptitude exam are mailed to New Jersey high school guidance and business departments each September. The exam is given in November and the highest scorers receive accounting scholarships to the college of their choice.

Financial data The stipend ranges up to $1,700 per year.

Duration Up to 5 years.

Additional information This program has been offered since 1960. It includes scholarships supported by each of the Big 4 accounting firms: Deloitte, Ernst & Young, KPMG, and PricewaterhouseCoopers.

Number awarded Varies each year; recently, 18 of these scholarships were awarded

Deadline October of each year.

[664]
NEWCOMEN-HARVARD SPECIAL AWARD
Harvard Business School
Attn: Business History Review
South Hall 104
Soldiers Field
Boston, MA 02163
(617) 495-1003   Fax: (617) 495-0594
Web: www.hbs.edu/bhr/awards.html

Purpose To recognize and reward graduate students and recent Ph.D.s whose article published in the *Business History Review* is judged most outstanding.

Eligibility This award is presented for the best article in the *Business History Review* written by a graduate student or recent Ph.D. Authors may not yet have published a book in the field of business history.

Financial data The award is $500.

Duration The award is granted annually.

Additional information This award, first offered in 1959, is sponsored by the Newcomen Society of the United States.

Number awarded 1 each volume year.

[665]
NFTE OPPORTUNITY AWARDS

National Foundation for Teaching Entrepreneurship
Attn: Director of National Alumni Services
120 Wall Street, 29th Floor
New York, NY 10005
(212) 232-3333   Toll-free: (800) 367-6383
Fax: (212) 232-2244   E-mail: nfte@nfte.com
Web: www.nfte.com/alumni/awards

Purpose To recognize and reward students and teachers who have participated in programs of the National Foundation for Teaching Entrepreneurship (NFTE) and submit essays on starting a business.

Eligibility This program is open to students who have used the NFTE entrepreneurship curriculum to overcome personal obstacles to start and operate their own business. Teachers are also eligible. Applicants must submit an essay, up to 500 words in length, on how starting a business changed their life or the life of 1 of their students.

Financial data The prize is $1,000.

Duration The prizes are awarded annually.

Number awarded 10 each year.

Deadline January or June of each year.

[666]
OHIO SOCIETY OF CPAS MANUSCRIPT CONTEST

Ohio Society of Certified Public Accountants
535 Metro Place
P.O. Box 1810
Dublin, OH 43017
(614) 764-2727   Toll-free: (800) 686-2727
E-mail: oscpa@ohio-cpa.com
Web: www.ohioscpa.com

Purpose To recognize and reward students at Ohio colleges and universities who submit outstanding manuscripts on a topic related to accounting.

Eligibility This competition is open to students enrolled at Ohio colleges and universities. Applicants must submit a manuscript, up to 10 pages in length, on a topic that changes annually but relates to accounting. Recently, students were invited to write on the topic: "Has the adoption of the Sarbanes-Oxley legislation increased investor confidence in public companies and financial reporting?" Each manuscript must be reviewed by a sponsoring faculty member who is responsible for ensuring that the manuscript conforms to the technical requirements. Each faculty member may serve as a sponsor on a maximum of 5 papers. Co-authored manuscripts are not eligible, nor are manuscripts that have been published or submitted for publication elsewhere. Selection is based on the manuscript's content (manuscript covers specific topic area, approach to coverage of topic indicates originality of thought, relevant and meaningful issues and problems concerning both sides of the subject are discussed, each subdivision of the paper is clearly segregated and is relevant to the discussion) and presentation (organization of the paper is logical and balanced, a clear and concise summary is provided that integrates the presentation into a coherent whole and gives a def-

inite conclusion, writing style clearly conveys meaning with structurally correct sentences and effective use of words, technical aspects of the paper are in good form).

Financial data The author of the first-place manuscript receives a plaque and a cash award of $1,500. The author of the second-place manuscript receives a cash award of $1,000. The sponsoring faculty members receive cash awards of $1,000 for first place and $750 for second place.

Duration The contest is held annually.

Additional information The first-place paper is considered for publication by the sponsor.

Number awarded 2 each year.

Deadline March of each year.

[667]
PICPA STUDENT WRITING COMPETITION

Pennsylvania Institute of Certified Public Accountants
Attn: Careers in Accounting Team
1650 Arch Street, 17th Floor
Philadelphia, PA 19103-2099
(215) 496-9272   Toll-free: (888) CPA-2001 (within PA)
Fax: (215) 496-9212   E-mail: schools@picpa.org
Web: www.cpazone.org/contawrd/studwrit.asp

Purpose To recognize and reward outstanding essays written by students in Pennsylvania on an accounting topic that changes annually.

Eligibility This competition is open to 1) accounting and business majors at Pennsylvania colleges and universities, and 2) Pennsylvania residents who attend college out-of-state. Candidates are invited to submit an essay on an issue (changes annually) that affects the accounting profession. Recently, the topic was: "Being the Best in Business." Essays should be approximately 1,500 words and include a 50- to 75-word abstract. Selection is based on content, method of presentation, and writing style.

Financial data First place is $2,000, second $1,200, and third $800. The top 3 schools receive, respectively, $1,000, $600, and $400.

Duration The competition is held annually.

Additional information The first-place manuscript is published in the fall issue of the *Pennsylvania CPA Journal*.

Number awarded 3 each year.

Deadline April of each year.

[668]
PUBLIC SERVICE ANNOUNCEMENT SCHOLARSHIP

Michigan Disability Sports Alliance
Attn: Publicity Committee-Scholarship
Michigan State University
211 IM Sports West
East Lansing, MI 48824
Web: www.MiDSA.org

Purpose To recognize and reward outstanding public service announcements (PSAs) created by undergraduate and graduate students in Michigan that promote and educate the public about the National Disability Sports Alliance.

Eligibility This competition is open to undergraduate and graduate students attending an accredited college or university in Michigan. Students entering this competition must be legal residents of the United States. They must create a 30-second PSA, a 45-second PSA, a 2 minute PSA, and a 10 to 12 minute Boccia Training Tape, all promoting and educating the general public about the National Disability Sports Alliance. Actual footage from the Michigan Sports Festival must be used. Students from any major can apply, but it is highly recommended that marketing, public relations, journalism, and media majors apply to add to their professional portfolios. To enter the competition, applicants must submit a preapplication, stating the area their PSA will encompass. After the initial application is reviewed, a press packet, along with press badge, is sent to the applicant, so that they can attend upcoming events. After that, students submit their completed PSAs.

Financial data The winner receives a $1,250 scholarship.

Duration The competition is held annually.

Additional information This program is sponsored by the Michigan Disability Sports Alliance, in conjunction with the National Disability Sports Alliance.

Number awarded 1 each year.

Deadline Preapplications are due in February. PSAs are due in June.

[669]
SHRM FOUNDATION GRADUATE STUDENT LEADERSHIP AWARD

Society for Human Resource Management
Attn: Student Program Manager
1800 Duke Street
Alexandria, VA 22314-3499
(703) 535-6084   Toll-free: (800) 283-SHRM
Fax: (703) 739-0399   TDD: (703) 548-6999
E-mail: SHRMStudent@shrm.org
Web: www.shrm.org/students/ags_published

Purpose To recognize and reward outstanding leadership skills by graduate student members of the Society for Human Resource Management (SHRM).

Eligibility This program is open to full-time graduate students who have completed their first 9 hours of graduate school, have maintained a GPA of 3.25 or higher, and are national student members of the society. Selection is based on leadership ability as demonstrated in an SHRM student chapter, commitment to the human resources profession, scholastic average and standing, and additional leadership activities, such as service to a campus organization and/or a community or charitable organization.

Financial data The award includes a $1,000 honorarium, a commemorative plaque, and complimentary registration to the society's annual conference and exposition.

Duration The award is offered annually.

Number awarded 1 each year.

Deadline February of each year.

[670]
SIEBEL SCHOLARS PROGRAM

Siebel Systems, Inc.
Attn: Program Manager
2207 Bridgepointe Parkway
San Mateo, CA 94404
(650) 295-6998   Toll-free: (800) 647-4300
Fax: (650) 295-5111
E-mail: monisha.perkash@siebel.com
Web: www.siebelscholars.com

Purpose To recognize and reward outstanding business and computer science graduate students at participating schools.

Eligibility This program was established to recognize outstanding graduate students at designated universities. For business administration, the schools are Harvard University, Massachusetts Institute of Technology, Northwestern University, Stanford University, University of Chicago, and the University of Pennsylvania. For computer science, the schools are Massachusetts Institute of Technology, Stanford University, Carnegie Mellon University, University of California at Berkeley, and University of Illinois at Urbana-Champaign. Nominees must be in their first year of their graduate program. Recipients are selected by the deans at each of these schools; selection is based on academic merit and leadership excellence.

Financial data Siebel Scholars receive a $25,000 cash award to defray tuition costs and expenses for the final year of their graduate studies.

Duration 1 year.

Additional information This program was launched in 2000.

Number awarded 5 at each of the participating schools.

[671]
TEXAS SHEEP AND GOAT RAISER'S AUXILIARY LETTER WRITING CONTEST

Texas Sheep and Goat Raiser's Auxiliary
c/o Doris Haby
P.O. Box 1496
Brackettville, TX 78832
(830) 563-3020   Fax: (830) 563-3019
E-mail: hghaby@aol.com

Purpose To recognize and reward the best letters on private property rights, written as part of this competition, by high school students to their congressperson.

Eligibility High school juniors and school seniors are invited to enter this competition; they must prepare a 1-page typewritten letter to their national senator and representative on a topic that changes periodically but relates to private property rights; recently, the topic was "Discuss the reasoning of our Founding Fathers for placing the language '...nor shall private property be taken for public use, with just compensation,' into the Fifth Amendment of our Bill of Rights and explain how private real property protects our liberty." Entrants must be U.S. citizens.

Financial data First prize is a $1,250 scholarship; second prize is a $1,000 scholarship; third prize is a $750 scholarship; fourth through tenth prizes are $100 U.S. savings bonds. Funds must be used for college study.

Duration The competition is held annually.

Additional information This program is co-sponsored by the Texas Sheep and Goat Raiser's Auxiliary and the American Land Foundation.

Number awarded 3 scholarship prizes and 7 savings bonds are awarded each year.

Deadline October of each year.

[672]
TEXAS YOUTH ENTREPRENEUR OF THE YEAR AWARD

Texas Christian University
Attn: M.J. Neeley School of Business
Ryffel Center for Entrepreneurial Studies
TCU Box 298530
Fort Worth, Texas 76129
(817) 257-6544   E-mail: g.laney@tcu.edu
Web: www.rces.tcu.edu/youth/index.org

Purpose To recognize and reward outstanding high school entrepreneurs in Texas for success in their own business.

Eligibility Open to high school students in Texas who have started and managed a business that has been in operation for at least 1 year. An application may be submitted by the student entrepreneur, family member, friend, teacher, or mentor. Finalists are interviewed.

Financial data The top winner receives a $5,000 award; the other winners receive $1,000 each. Funds may be used to offset tuition at any school of the student's choice.

Duration The competition is held annually.

Number awarded 6 each year: 1 top winner and 5 other winners.

Deadline December of each year.

[673]
UTAH CREDIT UNION SCHOLARSHIP CONTEST

Utah League of Credit Unions
Attn: Scholarship Contest
1805 South Redwood Road
Salt Lake City, UT 84104
(801) 972-3400   Toll-free: (800) 662-8684
Web: www.ulcu.com

Purpose To recognize and reward outstanding essays written by high school seniors in Utah on a topic that relates to banking but changes annually.

Eligibility Any Utah high school senior who is a credit union member or whose parents are credit union members is eligible. There is no limit on the number of students who may enter from any school. Students are invited to write an essay, less than 1,000 words in length, on a topic that changes annually but relates to banking or credit unions; recently, the topic was "What are credit unions, how do they differ from other financial institutions, and how can using them impact me?" Essays are evaluated on the following: content (100 points), organization (50 points), research (50 points), grammar (25 points), and presentation (25 points).

Financial data First prize is $1,500; second prize is $1,000; and third prize is $500.

Duration The competition is held annually.

Number awarded 3 each year.

Deadline September of each year.

[674]
YOUNG ENTREPRENEUR OF THE YEAR AWARDS

National Foundation for Teaching Entrepreneurship
Attn: Student/Alumni Awards Committee
120 Wall Street, 29th Floor
New York, NY 10005
(212) 232-3333   Toll-free: (800) 367-6383, ext. 336
Fax: (212) 232-2244   E-mail: nfte@nfte.com
Web: www.nfte.com/alumni/awards

Purpose To recognize and reward students and alumni who have participated in programs of the National Foundation for Teaching Entrepreneurship (NFTE) and have started or plan to start their own business.

Eligibility This program is open to students and alumni of the NFTE entrepreneurship program offered in high schools throughout the country. Applicants may enter in either of 2 categories: business plan (for plans for businesses not yet established) and operational business (for revenue-generating businesses). They must submit information describing their proposed or operating business, including a complete business plan. Selection is based on application presentation (neatness, legibility, visual appeal, and completeness); business viability (including profit potential and, for the operating business category, current revenue); social responsibility (knowledge of the community and how the business contributes to its well-being); and entrepreneurial spirit (use of innovative and/or creative business methods).

Financial data Awards are $750 for the business plan category or $1,000 for the operational business category. Funds may be used for the business or college education. Awardees also receive a commemorative plaque and an all-expense paid trip to New York City to receive the award.

Duration The awards are presented annually.

Additional information These awards were first offered in 1994.

Number awarded Up to 20 each year.

Deadline February of each year.

[675]
7 UP CHALLENGE

DECA
1908 Association Drive
Reston, VA 20191-1594
(703) 860-5000   Fax: (703) 860-4013
E-mail: decainc@aol.com
Web: www.deca.org/7UPChallenge/guidelines.html

Purpose To recognize and reward (with college scholarships) DECA members who develop outstanding advertising campaigns for display on the Internet.

Eligibility This competition is open to high school DECA members who submit entries in either of 2 categories: 1) a web campaign of at least 400 x 400 pixels with up to 4 links and up to 500K in size; or 2) a banner ad of approximately 450 x 60 pixels, 72 dpi, and up to 20K. In either category, the campaign must promote brand awareness of lemon-lime and/or cherry-flavored soft drinks, involve the consumer, and utilize the themes of college basketball and/or music. Entries are received in 2 rounds, with finalists selected in each category in each round. Grand winners are selected from among the finalists on the basis of how well and creatively the campaign or banner ad promotes the soft drinks, overall appearance, content of copy, ease of use, identification, layout, and impact.

Financial data   Each finalist receives a $500 award. The grand winners receive $2,500 college scholarships.

Duration   The competition is held annually.

Additional information   This program is sponsored by the Seven Up Division of Dr Pepper/Seven Up, Inc.

Number awarded   4 finalists are selected in each category in each round (for a total of 16 finalists); from among those, 2 grand winners (1 in each category) are selected.

Deadline   December of each year for the first round; March of each year for the second round.

Sponsoring Organization Index

The Sponsoring Organization Index makes it easy to identify agencies that offer financial aid specifically to undergraduate and graduate students in business and related fields. In this index, the sponsoring organizations are listed alphabetically, word by word. In addition, we've used an alphabetical code (within parentheses) to help you identify the type of funding offered by the organizations: S = Scholarships; F = Fellowships; G = Grants; and A = Awards. For example, if the name of a sponsoring organization is followed by (S) 141, a program sponsored by that organization is described in the Scholarships section, in entry 141. If that sponsoring organization's name is followed by another entry number—for example, (A) 600—the same or a different program sponsored by that organization is described in the Awards section, in entry 600. Remember: the numbers cited here refer to program entry numbers, not to page numbers in the book.

Institute for Humane Studies at George Mason University, (S) 178, (F) 486, (G) 604, 626

Institute for Supply Management, (G) 613

Institute of Management Accountants, (S) 184, 359, (F) 490, 573, (A) 654

Institute of Management Accountants. Pikes Peak Chapter, (S) 322, (F) 551

Insurance Women of Columbus, (S) 64

International Association of Administrative Professionals. New York State Division, (S) 189

International Association of Administrative Professionals. Texas–Louisiana Division, (S) 367

International Association of Food Industry Suppliers, (S) 248, (F) 516

International Dairy–Deli–Bakery Association, (S) 181, (F) 489

International Public Management Association for Human Resources, (S) 185, (F) 492

International Right of Way Association. New England Chapter 16, (S) 187

ITS Washington, (S) 413, (F) 593

ITT Hartford Insurance Company, (S) 192

James C. & Elizabeth R. Conner Foundation, (F) 494

James S. Kemper Foundation, (S) 207

Jewish Community Centers Association, (F) 495–496

John A. Hartford Foundation, (F) 438

John Deere & Company, (A) 645

Johnsonville Sausage, LLC, (S) 197

Junior Achievement, (S) 396, (F) 506

Junior Achievement of Delaware, Inc., (S) 318, (A) 652

Junior Achievement of Maine, Inc., (S) 200

Kansas Junior Livestock Association, (S) 201

Kansas Livestock Association, (S) 214

Kansas Livestock Foundation, (S) 201

Kansas Society of Certified Public Accountants, (S) 216–218, (F) 437, 502

Kentucky Society of Certified Public Accountants, (S) 209–210

Kern County Farm Bureau, Inc., (S) 68

Knight Ridder, Inc., (S) 215

KPMG Foundation, (F) 501, (A) 663

Kurzweil Foundation, (S) 294, (F) 540

LAGRANT FOUNDATION, (S) 219

Lambda Alpha International, (G) 616

Lang Family Foundation, (S) 7

League of United Latin American Citizens, (S) 147

Lee Enterprises/Madison Newspapers, Inc., (S) 225

Legacy, Inc., (S) 226, (F) 505

Liberty Mutual, (S) 229

Library Company of Philadelphia, (G) 597, 599, 621

Lincoln Community Foundation, (S) 221

Little Family Foundation, (F) 506

Maine Education Services, (S) 234

Maine Society of CPAs, (S) 6, 233

Malt–O–Meal Company, (S) 236

Marriott International, Inc., (S) 240

Maryland Association of Certified Public Accountants, (S) 244, (F) 513

Maryland Bankers Association, (A) 657

Maryland Federation of Business and Professional Women's Clubs, Inc., (S) 90, (F) 454

Massachusetts Society of Certified Public Accountants, (S) 126, 203, 314, (F) 457, 514, (A) 658

Michigan Association of Certified Public Accountants, (S) 251, (F) 521

Michigan Disability Sports Alliance, (A) 668

Michigan Press Association, (S) 252

Minnesota Society of Certified Public Accountants, (S) 262

Minnesota Space Grant Consortium, (S) 254, (F) 523

Miss America Pageant, (S) 256, (A) 659

Mississippi Society of Certified Public Accountants, (S) 257, (F) 525

Missouri DECA, (S) 194, 204, 208, 228, 258–259

Missouri Insurance Education Foundation, (S) 260–261

Missouri Society of Certified Public Accountants, (S) 224

Monsanto Company, (A) 631

Montana Broadcasters Association, (S) 246

Montana Meat Processors Association, (S) 263

Montana Society of Certified Public Accountants, (S) 264

Montana 4–H Foundation, (S) 263

Monterey County Farm Bureau, (S) 68

Morgan Stanley, (S) 266–267

Mortgage Bankers Association of the Carolinas, Inc., (S) 77

M&T Bank, (S) 268

Municipal Bond Investors Assurance Corporation, (S) 247

Mustard Seed Foundation, (F) 481

NAPSLO Educational Foundation, (S) 101, (F) 464

National Ad 2, (A) 660–661

National Association for the Advancement of Colored People, (S) 110, (F) 465

National Association of Black Accountants, (S) 19, 239, 269, 271, 327, 362, 374, (F) 425, 510, 527, 529, 556, 574, 578

National Association of Collegiate Directors of Athletics, (F) 499

National Association of Insurance Women, (S) 270, (F) 528

National Association of Tobacco Distributors, (S) 328, (F) 557

National Association of Water Companies, (F) 497

National Black MBA Association, (S) 272, (F) 530–531

National Black MBA Association. Dallas Chapter, (S) 91, (F) 455

National Black MBA Association. New York Chapter, (S) 250, (F) 519–520

National Black MBA Association. Twin Cities Chapter, (S) 380, (F) 579

National Black MBA Association. Washington, D.C. Chapter, (S) 95, (F) 459

National Candy Wholesalers Association, (S) 328, (F) 557

National Collegiate Athletic Association, (F) 472, 588

National Dairy Promotion and Research Board, (S) 274

National Dairy Shrine, (S) 273

National Defense Transportation Association. Scott–St. Louis Chapter, (S) 275

National Disability Sports Alliance, (A) 668

S–Scholarships   F–Fellowships   G–Grants   A–Awards

Tag and Label Manufacturers Institute, Inc., (S) 370
Tennessee Society of CPAs, (S) 363
Texas Business Hall of Fame, (F) 575
Texas Christian University. Neeley School of Business, (A) 672
Texas FFA Association, (S) 76, 127, 129, 193, 336, 355, 364, 414
Texas Higher Education Coordinating Board, (S) 365
Texas Sheep and Goat Raiser's Auxiliary, (A) 671
Texas Society of Certified Public Accountants, (S) 4, 378
Texas Telephone Association Foundation, (S) 379
Texas 4-H Foundation, (S) 366, 415
Theodore W. Batterman Foundation, (S) 368
Tommy Ramey Foundation, (S) 371
Truckload Carriers Association, (S) 377
Tulare County Farm Bureau, (S) 68

United Church of Christ. Council for Health and Human Service Ministries, (F) 580
United Negro College Fund, (S) 8, 35, 42, 75, 87, 97, 107, 138, 145, 229, 247, 266, 305, 319, 324, 381–382, 384, (F) 461, 549
United Parcel Service of America, Inc., (S) 384
University of California. Institute on Global Conflict and Cooperation, (G) 614
University of Virginia. Miller Center of Public Affairs, (G) 618
Urban Financial Services Coalition of Delaware, (S) 385
U.S. Agency for Healthcare Research and Quality, (G) 609
U.S. Corporation for National and Community Service, (F) 423
U.S. Department of Agriculture, (S) 325, 386, (F) 554
U.S. Department of Commerce. National Oceanic and Atmospheric Administration, (F) 533, (G) 619–620
U.S. Department of Energy, (G) 620
U.S. Department of Energy. Office of Economic Impact and Diversity, (S) 292
U.S. Department of Energy. Office of Environmental Management, (S) 121
U.S. Marine Corps, (S) 237, (F) 508
U.S. National Aeronautics and Space Administration, (S) 254, 383, 408, (F) 419, 523, (G) 596, 624–625
U.S. Navy. Naval Education and Training Command, (S) 360
U.S. Navy. Naval Medical Education and Training Command, (F) 517
US Pan Asian American Chamber of Commerce, (S) 59
Utah League of Credit Unions, (A) 673

Vermont Chamber of Commerce, (S) 213
Vermont Student Assistance Corporation, (S) 122, 191, 213, 388–389
Vermont Subcontractors Association, Inc., (S) 122
Vermont/New Hampshire Direct Marketing Group, (S) 389
Virginia Foundation for Independent Colleges, (S) 320
Virginia Organization of Nurse Executives, (F) 562
Virginia Society for Healthcare Human Resources Administration, (S) 391, (F) 581
Virginia Society of Certified Public Accountants Education Foundation, (S) 392–393, (F) 582
Vitale Caturano & Company CPAs PC, (S) 126

Wal-Mart Stores, Inc., (S) 394
Walgreens, (S) 395
Walt Disney Company Foundation, (S) 396
Washington Federation of Private Career Schools & Colleges, (S) 55
Washington Society of Certified Public Accountants, (S) 277, 400
Washington Society of Certified Public Accountants. Sammamish Valley Chapter, (S) 338
Washington State Environmental Health Association, (F) 590
Wausau Benefits, (S) 401
Wells Fargo Bank, (S) 403
Wilbur-Ellis Company, (S) 404
William Reese Company, (G) 599
Wisconsin DECA, (S) 406
Wisconsin Foundation for Independent Colleges, Inc., (S) 7, 36, 40, 159, 197, 220, 225, 343, 368, 401
Wisconsin Institute of Certified Public Accountants, (S) 334, 390, 407, (F) 587
Wisconsin Space Grant Consortium, (S) 408, (G) 624–625
WISS & Company, LLP, (S) 116
Wolf & Company, PC, (S) 203
Women's Transportation Seminar, (S) 232, 344, (F) 483
Women's Transportation Seminar. Colorado Chapter, (S) 410, (F) 589
Women's Transportation Seminar. Minnesota Chapter, (S) 411, (F) 591
Women's Transportation Seminar. Puget Sound Chapter, (S) 157, 412–413, (F) 555, 592–593
A World Connected, (A) 635

Yolo County Farm Bureau, (S) 68

Zonta International, (S) 190

Residency Index

Some programs listed in this book are restricted to residents of a particular county, state, or region. Others are open to applicants wherever they may live. The Residency Index will help you pinpoint programs available only to residents in your area as well as programs that have no residency restrictions at all (these are listed under the term "United States"). To use this index, look up the geographic areas that apply to you (always check the listings under "United States"), jot down the entry numbers listed after the type of funding that interests you (e.g., Scholarships, Grants), and use those numbers to find the program descriptions in the directory. To help you in your search, we've provided some "see also" references in each index entry. Remember: the numbers cited here refer to program entry numbers, not to page numbers in the book.

Meagher County, Montana: **Scholarships,** 246. *See also* Montana

Michigan: **Scholarships,** 251–252, 316, 404; **Fellowships,** 521; **Awards,** 668. *See also* Midwestern states; United States; names of specific cities and counties

Midwestern states: **Scholarships,** 5. *See also* United States; names of specific states

Minnesota: **Scholarships,** 45, 130, 236, 254, 262, 380, 404, 411; **Fellowships,** 439, 523, 579, 586, 591. *See also* Midwestern states; United States; names of specific cities and counties

Mississippi: **Scholarships,** 165, 257, 371; **Fellowships,** 525; **Awards,** 637. *See also* United States; names of specific cities and counties

Missouri: **Scholarships,** 34, 41, 66, 92, 128, 194, 204, 208, 224, 228, 258–261, 275; **Awards,** 637. *See also* Midwestern states; United States; names of specific cities and counties

Montana: **Scholarships,** 45, 130, 132, 158, 242, 246, 263–265, 404; **Fellowships,** 511. *See also* United States; names of specific cities and counties

Monterey, California: **Scholarships,** 381. *See also* California

Montgomery County, Maryland: **Scholarships,** 399; **Fellowships,** 584. *See also* Maryland

Nebraska: **Scholarships,** 128, 130, 144, 160, 221, 276, 304; **Fellowships,** 543. *See also* United States; Midwestern states; names of specific cities and counties

Nevada: **Scholarships,** 34, 348; **Fellowships,** 569. *See also* Southwestern states; United States; names of specific cities

New Castle, Delaware: **Scholarships,** 381. *See also* Delaware

New England states: **Scholarships,** 43, 102, 278, 397; **Fellowships,** 435, 534, 583. *See also* Northeastern states; United States; names of specific states

New Hampshire: **Scholarships,** 187, 229, 280–281, 323, 389; **Fellowships,** 535–536. *See also* New England states; Northeastern states; United States; names of specific cities and counties

New Jersey: **Scholarships,** 107, 116, 123, 139, 229, 247, 283–286, 299, 323; **Fellowships,** 537–538, 541; **Awards,** 662–663. *See also* Northeastern states; United States; names of specific cities and counties

New Mexico: **Scholarships,** 34, 41, 45, 287, 404; **Fellowships,** 539. *See also* Southwestern states; United States; names of specific cities and counties

New York: **Scholarships,** 113, 119, 128, 189, 229, 247, 268, 289–291, 299, 323; **Fellowships,** 466, 541. *See also* Northeastern states; United States; names of specific cities and counties

New York County, New York. *See* New York, New York

New York, New York: **Scholarships,** 250; **Fellowships,** 519–520. *See also* New York

North Attleboro, Massachusetts: **Scholarships,** 279. *See also* Massachusetts

North Carolina: **Scholarships,** 34, 128, 165, 296–297; **Awards,** 637. *See also* Southeastern states; United States; names of specific cities and counties

North Dakota: **Scholarships,** 45, 118, 130, 404; **Fellowships,** 439. *See also* Midwestern states; United States; names of specific cities

Northeastern states: **Scholarships,** 111. *See also* United States; names of specific states

Northern Marianas: **Scholarships,** 164; **Fellowships,** 480. *See also* United States

Ohio: **Scholarships,** 2, 64, 78, 128, 300–301, 404; **Awards,** 666. *See also* Midwestern states; United States; names of specific cities and counties

Oklahoma: **Scholarships,** 34, 45, 104, 128, 303; **Awards,** 637. *See also* Southwestern states; United States; names of specific cities and counties

Oneida County, Wisconsin: **Fellowships,** 439. *See also* Wisconsin

Oregon: **Scholarships,** 34, 45, 132, 174, 306–307, 309–310, 404; **Fellowships,** 544, 546. *See also* United States; names of specific cities and counties

Pennsylvania: **Scholarships,** 30, 128, 229, 268, 299, 317, 321, 323; **Fellowships,** 446, 468, 541; **Grants,** 595; **Awards,** 667. *See also* Northeastern states; United States; names of specific cities and counties

Pepin County, Wisconsin: **Fellowships,** 439. *See also* Wisconsin

Phillips County, Montana: **Scholarships,** 246. *See also* Montana

Pierce County, Wisconsin: **Fellowships,** 439. *See also* Wisconsin

Plainville, Massachusetts: **Scholarships,** 279. *See also* Massachusetts

Polk County, Wisconsin: **Fellowships,** 439. *See also* Wisconsin

Pondera County, Montana: **Scholarships,** 246. *See also* Montana

Portage County, Wisconsin: **Scholarships,** 220. *See also* Wisconsin

Price County, Wisconsin: **Fellowships,** 439. *See also* Wisconsin

Prince George's County, Maryland: **Scholarships,** 399; **Fellowships,** 584. *See also* Maryland

Prince William County, Virginia: **Scholarships,** 399; **Fellowships,** 584. *See also* Virginia

Puerto Rico: **Scholarships,** 29, 53, 99, 124, 164, 171, 179, 322, 337; **Fellowships,** 431, 441, 480, 551. *See also* United States

Queens County, New York. *See* New York, New York
Queens, New York. *See* New York, New York

Rhode Island: **Scholarships,** 57, 94, 175, 187, 279, 323, 329. *See also* New England states; Northeastern states; United States; names of specific cities

Richland County, Wisconsin: **Scholarships,** 220. *See also* Wisconsin

Richmond County, New York. *See* New York, New York

Rusk County, Wisconsin: **Fellowships,** 439. *See also* Wisconsin

Salem County, New Jersey: **Scholarships,** 318; **Awards,** 652. *See also* New Jersey

Samoa. *See* American Samoa

Tenability Index

Some programs listed in this book can be used only in specific cities, counties, states, or regions. Others may be used anywhere in the United States (or even abroad). The Tenability Index will help you locate funding that is restricted to a specific area as well as funding that has no tenability restrictions (these are listed under the term "United States"). To use this index, look up the geographic areas where you'd like to go (always check the listings under "United States"), jot down the entry numbers listed after the type of funding that interests you (e.g., Fellowships, Awards), and use those numbers to find the program descriptions in the directory. To help you in your search, we've provided some "see also" references in each index entry. Remember: the numbers cited here refer to program entry numbers, not to page numbers in the book.

Specialty Index

Use this index to access the funding opportunities available to support various specialties in business or related fields. For your convenience, the type of funding offered is clearly marked (Scholarships, Fellowships, etc.). Remember: the numbers cited in this index refer to program entry numbers, not to page numbers in the book.

Calendar Index

Since most financial aid programs have specific deadline dates, some may have already closed by the time you begin to look for funding. You can use the Calendar Index to identify which programs are still open. To do that, look at the funding type that interests you (Scholarships, Fellowships, etc.), think about when you'll be able to complete your application forms, go to the appropriate months, jot down the entry numbers listed there, and use those numbers to find the program descriptions in the directory. Keep in mind that the numbers cited here refer to program entry numbers, not to page numbers in the book. Note: not all sponsoring organizations supplied deadline information to us, so not all programs are listed in this index.

Scholarships:
January: 7, 35–36, 40, 46–47, 66–67, 72, 93, 97, 119, 123, 144, 154, 159, 163, 188, 192, 197, 205, 209, 224–225, 251, 285–286, 296, 299, 304, 316, 319, 322, 326, 361, 367–368, 371, 386, 396, 401
February: 8–10, 15, 18, 24, 34, 38–39, 42, 58–59, 69–70, 79, 82, 86, 92, 98, 102, 106, 112, 115, 120–121, 128, 130–131, 133, 137–138, 140–142, 149, 158, 164–166, 169, 174, 184, 194, 204, 208, 210–211, 227–228, 235–236, 238, 240, 249, 255, 258–259, 270, 275, 282, 292, 294–295, 307–311, 323–324, 332, 334, 340, 342, 348, 359, 366, 381, 383, 394–395, 399, 403–405, 407–408, 415
March: 3, 17, 20, 22, 28, 32, 44, 64, 75, 77, 84, 87, 91, 95, 104, 109, 111, 125, 160, 168, 173, 180–181, 183, 187, 199–200, 217, 219–220, 230–231, 242–243, 246, 254, 260–261, 265, 273, 276, 278–279, 284, 290, 293, 298, 305–306, 321, 343, 354, 357, 369–370, 372, 376, 379–380, 384–385, 388
April: 16, 21, 29, 41, 43, 45, 48, 51–53, 57, 65, 99, 108, 110, 116–117, 122, 124, 132, 136, 146, 148, 153, 171, 175, 179, 189, 191, 196, 201, 213–214, 218, 221, 234, 237, 244–245, 263, 267–268, 277, 287, 291, 297, 301, 303, 318, 325, 333, 337–338, 341, 345, 349, 353, 376, 392–393, 397–398, 400, 409
May: 2, 11, 14, 25, 31, 49, 56, 74, 90, 101, 105, 133, 139, 162, 167, 182, 185, 190, 212, 226, 241, 253, 274, 281, 315, 317, 328, 331, 347, 350, 352, 356, 377
June: 1, 61–62, 68, 81, 100, 114, 143, 152, 156, 181, 195, 206, 216, 223, 257, 329, 335, 339, 351, 373, 378, 389
July: 30, 37, 50, 113, 147, 360
August: 88–89, 133, 172, 198, 312, 391
September: 12, 96, 150, 181, 202, 250, 288, 371, 376, 402
October: 26, 78, 108, 155, 157, 170, 280–281, 330, 346, 382, 390, 412–413
November: 2, 33, 83, 114, 133–134, 232, 247–248, 313, 344, 375, 410–411
December: 19, 178, 181, 229, 239, 252, 269, 271, 289, 320, 327, 362, 374
Any time: 80

Fellowships:
January: 424, 452, 458, 461, 469, 471, 487, 491, 495–496, 499, 507, 515, 521, 533, 538, 541, 543, 549–552
February: 416, 419, 422, 428, 434, 437, 443, 456, 463, 472–474, 476, 480, 490, 509, 518, 524, 528, 540, 544–546, 553, 564, 566, 569, 573, 584–585, 587–588
March: 417–418, 421, 426–427, 430, 436, 438, 446, 451, 455, 459, 468, 475, 489, 497–498, 503, 511–512, 523, 534, 537, 572, 579, 590
April: 420, 431, 435, 441, 465, 478, 501, 513, 530–531, 554, 560–561, 565, 568, 582–583
May: 432, 440, 442, 448, 454, 464, 474, 492, 500, 505, 522, 536, 548, 557, 559, 571, 586
June: 444–445, 450, 467, 470, 477, 479, 489, 502, 504, 525, 563, 570, 577
July: 466
August: 453, 474, 508, 517, 581
September: 460, 489, 519–520, 562
October: 429, 439, 462, 484, 526, 535–536, 555, 558, 567, 592–593
November: 433, 452, 467, 474, 481, 483, 516, 547, 576, 589, 591
December: 425, 486, 488–489, 510, 527, 529, 556, 574, 578
Any time: 449

Grants:
January: 600, 608–611, 613–615, 618–619, 623
February: 596–597, 599, 601, 603–604, 616, 621, 624–625
March: 622, 626
May: 609
September: 609, 617
October: 605
November: 595, 598
December: 594
Any time: 602, 612, 620, 626

Awards:
January: 632, 636, 654, 657, 662, 665
February: 639, 646, 649, 668–669, 674